TANYA
PLIBERSEK

ALSO BY MARGARET SIMONS

Cry Me a River: The Tragedy of the Murray-Darling Basin (2020)

Penny Wong: Passion and Principle (2019)

Six Square Metres: Reflections from a Small Garden (2015)

Kerry Stokes: Self-Made Man (2013)

Journalism at the Crossroads: Crisis and Opportunity for the Press (2012)

Malcolm Fraser: The Political Memoirs (2010)

The Content Makers: Understanding the Media in Australia (2007)

Faith, Money and Power: What the Religious Revival Means for Politics (2007)

Latham's World: The New Politics of the Outsiders (2004)

Resurrection in a Bucket: The Rich and Fertile Story of Compost (2004)

The Meeting of the Waters: The Hindmarsh Island Affair (2003)

Fit to Print: Inside the Canberra Press Gallery (1999)

Wheelbarrows, Chooks and Children (1999)

The Truth Teller (1996)

The Ruthless Garden (1993)

TANYA PLIBERSEK

On Her Own Terms

THE BIOGRAPHY BY

MARGARET SIMONS

Published by Black Inc.,
an imprint of Schwartz Books Pty Ltd
22–24 Northumberland Street
Collingwood VIC 3066, Australia
enquiries@blackincbooks.com
www.blackincbooks.com

9781760643386 (paperback)
9781743823040 (ebook)

 A catalogue record for this
book is available from the
National Library of Australia

Cover design by Tristan Main
Text design and typesetting by Typography Studio
Cover image by Kym Smith / Newspix
Index by Belinda Nemec

Printed in Australia by McPherson's Printing Group.

CONTENTS

PREFACE

When I was asked by my publisher to consider writing a biography of Tanya Plibersek, I didn't leap at the chance.

She had always struck me, from what I had seen on television and media appearances, as more than competent and an excellent communicator, but I didn't understand the particular passion of her fan club.

By the time this project was suggested to me in early 2021, it was clear she was the most likely person to replace Anthony Albanese if he failed to retain the leadership, or if he lost the 2022 election. The fact that she was a possible future prime minister made her inherently interesting and worthy of a biography, yet still I hesitated. Taking on a project of this kind means that the subject will dominate one's waking thoughts for at least two years. That is no small commitment. Was Plibersek sufficiently absorbing?

I started with a quick survey of what journalists had already written. Two things drew me. First, I found out that she loved the work of Jane Austen. That was something we had in common.

Even more intriguing, the Austen heroine she most identified with was Elinor Dashwood. It is rare, in fiction as in politics, for sensibleness to be cast as an heroic virtue. That Plibersek aspired to such sense appealed to me greatly.

The second thing that drew me was her family history. I have always been moved by the stories of the young men and women who moved half a world away from Europe after the trauma of the Second World War. In many ways, Joe and Rose Plibersek are the true heroes of this narrative.

And so, I was persuaded.

I approached Plibersek's office seeking cooperation in March 2021. The response was cautious. A concern was that I should let it be known that the biography was not Plibersek's idea, and not at her urging. Plibersek's staff referred to the preface I wrote for the biography I wrote of Penny Wong, the first words of which were 'Penny Wong did not want this book to be written.' Would I write something similar for this book? It was clear that, at a sensitive time, Plibersek did not want to be seen as seeking personal publicity.

However, unlike Wong, who was hostile to the project until very late in its progress (at which point she agreed to be interviewed), Plibersek chose to cooperate from the start in the interest of having some agency, given the book was to be written with or without her cooperation. She helped me with introductions to her brother and mother. Her husband and eventually her two eldest children spoke to me. She agreed to eight interviews, six before the 2022 election and two afterwards. About half of these were conducted by Zoom, due to pandemic lockdowns in my hometown of Melbourne. The rest were in her electorate office or her home.

One interview is clearly missing from this account. I was not able to speak to Anthony Albanese, despite several requests. At one stage I was told he would ring me and give me 'ten minutes'. The call never came, and no response was received to my attempts to follow up.

The interviews with Plibersek and her family were on the condition that any quotes or information I wanted to attribute were cleared with them before publication, and that she would also see a proof of the book and have the opportunity to correct any factual inaccuracies. Other than this, she was not given any say over how I chose to present the material, who else I spoke to, or the text. Anna, on the other hand, was given control over the small section of the book which tells of her experience. When the time for quote-checking came, she made only minor amendments and, in some cases, additions.

A biographer hears many things, and in the case of a living subject whose career is not over, has to make a judgement about what is rightly kept private and what the public deserves to know. It is impossible to give details of how I made these decisions without revealing the substance of the material that I chose not to use. In most cases, it was an easy call because the material concerned entirely private matters.

In other cases, the material lay on the boundary of private and public life. Where I chose not to reveal it was because, after substantial research, I concluded that the events did not have a significant impact on the story of Plibersek the politician – and on the other hand, publication could harm people not in public life.

These were not easy judgement calls. Some might have decided differently. But they were decisions carefully made.

Plibersek turned out to be an absorbing subject. Despite her cooperation with this book, she was always cautious in self-revelation. She was a complex and layered subject, as I hope this book reveals.

THE SPIDER

I t must have seemed like the biggest sky in the world, and the red sand and mauve saltbush the strangest of landscapes. It was 1953 in a tent camp a couple of hundred kilometres east of Broken Hill – a remote spot in one of the sparsest populated countries in the world. Josef Plibersek, a skinny, blond 21-year-old, had arrived in Australia only six weeks previously on a ship called the *Seven Seas* – a troop carrier hurriedly converted for refugees from the chaos of post-war Europe.

Conditions on board had been crowded and harsh, but as Josef told an interviewer later in his life, he was young and could put up with anything.[1] On board, he signed an agreement that he would learn English as soon as possible when he got to Australia. He was told he was heading for a land of opportunity.

The ship landed in Melbourne and within hours he was on a train to Wodonga and the displaced persons' camp at Bonegilla. He slept in a hut with three other single men. Conditions were primitive, but there was a bonus. For the first time in his life there was plenty of food – great heaped mounds of meat and potatoes, served in big communal canteens. You could take as much as you wanted. It was extraordinary, but he couldn't get used to the tea. 'My goodness, it was more like a coffee. There was no coffee around, of course.' He learned that these Australians drank their tea with milk – just one of many strange habits. He loaded his tea with extra milk and learned to get it down.

Under the terms of his contract with the Australian government, Josef had agreed to work for two years anywhere the government told him to go. After five weeks he was put on another train to Sydney, then transported to the great arid plain between Menindee and Broken Hill.

There he was given a tent, a billy, some flour, sugar and a rifle so he could hunt rabbits to sustain himself. He was to work as a labourer on the Parkes to Broken Hill railway, a section of the transnational track that was part of Australia's fever of nation-building.

On that first evening, camped out in the vastness of the Australian inland – as bereft and alone as a man could be – he found a big spider in his tent. It was a fortunate creature: in Plibersek's home in Slovenia, spiders were believed to be a sign of good luck and killing them brought misfortune.

His daughter, Tanya Plibersek, remembers him telling the story. She tears up recounting it. 'He was trying to make peace with the country he found himself in,' she says. 'He thought that the attitude he displayed to this spider would set the pattern for his attitude to his new country.'

Josef carefully picked the spider up, took it outside and set it free.

Her father is the subject of many of Tanya Plibersek's earliest memories. She would sit on his lap when he came home from work and fall asleep with the studs of his overalls making impressions against her cheek. 'It was the best place to be in the world.'

Josef Plibersek grew up on a smallholding in the mountains of Slovenia, near the Austrian border. His family's subsistence farm was carved out of the pine forest. It was a beautiful place – crisp mountain air, and in spring the blossom from the orchards blew about like pink snow. The family ran a few cows for milk, pigs for meat and grew corn and vegetables. They grew wine grapes and plum, cherry and pear trees from which they made wine and plum brandy. But for as long as he could remember, Josef had been hungry most of the time – and he had rarely felt safe. He would milk the cows each morning, then run five kilometres down the mountain in bare feet to school. He was the youngest of seven children and had always understood that this meant the farm would go to his older brothers, not to him. He would have to make his own way. It was a hard life. Once, clearing out the barn, he put a pitchfork through his foot. His mother's response was to tell him to toughen up and get on with it. Josef's father had died when he was about seven. He remembered him as a calm, quiet man – but those memories were limited and few. His brothers were the heads of the family, and his older sisters cared for him, worked the fields and tried to keep everyone fed.

It is extraordinary that Slovenia – a small country squeezed between Italy, Austria and Hungary, touching the Alps and bordering the Adriatic Sea – has managed to maintain such a strong sense of identity. For most of history, it was part of other countries' empires – the Roman empire, the Hungarian empire, the French empire and then the Austro-Hungarian empire, repeatedly occupied, invaded and exploited. After the First World War, it became part of the State of Slovenes, Croats and Serbs, which then merged with Serbia to become the new nation of Yugoslavia. Through all this, the Slovenians maintained their language, culture and sense of national pride. Religion was central. The Pliberseks, like almost all Slovenians, were Roman Catholics. The faith was a source of meaning, resilience, purpose and consolation.

In 1941, when Josef was approaching his ninth birthday, Slovenia was invaded by the Axis powers – the coalition on Nazi Germany's side in the Second World War. Different parts of the country were occupied by successive waves of Germans, Italians and Hungarians, each seeking to annex part of the territory. The Pliberseks' region was occupied by Germany, and Hitler's plan was to 'Germanise' the population. Almost overnight, Josef and his schoolmates had to speak German at school and were punished, often beaten, for using their own language or singing traditional songs. At home, Axis troops seized the family's stores of food. His brothers were conscripted to fight on the Russian front.

Josef used to sleep in the barn. One night, he woke to find his older brother, Alojez, had returned. He had been injured on the Russian front and taken to Austria to recover. There, he escaped and crossed the border to find his way home. News of his return spread quickly, and within a few days the Yugoslav partisans – the resistance to the occupation – came to visit. As the family recalls the story: 'They said to him at gunpoint, would you like to volunteer to join us, or will we kill you now?' The older Plibersek didn't need the compulsion. He willingly went with them and fought a guerrilla war of resistance, hiding in the mountains. He was shot and treated in a secret hospital hidden in the forest near the family farm, and by the end of the war was a decorated hero. Two other Plibersek brothers also fought with the partisans.

In 1945 the Germans retreated and were replaced by Russian soldiers. In the family storytelling, they were even worse than the Nazis. They took more food, and families learned that women should be hidden when they came to call, or they would be raped. The next year the British prime minister, Winston Churchill, gave his famous speech declaring that an iron curtain was falling across Europe, as the Soviet Union imposed communism on its occupied territories.

At the end of the war, aged fourteen, Josef left school to work on the family farm, then went to trade school and trained to be a plumber and sheet-metal worker. He worked as an apprentice for the local council in the eastern border city of Marburg, or Maribor as it was called after the war. When he had his qualifications, he got a job with a state-owned building company. As a government employee, he was expected to join the Communist Party – and that meant giving up his religion.

He recalled his thinking in later years. 'Once you become a member of the Communist Party, you were separated from your church. And to me that was not acceptable.' He wanted to marry and have children, but if he left his church there would be only a civil ceremony. This, too, was 'unacceptable'. Almost as bad, he could see no way, in what was now communist Yugoslavia, to earn enough money to support a wife and children and give them a decent life.

In December 1951, Josef swam a river to cross into Austria. He was jailed for five weeks for crossing illegally, then transferred to a refugee camp swollen with the displaced people of Europe. There were Jews released from concentration camps, Nazis on the run and many people, like Josef, escaping communism and poverty, intent on finding a better life. The refugees were allowed to work, and Josef earned money as a plumber in a nearby town, but his life was on hold, and he was impatient. He told the camp authorities he didn't care where he went. He just wanted to migrate to a country that offered a better life. Which country could accept him fastest?

The answer, he was told, was Australia. It was desperate for young men like him. In the post-war years, Australia had an expanding economy and an acute shortage of labour, particularly for the big nation-building projects of the inland – coalmining, timber getting and steel production. Australian workers could take their pick of jobs in the booming economy, and they were moving to cleaner, better-paid and easier work in manufacturing and service industries. In particular, the Commonwealth Railways Commissioner was unable to recruit fettlers for the Trans-Australian Railway.

So began the great wave of post-war immigration, presided over by immigration minister Arthur Calwell. At first, Calwell wanted only British migrants, but there weren't enough of them to meet the needs of industry. From 1947 onwards, the government turned its eyes to the estimated 8 million people in the European refugee camps. There was, Calwell said, 'splendid human material' in the camps. He worried the 'whole of the cream' would be skimmed by other governments, and so Australia began to recruit with urgency to get 'the best migrant types'.[2] At first only Baltic people were accepted, then that expanded to include Ukrainians and Slovenians. A blanket ban on Jews was removed for 'exceptionally good cases' who agreed to work in remote areas.[3] By 1949, all European races were deemed acceptable.

Josef Plibersek was accepted in the last year of the displaced persons scheme, in June 1952, and arrived in 1953, after it had officially ended.[4] Harold Holt was now immigration minister and had softened the early insistence that migrants must assimilate instantly. In 1950, Prime Minister Menzies had said, 'We must say to them ... that whatever may be the circumstances of the past ... in a few years they will all be Australians, they will all be British, and they will all be, as we are, the King's men and the King's women.' Holt said, 'You get the fully assimilated migrant perhaps in the second generation. You don't expect it in the first.'[5]

Josef was interviewed twice before he was accepted for entry to Australia. He was asked whether he had any political connections – Australia was fearful of importing either Nazis or communists. He said he had none. He told his interrogators he had left his home in search of economic opportunity and to avoid military service. His physical examination cleared him of tuberculosis and diabetes. His lungs, eyes and hearing were judged to be good. He had no criminal record – though he declared that he had once received a fine for riding his bike on a foot-path. He was bilingual, speaking both German and Slovenian, but spoke no English. He was, the authorities concluded, a 'good type'. The photo attached to his papers in Australia's national archives shows a blond, fair-skinned man – barely more than a boy – his hair in carefully combed waves back from a high forehead, his eyes a little uneven, staring straight at the camera.[6]

He looks strikingly like his daughter, Tanya Plibersek – the second generation that Holt had predicted would be 'fully assimilated'.

* * *

The Parkes to Broken Hill railway line was used mainly by steam loco-motives and, three days a week, the diesel Silver City Comet. The reason Josef Plibersek was needed, along with dozens of other labourers, was that the sleepers had been laid on sand, with insufficient ballast. When the big trains went by, the sand rose like red smoke, leaving the track even less well supported. An army of labourers, or fettlers, was needed to maintain the track. They worked with picks and shovels, travelling along the line on hand-powered vehicles, setting up camp in a new place each night. It was the kind of work that Australians didn't want to do. The loneliness was intense. Josef was upset that he was doing unskilled labouring, rather than using his qualifications as a plumber, which the Australian authorities didn't recognise.[7]

Fortunately for him, the scheme under which new migrants were obliged to work wherever they were sent was already in disarray. In practice, the government had found it was impossible to track the migrants or prevent them from taking better jobs. A few months after his arrival, the obligation was dropped, and Josef was free to look for other work. He briefly considered buying a small parcel of farmland in the Menindee Lakes area, but quickly decided the land was too harsh and dry. Meanwhile, word of a new, giant project in the distant moun-tains was spreading among the refugee fettlers. It was said to be paying top wages. It was called the Snowy Mountains Scheme.

As soon as he was able to be freed from his contract, Plibersek left the railway and made his way to the town of Cooma, in southern New

South Wales, where he presented himself at the employment office. His English was still rudimentary, but he had a stroke of good luck – the employment officer was Slovenian. By that night, he had a bed in one of the barracks and a few days' work putting a roof on a shed intended to house the explosives and detonators that were being used to blast tunnels out of the mountains to build one of the world's greatest hydroelectricity schemes. He had to buy his own tools and to learn the imperial system of measurements in quick time.

He later recalled, 'When you're young, you're eager to learn … and the most important thing is you must never say to yourself, "I can't do that." If you say that to yourself once or twice, you have convinced yourself you can't do it. So I really tried hard.' When his work was inspected a few days later, his supervisor was impressed. Within four months, more plumbers had been employed, and Josef had been made a foreman. The Snowy Mountains Scheme was a wellspring of opportunity. As Josef later recalled, 'Once I was in the Snowy, everything went well. The money was good, the food was good. For me that was the start of everything.' At first he was employed under a huge roof to build houses – more than 180 of them over sixteen months – in prefabricated halves before they were put on a truck and taken up the mountain to the new work sites. 'It was a neat job, a clean job and well protected.' When that was done, he followed the project up the mountain to Tumut Point. For the first time in his life, he had a room to himself. It was 'Fantastic. I had a little table and one chair and the room was just big enough to turn myself around … we had a [heating] pipe going underneath the ceilings and I used to throw my wet gear on top of it, and the next day I was ready for work with dry clothes.' He worked six days a week. Sunday was a day for prayer and laundry. There were so many migrant workers that there was no prejudice. He found countrymen – and soon the canteens had divided into tables based on nationality and common languages.[8] Unlike many, Josef didn't drink or gamble, but saved all his money. 'I knew my future … I'm going to buy a house, I'm going to get married, I'm going to raise a family.' The only money he spent was to send letters back to his mother in Slovenia.

There were serious accidents in the tunnels, with dozens of lives lost. Josef needed an operation after he fell off a truck and damaged his back.

Later, he was exposed to asbestos in a boiler-house accident. But he loved the work and the community of workers. 'We were all proud to be new Australians and proud to be working for a good company with good money, good conditions, and building something worthwhile.'

Josef Plibersek had arrived. He was now part of the country and building its future.

*   *   *

There is a painting by the Swiss-born artist Sali Herman titled *The Women of Paddington, 1950*. Two women, both in calf-length skirts, are standing outside that suburb's iconic terrace houses, the peeling paint only partly offset by flowers in hanging baskets. Both hold babies. There are more children at heel – a toddler clinging to the skirts, a baby in a crib on the veranda and another sitting wide-legged on the footpath. As Herman recorded, the houses were cramped and the streets were the place to socialise. In other pictures he trowelled on the paint to show the terraces seemingly leaning against each other behind a foreground of tumble-down fences and untended grass.[9]

Today, those terraces are in the federal electorate of Wentworth, which neighbours Tanya Plibersek's seat of Sydney. Paddington is one of the wealthiest suburbs in Australia, and these houses some of the most expensive. But when Josef Plibersek was making his way, it was a slum – home to recently arrived migrants and a centre of the Slovenian community. This was where Josef Plibersek came on his rare breaks from work on the Snowy.

One evening in 1956 he went to a Slovenian community dance at the Paddington Town Hall. There he met a young woman who had been in the country only a few weeks. She was the beneficiary of sponsorship from the Federal Catholic Immigration Committee – one of the church- and community-based organisations that had partnered with government under the 'populate or perish' imperative when the formal displaced persons' scheme had ended. Josef and Rozalija Repic fell into conversation. They danced. They discovered that they had been brought up in the same region of Slovenia, both on subsistence farms about thirty kilometres apart. From the Plibersek family farm in Kočno, you can look down to the plains and see where Rozalija – now known as Rose – was brought up in the village of Podvinci, near Ptuj. Rose remembers that first meeting with Josef. 'He had beautiful blue eyes. He was a nice man, such a nice man.' On her side, at least, it was not love at first sight, but Josef was clear from that first meeting about his intentions. He wanted to marry her. When he returned to the Snowy, they wrote to each other. 'You get to know a lot about someone from the way they write a letter,' she recalls.[10]

Rose was probably twenty-four years old when they met. She can't be sure. Whereas Josef Plibersek left a paper-trail behind him, there are no easily available public records recording Rozalija's existence until she migrated to Australia. Tanya Plibersek says she knows so little about this side of her family that when she is asked for the family medical history, on her mother's side there are mainly blanks. The family has managed to determine that the birth date that was recorded on Rozalija's official papers – August 1933 – is wrong.[11] Combing through church records, they found a record of her birth in April that year. But Rozalija didn't know her birthday, because when she was a child nobody ever celebrated it. When the immigration officials asked for a date, she made one up. Tanya has no hesitation in describing her mother as a victim of child abuse. Rose doesn't use those words. She says her upbringing was 'strict' or 'tough'.

Rose's mother died when she was about five, probably from complications after giving birth to Rose's youngest brother, Anton. Her father remarried quickly to a woman who has entered the Plibersek family lore as, in Tanya's words, 'a classic wicked stepmother ... she was physically abusive. My mother has a pretty strong personality, so perhaps she copped it more than the other children. My grandfather never protected any of them, and he had a pretty harsh parenting style himself.'

Why child abuse, rather than 'strict parenting', which is the term Rose uses? Tanya recounts a 'creative punishment' inflicted on her mother. The family grew cobs of corn and used the dried kernels for stock and chicken feed. When Rozalija and her siblings had been 'naughty', their father would scatter the dried kernels on the ground and force them to kneel on them. The only emotional warmth came from Rose's siblings, but she was sent away from them before she became a teenager. She lived with other relatives as a domestic servant. She remembers the Russians coming through the town, and the girls, particularly the youngest girls, being hidden in the cellar for fear of rape.

Rose has always been reluctant to speak in detail about her childhood, but in an interview for this book said, 'Perhaps I missed out on something that I was not able to give my children.' This is part of her enduring pain, and part of the grief that haunts her. It is not a verdict shared by her children. Rather, her eldest son, Ray Plibersek, says, 'The gap between what my parents had growing up, in the way of love and security, and what they delivered to us, was huge.'

After the war, Rozalija moved to the capital of Slovenia, Ljubljana, and worked in a kindergarten before being taken on as a nanny and housemaid by a war widow. When the war ended, there was nothing to hold her in Yugoslavia. Always questing, always adventurous and rebellious, she decided she wanted to see the world. She crossed the border – illegally – into Italy, and once in Milan began to enquire about immigration. She thought she would go to California, because she had heard about it, but she soon discovered that she could be accepted by Australia much more quickly. She knew nothing about the country, but the Catholic Church said it would sponsor her. She boarded a flight in Milan in 1955 and arrived in Sydney on 14 June. On her arrival card she gave her occupation as 'domestic' and her intended address as the Federal Catholic Immigration Committee in Elizabeth Street, Sydney. The purpose of her visit was described as 'resettlement – indefinite'. She signed with a round, cursive script.[12] She says today that she never intended to stay. She was going to earn money in Australia and then travel to other places. 'I wanted to see everything there is to see.'

For the first few weeks, she lived in the harbourside Sydney suburb of Rose Bay, in a billet organised by her sponsoring organisation. But Rose had a remote family connection in Australia. The sister of her sister's husband, Kristina Hoiker (née Bernhard), and her husband were living in the evocatively named suburb of Oyster Bay, on the outskirts of the city. By the time of that Paddington Town Hall dance, Rose was living with them and working in a shoe factory in inner-city Redfern, catching a bus and train back and forth each day.

Less than a year after they met, Rozalija and Josef, or Rose and Joe as they had now become, were married in the Como West Catholic Church. It was still a long-distance relationship. Rose continued to live with Kristina in an increasingly awkward and unfriendly arrangement. Kristina was 'a hard woman', recalls Rose. It was lonely. Rose still spoke hardly any English. Waiting to catch the bus to her job in Redfern, she would sometimes be abused for not speaking English. 'People would say, if you can't speak English you should go back to where you came from,' she remembers. She fell pregnant almost immediately after the marriage, and on Christmas Day 1957 gave birth to a boy they called Raymond Joseph. He was an unsettled infant, crying day and night. Kristina doted on the child but was hard on the mother. She refused to let Rose use the new washing machine to launder nappies. Joe continued to work on the Snowy, and was home so infrequently that when he came, the baby was frightened of him.

Joe was not waiting for the future to arrive but doing everything he could to build it. He was saving money with more dedication than ever before. In the months before Rose gave birth, she had bought a ticket in a workplace raffle and won £250. This, together with Joe's savings, meant they had been able, on 3 October 1957, to buy a newly subdivided block of land at 3 Carvers Road, Oyster Bay, for £750.[13] From then on, whenever Joe could get a break from the Snowy, he worked on building their new home.

Why did they choose Oyster Bay? Rose says it was partly because she was already familiar with the suburb. As well, it was affordable. They might have felt less isolated, and suffered from less prejudice, if they had moved to the inner-city southern European communities, but that would have meant slum-living, and renting. Joe and Rose liked Oyster Bay because it was semi-rural, with clean air and big trees. Twenty-six kilometres south of the centre of Sydney, it was a working-class suburb – their neighbours were tradespeople and factory workers. It was also overwhelmingly white and Anglo-Saxon. The Pliberseks – Joe still with a strong accent and Rose not fluent in English – stood out as foreigners.

All over Sydney, the outer suburbs were growing fast, fibro houses springing up alongside unsealed roads, well ahead of the capacity and willingness of governments to provide services. These post-war, baby-boom suburbs were the childhood homes of many future Labor Party politicians. Paul Keating grew up in Bankstown, Mark Latham in Liverpool. But Oyster Bay was different to the flat plains of the western suburbs. It was on one of the most beautiful stretches of coast in the country, and the landscape redeemed what otherwise might have been bland and ugly as buildings were thrown up at speed. The bay from which the suburb took its name was on the estuary of the Georges River as it entered Botany Bay. A previous generation of local children had been able to crack open oysters on the rocks of the coastline. It was still a wild, exhilarating place of rolling hills, creeks wending their way to the river and glimpses of the Georges River. This was one of a cluster of fast-growing suburbs on the crenelated peninsula that jutted out between Botany Bay and the Royal National Park.

Oyster Bay is part of the Sutherland Shire, which today has entered the national consciousness as a collection of quintessentially conservative, white Australian suburbs. This is the home of former prime minister Scott Morrison and his electorate of Cook, named after Lieutenant (later Captain) James Cook, who landed at Kurnell in 1770 and laid claim to the continent for the British crown. The area where the Pliberseks built their house, and where Rose still lives, is now in the federal electorate of Hughes, which until the 2022 election was held by Craig Kelly – Liberal Party renegade and later leader of the United Australia Party. The Sutherland Shire includes Cronulla Beach, which takes its name from an Aboriginal word meaning 'place of pink seashells'. Cronulla is a centre of surfie culture, the backdrop for the novel and film *Puberty Blues*, and, in 2005, the setting for race riots during which a mob attacked Middle Eastern youths.

But for the Plibersek family, Oyster Bay was a wonderful place – somewhere their children could grow up happy, healthy and with all the opportunities their parents had lacked. In 2019, Tanya Plibersek appeared at the Byron Bay Writers' Festival and was invited to play a game in which she was to say the first thing that entered her mind in response to a phrase or word. The first term thrown at her was 'Oyster Bay'. Without drawing breath, she responded, 'Trees.'

Soon, Rose was pregnant again. A second son, Fred Phillip Plibersek – who always went by Phillip – was born on 19 April 1960. By then, the family were living in their new house at 3 Carvers Road. They moved in as soon as the roof was on, sitting on crates until they could afford furniture. Rose did the washing with a scrubbing board in the back yard, which was soon planted with vegetables and grape vines, with space for a chicken pen. When she could afford a copper and a wringer, it was regarded as a labour-saving device. Washing machines came much later. Until Ray was eight years old, if he wanted to watch television he had to go to a neighbour's house.

Joe left the Snowy when the house was complete and began to work as a plumber for a large building business, picking up side jobs on the weekends. Despite having worked as a plumber for years on the Snowy, his qualifications were still not formally recognised in Australia. Ray's earliest memories include his father coming home after a day's work, eating an early dinner, then spreading his technical college homework over the dining table and drawing diagrams of drainage. It was an ethos he and Phillip were encouraged to copy. 'We were always aware that we should study, that this was an opportunity our parents hadn't had.'

First children are, the folklore goes, more likely to be responsible, sober citizens. First children of migrants bear a particular burden. From an early age, they become the point of liaison between their parents and the wider world. Today, Ray Plibersek has no doubt that this combination formed his character. He is a lawyer and active in Labor Party politics. Until recently he was a Labor councillor for the Sutherland City Council. Yet despite being outwardly entirely 'assimilated', in Harold Holt's words, he regards English as his second language. Until he started school at the state primary in Oyster Bay, he spoke only Slovenian, and he was burdened with a name the other children struggled to pronounce. He had no option but to learn English quickly, and he then became Rose's ambassador – translating for her, filling in forms, explaining things to her. But when acting on his own behalf, he says, he has always been shy.

As soon as they were old enough, the boys would go with their father on weekends to help him with his plumbing jobs, learning practical skills and absorbing his work ethic. Ray still has scars from injuries

acquired on building sites as a child, but he loved working alongside
and talking to his father – and at the end of the day he would be paid
for his efforts. For Ray and Phillip, Oyster Bay was a wonderland: they
rode their bikes around the gradually urbanising streets, caught tad-
poles in the creek at the end of the road and got up to mischief. The
boys became expert bombmakers, making explosives out of firecrack-
ers. In one week, they blew up a few letterboxes in the surrounding
streets, then realised that the fact their own letterbox was unexploded
was suspicious. They blew it up too, to throw their neighbours, and
their parents, off the case.

Meanwhile, in the evenings, Joe and Rose were taking advantage
of the first modest security they had ever known to indulge their thirst
for learning. Joe subscribed to *Reader's Digest* and ordered its condensed
versions of books from the canon of English literature. Joe maintained
a subscription to *National Geographic* magazine, and *New Scientist*. As
soon as they could afford a record player, pop and classical music filled
the house. Later, the children would be taken to the opera or the theatre
whenever money allowed. They spoke Slovenian at home on Joe's insistence, but heard lots of other languages as well thanks to the frequent
visitors from the wider migrant community: German, Serbian and Cro-
ation among them.

The boys were close, but as they grew older it became increasingly
apparent that they were very different in personality. Ray says, 'I was
always the sensitive, responsible older brother, whereas Phillip was a bit
more – well, not exactly a black sheep, but a bit less responsible. A bit
more fun-loving. Aggressive is not the right word. Hard is not the right
word either. But he liked to muck around. I was the caring, responsible
one. Phil would be the troublemaker.' Today, Ray sees his sister, Tanya,
as combining both these sides of the family personality. They have often
discussed how she might be different if, like him, she had been the first
born, and forced to help their parents navigate the new country. Instead,
by the time she came along, the family was established. Ray says, 'Like
me, she's got a caring, soft, considerate side. But like Phillip, she also has
a toughness, and a rebelliousness, and,' he pauses, 'when she was younger,
she was a bit wild.'

Joe and Rose had always wanted three children, but for years after Phillip's birth, Rose didn't get pregnant. The family, to Ray's mind, had a neat symmetry to it – two adults, two children. 'It was a loving family, and home was somewhere we always felt safe.' He remembers feeling resentful when, in mid-1969, at the age of eleven, he was informed that his mother was pregnant again. 'I thought it would upset things. That we were fine as we were.' But the minute his baby sister was born, he fell in love.

Many biographers of prime ministers – who have almost all been male – have observed that they were the centre of doting attention from their mothers and sisters. This, it has been hypothesised, is what gave them the confidence and self-belief to conceive of themselves as leaders. In the case of Tanya Plibersek, the gender aspect of this dynamic is reversed. From the moment of her birth, she was the centre of adoring attention not only from both her parents, but also from her two older brothers.

Ray remembers pestering his mother for a chance to nurse Tanya with a bottle. In the evenings he would tuck her up in his bed and read to her. He had been a restless baby, but Tanya was chubby, happy and pretty. She became a striking toddler with platinum-blonde hair. Her brothers took her everywhere, including her in all their adventures. Ray put a pillow on the back of his bike and cycled with her all over the suburb. Tanya remembers Phillip riding with her on the back of his bike in heavy rain, then losing control on one of Oyster Bay's steep hills when his brakes failed. She was six years old. Phillip had to tell her to jump for her life. It was, she recalls, 'messy but spectacular'. In the evenings the boys would play and talk in their bedrooms, and little Tanya was always there. 'We were always talking to her and playing with her, and when we would argue she would sit there and watch, taking it all in,' says Ray.

Ray was aware, when Tanya started primary school, that his little sister was very bright – and that she had also benefited from watching him and Phillip. The two boys were now teenagers, and often argued about politics. It continued when they started university. Ray was studying law and history and was politicised by his course, acquiring an intense awareness of the impact of the dispossession of Australia's first people. Phillip was studying geology. He was not necessarily right-wing. Ray never knew how Phillip voted, but Phillip didn't like 'greenies' and was pro-mining. As they grew older, the arguments between the two brothers became increasingly passionate. Their raised voices would fill the house. They argued about land rights, about uranium mining, and about whether government should intervene to help make people's lives better or whether, as Phillip would assert, people should be self-reliant and pull themselves up the ladders of opportunity.

And there, sitting on the floor or the bed listening to them, was Tanya. Ray says: 'She was a smart little girl. And she's being stimulated by these discussions. So she's grown up with exposure to all these ideas ahead of most of her peers.' Unlike him, Tanya was socially confident, and always popular. He was immensely proud of her, and hugely protective.

There is a story that has entered the Plibersek family folklore, honed from many tellings, which the family sees as summing up the relationship of Tanya to her brothers – and the difference between these two formative figures in her life. It concerns the rubber tree that used to stand in the front yard of 3 Carvers Road. It was to be cut down because the roots were interfering with the drains. Tanya, about four years old at the time, was distressed at the thought of losing it. Phil took her outside to 'say goodbye to the tree'. Ray remembers: 'I was inside and I heard her screaming, "Ray, Ray, help me," and I rushed out, and there was Tanya hanging by her arms from the tree, maybe three or four feet off the ground. And my brother is just sitting there looking at her. And she says, "Ray, rescue me." And I said to Phillip, "Why don't you help Tanya?" And he said, "No, I just put her up there. I just wanted to see how long until she falls."'

This story is told as a joke, but with an edge. Meanwhile, in a blog of family memories written many years later, Tanya described her brother Phillip as:

> experienced at both physical and psychological torture ... He often experimented on me: physical endurance, and Pavlovian behavioural experiments. Phil wanted to see how many times I would do his bidding without reward. He would give me 20 cents and his lolly order (liquorice bullets, spearmint leaves, choccos, or sherbet fountains depending on his mood) and tell me if I got his

lollies he might give me one. Sometimes he would, sometimes not. If he didn't give me one twice or three times in a row I would refuse to go the next time. It was a delicate balancing act. Why didn't I just steal a lolly or two on the way home? Because he would punch me in the arm. Or poke me in the ribs. He habitually poked me in the ribs when we passed each other on the stairs, until I learnt a contorted defensive position which covered both my head and sides.[14]

But Phillip was also the best fun. She remembers: 'Phil made the best paper aeroplanes and could usually be tempted from his study to do it. He told good scary stories – so scary that I am still frightened of vampires (he told me there was one under his bed. I was sitting on it at the time). Even as a child, his mischievousness was one of his most fun and attractive qualities.'[15] And so the pattern was set: Phil as the charismatic risk taker, Ray as the responsible caretaker, and Tanya absorbing all those qualities.

It was Phillip, she says, who first told her that she was especially smart, and that she had a duty to do something with those talents. The boys themselves were no slouches intellectually. Ray went on to get honours in history and a masters degree in law. Phil got first-class honours in geology. Ray would come home from university and see Tanya selling flowers at the railway station – an after-school job that, he says proudly, she was very good at 'because she was always smiling'.

Ray left home when Tanya was still in high school, to take up his first job as a land-rights lawyer in the Northern Territory, but he kept in close touch. Today, living back in Oyster Bay, he often goes to parliament to watch her speak, and he attends her political functions when he can. During the 2022 election campaign, he could be seen on the edge of a shot on the television news, protectively holding an umbrella over his sister's head as she addressed the media.

There is a joke between Ray and Tanya. When they cross a busy road together, he still puts out a hand to protect her as the cars whizz past, a habit acquired when she was a little girl. She will brush his had aside and say, 'Ray, I am an adult woman now.' And he says, 'Of course you are.'

*   *   *

Tanya's earliest memories are of the house and garden at Carvers Road. 'I remember sitting in the back yard, eating things off the tree – white peaches and figs and mandarins and things still warm from the sun. I remember helping my mother cook, making apple strudel. She'd peel the apples and I'd get to eat the long snake of apple skin and drink the juice after she'd grated the apples by hand. I remember helping her put the washing through the mangle, and walking up to the shops at Jannali, and she would give me a little bag or a little box of things to carry to make me feel helpful. I remember standing at the window when I could barely see over the sill and watching the other kids going to school, and saying, "When can I go to school, how old do I have to be?" I remember sitting on my dad's lap watching the news.'

Joe liked Gough Whitlam, but he did not talk to his daughter much about politics. She doesn't know how her parents voted, but they communicated 'by their lived example' clear values. They showed her that it was important to look after the people around you. By the time Tanya could speak, her mother had overcome her language difficulties and made friends in the community. Over time, she became a local identity, and Tanya watched as she talked to neighbours over cups of tea and biscuits fresh from the oven. The Pliberseks were the kind of people who helped others. They were always welcoming people into their home, the kettle always on, the biscuit tin always full. As well as their immediate neighbours, they kept up with the Slovenian community. Tanya remembers frequent gatherings at their home. Her mother has maintained friendships from this time for the whole of her life. For example, Rose was the only visitor to a woman dying of cancer who had sometimes looked after Tanya as a child. There were darker moments, too – conversations that had a lasting impact on the little girl. Tanya remembers gradually becoming aware, from conversations between her mother and her friends, that not all homes were as safe as hers.

Although politics wasn't discussed much, Joe had a keen interest in current affairs. Tanya was sent across the road to buy the newspaper. Joe would come home from work, greet the family, then settle down to read. He always had the radio on when working, and he paid attention to the news. Little Tanya's first political statement was on her father's lap in front of the television. Gough Whitlam was on the news, and Tanya said to her father, 'He's a good man, isn't he, Daddy?'

The family had dinner together, sitting around the dining-room table. As well as talking about their days, they would discuss the news. The arguments between Ray and Phil were now commonplace, and from late primary school, Tanya was holding her own. She could be fierce, certain and passionate in her opinions, increasingly siding with Ray. Joe was a watchful and moderating presence. Tanya recalls that they were never reprimanded for passionate argument, but he insisted that they listen respectfully to one another. 'My father often said to me, if I was in full flight about something, "You've got to listen, you've got to learn to listen to the views of others." I have never forgotten that. It was an important lesson for me.'

From a young age, Tanya was aware that her parents had very different temperaments, and a different attitude to Australia. Her father was calm and rational. He never lost his temper. She recalls that they argued, but 'never attacked each other personally or belittled each other. Their arguments were two equals disagreeing ... the arguments were sort of lopsided sometimes, with her getting quite heated and emotional and him usually deflecting to humour if he could, and frustrating her even more. But they really loved and respected one another.' Joe's feeling for Australia was one of unalloyed gratitude. Her mother, however, had never meant to leave Slovenia for good. She had intended to travel beyond Australia and then to return home. Despite her happy marriage, there was a sense of grief that marrying had meant giving up those intentions. As well, there was her mother's traumatic childhood. It was rarely discussed explicitly. Tanya had to press her mother for information, and even today she is not sure of many details. But the knowledge of past pain, mixed with gratitude for current blessings, was part of the family atmospherics. Tanya remembers the day her mother got a letter telling her that her brother had died. 'It was the first time I ever saw her cry, sitting on the back steps. I heard her first, and I went out and saw her crying. I didn't know before that that adults could cry.'

Tanya loved and was close to both her parents, but she identified with her father. She aspired to imitate his rationality and his even temper, and she worked at it. The family's Slovenian heritage was defining. Tanya and the boys spoke Slovenian at home, and Ray and Tanya still speak Slovenian to Rose. At first, Tanya was ashamed of being different. She began her formal education at the Oyster Bay Primary School, walking there each day with her mother. When they got within earshot of her classmates and their parents, she would beg her mother to speak English. One of Tanya's teachers was married to a Slovenian, and he spoke the language. 'I understood him perfectly, but I wanted to sink through the floor, because I was embarrassed, and it made me different,' she recalls. But by the end of primary school, Tanya had changed her attitude. Now, she was intensely proud of her difference and of her heritage.

Wrapped into all this – indivisible from the routines of family life and identity – was the Catholic Church. The week was punctuated by worship, confession and forgiveness. They attended the Slovenian church in Merrylands, where the service was accompanied and framed by community and cultural gatherings. They also went to St Joseph's Catholic Church, a stone's throw from the Carvers Road house, for mass and confession every weekend. Ray, Phillip and Tanya would go in the morning, because she wanted to watch Disney on television on Sunday night. Her parents went later. Not attending was simply never considered, unless one of them was ill. The family did not ostentatiously display their religiosity, but the expectations around it were strong. 'It was always clear to me that my parents expected that so long as I lived in their house, I would go to mass and confession,' Tanya recalls.

Catholicism – her understanding of its values, its culture and the network of believers and cultural Catholics throughout social and political life – is the warp and weft of Tanya Plibersek. In our interviews she claimed that she was no longer a believer. She said she valued the sense of belonging to the church, and that she finds great beauty in the ceremony and ritual. But as a feminist, there was a tension with the church's record of male domination, its opposition to contraception and abortion. She describes herself as a cultural Catholic. 'I believe in many of the teachings of the church, but not literally everything in the book.

Do I believe I will be reunited with my father in heaven? I don't believe that. And I do, in a way, regret that. But the fact is I can't buy the whole package.' She told me she still went to mass sometimes, to keep her mother company.

But her friend Kim Williams scoffs at the suggestion that this is the only reason. Tanya, he says, 'has a truly Christian heart. She is an old-fashioned lefty Catholic. I think she goes to mass out of personal need.' He recalls 'an almighty row' at a dinner party he hosted between former NSW Labor minister Michael Egan and Tanya about the role of the church. Egan, also a Catholic, was defending the Christian Brothers in the face of the reputational damage caused by sexual abuse. Tanya and Williams were confronting him with the systemic failures of the order, as revealed by the Royal Commission into Institutional Sexual Abuse. Recalls Williams: 'Michael was accusing us of being anti-Catholic. We both said, "No, don't be so simplistic and foolish." And Tanya said, "Fuck you, Michael. I'm the one that still goes to mass. Not you."'

Catholicism is part of many of her childhood memories, from the momentous to the mundane. The family kept chickens, and Tanya had a bantam that was her special pet. She used to read to it from a book, *My Book of Bible Firsts*; the chicken pooed on the page. She was confirmed at St Joseph's, made her first communion there, and later she was married at St Patrick's, Sutherland.

In 2022, Tanya delivered the Daniel Mannix Memorial Lecture at Newman College, Melbourne. Named for Australia's most famous and politically active Catholic archbishop, the annual event is a landmark in the political and intellectual life of Catholic Australia. Previous lecturers included the head of the 1950s anti-communist movement, Bob Santamaria, and former prime minister Malcolm Fraser. Tanya was the choice of the college rector, Father Frank Brennan, known for his activism on human rights on behalf of refugees. He had made a point of getting to know Tanya early in her political career.

Surrounded by the college alumni, Tanya spoke openly about her faith and said her values were drawn from Catholicism. 'My youth was marked by the checkpoints and rituals of the church,' she said. She recalled struggling to come up with weighty sins at confession – 'something more than "I was fighting with my brother" – the cost of which was usually a pretty mild three Hail Marys.'

There was 'no longer a single pulpit or a universal source of truth', she continued. 'But it's clear to me that, even in our fractured world, the timeless lessons of Christ continue to inform progressive politics today. Love thy neighbour. Turn the other cheek. The first will be last and the last will be first. The meek shall inherit the earth … These are simple statements. But that shouldn't hide just how radical they are.' Had the audience ever tried to love their neighbours, she asked. 'All of them?'[16]

Tanya's faith is visible in some of her habits of speech. One of her favourite phrases in describing people she likes or admires is 'decent human being'. She used those words when farewelling the departing presenter of ABC Radio National's *Breakfast* program, Fran Kelly, saying Kelly had demonstrated that it was possible, in public life, to be both a good journalist and 'a decent human being'. She used the same phrase in almost every one of our interviews in talking about colleagues and mentors, and in talking about her father. Tears in her eyes, she said Josef was a 'decent human being' and then, after a breath, 'a beautiful man, an absolutely beautiful man'. She described her early mentor, Senator Bruce Childs, as another 'beautiful man'. And she used the same terms when referring to her own aspirations. She wanted to be a 'decent human being', to make a difference, and to live a large and useful life.

*   *   *

Around 1970, Joe Plibersek got a job as a plumber with Qantas. As well as better wages and job security, a primary motivation was that staff of the airline could access cheap standby airfares. After years of separation from Slovenia, Joe and Rose wanted to go home.

On the first trip, in 1970, baby Tanya was left behind with friends, but Ray remembers the flight and then the train journey. His father was tense as great-coated agents of the communist government walked the train, checking papers, 'like something out of a Le Carré novel'. Josef had, after all, left the country illegally. Would there be consequences now? But all was well. When the train pulled into the station the platform was full of family members Ray had never met. It was overwhelming.

From then on, thanks to the cheap tickets, the family travelled almost every second year to Slovenia, and more widely through Europe and the Pacific. Tanya can't remember a time when international travel wasn't part of her life. This, together with her parents' passion for education and culture, gave her what others would later describe as a middle-class polish and urbanity. In adult life, people tended to assume on meeting her that she came from a well-off family. The truth was that Joe and Rose never had much money, but any surplus was spent on education, literature, the arts and travel. This, too, was how they demonstrated their values to their children.

With Tanya's birth, the family outgrew Carvers Road. Rose and Joe bought another block of land nearby, and from 1974 worked on building a new house, aided by Phillip and Ray. This was a much larger home, constructed in the chocolate-coloured brick that was fashionable in the 1970s. There were five bedrooms upstairs, a big living area downstairs, and, once again, a backyard for fruit trees, vegetables and chickens. Rose Plibersek still lives there today, and the house has barely changed since the children filled the upstairs bedrooms. There is the same furniture. Photos and mementos of her children and grand-children are on every surface. Ray lives with his family nearby and comes by most days, calling out to her in Slovenian as he pushes open the back door.

Tanya Plibersek was a precocious primary-school student. It seems that feminism was always a part of her, even before she knew the word. In primary school she remembers questioning why boys and girls had to line up for class in separate lines, and why all the doctors were men and the nurses women. She remembers pestering Ray to explain things to her – such as the difference between communism and capitalism. 'He'd explain, and then before we talked again, I'd forget what the words meant, and I'd say to him things like "communism is the one that is about sharing with people, right?"' It was Ray – by now a member of the Labor Party – who talked to her about politics, including explaining what was happening during the dismissal of the Whitlam government and the election of the Fraser government in 1975, when she was approaching her sixth birthday, and he was in his first year at university.

Ray says Tanya was recognised as one of the brightest students in her primary school and was offered a place in selective 'opportunity classes' in the last two years of primary school. It was her choice to stay local, and she moved on to Jannali Girls' High School. It was far from multi-cultural. Phillip and Ray had gone to the boys' school on the other side of the road. Phillip's nickname had been 'pineapple' because his surname was regarded as too difficult to pronounce – 'too many p's', one of his classmates recalled.[17] Among the 800 or so girls in Tanya's school, she was one of very few who came from a non-Anglo background. She remembers only one Aboriginal student. If she was teased, she doesn't remember it. She strode into high school, keen for the next stage of her life – impatient, even.

It was an ugly campus, typical of the hastily constructed schools in the baby-boomer suburbs. She recalls it as resembling the set of the television series *Prisoner*, 'as though they got some plans for concrete school buildings from East Germany in the 1970s'.

By now, Ray had left home. Phillip was still a university student, but he soon moved away as well. Almost as soon as he had graduated, he was travelling throughout the Pacific Rim, working for mining companies, but for much of Tanya's school and university career he had a flat in inner-suburban Sydney. If Tanya had a wild side at high school – if she tried drugs, if she drank underage – it was almost certainly at one of Phillip's parties, says Ray. 'He used to take her to see bands. He liked live music. He liked fast motorbikes. He loved taking risks, and she had that side, too.' Rose remembers how Phillip would come back to Oyster Bay to visit, riding his Ducati motorbike and cradling a treat of fresh croissants, warm from the bakery, under his leather jacket. He would embrace her, then roar off again to the shops because she had only low-fat milk in the fridge and he insisted on full cream in his coffee. Phillip and Rose had a special bond, family friends remember. If Tanya identified with her father, Phillip was more like his mother.

Tanya claims she was a nerd at high school, 'a girly swot', but she was also popular. There were always friends gathered around the kitchen table after school. Rose would bake for them. 'So much laughter and chatter,' recalls Rose.

Despite the unprepossessing buildings, the teaching at Jannali was excellent. Tanya recalls a strong cohort of feminist women teachers. 'They were wonderful, caring staff who were committed to the ideals of public education.' She keeps in touch with several of the women who taught her. Particularly influential was Diana Lewis, a visual arts teacher who taught Tanya in every year of high school. Lewis remembers Tanya as one of the most rewarding students she ever encountered. In the early years of high school, Tanya was 'a bit of a naughty girl, a bit of a rebel ... She was intelligent beyond her years. So I think she stood up for what she believed in right back then.' Sometimes in those early years, Lewis thought that Tanya was bored. She was at the centre of a strong group of intelligent girls who would get annoyed with other students if they disrupted the class or failed to apply themselves. 'At Year Eight, she was at Year Eleven level in most subjects, and she found other students frustrating ... She would bait them. She didn't suffer fools gladly.'

From early in high school, Tanya was on the student representative council. She later joined the debating team, in which she excelled. She could argue, as Lewis remembers, 'that black was white and white was black'. After one debate, another girl said to her, 'You are going to be a politician.' Joe and Rose would turn up to parent–teacher meetings, humble, expressing nothing but gratitude for the teachers, and glowing with pride as they heard of the achievements of their clever daughter.

When Tanya was in Year Twelve, Lewis was scheduled to teach her art history subject in a room that didn't have curtains to block the windows. Showing slides was central to the teaching. 'I was a bit put out, but Tanya was enraged,' Lewis remembers. Tanya organised a petition among the students and took it to the principal. 'And lo and behold, our room was changed,' says Lewis.

By her senior years of high school, Tanya had a boyfriend – Matt Brown, a Sutherland Shire boy who went on to be an ABC journalist. Their classmates recall it as a passionate affair; the gossip was that they planned to marry. Tanya says, 'I don't think anyone was thinking about marriage at seventeen.' The relationship endured into university, and they remain friends today.

Tanya was an all-round good student, Lewis says, but her strength was writing. Her essays were 'extraordinary. I had never read student essays like it. She answered the question intelligently with the most compelling argument. Her choice of language was superb.'

Lewis used to take the students into the city to visit the Art Gallery of New South Wales, or further afield to the National Gallery in Canberra. For most of the students, going into the city or to Canberra was a big deal. Sutherland Shire kids tended to be insular – there was a motto that people were born in the Shire and died in the Shire, without going anywhere else. That wasn't true for the well-travelled Pliberseks, but Tanya nevertheless remembers those excursions as enormously exciting, thanks to how Lewis brought the pictures and their history to life. Whenever she travels, she takes the time to visit artistic historical sites, and when she visits the gift shop, she buys a postcard to send to Diana Lewis.

Despite its conservative tinge, the Sutherland Shire was home to a cohort of left-wing Labor members and strong, progressive women. Plibersek remembers environmental activist Genevieve Rankin, who went on to be mayor of Sutherland Shire and was the first president of the NSW Welfare Workers' Union. Another important figure was Hazel Wilson, a Labor Sutherland Shire councillor and later an ALP state candidate. These women organised the local presence in the big Palm Sunday peace marches of the 1980s, protesting against Ronald Reagan's 'Star Wars' defence plan, against uranium mining in Australia, and, closer to home, against the Lucas Heights nuclear reactor, which was on the edges of the Sutherland Shire, just a dozen kilometres from Tanya's home. Tanya was an enthusiastic participant in the marches from her earliest years in high school.

Then, in 1985, at the age of fifteen, she represented the school at an International Youth Year function in the Sutherland Civic Centre. The young people were broken up into groups to discuss different topics. Tanya's group was meant to discuss how to prevent young people using drugs, and at the end of the session, she was chosen to present their conclusions in a public address. Tanya can't remember what she said, but it must have been good. As she left the stage, she was approached by Hazel Wilson, who told her that with views like hers, she should join the Labor Party.

Within days, she had acted on that advice.

2

SENSE AND SENSIBILITY

I t was Alisson Cobin, Tanya Plibersek's Year Eleven English teacher at Jannali Girls' High, who introduced her to the work of Jane Austen. The nineteenth-century English novelist remains Plibersek's favourite author. Almost every media profile of Plibersek mentions her love of Austen, often suggesting it is somehow quaint for a feminist to admire what those who know no better think of as antiquated chick-lit about genteel romance. Julia Gillard recounts how Tanya would often, on the plane out of Canberra on a Thursday night, be reading Austen or George Eliot or some other nineteenth-century work of fiction when everyone else was sleeping or working.

But to diminish Austen is to misunderstand her genius. It is also to misunderstand Tanya Plibersek.

Plibersek says she has read Austen's six major novels between fifteen and twenty times each. She returns, at times of stress, to *Pride and Prejudice*, which is probably Austen's best-known book. Why does she like Austen?

'I like the subtlety of it. I like the sense of humour. I like the minute observation. I like that she can find rich human experience in a small circle of people. I like that every time I read one of the books, I find something new in it.'

When she first read *Pride and Prejudice*, she identified with Elizabeth, the central character, and shared her embarrassment at the conduct of her mother, the socially gauche Mrs Bennet, whose central preoccupation is finding husbands for her five daughters. But after becoming a mother herself, she saw it differently. She was angry at the way Mrs Bennet was treated by all the other characters. 'What a reasonable thing to be worried about your five daughters and whether they are going to have a roof over their heads and food on their plates. And to be made a figure of fun for that is so wrong . . . but what incredible writing that you can come to a completely different conclusion on the characters. And Mr Bennet, you know, in the early days when you're on Lizzie's side he seems like a totally cool dad. And as you get older you think, "What a completely irresponsible man."'

Plibersek's description of her relationship with the book is, appropriately, an echo of the novel's main theme – which as the title suggests is about a journey from pride and prejudice to a more humble, mature and nuanced understanding of the world and its people. That's a journey Plibersek has also traced, according to those close to her, from the fierce, opinionated teenager – Diana Lewis's 'naughty girl' – to a woman who speaks of compromise in the pursuit of incremental reform.

There is one Austen book with which Tanya particularly identifies.

Sense and Sensibility is about the Dashwood family – a mother and three daughters left in straitened circumstances after the death of the father. The relationship between the two eldest daughters, Elinor and Marianne, drives the narrative. They are devoted to each other, unquestionably on each other's side, but also locked in mutual frustration, each with the other.

Marianne, the younger of the two, represents sensibility. She is characterised by an overwrought romanticism. In Austen's words: 'She was sensible and clever, but eager in everything; her sorrows, her joys, could have no moderation. She was generous, amiable, interesting; she was everything but prudent.'

For Marianne, no emotion is experienced in moderation, and no strong feeling remains unexpressed. She goes into raptures over falling leaves: 'Oh . . . with what transporting sensations have I formerly seen them fall! How have I delighted, as I walked, to see them driven in showers about me by the wind!' And, of course, she falls in love and is almost ruined by her failure to moderate her behaviour to the expectations of society and the exigencies of the time.

Elinor, on the other hand, is sense. She 'possessed a strength of understanding and a coolness of judgment which qualified her, though only nineteen, to be the counsellor of her mother, and enabled her frequently to counteract, to the advantage of them all, that eagerness of mind ... which must have generally led to imprudence. She had an excellent heart; – her disposition was affectionate and her feelings were strong; but she knew how to govern them; it was a knowledge which her mother had yet to learn, and which [Marianne] had resolved never to be taught.'

Tanya Plibersek is clear. In her family of origin, 'I was Elinor. No doubt about it.' As an adult she still identifies with Elinor and aspires to be like her. Austen, she says, provides a corrective in *Sense and Sensibility* to 'melodrama, the idea that all strong emotions must be constantly on display'.

There is no doubt that Elinor is the hero of Austen's tale. She is the exemplar of what, more than a hundred years after Austen was writing, Ernest Hemingway would depict as the defining characteristic of a hero, the definition of true courage – 'grace under pressure'.[1] Hemingway saw this as characteristic only of men. Part of Austen's genius is to show a female version of this virtue, within the confines of society at her time, and to make Elinor interesting – despite her common-sense exterior.

But Elinor can also be annoying. She is constantly trying to get her younger sister to moderate her emotions, to manage herself, to look on the bright side. 'Exert yourself, dear Marianne,' she tells her sister when she is in floods of tears over lost love. 'Think of your mother; think of her misery while you suffer; for her sake you must exert yourself.' When Elinor speaks of the man she loves, she says: 'I do not attempt to deny ... that I think very highly of him – that I greatly esteem, that I like him.' To which Marianne responds, 'Esteem him! Like him! Cold-hearted Elinor! Oh, worse than cold hearted. Ashamed of being otherwise! Use those words again, and I will leave the room this moment.' The reader can be forgiven for being a bit on Marianne's side in her frustration with Elinor's emotional withholding. Meanwhile, Tanya's husband, Michael Coutts-Trotter, says of his wife: 'She never loses her cool in an argument. I will end up incoherent and spluttering, and she will be Zen-like. It's just absolutely infuriating.'[2]

Not many people dislike Tanya Plibersek – but quite a few find her frustrating. An unnamed 'senior Liberal' once said of her to a journalist,

'I can't stand all that passive-aggressive "let's take the politics out of it" stuff. But God it works.'[3] On her own side of politics, she has an adoring fan club and many admirers. The people who are opposed to these groups are not so much enemies as Plibersek-sceptics. They think that while she is good, she is not quite as good as people who don't know her tend to think. Plibersek-sceptics use words like 'opaque', 'plays her cards close to her chest' and even 'bland'. Her fans refer to these same qualities, but in more positive terms. They describe her as 'impeccably proper', 'always discreet', 'the ultimate professional', and 'always considered, always respectful' of people, in a way unusual in the passionate, often dysfunctional and sometimes abusive world of the Australian Labor Party. Says another who stands between the fans and the sceptics: 'Strokes of dramatic policy insight are not her game, but she is a very good communicator and a very capable woman, and a very good listener. And these are under-rated skills.'

Plibersek is particularly recognised as a good media communicator – one of the best in the parliamentary Labor Party. But in her speeches, while there is plenty of sense and a workmanlike construction of ideas and values, there is little passion or rousing prose. She is a good communicator, but not usually an orator. Her colleagues ask each other whether Plibersek has 'the vision thing'.

Plibersek does not always cloak her passions. Around a dinner table with trusted confidants, she can argue tough. Kim Williams says she 'does anger explosively, with passion and with great indignation and very, very solid, purposeful engagement. It is very impressive.' Her political history is dotted with examples of this passion – including colourful language and personal attacks later regretted. Immediately after the 2022 election, she was ticked off by the new prime minister, Anthony Albanese, for comparing the appearance of opposition leader Peter Dutton to Voldemort, the archvillain of the Harry Potter books.[4] It was wrong, she admitted later, to focus on people's personal appearance, and she apologised unreservedly. But four years before, in parliament, she had compared Dutton to a Chucky doll – the evil toy possessed by a serial killer in the *Child's Play* horror-movie franchise. Dutton was, she said, 'like a really scary wooden puppet come to life, with the hand of the member for Warringah [then

Tony Abbott] up his, um, back! He's back, like Chucky! He's back, like Glenn Close in *Fatal Attraction*! That's right.'[5] Dutton, meanwhile, was once made to withdraw an unparliamentary epithet he hurled at her – the comparatively mild 'nasty Tanya'.[6] Tanya has been ejected from parliament her fair share of times for words thrown across the aisle.

So Plibersek does not always behave with the extraordinary restraint and dignity of Elinor Dashwood. Yet it is Elinor's virtues to which she aspires, and it is those quiet yet heroic qualities – grace under pressure, restraint, discipline, decency, common sense and perhaps most of all kindness – that she is happiest to be recognised for.

But if Tanya is Elinor, who is Marianne?

I asked her this question in our first interview, and she began to answer. 'There's no real Marianne in our family. I mean, maybe my brother Phillip was a bit of a Marianne. But I am definitely the Elinor.'

Asked to explain, she backed away. 'I don't really want to talk about any of that. Can we just talk about the facts until I know you better? You're asking for a kind of a self-analysis, and I don't really know you well enough for that, to be honest.'

We never did talk about Phillip, much. When I asked about him later, she said she didn't want to use his story in a cheap way, just to be 'relatable as a politician'.

But as the research for the book proceeded, I saw other candidates for Marianne – that gorgeous, bright and passionate girl, with her hunger for life and her incapacity to self-manage. I hope the reader of these pages is acute enough not to need each candidate to be highlighted and underlined as they make their appearance to get the point. As well, Tanya's occasional missteps and excesses – few, but potent – suggest her Marianne is internal, and part of her own passionate nature.

Finally – and perhaps it pushes the metaphor too far – one candidate for the Marianne to Tanya's Elinor might well be the Australian Labor Party itself.

By the final pages of *Sense and Sensibility*, Marianne has learned from her sister, and has resolved to manage herself better, fighting back heartbreak and anger with a resolve to put a good face on things and be cheerful. She says to Elinor: 'I saw in my own behaviour ... nothing but

a series of imprudence towards myself, and want of kindness to others ...
Had I died, it would have been self-destruction.'

*   *   *

Tanya Plibersek joined the Como Jannali branch of the ALP at the age of
fifteen. Meetings were held in the Oyster Bay Community Hall, which
was diagonally opposite her home. There, she met the progressives of
the Sutherland Shire, including, as she remembers, 'wonderful feminist women'. Plibersek is remembered by other branch members from
the time as an impressive young woman, more than ready to speak up
despite her age and her relatively recent arrival. She was, remembers one,
'fierce, very impressive, very uncompromising'.

Robert Tickner, previously principal solicitor for the NSW Aboriginal
Legal Service, had been elected as the Labor member for the federal electorate of Hughes, which included Oyster Bay, the year before Plibersek
joined the party. Tickner was to go on to serve as Minister for Aboriginal
and Torres Strait Islander Affairs in the Hawke and Keating governments. He remembers becoming aware of this recruit to the party – 'an
impressive young woman with an old head on young shoulders'. 'She
had a real presence about her,' he recalls. He sees little disjunct between
the self-confident young teenager he met then and Plibersek today. 'She
always had a serious purpose to her. She was always extremely articulate,
deferential, polite, unassuming, but strong. And hugely impressive to all
that who met her.'

Shortly after joining the branch, Plibersek also joined Young Labor,
where she met a man six years older than herself, an economics graduate
from Sydney University. Anthony Albanese and Tanya Plibersek were
both from working-class roots, but in other ways their backgrounds were
very different. Plibersek had the benefits of a devoted family and relative financial security, although not wealth. Albanese had been raised in
public housing by a single mother who was disabled with arthritis. He
was her carer as well as her son. Money was always short, and life was a
struggle.

Albanese had grown to be a shrewd politician and a fighter – passionate, emotional and with a strong strategic sense. He was tribal in

his loyalties and his enmities. Through his activism in student politics and Young Labor, he had been identified as a talent by the elders of the NSW Labor Left. They decided he needed a father figure to settle him down, and a position had been found for him on the staff of the Minister for Local Government, Tom Uren.[7] When Tanya met him, he was already a dominant figure in Young Labor – but also on a massive learning curve as he wrote reports for his new boss. They were often critiques of the policies of Prime Minister Bob Hawke and Treasurer Paul Keating. The first time Albanese went to Canberra to accompany Uren was also the first time he had been on an aeroplane. He walked into a committee room at Parliament House and, as he later recalled, 'just blurted out this big spiel about how exciting it was to go on a plane – and a car to pick you up. I told him about how exciting it was – that my mum and all the neighbours came to look at this car.'[8]

This was a long way from the experience of Plibersek, who had been travelling internationally for as long as she could remember. Yet Albanese was her senior – six years older and with a position in the party structure. She was too young and too junior to have a great deal to do with him at this stage – but neither forgot the other.

Plibersek's first stint as a member of the ALP lasted a bit longer than a year. The Hawke government had decided to allow uranium mining in Australia. The left of the party was marginalised, and there was a revolt. Thousands of members walked out to join the Nuclear Disarmament Party, which surged to prominence in the lead-up to the 1984 federal election.

Uranium policy was a common topic of debate at the Como Jannali branch meetings. Tickner had been campaigning against nuclear weapons since his teens, and he was one of those struggling to reconcile the new policy with his own position. That got harder when, in August 1986, Hawke granted permission for Queensland Mines – owner of the Nabarlek project – to export 2600 tonnes of uranium to France, even though France was testing nuclear weapons in the Pacific. Hawke was also backtracking on Aboriginal land rights. On coming to government, party policy had been to implement national uniform land-rights legislation, but the government had watered down the powers of traditional owners to restrict mining on their land. In mid-1985 it was announced that even this weaker land-rights legislation, which by this stage pleased nobody, would be indefinitely deferred.

These two issues – concern over the nuclear threat, and Aboriginal land rights – had been at the heart of Plibersek's nascent political commitment ever since she had sat on her brothers' beds and listened to Ray argue with Phillip. She was outraged and disgusted. When the party sent her a membership renewal form, she wrote a letter on the back telling them she had been trying to telephone them to cancel her membership. She put some fire into it: 'I felt like it was a gesture that I hoped people would listen to. I now realise that head office was probably getting a million of these cross letters from idealistic young Labor Party people.' Extraordinarily, her letter was kept somewhere in the cavernous filing cabinets of ALP headquarters. More than ten years later it was disinterred and used against her.

Plibersek was out of the party, but not out of the networks that surrounded it. In particular, she remained in touch with Genevieve Rankin. Another lasting contact was Joy Goodsell, who headed the Sutherland Shire's family services division and was later a co-founder of the NSW Domestic Violence Coalition. These were contacts Plibersek maintained for decades. She also watched, with something approaching fan-girl enthusiasm, the activities of some of the left-wing feminists involved in state Labor politics, including Labor MP Ann Symonds and, later, academic Meredith Burgmann, who was elected to state parliament in 1991 after years as a human rights activist. Tanya remained aware, at a distance, of the doings of Anthony Albanese and his rise through the ranks, including, in 1989, his election to the most senior Left position in the state party, assistant general secretary of the NSW branch. But she had decided, with the certainty of opinion that characterised her at the time, that the Australian Labor Party was not for her.

At the end of 1987, just after her eighteenth birthday, Tanya Plibersek graduated as the dux of Jannali Girls' High School. She was an unusual and impressive graduate. Born and raised in the Shire – stereotypically seen as narrow, white and insular – she had the stability and self-worth that came from the focus, love and attention of her family, and the breadth that came from regular international travel. She was a nerd – dedicated to study and taking all that her excellent teachers had to offer her. She was politically engaged and well informed. In the next few years, people who didn't know her background tended to assume that she had had the benefits of a private school education and a middle-class upbringing, such was her polish and easy self-confidence. She could be self-righteous. She was hard on herself, but also sometimes hard on others – quick to judge and condemn those who held views different to her own. Despite this, people found her likeable, with a conspicuous brand of compassion for others. She was also a fully formed feminist. Feminism had always been a part of her make-up, from before she knew the word.

From this time on, those who have spent time with Tanya Plibersek offer a consistent kind of anecdote about what one friend calls her 'conspicuous compassion'. There are many, many stories of being with her – driving or walking in the street – and being delayed because Tanya insisted on stopping when she saw a homeless person unconscious, or someone who appeared to be lost or troubled. Anna Coutts-Trotter, her daughter, talks about a day they were in a rush to be somewhere, and her mother noticed an old lady seeking directions. They stopped. It turned out she was heading the wrong way in search of a shop selling washing machines. They gave her a lift to one shop, then another – their own appointment forgotten or indefinitely postponed.

There are darker stories – the Aboriginal man living in a dangerous boarding house, his fingers literally rotting off his hands because of circulation problems, and how Plibersek intervened to get him to hospital to have his fingers amputated, almost certainly saving his life. Was he one of her electors? Anna isn't sure. 'It doesn't matter. She would have done it anyway.' More trivially, it is always Tanya who offers directions to tourists trying to find their way. And, always, she cooks for people. She is a feeder. She makes soups for visitors to her parliamentary office, pressing the little workplace kitchen to the max. She hosts great dinner parties. She delivers homecooked food to the elderly in her street.

There are so many stories of Plibersek going out of her way to do good deeds, and some of them are so striking, that to relate them all would be saccharine. They are also strangely challenging, even confronting, to consider. How can a woman, so busy already, find time and headspace to go out of her way to intervene so intensely in the lives of others? She tells her children that while she wants them to be many things, if she could choose just one character trait she would like them to display, it would be kindness.

Perhaps the stories of Plibersek's conspicuous compassion are challenging because they create the inevitable reflection: if she can be so kind, if she can go out of her way so often, why don't I? Or perhaps they are confronting because they raise a question about her boundaries. One of her long-term colleagues says that, at times, Tanya's empathy can be 'a bit much. Like just over the top. And you wonder what's behind that, and then you feel bad for wondering, because maybe it's you who is inadequate.' Some say she is a rescuer, pathologising behaviour she would characterise as merely kind. But she is the first to admit that she gets her greatest satisfaction when she can see that her work – whether as a minister or a local member or even as a neighbour – has improved individual lives.

One close observer of Tanya over the years remarks that she has 'a natural temperament that leads her to listen to every hard-luck story going around. And some of that is admirable. But all that energy put in to being the advocate of the dispossessed is energy you are not putting into things that get you further in politics, and might actually affect your ability to make a difference.' Plibersek, this person says, started as a 'naive idealist' with an unsullied faith in big government and its ability to fix people's lives. 'She has matured from that, but she would still struggle with the proposition that government can't always fix social problems, and government can waste a lot of money trying.'

Plibersek's husband says she enjoys being a local member as much as or more than being a minister, because 'she loves the chance to be able to do useful things for people. We've got a number of older people who live near us, and in lockdown she was cooking meals for the neighbours. Wherever we've lived, she's been the woman in the wide-brimmed hat who waters the street trees to make sure they stay alive during a drought.'[9]

By the middle years of high school, Tanya wanted to be a social worker. She wanted to help people, and to be useful. Then in her final years, as her interest in politics grew, she began to consider journalism. She was aware of the media's place in the engine room of politics and democracy. In Year Ten, she did work experience at the afternoon tabloid *Sun* newspaper – then owned by Fairfax and seen as the afternoon companion to *The Sydney Morning Herald*. She loved the newsroom – the energy and sharp intelligence of newspaper people, and the sense of public consequence to their work. She recalls: 'I was interested in politics. I was interested in history. I was interested in writing, so it seemed like a great career.' She chose to study journalism before her high-school boyfriend, Matt Brown, who was to go on to be one of the Australian Broadcasting Corporation's longest-standing foreign correspondents, reporting from the Middle East and Indonesia. At the beginning of 1988, Plibersek and Brown both enrolled in a Bachelor of Communications at the University of Technology, Sydney.

UTS, previously the NSW Institute of Technology, had been established during the Hawke government's reform of higher education, under which big, multi-campus universities were created by merging smaller institutions, such as teachers' and technical colleges. The institution had acquired university status only the year before Plibersek joined the student body, and was growing quickly, taking in the Ku-ring-gai College of Advanced Education and the Institute of Technical and Adult Teacher Education. The Labor Party reforms had also included the introduction of fees for tertiary education, together with a system of student loans. A generation of progressive students were shaped by their opposition to student fees. On the other side of the nation, in Western Australia, a young activist called Adam Bandt decided their introduction meant he could not be part of the Labor Party. He went on to explore socialist politics, before joining and eventually leading the Greens. In Adelaide, a young Penny Wong demonstrated outside the state ALP conference against the changes – and was persuaded by one of the attendees that if she was serious, she should join the party and argue her case from inside the room, rather than protesting impotently outside it.

Meanwhile, Plibersek had already decided that the Labor Party was not for her, and the student fees issue seemed to confirm the correctness of that decision. There was little at UTS to encourage her to reconsider. The prevailing ethos of campus politics was contempt for both the major political parties. There was no Labor or Liberal club at the university. Rather, progressively oriented students prided themselves on being 'independent' of the parties. There were two elected student bodies – the Students' Association, which was the political and representative organisation, and the Student Union, which was a not-for-profit business charged with running the cafeterias and bars and providing services.

Lisa Brockwell studied alongside Tanya in the Bachelor of Communications and went on to be president of the Students' Association. She recalls being taken aback, when she attended national student conferences, at the extent to which other campuses organised themselves along party-political lines. That was not the UTS style. 'UTS was refreshing in that way,' she recalls. It was radical, but non-aligned – left-wing and progressive, but mostly contemptuous of the direction of the Labor Party under Prime Minister Hawke. There was an intellectual freedom to the lack of formal political alignment, remembers Brockwell. Her predecessor as president, Ben Oquist, ran a Greens group on campus, but it was not formally affiliated with the political party. Oquist, nevertheless, went on to have a career with the Greens, serving as chief of staff to its leader, Bob Brown, before becoming executive director of left-leaning think tank the Australia Institute.

The Bachelor of Communications was located in an innovative faculty, reflected in the fact that when Plibersek enrolled, there was a policy of not giving students grades. The policy was already under challenge and in future years it was abandoned, but the fact that it existed at all reflected the nonconformist vibe.

For most of the history of Australian journalism, training had been on the job, through cadetships and copy-boy positions in newsrooms. In the 1980s, university journalism courses were proliferating but were far from established as the conventional method of entering the profession. The hard-bitten, street-smart but relatively uneducated men who ran most newsrooms were hostile to tertiary education in journalism, harbouring a romantic notion that journalists were born, not made. University journalism courses, the narrative in newsrooms went, were about 'training troublemakers', and the groundbreaking course at UTS was seen as an exemplar of the trend.[10] The UTS Bachelor of Communicatons was, by the time Plibersek enrolled, a big, well-established course with alumni already making their way, particularly at the ABC.

The degree was taught at the main campus on Sydney's Broadway, opposite Central Station, next to the building that housed the Fairfax newspapers and a stone's throw from the ABC headquarters. The campus was centred on a brutalist 1970s brown brick tower – later voted the ugliest building in Sydney. It was a broad-ranging course, encompassing different specialities. As well as journalism, students could study public relations or creative writing. It was a strongly practice-based course, but there were also units in political economy and a quota of media theory.

There were some giants among the teaching staff. The notable narrative poet Dorothy Porter taught creative writing. Julianne Schultz, a former Fairfax and ABC reporter and *Four Corners* producer, taught journalism. So did Alan Knight, formerly of the ABC and before that a correspondent for the *Nation Review*. The broader faculty included Ann Curthoys and Liz Jacka, both leading feminist scholars. But one woman, first as a casual teacher and from 1991 as a full-time staff member, came to have a particular influence on UTS journalism.

Wendy Bacon was an investigative journalist and a leading member of the previous generation of political activists. She had been a late member of the Sydney Push – an intellectual subculture with left-wing, libertarian politics that in its earlier incarnation had included Germaine Greer, Robert Hughes, Clive James and Frank Moorhouse. She was influenced by Sydney libertarianism, and had worked as a journalist for *Nation*, the *Nation Review* and other independent publications. She was anti-apartheid, anti-censorship and opposed to Australia's involvement in the Vietnam War. By disposition and thanks to her work as a journalist, Bacon had become deeply sceptical of the Australian Labor Party, its culture and power structures. She wrote later in her career, 'I want my journalism to be useful to those who resist abuses of power and seek social justice rather than supporting existing power structures, which is what a lot of journalism does. My emphasis is on information that I hope will empower people to take action.'[11]

Bacon had been awarded Australian journalism's highest prize, the Walkley Award, in 1984, for a series of articles for the *National*

Times about NSW police corruption. She had also been involved in reporting one of the most controversial episodes in Australian journalism – the publication of the so-called *Age* tapes and allegations against Lionel Murphy, a High Court judge and former attorney-general in the Whitlam Labor government. This was one of the most sensational corruption scandals in Australian political history, the subject of three parliamentary inquiries and two criminal trials. The last of the inquiries ended when Murphy died of cancer in 1986. Bacon had also investigated former NSW Labor premier Neville Wran, who faced the Street Royal Commission in 1983 over claims by the ABC's *Four Corners* that he had tried to influence the magistracy over the 1977 committal of Kevin Humphries, charged with misappropriation of funds.

Plibersek was deeply impressed by Bacon. She found her exciting and 'enormously generous and inspiring' – but when her brother Ray heard her singing Bacon's praises, he 'was in my ear saying Wendy Bacon was the devil because she was one of the ones who had hounded Lionel Murphy to his death. Which was a bit of a contrast to my first-hand experience of her. She was encouraging to all of us. She was endlessly patient and kind. She was wonderful.'

Journalism students at UTS were encouraged to think of themselves as reporters from the earliest days of their degree. The teaching staff had established the Australian Centre for Independent Journalism, which ran its own media outlets for which students were expected to write. They were encouraged to complete ambitious investigative projects. That meant hours of work, well beyond the normal commitment of undergraduates to their study. The teaching staff took on the roles of both tutors and editors. Bacon remembers getting to know this early intake of students well, and joining them for long sessions in the underground coffee shop at the foot of the brutalist tower.

It was a stellar cohort, remembered today as one of the best groups of journalists UTS has produced. Tim Palmer, who became a senior journalist and foreign correspondent at the ABC, was a mature-age student. A few years ahead of Plibersek, Steven Lewis went on to be a senior member of the Canberra press gallery. Matt Brown, Plibersek's boyfriend, was another student headed for a high-powered career.

Stephen McDonell, later the ABC's China correspondent, was studying journalism at Master's level, as was Peter Cronau, later a Walkley
Award–winning *Four Corners* journalist. Interestingly, some of the
strongest students, including McDonnell, Brown, Brockwell and
Plibersek, were from the Sutherland Shire. Bacon remembers 'all these
interesting young progressives coming from the Shire' as a distinguish-
ing feature of the group.

Because there were no grades, there is no objective record of Plibersek's academic achievement, but she is remembered as having been as
strong as any of her peers in this particularly strong cohort, but not head
and shoulders above the rest. Bacon recalls, 'I would not have said Tanya
stood out, but that is because it was a very strong group. You had to be
in the top 6 per cent of the state to get into the course. She was potentially a very good reporter and feature writer.' Bacon liked her. Tanya
came to her home and looked after her children on several occasions and
was great with the kids. 'Tanya was a very warm and likeable person.'

Terry Flew was a new arrival at UTS. He had come from Sydney
University, where a few years before he had studied political economy
with fellow undergraduate Anthony Albanese. He went on to teach
Plibersek, and today often reflects on the similarities and differences
between the two. Albanese, he recalls, was a Labor Party person right
from the start. He was clearly studying political economy because of its
relevance to politics, and there was already the expectation he would go
on to a political career. Plibersek was a different kind of activist. She was
certainly politically engaged – Flew remembers seeing her at the regular
'Politics in the Pub' sessions – but she was 'more of a social movement
kind of activist, and that was the vibe of UTS at the time'.

Tim Palmer, meanwhile, remembers studying an Australian politics unit alongside Plibersek. Each student had to do a research project,
and Palmer, 'being that annoying mature age student who does all the
reading', had embarked on a 'wonkish and arcane' study of how independents could use the preferential voting system to gain seats. 'Everyone
else in that class was bored brainless by it, but not Tanya. She was right
into it. It really struck me that she was very different. She was engaged
with politics, but she was also interested in how it actually worked.

How all the pieces fitted together. The machinery. She was politically nerdish, and I really liked that about her.'

Plibersek retains strong friendships from her time at UTS. Palmer, McDonell and Brown remain close friends. But in 1988, it took a while for her to find her feet. After the first year of her degree, she took a year off. She worked for six months, at first washing dishes at the Sutherland District Trade Union Club, or the Tradies, as it was known locally, before graduating to waiting tables in the à la carte restaurant, the Waratah Room, with its flocked wallpaper and carved wooden panels of Australian native flowers. She used the money she saved to go overseas.

Most young people, if they take a gap year, do it between school and university. Why did Plibersek wait a year? She says today that she had been excited to start her degree and had not wanted to wait: 'I had my heart set on it.' Despite her experience with overseas travel, she recalls, she was nervous about travelling on her own. There were probably other reasons. Years later, she would tell a reporter writing about the advantages of reaching middle age that she had been very unhappy around the time of her nineteenth birthday, which was towards the end of her first year of university. 'I finally knew I'd never be a child prodigy ... I didn't feel I had a lot of friends at uni, and I'd just broken up with my boyfriend.'[12]

She travelled on her own, picking up occasional companions on the way. She journeyed through Europe, including a visit to relatives in Yugoslavia and time in Belgium, France, Morocco, Turkey, Germany, the United Kingdom, Greece and Czechoslovakia. She wanted to see in person the things she had learned about in Diana Lewis's art classes. In Turkey she went to the ruins of the Mausoleum at Halicarnassus and the galleries and museums in Bodrum. In Crete, she went to Knossos; in Paris, to the Pompidou Centre. 'I spent a lot of time in museums,' she remembers. 'It was not a party trip. It was a serious trip. A nerd's trip.'

By the start of first semester in 1990, Plibersek had returned to Sydney and to her degree. It was from this point that her life on campus took off. By now, the students who gathered in the UTS cafes had been joined by another young man. He was a few years older than most of his classmates and seemed to stand slightly apart from them. He had a seriousness about him, even a sadness, Wendy Bacon recalls. She remembers him as being 'more polished than the others, more professional and probably more right-wing'. He would turn up to campus in a suit because he was already working for the public relations company Turnbull Fox Phillips. His name was Michael Coutts-Trotter. Like Plibersek, Coutts-Trotter was a strong student, although Bacon says it was clear from the start that he was more likely to become a political staffer or a bureaucrat than a journalist.

Tim Palmer had known Coutts-Trotter for years. The two men had shared a cheap flat above a pizza shop in the suburb of Artarmon. Palmer recalls that in summer they could see a heat shimmer rise through the floorboards every time the ovens were opened downstairs. There were some wild times, including a party that attracted scores of gatecrashers, followed by the police riot squad and eventually gun-toting tow-truck drivers trying to keep the peace. Sometimes the pair would ride together on Coutts-Trotter's motorbike into the city to see gigs, done up in New York Dolls–style paisley shirts, plush jackets and eyeliner. But as the years went on, Palmer had witnessed his friend's descent into drug addiction and crime. Just a few years before Coutts-Trotter joined the UTS cohort, Palmer had been one of his more regular visitors to the various jails where he served time. Unbeknown to most of his classmates and teachers, Coutts-Trotter was still on parole.

Meanwhile, Plibersek was throwing herself into her journalistic work, and into the political life of the campus. On 30 June 1991, her name appeared in mainstream media for the first time, in the by-line of a story written with two fellow students and published in *The Sydney Morning Herald*. It concerned the Lucas Heights nuclear research plant in the Sutherland Shire, just thirteen kilometres from the Plibersek family home. Lucas Heights was, Plibersek and her co-authors reported, holding more than 1500 radioactive fuel rods and didn't know what to do with them.[13]

Later, she wrote a longer story on the same subject for the university newspaper, *Vertigo*. Lucas Heights had been the site of Australia's only nuclear research reactors for over thirty years, but they were ageing and there were moves to build bigger and better reactors. The Sutherland Shire Council was implacably opposed, and Plibersek drew on her old contacts from Oyster Bay days, including Genevieve Rankin, who was on the front line of local opposition. Plibersek used her local knowledge. She wrote:

> All roads out of the area take residents closer to the reactor before they can escape the suburb. A primary school sits by the exclusion boundary fence. In the event of an accident these children, and their parents at home, would be told not to go outside until any radiation cloud had dispersed.

Plibersek reported a meeting of the activists at Darling Harbour. The newly launched *Rainbow Warrior* – successor to the Greenpeace vessel that had been blown up by the French in New Zealand seven years before – was floating in the background. Plibersek recapped the history of opposition to nuclear industries and in her final paragraphs showed some of the flair that had led Bacon to conclude she would make a good feature writer. As the protest meeting wound up, 'the sound of a throbbing ferry combined with the animal yowl of what sounds like a bucks' party motored past on Darling Harbour. "Arr fuck off ya greenies". "Good on the French", "Blow it up! Blow it up!" and six hairy white buttholes salute the public spirit of the gathered faithful. "There's the informed opposition," laughs Genevieve Rankin.'[14]

By 1991, Plibersek was involved in a loose women's collective that spanned the different campuses of UTS. She became the central figure in a controversy that filled the pages of *Vertigo* for weeks. It concerned the Student Union bookshop's generous stock of the kind of pornography that had to be sold in wrappers. The Students' Association women's officers had asked the union to stop selling the magazines, and the board had agreed, but at the next meeting, the decision was overturned. The mover of the motion to rescind the previous decision was Steve Lewis.

Lewis was by now working for the *Australian Financial Review* and was the new father of twins. All this had taken him out of student politics, but he was still on the board of the student union. He thought the move to stop the sale of pornography was an attack on freedom of speech. He argued that some of the titles had creative and artistic merit, including gay and alternative pornography. But as Plibersek remembers, there was nothing obscure or artistic about most of the titles on sale. 'It was good old-fashioned meat-and-potatoes porn.'

Plibersek wrote a long article questioning the union's involvement 'in providing a service which presents women as voiceless spectacles for men to masturbate over. Universities must be places of equality where individuals are judged on their ability, not the size of their norks.' There were plenty of other pornography outlets on Broadway, she said. 'The nearest adult shop is only two blocks away. If students and staff want to read category-one mags, surely they could carry their aching loins two blocks down George Street.'[15]

Lewis replied in a letter in the next edition:

I suggested to your 'reporter' Tanya Plibersek that because pornography was such a complex and emotive issue, it required a structured and rational debate. Alas in the best traditions of student journalism her article ... was neither. Instead it contained the tired old propaganda of the feminist thought police whose definition of democracy is to ban whatever they don't like.[16]

The following edition carried a reply from Plibersek and a full page of letters from other students. Plibersek wrote that Lewis's response was so 'facile' that it made her 'heart sick':

Pornography constructs the way men see women, and the way some women see themselves. It saddens me deeply that Mr Lewis (and the other correspondents) have not got the 'penetration' to see this issue for what it truly is ... Women are faced with the harsh reality of sexism every day. Why should we be subjected to it at university also? And why especially from a body that we pay and belong to? ... Good sex has more to do with personality, warmth, humour and patience than lipstick and a good perm. Pornography doesn't reflect this.[17]

Today, Lewis is a veteran political journalist, having had a long career with Murdoch's News Corporation. He has been in touch with and written about Plibersek many times since their UTS stoush. He remembers ruefully being 'beaten up in the student newspaper' and a debate with Plibersek on the student radio station 2SER in which she was 'terrific...we had a robust exchange'. He says they have chatted about their student clashes a few times over the years, that he is a big fan of hers and that there are no hard feelings.

When I put that to her, she smiled and didn't comment, but wryly recalled the 'brief shining moment when the UTS Union was not profiting off women's bodies' before Lewis interceded with his rescission motion. Were there hard feelings? 'It was a good debate to have at the time.'

When the Students' Association elections were held shortly after the pornography controversy, Tanya Plibersek was a candidate for the post of women's officer as one half of a team with fellow student Cassandra Bennett. They were on a ticket titled 'Focus', including Lisa Brockwell running for president, with a progressive if slightly diffuse agenda. Three threads of policy united the candidates: women's issues, gay and lesbian rights, and the environment.

Plibersek and Bennett were running against a team of three second-year, part-time communications undergraduates. Their competitors had a grab-bag of policies, including putting tampon and condom machines in the women's toilets. Plibersek and Bennett, on the other hand, focused on women's safety. Sexual harassment, they wrote in their campaign pitch, was a 'barrier to women's learning':

> As [women's officers] we will always be available to women wanting to take action in cases of sexual harassment. We don't have to be scared of the repercussions of approaching lecturers or other students to tell them that their behaviour is inappropriate... How can we participate fully in university life if we're scared to walk across our campuses at night?' They promised to lobby for women's rooms on every campus, 'where we can relax without having our norks stared at'.[18]

The Focus ticket swamped the elections, winning more than 80 per cent of the vote for most of the office-bearing positions, including the editorship of *Vertigo*, whose reporter described the contest as 'the most one-sided election since Daryl Braithwaite won King of Pop in 1976'. Why was the election 'such a bore', the reporter asked. Answering his own question, he said it was because of the lack of a political culture at the university. The Young Liberals had 'crawled back under a rock' after an anaemic showing the previous year, and 'apart from the odd angry Trot wandering about, UTS is removed from the outside political world, and it was noticeable that all parties ran as independent groups'.[19]

Plibersek and Bennett set out to deliver on their election promises. They are remembered as active women's officers. Plibersek recalls that they dealt with 'quite serious' complaints of sexual harassment and took action to make women safer on the Ku-ring-gai campus, which was inside a national park in Sydney's northern suburbs. It was a bush campus, with the car park a long distance from the main buildings. 'We asked the security guards to walk women to their cars if they were there very late at night, so it was practical things around sexual harassment and sexual assault and safety on campus,' Plibersek recalls.

Together, Bennett and Plibersek wrote a regular column in *Vertigo*, titled 'Salvation Jane'. Plibersek maintained a regular spot on the student radio station 2SER, talking about subjects such as 'the feminisation of poverty'. She encouraged women to write to the National Working Party on the Portrayal of Women in the Media, set up by the federal government.

It was in *Vertigo* that Plibersek confided to her readers that she had a pervasive fear of sexual violence. She wrote:

> When I was about 18, I had a terrifying David Lynch type dream. Five years later it still makes me nauseous. I woke with the profound certainty that my end would be bloody and sexually violent. I was sad for myself but strangely calm: the choice was to try to prolong life by staying home or to go into the world for my 'one crowded hour' and accept the inevitable. I no longer believe that this end is inevitable, but I know the spectre of sexual violence will haunt me till I shuffle out with old age.

She asked, 'Can men be feminists?' and answered herself: 'no, no, no'. 'Men have no idea about the constant fear of violence that most women feel,' she wrote. 'Not a single day goes by when I don't consider the potential of violence. Waiting at the bus stop and a group of yobs drives past ... even in the middle of the day.'

She referred, in this piece, to 'my friend Matt', who slept with his window open, even though it faced the street, and 'Michael', who was careless about walking through the park at night. These were examples of men who did not need to worry about sexual violence.[20]

The Matt she was writing about was Matt Brown, to whom she was still close.

The Michael was, of course, Michael Coutts-Trotter.

*   *   *

Tanya Plibersek has described her family's story as being about Australia – the opportunities it offers. More particularly, it is possible to see her story, and that of Michael Coutts-Trotter, as a story about Sydney – the first European colony in Australia, founded at Botany Bay just down the road from where she grew up, and the few square kilometres of harbour, parks, glittering homes and desperate poverty that make up her electorate, which forms the city's heart.

Sydney is called the Emerald City, a name that comes from a 1987 work by Australia's most successful playwright, David Williamson – 'part love letter, part hate mail' to the city, said the publicity for the play. Sydney is a city of subtropical abundance, of wealth and promise. In *The Wizard of Oz*, the Emerald City is the ultimate destination and the seat of power. When Dorothy reaches it, she finds the wizard at its heart appears as a giant ghostly head, but when her dog, Toto, pulls back the curtain, the Wizard is revealed as an ordinary man, his power based on deception.

Sydney has also been called Sin City, because of the grip organised crime had on the city in the second half of the twentieth century – its vice, drugs, bookmakers and narcotics dealers, and the flashy illegal casinos that bankrolled corruption. No other Australian city is so rich in stories and contrasts, in sheer physical beauty, and in desperation.

Tanya Plibersek and Michael Coutts-Trotter have been referred to as one of the power couples of Sydney, their names mentioned alongside former prime minister Malcolm Turnbull and his wife, Lucy, a former lord mayor. At the time of writing, Coutts-Trotter is the most senior public servant in the NSW government, serving as head of the Department of Premier and Cabinet, the personal pick of the Liberal premier, Dominic Perrottet.

Coutts-Trotter's story, worthy of a book on its own, has become well-honed over the years – recapped often for the media and other audiences and mentioned in Plibersek's speeches a number of times. Before the 2022 federal election, she mentioned it in her Mannix address as an example of the power of faith, and the continuing role of the Catholic Church in forming her values:

> The resurrection is not something we can prove or disprove. It can only be arrived at by faith; or rejected by scepticism. But what we do know is that, for countless people since, the life of Jesus has offered a beacon of practical inspiration. To do good work. To help our fellow human. To live out faith, to live our values, through action … When my husband was struggling to get clean from his heroin addiction, it was the Salvation Army that took him in and gave him the support he needed.[21]

At various times over the years of their partnership, it has been suggested that Michael Coutts-Trotter's criminal record might inhibit her career. Could Australians tolerate a prime minister, for example, who had a convicted drug dealer as a husband? In an interview for this book, Coutts-Trotter himself referenced that concern. There was no dirt to be had on his wife, he assured me. She was exactly as she appeared. She was the same 'articulate, compassionate, intelligent person' at home as she was in public. 'There's no dirt file on Tanya,' he said. 'I'm as close to a dirt file as it comes.'

And this is true. There is not a ghost of scandal concerning Plibersek's public life – no hint of corruption or rorts. Even her rivals – she has few enemies – do not suggest it. And any dirt associated with Michael has long since been redeemed. His narrative has become one of the archetypal redemption stories of the Emerald Sin City. There are those who say Tanya Plibersek rescued Michael Coutts-Trotter. This is not true. By the time they met, he was well advanced in rescuing himself.

In 2007, when he was director-general of the NSW Department of Education, Coutts-Trotter was invited back to his old school, the exclusive, Jesuit-run Saint Ignatius College, Riverview, to speak to the students. He gave an extraordinary speech. It wasn't the first time he had told his story, but on this occasion even those who already knew it were moved to tears. As for the students, it was the kind of occasion they are never likely to forget. He told them he was not only a Riverview old boy. He also had 'other affiliations':

> I'm an old boy of the Salvation Army's William Booth drug and alcohol rehab, and of six prisons including Long Bay, Parramatta and Bathurst. There are some places you want to return to as an old boy, and some you don't.

There was a lot on offer at Riverview, he told the boys, and he had passed over almost all the opportunities that were now available to them. He had been a rower, which taught him 'physical courage, fellowship, the unexpected pleasures of responsibility, and, although we never named it, a sense of the divine out there on the water at sunset'. But as for the rest – he had failed to take advantage.

Four years after he left school, he was facing jail:

> Six and a half stone, psychotic from lack of drugs and lack of sleep, charged with conspiracy to import half a kilo of heroin and humiliated by the things I'd done, and the things I'd failed to do, in using and selling drugs. Anything I'd glimpsed of what is fine in humanity, and what could have been fine in me, was gone in a fog of greed, selfishness, self-pity and despair.[22]

Pictures of Coutts-Trotter from that time show him gaunt and floppy-haired, with a death's head tattooed on his biceps – a tattoo he retains.

Coutts-Trotter has deep roots in the history of New South Wales, and Sydney. On his mother's side, he is a Meagher – which is a resonant name for those steeped in the culture and history of the Catholic Church in the state. John Meagher and Co. was, for close to a century, the dominant retail chain in the western districts of New South Wales. Its founder, John Meagher, was Michael Coutts-Trotter's great-great-grandfather. Born in 1837 in County Clare, Ireland, he arrived in Sydney about 1859 and opened his first store in Bathurst, followed by branches throughout the central and western districts of the state. He stood unsuccessfully for the seat of Bathurst in the 1885 elections, was active at the Bathurst conference for federation, and entertained leading federationists, including Australia's first prime minister, Edmund Barton, at his home. In 1900, he was appointed by the governor as a lifetime member of the NSW Legislative Council as a protectionist and an advocate of state aid for Catholic Schools. Meanwhile, Ben Chifley, future Labor prime minister, worked as a cashier and shop boy in Meagher's Bathurst store.[23]

In Australia's Catholic community, Meagher and his descendants are remembered as dedicated believers and generous donors to Catholic orders. Meagher funded the Sisters of Mercy orphanage at Bathurst. When Saint Ignatius College, Riverview, was founded in 1880, it became the school of choice for the males of the family. Meaghers are littered through the history of the college and the Jesuit order in Australia. Some became missionaries or nuns. There was a Father John Meagher who was rector of Riverview in the 1930s, and later head of the Jesuit order in Australia. Roddy Meagher, a judge of the NSW Court of Appeal, was his nephew. Michael Coutts-Trotter has two uncles – Paddy and Geoffrey Meagher – who were Jesuit priests in India.

On his father's side, Coutts-Trotter's lineage runs through British colonialism and the law. His father, Paul Coutts-Trotter, was the son of Sir Murray Coutts-Trotter, British barrister and chief justice of the Madras High Court from 1924 to his death in 1929. He was knighted in 1924.

Michael's great-aunt was a suffragette, campaigning for the right for women to vote, which was then restricted in Britain to those over thirty years of age, to be extended to the same age as for men. In 1928, Prudence Coutts-Trotter's fame spread to Australia in a report of demonstrations outside 10 Downing Street and Buckingham Palace, during which a group of women had tried to deliver a petition to the king. The women, the report said, had engaged in a 'maidenly strategy' by which some distracted the constables at the gate of Buckingham Palace 'as a barrage for Miss Coutts-Trotter, who endeavoured to storm the Privy Purse Door, but another constable appeared and slammed the door. He gathered up the struggling Miss Coutts-Trotter and deposited her in the street.'[24]

Michael's parents, Paul Coutts-Trotter and Helen Meagher, met in London. Paul was fifty-four when they married and Helen twenty-four years younger. Paul had fought in Crete during the Second World War and became a prisoner of war. Despite his privileged background and a career as a stockbroker, Paul finished his working life as the butler to one of the heirs of the Wills tobacco fortune. Paul, Helen and Michael lived in a small flat on the top corner of a splendid ten-bedroom lodge in the Cotsworlds. Helen worked as a cook for the Wills household. Michael also had three half siblings from Paul's previous marriage.

In 1976, when Michael was eleven years old, the family moved suddenly back to Australia and the Meagher family seat of Milton, in Cootamundra. Michael was sent to board at Riverview, like generations of Meaghers before him, on a scholarship.

Just three months later, Paul Coutts-Trotter died from brain cancer.[25] The young Michael was already struggling to find his feet in the new country. He stuck out among his classmates because of his English accent, and he lacked any emotional connection to his new country. His father's death was 'trauma upon trauma', in the words of one of his classmates. 'He was adrift.' Meanwhile, his mother, Helen, worked as a cleaner to support herself and her son.

Michael started drinking by the time he was twelve years old. As he later told the boys at Riverview, by the end of his school years, he was addicted to heroin. He sat for his HSC exams aged sixteen, a week after taking a lot of hallucinogens. Soon after finishing school, he had moved out of home and was living above the pizza shop with Tim Palmer, afloat on the tide of heroin then flooding the inner suburbs of Sydney.[26]

The crime for which Coutts-Trotter went to jail was more serious, and more premeditated, than trading a little drugs on the side to fund his habit. He was living with his girlfriend – also an addict – when their dealers were caught by the police and offered to sell their business to the couple to fund their bail. Coutts-Trotter took up the offer. The decision to go from small-time dealer to the big time was his own, he has always said. Addiction was not an excuse. 'I deserved to go to jail,' he told the Riverview boys.

His downfall was a scheme to import half a kilogram of heroin from Thailand. A joint Commonwealth–NSW police task force was on to the plot, and he was arrested at the age of nineteen, after picking up the package from the Redfern Mail Exchange. The police were hard on him. He later told his daughter that he had been suspended out of a window, held by his feet. He spent about six weeks on remand in Long Bay jail. Even there, the Catholic networks helped and saved him. 'There's a job called "the sweeper", who cleans the prison wing,' he told the media in 2007. 'The sweeper was a fellow who had been sentenced for murder, but he had a radical nun defending him, convinced he was innocent. She had connections through the nuns' community to my family ... and when I arrived as a nineteen-year-old looking like a scared rabbit, this fellow took me aside and got me a job as assistant sweeper. It was one of the plum jobs. So, you know, odd things happened. I've just been extraordinarily lucky in all sorts of ways.'[27]

He was bailed to the Salvation Army's rehabilitation program and spent about ten months at the order's dairy and piggery farm, Miracle Haven, in Morisset on the New South Wales central coast. He remembers having to deal with heroin withdrawal at the same time as helping male pigs to mount sows as part of the breeding program. He told the boys at Riverview: 'I got physically well, lost the certainty that there was no God and learned how to ask for help.' He returned to Sydney and the Salvation Army William Booth House, attending regular Narcotics Anonymous meetings.

'Every night in Sydney in draughty church halls,' he told the Riverview boys, 'people perch on uncomfortable metal chairs and tell each other what their lives were like when they used drugs, what happened, and what things are like now. People who couldn't go a day without pills or powder, going days and months and years without drugs – with nothing other than the faith, and sometimes not even faith, just hope that sitting in those rooms and trying to tell the truth about themselves, and listen to the truth from others, would change their lives. And it did. And it does. Every night, alchemy: human frailty transformed into strength, even beauty, by a mystery of hope and fellowship.'

It was while he was securing his recovery, on bail and knowing that he would likely soon be jailed, that his life took a formative turn. Coutts-Trotter had a friend who worked with Lesley Brydon, founder and head of the Fox Communications public relations company. Brydon was well known in Sydney in 1985, not only as a respected PR professional, but also as the wife of Peter Wherrett, a motoring journalist who was a household name as the presenter of the ABC's television program *Torque*. The couple were in the middle of a divorce – as amicable as these things can be. Wherrett was later to live as a woman, taking the name of Pip. It was, in other words, a tumultuous time for Brydon when Michael's friend asked if she would consider employing someone who was in rehabilitation from a drug habit.

Brydon was looking for a 'boy Friday' – someone to work a few hours a day to collect and post the mail, walk her dog and do other office chores. She responded that she was prepared to give anyone a chance. She was happy to meet him, and it would depend on how they got on. Brydon remembers: 'Michael came in and he was an impossibly tall, skinny man. He was quite gaunt because of his background. But he walked up to me and extended his hand and he said, "Thank you so much for seeing me." He looked me in the eye and gave me a firm handshake and his manner convinced me that I wanted to give him a chance.'

Michael was 'very open' with Brydon about his habit and rehabilitation – but he didn't tell her he was on bail and facing drug-dealing charges. She often wonders if she would have given him the job had she known. 'I think I would have, because quite quickly there was a relationship there, and I relied on that relationship, and I wasn't wrong to do so.' She paid him $225 a week. Over the course of ten months, he became 'part of the team ... most of my employees at the time were female and they were all great girls and we all became very, very fond of him.' Then one afternoon Michael said he would not be able to come the following day, because he was due in court.

'And then he told me about the dealing charge. I was quite shocked, but it didn't change my feelings about him at all. And anyway, he went off to court and his mother, Helen, rang me the following morning after the court case and said he had been sentenced for nine years with a four-and-a-half-year non-parole period, and I was simply flabbergasted.' Coutts-Trotter had pleaded guilty. Brydon went out to visit him at Long Bay jail the following day. 'I said you'd better tell me everything because this is just dreadful.'

By this stage, Coutts-Trotter was twenty-one years old and had enrolled at UTS. Brydon thought his sentence a horrific waste of his potential. 'He was obviously damaged, but he was charming and intelligent. He was very dignified and polite, modest. And I thought he had huge potential and that he could work through his problems. So to find that he was facing up to nine years in jail just threw me entirely.' She decided to fund an appeal, seeking help from criminal lawyer Terry Buddin (later Director of Public Prosecutions in the ACT and now Inspector of the Law Enforcement Conduct Commission of NSW) against the sentence. The appeal was unsuccessful.

Brydon's staff established a roster of visits. Meanwhile, Coutts-Trotter wrote for a street magazine called *Billy Blue*. His column 'Letter from the Can' was published under the pseudonym 'Con'. He wrote about the food, about his cell mate using the toilet: 'We usually coordinate our bowel movements with the 8.30 to 3.30 period when we aren't locked in. Something has obviously upset his equilibrium – not getting a visit is the cause, I think. I wish his people would be more regular so he can follow suit.'[28] Later, from the Bathurst jail, he wrote under his own name, in a lyrical style, about spending the Easter weekend sitting by a big window overlooking the golf course, with the famous Bathurst racetrack just out of sight:

> For three weeks beforehand, the sky hung over us like a gaol blanket; grey and heavy all the way to the horizon ... I was sure the Easter weekend would be rained out but when it came the sun came with it ... The sun angled in through the glass and warmed my chest. I could smell my jumper needed washing.

Listening to the sound of the motorbikes on the racetrack, he recalled:

> I used to love riding through the tunnel under the Cross. Midnight,
> maybe later, the air cool enough to chill me a little and not many
> cars about ... If I had 160 horses crammed into the frame beneath
> me I wouldn't steer it around a mountain, I'd fly in to the heat of
> the Nullarbor or maybe down the Pan Pacific Highway until the
> land ran out. Crack the throttle until the wind tore the jumper off
> my back ... leave its greasy, cramped, gaol smell in a pile beside
> the road.[29]

Coutts-Trotter spent time in maximum security, where he witnessed
a man being disembowelled and several stabbings. Jails were awash with
drugs, but he stayed clean. In Long Bay, there was a Narcotics Anonymous meeting every Saturday at noon, which would be announced over
the loudspeakers. Coutts-Trotter recalled, 'I would be the only person
who would walk across the yard to go, and people would just abuse you
for doing it ... but I'd had enough time in rehab to deal with it, and I
was hanging on, by my fingernails sometimes.'

He had the support of his family – his mother, and an uncle who
was the closest thing he had to a father. Brydon made it clear that when
he got out of jail, there would be a job waiting for him as one of her
public relations consultants. He was an exemplary prisoner and was
granted parole in 1988 after serving just two years and nine months of
his sentence. He returned to work for Brydon's company, which had now
become Turnbull Fox Phillips.

Wendy Bacon remembers teaching Coutts-Trotter, Plibersek and
Matt Brown in an investigative journalism subject. Coutts-Trotter did a
'terrific project' examining the sale of a government building. Plibersek
and Coutts-Trotter shared another class that semester, before having a
semester apart. In 1991 they were again in the same tutorial, and on
opposite sides of a debate about freedom of speech. The example under
discussion was a controversy about the song 'Fuck Tha Police' by the
American hip-hop group NWA. The ABC youth radio station, Triple J,
had been one of the few radio stations in the world to play it, until ABC

management banned it after a campaign by police and Liberal politicians. Triple J staff went on strike and played NWA's 'Express Yourself' for twenty-four hours in protest.

Ironically, Coutts-Trotter, on parole and a victim of police brutality, was on the side of the police and in favour of the song being banned. Plibersek argued for freedom of speech. He remembers, 'She was formidable, super bright, absolutely gorgeous and just lovely.' He invited her out when they passed each other on the escalators at Central Station. He was going up, she was going down; he had to run against the direction of the escalator to stay close enough to speak to her. They went to a Thai restaurant on Oxford Street and almost immediately fell into an easy conversation.

It was courageous of him to tell her, on that first date, the truth about his history, including that he was still on parole. Today he says his Catholic upbringing meant that 'confession came easily to me'. As well, he had attended many meetings of Narcotics Anonymous and grown used to standing in front of strangers and being honest and revealing. But more than this, from the earliest moments he knew he wanted something to come of this date. 'I just felt a compulsion to intimacy with her. And telling her my story seemed to be, if nothing else, a short cut to intimacy.'

If Plibersek was shocked, she didn't show it. Coutts-Trotter remembers, 'Her response was one of just warm curiosity ... [She] wasn't guarded. She wasn't obviously taken aback. She just seemed curious.' They shared a serve of sticky date pudding for dessert. Perhaps the more remarkable thing, and the thing that is most revealing of the complexities of Plibersek's character, her sense and sensibility, is that she not only agreed to see him again, not only took him back to her brother Phillip's flat, where they lay chastely in bed in the spare room and talked all night, and was not only kind and understanding.[30]

That night, she fell in love with him. And he with her.

Soon, he was taken to meet the family. This, he recalls, revealed something of his own prejudices. Tanya was so poised, confident and articulate that he assumed he would be meeting professional people. Instead, there was Joe the plumber and Rose the factory worker turned homemaker. He is sure that Ray looked him over carefully, but the family accepted him without question. Now a parent himself, he appreciates how extraordinary that was. 'They were just extremely matter-of-fact, and as warm and welcoming to me as they were to everybody else who came to their home.' Rose recalls that when Tanya first brought Michael home, 'My husband says, "Tanya, you know what you are doing."' They both had faith in their daughter's judgement.

A common bond between the cultures of Ireland and Slovenia was the Catholic faith. In the Plibersek home, Michael found the same routines with which he had been brought up – the regular attendance at mass, the gossip afterwards over the dinner table about the priest, and complaints and commentary about the homily: 'All the things that happen in Catholic households across the world.'

Tanya, he says, was 'a more hard-edged person' than she is today. She was a 'deeply scary women's officer'. They had some fierce rows in those early years. Their worst ever, he says, was about electricity privatisation. He was driving their little white Toyota Corolla over the Anzac Bridge, and they were arguing so fiercely – him for it, her against – that she tried to pull the handbrake so she could get out of the car. Tanya disputes this account. She says she would never do anything so dangerous. But they have always shared fundamental values, Michael says. 'I think as she gets older and I get older, we kind of move closer to one another. She's more centrist than she was. And I'm less sort of provocatively doctrinaire ... I think the thing that's changed as she's got older is she's much less hard on other people, but she remains, in my view, way too hard on herself.'

He has visited the Slovenian family many times with Tanya. Today, they own an apartment in a building in the capital, Ljubljana – an impulse purchase to give them and their children an anchor in the old country.

Travelling in the rural areas of Slovenia, Michael fancies he has seen the antecedents for his 'beautiful, kind, unstoppable' wife and her extraordinary resilience and ability to work. 'She's got the constitution of a Slovenian farmer. You see black and white photographs of women hauling ploughs in the fields ... And you know, in another time and another place, that would be Tanya, keeping going. Keeping everything together.' She is never still. 'Working and working. She is just remarkably robust. She is unstoppable.'

* * *

The year in which Tanya Plibersek served as UTS women's officer – 1992 – was also her honours year. It was unusual at that time
for journalism students to do honours. Most were keen to get into the
industry as fast as possible. Today, she says she did an honours year primarily because she was involved in student politics and needed to stay
enrolled to hold the women's officer post.

Bacon supervised her thesis, which had to be presented as a piece of
journalistic practice. Titled 'Smoke Signals: Cigarette Advertising Aimed
at Women in Developing Countries', Plibersek's thesis was pitched as a
booklet that could be published by the Australian Centre for Independent Journalism and distributed to 'health workers and acitivists, feminsts
and womens' organisations' (spelling mistakes in original). It could also,
the foreword asserted, be transformed into a series of feature articles.

The topic was motivated partly by her admiration for the subversive
group BUGA-UP (Billboards Using Graffiti Against Unhelpful Promotions), which, operating on the edges of the law, made witty amendments
to billboards advertising tobacco and other products. As well, Matt
Brown had a sister who was a women's health worker, which led Tanya
to an awareness of how hard women can find it to give up smoking – and
how cigarettes were pitched at them as a 'little treat'. Tobacco advertising had begun to be phased out by the Whitlam government, and was
banned on television and radio, but print advertising and billboards were
still legal. When it came to cigarette advertising, Plibersek regarded the
free speech argument with the same contempt she had the previous year
directed at pornographers.

In the introduction to her thesis, she argued that cigarette marketers
had appropriated the language of feminism to try to associate cigarettes
with liberation. Meanwhile, in the developing world, women who were
entering the workforce for the first time, perhaps delaying marriage, were
also increasingly likely to smoke. She shared an anecdote from her travels:

Cramped on a slow Egyptian bus, we crawl North along the Red Sea
Coast. The desert ends abruptly, crumbling straight into the ocean.

Just salt and dust. The red sunset quickly turns the earth black, and the bus hostess offers us a cigarette. She is Egyptian, but she is the first Egyptian woman I have seen who wears short sleeves, a knee length skirt, blue eyeshadow and a defiant look. Her cigarettes are Western – she can afford them. She can afford to offer them ... She offers her cigarettes to men, treating men as equals. The men salivate. Is she sexually available? What else could this display mean? Why is she working? Obviously, her family can't afford to keep her securely at home. Do the men imagine that she could work by choice?

Plibersek asked how 'a thin sheet of paper wrapped around the shredded leaves and twigs of a south American plant, containing fifty carcinogens and hundreds of poisonous substances ... can allow women to feel "exciting" and "adventurous"'. Cigarette advertisers, she argued, had recognised the fears and insecurities of modern women and success-fully offered cigarettes as a 'solution'.

What followed was a lengthy piece of journalism in three parts: the first dealt with the history of cigarette advertising aimed at women, the second was an overview of the markets in developing nations, and the last an in-depth case study of the launch of 'Ms' cigarettes in India, marketed under the motto 'A lady's privilege'. She drew on fem-inist literature such as Anne Summers' book *Damned Whores and God's Police*, and the work of Betty Friedan.

It was, Bacon recalls, 'a solid piece of research for a young person'.

Plibersek ended the thesis with thanks 'to all the people who fed me, indulged me and consoled me through this ordeal (especially Wendy Bacon, the Queen of Early Mornings. May your lungs stay pink and healthy).'[31] The early mornings were a reference to the fact they used to meet in cafes at the crack of dawn, as Bacon juggled her work as an aca-demic with caring for her young children.

Meanwhile, Plibersek continued to write for *Vertigo*. In late 1992, in one of her last Salvation Jane columns, Plibersek and her fellow women's officer, Cassandra Bennett, wrote a critique of the Liberal Party's 'Fight-back' economic policy, saying it was no good for women, unless 'you were a stay-at-home mum whose husband has an above average wage that he's prepared to share with you'. The package, the article said, would push more responsibility for care of children onto the family unit, 'and that means women. That means free labour.'

The cuts in government spending would hit women hardest, and the Liberals' proposed goods and services tax represented 'a system of incentives and rewards for the wealthy at the expense of the poor. The supposed trickle-down outcome is a piss-on effect of the nastiest variety, and it is women who will be stung the hardest.'

But Plibersek was almost equally critical of Labor. Their approach was 'hardly better', she said: 'Hewson's package merely represents a more ruthless and damaging approach. Moreover any government that places a luxury tax on tampons and pads, and then imports caviar tax-free ought to be shot.'[32]

When she submitted her thesis at the end of 1992, Plibersek gave her address as 16/29 Elizabeth Bay Road, Elizabeth Bay 2011. This was a tiny one-bedroom flat in The Emerson – one of the run-down but charming art-deco buildings that characterised the suburb. There was a nook for a desk, with views of Rushcutters Bay, a tiny kitchen and living area. She had lived in a variety of student share houses during her university years, but this was the first home she shared with Michael Coutts-Trotter. They were owners, having bought it in both their names.

Plibersek continued to write for *Vertigo* even after she graduated, including a three-page history of Yugoslavia, starting with an eyewitness account of Slovenia's declaration of independence on 26 June 1991. 'I half ran to the town square. I couldn't see and I could barely hear, but I cheered with everyone else when the announcement was made that Slovenia was officially independent.' She was in the market place the next day and saw the beginning of the fighting, as the Serbian army crossed the southern border and bombed the airport while '[t]he grandmothers, in their patterned cotton shifts and colourful scarves, continued to sell wild mushrooms, raspberries and camomile tea'. She attacked the stereotype of 'mad Yugoslavs' always at each other's throats: 'This simplification disgusts me.'[33]

In another piece she reported on the making of a South Korean drama series about the Vietnam war. Her article was illustrated with a confronting image of a US soldier holding a shredded corpse.[34] The next issue of *Vertigo* contained a letter from a student councillor protesting the image: 'This was obscene and you printed it anyway.' Tanya wrote a sharp response: 'I agree totally that what is depicted is an offence to humanity. What is depicted is war.' She had taken the picture herself in the Museum of War Atrocities in Ho Chi Minh City.[35]

After the re-election of the Keating government in March 1993, *Vertigo* ran a tongue-in-cheek survey of the new ministry, based on questions sent out by Tanya. Only four ministers responded – Ross Free, minister for schools, education and training; Frank Walker, special minister of state; Graham Richardson, minister for health and Bob McMullan, minister for the arts. In the last question, Plibersek asked the ministers who would be the first Australian president. Free said he was not sure. Richardson said 'me'. McMullan said, 'It won't be [Liberal MP] Bronwyn Bishop.' But Walker replied: 'Tanya Plibersek, former member of the Como Jannali ALP Branch and Young Labor.' Plibersek commented, in square brackets, 'I swear I have never met this man, nor paid him any money.'[36]

Meanwhile, Plibersek had applied for one of the most prized opportunities for recent journalism graduates: a cadetship at the Australian Broadcasting Corporation. Wendy Bacon wrote her a reference – not something she did lightly, or for every graduate. Plibersek got to the final round of interviews. Nervous, she sought advice from friends about how to present herself. She was told that she might come across as being too softly spoken and gentle: 'They'll want someone who's more aggressive for this type of job.' She took the advice on board and ramped up her presentation accordingly – and was devastated when she failed. She asked for feedback and was told that she had come across 'as someone who might be difficult to work with'.

Plibersek says she has never forgotten this lesson. 'If I had been more myself, I still may not have got the job, but it wouldn't have been because I seemed difficult to work with. It would have been for some other, probably more valid, reason. Anyway, it was a good lesson. Never try to pretend that you're something you're not in an interview.'

Plibersek did not apply for any other jobs in journalism. The ABC was the pinnacle for young progressives wanting to work in the industry, and she had set all her hopes on getting in.

Perhaps she would have applied to other media companies, given time, but just weeks after she got the knockback, she saw what she thought was her dream job advertised – for an entry-level research officer at the newly established Ministry for the Status and Advancement of Women, working in the Domestic Violence Unit. From the day she saw the advertisement, she put all her eggs in that basket and focused on getting the job. This time, she succeeded. Apart from part-time jobs at school and to support herself at university, this was to be the only job outside politics she has ever held. She started in mid-1993 and lasted less than a year.

3

SEEKING SYDNEY

People ask how someone like Tanya Plibersek, so *nice,* could possibly have survived and prospered within the notoriously thuggish politics of the NSW branch of the Australian Labor Party. It is one of the remarkable things about her. Almost alone of her NSW colleagues, she has maintained relatively clean hands in the party's constant internal wars. In interviews for this book, Plibersek described the work of factional deals and negotiations as like the human resources department of a large organisation. It was important work, someone had to do it, but it was not her thing, and she did as little of it as she could get away with. Her rise despite this is a testament to her talents. On the other hand, she probably would have risen faster, and perhaps further, if she had not held herself aloof. In the early years of her career, she was the beneficiary of battles fought by others – perhaps chiefly by Anthony Albanese. Some people resent her for that. The battles Albanese fought are part of the prehistory to Plibersek's entry into politics and formed the context for her progression.

Andrew Leigh, now an assistant minister in the Albanese government, has also been an academic. In 2000 he wrote a paper based on interviews with the people involved in the almighty battles within the Left faction of the NSW ALP in the late 1980s and early 1990s. Factionalism in the ALP, he wrote, was 'like the role of the Mafia in Italian politics, few outside the system seem to understand the power networks, whilst few inside are prepared to share their thoughts with the outside world. Yet without understanding factions, it is impossible to properly comprehend the Labor Party.'[1]

It is hard to recreate the atmosphere of inner-Sydney left-wing Labor politics at that time. Probe the memories of the people who were there, and you get stories of half-drunken encounters at pub fundraisers, fierce rows about the direction of the Hawke and Keating governments, and heated branch meetings in local halls. It was internecine and passionate. Everyone knew everyone else.

The Left faction of the party was very different then. Largely excluded from power, it saw itself as an opposition within the party, or at least a ginger group. Tom Uren, Anthony Albanese's boss, was one of Bob Hawke's strongest critics. The Left, including Albanese, opposed many of the major reforms of the period, from privatisation to cutting tariffs, exporting uranium, and introducing fees and loans for higher education. When treasurer Paul Keating brought down a budget, the staff of Left MPs would stay up all night combing through it and produce the faction's own, often critical response. But during the late 1980s and into the 1990s, the power of the Left was growing. It scored some significant victories over the Right, and that meant struggle, including within the faction.

By the time she graduated from UTS, Plibersek was part of several interlinked networks that overlapped with the Australian Labor Party. There were the progressive women from the Sutherland Shire. There were the feminists she had met at conferences and forums during her time as women's officer at UTS. As well, she admired pioneering NSW female parliamentarians, including Ann Symonds and Meredith Burgmann. Plibersek recalls: 'If I heard either of them was giving a talk, I would always go.'

In 1991, when she first met Plibersek, Burgmann was a candidate for the NSW Legislative Council. She was contesting the position at Albanese's 'unrelenting' urging.[2] Albanese later said he had recruited Burgmann because as well as being a good candidate, she was 'more than anyone else part of the Vietnam, anti-apartheid, activist generation. She sent a huge message to the Whitlamite Left, if you like, that you should be in the Labor Party.'[3] Plibersek was not on Albanese's radar at the time, but she was an exemplar of the kind of person he was talking about – engaged with Labor, part of the broad progressive movements within Australia, but not in the party. Sure enough, Plibersek was drawn to Burgmann's example.

Burgmann, an academic, unionist and activist, had been a member of the party for almost all her adult life. A leader of anti–Vietnam War protests and an activist against apartheid, she had been arrested twenty-one times and spent time in prison. She first met Albanese in the Criterion Hotel on the corner of Liverpool and Sussex streets, when he was just nineteen. He introduced himself to her as Albo and insisted on being called that. 'Even then he had such joie de vivre and self confidence that I actually remember meeting him. I doubt if I would remember meeting any other nineteen-year-old in the Criterion on a Friday night after many gins,' she wrote later.[4] They became friends and allies, but there were rows – nights that ended with them standing at opposite ends of the room, both in tears – although, she remembers, he wept more easily than she did.

'He saw me as too centred on inner-city concerns and kept hammering me about the need for the Left to broaden itself out to the western suburbs.' But they agreed on their core values, and on the need to engage with broad progressive movements in society – environmentalists, feminists and others – and to draw them to the Labor cause. Over time, despite the fact that Albanese was sixteen years younger than her, Burgmann came to regard him as a political mentor. He was tactically among the smartest Labor people she had ever known. 'I once said to him that I was getting better and I could now think three steps ahead and he just laughed at me and said "yeah, but I'm eleven steps ahead" and I reckon that's probably true. He's the master of the long game.'[5]

Burgmann and Plibersek met in what Tanya recalls as a 'fan-girl moment' at a fundraiser for Genevieve Rankin's tilt at state parliament, held at the Sutherland District Trade Union Club. Burgmann had given a speech and then gone to the bathroom. Burgmann had had a few drinks, she remembers, as had most people at the event, 'and we were all pretty cheerful'. As she washed her hands she was approached by a young undergraduate student – Plibersek. 'And I remember her not quite accosting me, but coming up to me and talking about how much she wanted to be like me, and that I was one of the people that she thought about a lot. It was quite touching, really.'

Even in that unpromising environment, Burgmann was impressed. She recalls that Plibersek was 'someone you remembered, even though she was so young. She was charismatic, which is more than you would normally say about a student, and she was very interested in and good on women's issues.' From then on, Plibersek remained in Burgmann's broader circle – often at the same events, demonstrations and public speeches, always articulate, confident and impressive – but not on the inside. She had not yet rejoined the Labor Party.

Meanwhile, an almighty battle was underway.

The politics of Labor's factions are deeply unappealing to most outsiders – and to some insiders. Former prime minister Kevin Rudd has described factions, particularly those in NSW, as a cancer on the party. They are usually mentioned in the media with only negative connotations. But just as political parties are part of a mature, orderly democracy, party factions are part of the machinery by which large groups of people with different values and priorities nevertheless manage to work together. Through the factions, the cats are herded and power distributed. Three times in its history, the Labor Party has split. Each time has been devastating. The factional system is, in some ways, the contemporary alternative to splitting – which is one of the reasons the hatreds involved can be so intense.

After Plibersek's brief acquaintance with Albanese in Young Labor when she was fifteen years old, he had fought battles for control of Young Labor against a hostile takeover attempt from the Right. While she was still at university, he had been engaged in conflicts which, with the benefit of hindsight, can be seen as crucial to the formation of the contemporary party. These saw the NSW Left become one of the most powerful factions in the party, with personalities to rival those of the big men of the Right – Hawke, Keating and Graham Richardson. The fact that today the leadership of the government is dominated by Left faction members – Albanese as prime minister, Penny Wong as leader in the Senate – is partly the legacy of those battles. But in the process of acquiring power, the Left has itself been changed. It is no longer an internal opposition to the leadership of the party. It now *is* the leadership – and at the 2022 election, presented a small target rather than a radical agenda.

Labor's long period in government from 1983 had cemented the role of factions and institutionalised them. Three had formed – the Right, the Left and the Centre Left. They operated, often, like mini parties, with their own office bearers, newsletters and even policies. As they became entrenched, their power was both constrained and amplified by agreements under which frontbench and parliamentary committee appointments were shared out by the factional leaders, based loosely on the factional representation in caucus. By the end of the Hawke and Keating governments, power within the ALP depended largely on having influence within a faction, rather than within the party as a whole. Inevitably, that meant the wars were not only between factions, but within them.

When Plibersek met Burgmann, the NSW Left had split into two 'fractions', commonly known as the Hard Left and the Soft Left. The division was partly ideological. Members of the Hard Left saw the Soft Left as too cynical, and too ready to capitulate to the Hawke–Keating market-based agenda. The Hard Left was more open to connections with broader left groups outside the party.

But the split was also largely about personalities. The Soft Left was dominated by the Ferguson family – patriarch Jack Ferguson, former deputy premier in the NSW Wran government, and his sons Martin and Laurie, both of whom became federal MPs in the 1990s. The Hard Left, on the other hand, was dominated by people such as Tom Uren, Senator Bruce Childs and, as time went by, Albanese himself.

A key battle had been fought in 1989, the year Plibersek had spent travelling the world in her gap year. The position of assistant general secretary of the NSW branch of the party became vacant when the incumbent, John Faulkner, was elected to the Senate. It was a key post, and it was reserved for the Left. The first person to hold it had been Bruce Childs. Both he and Faulkner had suffered from constant bastardry and bullying from the Right. The stories that are told of the terrible things left in office drawers could fill a book. There had never been a ballot for this position: the Left simply chose the candidate. This time, too, it was assumed that the Soft Left candidate would sail through. Albanese had different ideas. He contested the position and won, making him the effective leader of the Hard Left fraction, if not the Left as a whole, in the NSW administrative party.[6]

From this key position, and before the Labor Party adopted affirmative action policies mandating the selection of women candidates for winnable seats, Albanese was important in organising women into both state and federal parliament. Burgmann was one beneficiary. Others were Linda Burney, Carmel Tebbutt and Penny Sharpe. Albanese was also close to Jeannette McHugh. She had won the eastern suburbs seat of Phillip in 1983, becoming the first woman from New South Wales to be elected to federal parliament. When Phillip was abolished in a redistribution, Albanese organised for her to move to Grayndler, in the inner western suburbs. It was understood between them that she was keeping the seat warm for him. He was not yet ready to run; he had more work to do as assistant secretary of the NSW branch. But after another three-year term McHugh would be sixty-two and likely willing to retire, and that would give him his chance to enter the federal parliament.[7]

The fractional wars between Hard Left and Soft Left continued. In some dusty corners of the party, they are still being fought. But with hindsight, it is possible to pronounce a winner: the Hard Left. Its ascendancy within the NSW machine was reflected in stronger representation in the federal parliament, with its two highest-profile representatives being Albanese, who was elected as the member for Grayndler in 1996 – and Tanya Plibersek, who would be elected to the federal parliament in 1998.

* * *

Working in the NSW public service, in the Ministry for the Status and Advancement of Women, changed Plibersek's mind about the merits of being a member of the ALP. After decades of Labor rule in New South Wales, the Liberal Party had come to government in 1988, with Nick Greiner as premier. He was forced to resign in 1992 after an Independent Commission Against Corruption (ICAC) investigation and was succeeded by John Fahey. Fahey restructured what had been the Women's Coordination Unit within the Department of Family Services and created a new ministry, the first state government ministry devoted to women's issues. The first Minister for the Status and Advancement of Women was Kerry Chikarovski, a rising star in the Liberal Party who was often spoken of as a possible future premier.

Under Chikarovski's watch, the ministry came to be known among the wags in the public service as the Ministry for the Advancement of Women of Status. Her focus was on helping already high-achieving women break through glass ceilings in the corporate world and in politics. For Plibersek, as the new entry-level research officer in the Domestic Violence Unit, this emphasis was more than frustrating. It made her angry. Plibersek's job was to compile research reports and provide executive support to the NSW Council on Violence Against Women. She remembers working with police crime databases to examine how apprehended violence orders were working in practice. She was in touch with frontline workers who were trying to help women to find safe housing or to get decent jobs. This, Plibersek thought, should be the main work of the ministry, but in her view these women 'were basically treated as embarrassing issues'.

She liked and admired her direct boss, Julie Stewart, who was the head of the four-person Domestic Violence Unit. But the head of the ministry, Jane Bridge, was a career public servant who was, Plibersek says today, 'clearly very networked into the Liberal Party. She was a political appointment.' Stewart was on the interview panel when Plibersek applied for the job and remembers Plibersek's performance. 'She was stunning. She was very young, but she was so worldly and assured about her politics and her ideas. The thing I can't forget is that at the end of the interview, she asked, "Have I mentioned enthusiasm?" And then she went on to give this amazing speech about how enthusiastic she was.'

The atmosphere in the office, however, was toxic. A lot of staff had already left. More were to leave over the next year. Stewart was under enormous pressure from Bridge. She recalls that 'people were too scared to talk to each other or to do anything'. She was feeling brow-beaten, intimidated and under siege, and to her own surprise increasingly came to rely on the 'wisdom and morality and clear vision' of Plibersek, her newest and youngest recruit.

One of the issues was how money was spent. There had been lavish office fit-outs, grooming advice for Bridge and monogrammed crockery. More seriously, there was a suspicion of corruption. In one case a boardroom table had been moved from the ministry office to the offices of Bridge's husband, who was an architect in private practice.

Plibersek, Stewart recalls, was 'on to that right away', and set about using some of the investigative journalism skills she had learned at UTS – doing company searches and getting statutory declarations from key sources, including the truck driver who delivered the table. 'It was her initiative. She just had so much guts.' Meanwhile, the Domestic Violence Unit was working on a strategic plan but was constantly thwarted. Key research reports were drafted but were not released by the government. Stewart had been told that Chikarovski didn't want to be associated with women as victims.

Plibersek, increasingly angry and frustrated, reflected that the feminist Labor women she knew – people like Burgmann, Rankin and Symonds – had a much better understanding of the issues. 'I didn't feel the government of the day was particularly interested in the sort of change that you'd have to make to really drive gender equality and reduce rates of violence against women,' she recalls.

Could she rejoin the party that had disappointed her, some of whose policies she still disagreed with? She decided that she could and should. 'I got into the headspace of "There's no point being on the outside throwing stones." I wanted to be part of making the change happen. And I thought the Labor Party might be an imperfect vehicle, but it is the best available, and some of the people I most respect are part of it.' She doesn't remember exactly when she rejoined the party, but by the end of 1993 she was once again a member. By early 1994, she was looking for another job.

In October of that year, the NSW Labor opposition began a sustained attack on Kerry Chikarovski, Jane Bridge and the ministry. Burgmann led the charge. In budget estimates hearings, she told how 'tough' women from the ministry had been coming to her in tears because of their difficulties dealing with Bridge. There had been a staff turnover of almost 50 per cent in the preceding year. About $68,000 had been spent on office refurbishments, money that should have gone to the domestic violence budget. Staff were frustrated with the lack of output. The report on the results of a phone-in for sexual assault victims, held in October 1992, had not been released until almost a year later, though it was ready within three months. The original recommendations were watered down, to the disappointment of community workers who had given their time to the project. Another report, resulting from an inquiry into Aboriginal women and the law, had been written a year previously but still not released. A letter from seven local domestic violence committees to Chikarovski blamed Bridge's 'inability to get along with staff' for preventing the 'proper functioning of the Domestic Violence Advisory Council'.[8]

Some of the allegations Burgmann made were much more personal, including claims that Bridge had spent taxpayers' money on advice about how to dress and do her make-up. And she raised the matter of the boardroom table.[9] Today, Burgmann says her memories of what prompted her attacks on Bridge, and where she got her information, are dim. She doesn't think that Plibersek was one of those providing information. But it seems clear, from a variety of contextual information and interviews with those involved, that Plibersek must have been a key source for Burgmann's parliamentary attacks. In other words, Plibersek either leaked or blew the whistle, depending on your point of view. It was a serious thing for a public servant to do. Asked about this directly in interviews for this book, Plibersek would only say, 'No comment.' Would she correct the record if the assumption was wrong? 'Well, no comment on that either, because then I would be commenting.'

The government stood behind Bridge and Chikarovski and both survived the attack. As for the boardroom table, the government pointed out that the same allegations had been made to the Independent Commission Against Corruption by an anonymous complainant more than a year before. ICAC had considered the allegations and dismissed them.

On 21 October 1994, Tanya Plibersek's name appeared for the second time in a mainstream media article reporting Burgmann's attacks. Plibersek was described as a former employee of the ministry who had left after just ten months 'because she found the work environment intolerable'. 'It was unhappy, unproductive and work was continually frustrated,' she said. 'The ministry did some very good work for privileged women but mainstream issues like domestic violence and sexual assault fell off the agenda and the needs of the majority of women in NSW just weren't being met.'[10]

Defending Chikarovski and Bridge in parliament the following week, the government MLC Helen Sham-Ho alluded to the interview, without naming Plibersek. Most of the women who had left the ministry had gone on to more senior positions, she said, and noted that they included 'a young woman who has spent the past few days happily giving interviews to the media about the alleged unhappiness inside the Ministry. It will not surprise members to discover that this young woman now works for a Labor Senator and just happens to be a member of the Labor Party and a colleague of the Hon. Dr Meredith Burgmann.'[11]

When she rejoined the Labor Party, Plibersek was immediately embraced by an informal women's network, operating within the neighbouring electorates of Sydney and Jeannette McHugh's seat of Grayndler. The co-convenor of the network was Jill Lay, another long-term contact of Plibersek, later to become the manager of her electorate office. Symonds and Burgmann were also involved. McHugh met Plibersek in Labor Party circles around Sydney. She has a distinct memory of sitting with her in a cafe after one event. As the two women talked, Plibersek was mistaken by the waiter as McHugh's daughter. McHugh recalls, 'I was so thrilled because here was this brilliant young woman and people thought she was related to me.'

McHugh was a long-term left-wing and feminist activist, but an eastern suburbs member of the middle class – somewhat out of place in working-class Grayndler. She was married to the barrister Michael McHugh, a High Court judge. She was one of Albanese's closest supporters, effectively holding Grayndler for the Hard Left until he was ready to enter parliament. Now she was a passionate Plibersek supporter as well.

At the same time as she was making these connections, Plibersek's relationship with Coutts-Trotter had carried her into other important networks. One of her closest female friends is Phillipa McGuinness, generally called Pip, an author and publisher. The two women met through their partners, when Tanya was still completing her honours thesis. Pip's partner was Adam Suckling, who was a colleague of Coutts-Trotter in public relations. 'The four of us have been tight ever since,' says McGuinness. They have dined together, holidayed together and supported each other through triumph and tragedy. A Catholic background is one of the bonds between Plibersek, Coutts-Trotter and McGuinness. Suckling, they joke, is 'the token Protestant'.

Suckling moved on to work with the arts administrator and media executive Kim Williams, who was later chief executive of Foxtel and for a brief period CEO of News Limited. Suckling was director of policy and corporate affairs for Foxtel, and then for News Corporation as a whole. Williams – who was married to Gough Whitlam's daughter, Catherine Dovey – also became part of their circle.

Given these networks, it is hardly surprising that Plibersek heard that Senator Bruce Childs was looking for a new member of staff. McGuinness believes it was Suckling who told her about the job. At this stage, says McGuinness, there was no suggestion that Plibersek might one day become a parliamentarian. She was like the rest of them – ambitious in the sense of wanting to achieve something, to make a difference, but not necessarily for any particular job. 'I don't think she ever at that time articulated that she might want a political career. She never spoke about it.' The suggestion from Suckling that she apply to join Childs' staff was 'without a scintilla of the idea that this will help you in your political career. It would have been like, "You're interested in policy. I've heard Bruce Childs is a really good man doing good work. Would you like to talk to him about a job?"' Plibersek, on the other hand, thinks it was Ann Symonds who first alerted her that the job was available. It could easily have been both of them, given the way the networks operated.

Plibersek made an appointment and went to see Childs, taking a portfolio of her work and a letter presenting her case. He was much more interested in understanding why she had joined the Labor Party so young, and why she had left. 'I told him, and I don't think it did me any harm in his eyes, that I left over uranium mining and land rights.' They knew people in common. They swapped names: the Sutherland Shire women, Hazel Wilson, Genevieve Rankin and Joy Goodsell. Plibersek mentioned that she knew Robert Tickner, and that he had been kind to her when she was still in high school. 'I don't know if he had rung any of them and asked them about me,' she says. In any case, he hired her on the spot.

* * *

In the first speech Plibersek gave in federal parliament, she described Bruce Childs as 'the finest example of a self-effacing, modest collectivist'. She remembers him as being 'a fantastic role model, a very lovely, decent, hardworking, principled, honourable person'.[12] In interviews for this book, she credited him with teaching her that it is possible to be passionately engaged in politics without becoming 'a nasty human being'.

Born in Mascot in 1934, Childs was the son of a carriage maker who had been ruined in the Great Depression. After leaving school, Childs became a printer's apprentice and then a unionist. *The Biographical Dictionary of the Australian Senate* records that his first meeting of the NSW Labor Council was a 'touchstone' for his later career. 'That's the leadership up there,' advised the older officials in his delegation, pointing to the presidium. 'If you have any doubts on an issue, always vote against the bastards.'[13]

Childs came of age on the eve of the Labor split in 1955, and from then on was firmly part of the Left of the party. He opposed the Vietnam War. He supported women's liberation and a greater role for women in the ALP. He was the convenor of the Nuclear Disarmament Coordinating Committee and a convenor of the Palm Sunday peace marches that had been part of Plibersek's political awakening as a teenager. Childs was not a high-profile senator, but he devoted himself to the important work of Senate committees. In his final speech to the Senate, he said he had never identified with being a politician, but 'I really do identify with being a parliamentarian'. This was an attitude he passed on to Plibersek.

But within the internal politics of the party, Childs was a warrior, and one of the chief antagonists of Hawke and of the Right. In 1986 – the year the teenage Plibersek had left the party – Childs issued a press release stating that the Hawke government's decision to sell uranium to France exemplified its 'failure to implement the party platform'. In January 1991, the year that Plibersek ran for and won the post of women's officer at UTS, Childs, together with senators Margaret Reynolds and John Coates, abstained from voting on a motion of support for Australia's involvement in the first Gulf War.

Due to her position on his staff, her friendships within the women's network and her own convictions, Plibersek inevitably became identified with the Hard Left. At that time, she says, she felt 'very strongly' about the ideological differences between the factions and believed that the Soft Left were too conciliatory with the Hawke–Keating agenda and 'much more inclined to do a deal with the Right on things that I couldn't agree with'.

On Childs' staff, as well as becoming a policy adviser and researcher, she got a crash course in the importance of electoral work. She learned the difference the 'authority of the MP's office' could make to ordinary people's lives. She helped Childs get more housing for an Aboriginal community. Together, they toured the rural areas of the state in the weeks when parliament wasn't sitting. When Childs organised a trip with other parliamentarians as part of a protest against nuclear testing in the Pacific, Plibersek's job was to find the boat. She loved the work.

She also got her first taste of parliamentary politics, spending every sitting week with Childs in Canberra, watching him in the Senate and on Senate committees. Childs was under pressure to retire at the next election to make way for union leader George Campbell, but he was not ready to go. The women of the Left were on his side. Seventy-one prominent ALP women signed a letter to the ALP Left caucus supporting him, and his position was saved, on the understanding that he would retire at the end of his next term. He finally resigned from the Senate on 10 September 1997 and was succeeded by Campbell. Plibersek stayed on Campbell's staff for the months between Childs' retirement and her own entry to parliament – but it is Childs whom she credits as her mentor.

When Tanya began working for Childs, Coutts-Trotter was still completing his degree at UTS, studying part-time while working as a public relations consultant at Turnbull Fox Phillips. Brydon surrendered control of the company but stayed in touch with Michael, who was by now, she says, 'a very accomplished and capable young consultant'. Coutts-Trotter handled the account for the government-owned telephone services provider, Telecom, in the lead-up to its privatisation by the Hawke government. That work brought him into contact with Michael Egan, who was the NSW treasurer in the recently elected Carr Labor government.

Coutts-Trotter had for a long time wanted to work as a Labor Party political staffer. When he graduated, he applied for a job as a press secretary for the then deputy prime minister, Brian Howe. He got the job, but the appointment was overruled by the prime minister's office. Now, Egan had taken 'a shine to him', in Brydon's words. She remembers

Coutts-Trotter coming to her and saying Egan had offered him a job as a press secretary. What did she think? 'I said, "Have you told him about your chequered past?" and he said no, he thought he'd talk to me first.' She recommended that he have a frank conversation with Egan.

Egan has retold the story of that conversation many times. He was a working-class Catholic, and a former union official. He had been educated in an impoverished Catholic school in the Sutherland Shire – not very far from Jannali Girls' High, but twenty years before Tanya went there. He was later to recall the struggles his school went through. 'Money, or lack of it, was the main problem. In those days, there was no state aid for non-government schools and the predominantly working-class parents of Sutherland were not exactly rolling in it either.'[14] It was a background about as far removed as possible from that of Riverview boy Coutts-Trotter, but for the common thread of Catholicism. Coutts-Trotter made his confession – a criminal past. Egan looked him up and down and said that he wasn't bothered by any of that. Rather, 'I don't like the fact you have a hyphenated name or been educated by the Jesuits'.[15] He warned Coutts-Trotter that if he took the job, it was inevitable that his background would come out.

Egan was right. It took about six months. Tim Palmer, by then working at the ABC, heard on the journalistic grapevine that his old friend was about to feature in a story in the Murdoch press. He got in touch with Carr's press secretary and other government contacts. 'I said to them, "This story is going to come out, and are you guys going to stand by him? Because if you are, give me a guarantee. And if not, I am going to beat them to the story, and publish it not as a "gotcha" story but as a favourable story.' And to their credit, they said straight-away that they were rock solid, that they would stand by him. By then, they loved him. They thought he was great.' Palmer stood back and let events play out.

On Sunday, 12 November 1995, the *Sunday Telegraph Mirror* carried a small article on an inside page. It didn't name Coutts-Trotter or Egan. The first paragraph read, 'A man jailed for his role in a $500,000 drug trafficking operation has become a key adviser to a senior State Government minister.' The man's jail sentence, the newspaper reported, had ended only in May that year – six weeks after the election of the Carr government. There was a political context to the story. Carr was locked in a battle within the party over an election promise to introduce automatic life sentences for major drug traffickers and killers. This looked like hypocrisy.[16] The story was picked up by television and radio. Brydon rang Coutts-Trotter. 'What are you going to do?' she asked. He replied that he was going to put out a statement and tell his story.

The result was a front-page article spilling into the inside pages in the following Tuesday's *Daily Telegraph*. There was a picture of Coutts-Trotter – still thin, but no longer gaunt – on the steps of NSW Parliament House with Egan by his side. 'Paid My Debt' was the headline. It was the first of many confessional interviews over the years. The positioning of Coutts-Trotter as a story of redemption had begun.

He told the media that 'I do not believe I should be placed on trial again for events which took place more than 12 years ago … as a teenager I did something very wrong. I faced the consequences of those actions and paid my debt in full.' Brydon was quoted, describing Coutts-Trotter's experience as a 'remarkable story of rehabilitation'. Egan described him as 'without peer in his profession … and one of the most fabulous human beings I have ever met.'[17]

In the same edition, Mark Day used the story to give Carr a caning. Carr and Egan, said Day, had 'made the perfectly reasonable judgement that although he had been an alcoholic at 13, a drug addict at 16, a heroin courier at 18 and a jailbird at 21, he was now 31 and reformed'. Coutts-Trotter 'deserves to be applauded, not condemned', said Day, and that meant that Carr should break his election promise to force judges to jail people involved in drug pushing.[18] The story filled the media for a week. None of the publicity mentioned Plibersek, who was then a virtually unknown junior staffer for Childs. But she was watching, and she was worried. This was the beginning of one of her most peculiar alliances.

Radio shock-jock Alan Jones was in 1995 at the height of his powers: number one on Sydney radio and author of a well-read newspaper column. His biographer Chris Masters would later describe him as the 'godfather' of Sydney's urban jungle at this time, using his influence and perceived power to demand attention from politicians, who feared him.[19] He adopted causes both deserving and dubious, and in the years to come was constantly at the centre of controversy. In 2005 he would help to incite the race riots at Cronulla, in the Sutherland Shire, by describing Lebanese Muslims as 'vermin' who 'rape and pillage a nation that's taken them in'. A court later found that he had 'incited hatred, serious contempt and severe ridicule of Lebanese Muslims'.[20] When Julia Gillard was prime minister, Jones notoriously suggested she should be put in a chaff bag and dumped at sea, and that her father had 'died of shame' because of his daughter's supposed lies.[21] But in 1995, Alan Jones came down on the side of Michael Coutts-Trotter. In one of his radio rants, he echoed Mark Day's line. He told his audience that he knew Coutts-Trotter personally, having dealt with him in his role as Egan's press secretary. He had been impressed. Coutts-Trotter was good at his job and should be left alone. With two of Sydney's most powerful media figures – both on the right of politics – backing Coutts-Trotter, he was effectively inoculated from the most likely sources of attacks.

A few years later, when Plibersek was a backbench MP, Jones helped her again, intervening in a campaign she was running to secure a pay rise for disability-sector workers during a dispute between the Carr and Howard governments. Plibersek has continued to make time for Jones. Until he was dropped from the station, she had a regular spot on his Sky News television show, appearing each week among the after-dark line-up of right-wing commentators. Jones would often introduce her as the woman who should be leading the Labor Party. Plibersek has appeared on Jones' self-broadcast YouTube channel since he was sacked from mainstream media. It mystifies her colleagues. Jeannette McHugh describes it as 'one of the few things I will never understand about Tanya, and most of what she does I think is terrific'.

So is Alan Jones a friend? Asked this question in interviews for this book, Plibersek shifted uncomfortably. She and Coutts-Trotter have been to Christmas drinks at Jones' home. There have been months and months when she has refused to deal with him or to appear on his shows. It took her a long time to speak to him after his treatment of Gillard. They have had plenty of arguments, both on and off the air, she says. They are under no illusions that they agree politically.

But is he a friend? 'Yes, he is a friend. There is a lot I can't agree with, but I have seen him do some things that are really generous as well, and I acknowledge that.'

She makes the obvious political point: that Labor is lost if it speaks only to those who already agree with its polices. It is Jones' audience she seeks, not him. She skips straight to one of her well-honed anecdotes from childhood – when Ray and Phillip would argue over the dining table, and Joe Plibersek would tell them that they must listen as much as they spoke, that they should try to understand points of view with which they did not agree. She says this is one of the most useful lessons her father taught her, and that she remembers it often

There is also, she acknowledges, a lasting gratitude. Jones backed her partner at a time when, arguably, he could have brought him down. Nevertheless, many of Plibersek's allies find her friendship with Jones utterly inexplicable. But Jones and Plibersek have one thing in common which she does not nominate. Both of them are known for intervening on an individual basis in response to hard-luck stories. Despite their deep differences, I suspect they recognise that instinct in each other. She would call it kindness.

Coutts-Trotter survived the revelation of his criminal past. The media stories would be revived periodically through his career, every time he got a new job. But from now on, it was no secret. He was inoculated against scandal. Egan became a close friend of Coutts-Trotter and Plibersek. He is the godfather of their eldest child, Anna.

*   *   *

Early in 1995, Plibersek enrolled in a Master of Politics and Public Policy at Macquarie University. She says she did it 'for fun' but also to dive into the issues of good governance that she was watching in real life, observing Childs and his work on Senate committees. The degree, she thought, would give her the chance to dive deeper than the fast pace and deadline-driven work of being a political staffer allowed. Her father's voice was also with her. He had told her as a child: 'You don't need a reason to learn something new.'

The degree was new – Plibersek was part of its second intake. It had been designed by Professor Geoffrey Hawker, a specialist in public policy who had previously worked for the landmark 1976 Royal Commission on Australian Government Administration, presided over by H.C. 'Nugget' Coombs. The degree was aimed at people who were working at the intersection of politics and public policy – future politicians, but also consultants, local government staff and lobbyists. It was a one-year course if studied full-time, but most students, like Tanya, were part-time, holding down full-time jobs. It was, remembers Hawker, 'a chummy little program', taught in the evenings to about ten students. Hawker remembers Tanya turning up in 'long woollen multicoloured stockings ... she was bright, on the ball, progressive, quick and witty and warm'.

Plibersek says doing the master's taught her 'a methodical approach to policy development'. She particularly remembers a unit of case studies on 'how things go right and how things go wrong in program development'. She has consciously applied those lessons in her work as a minister. 'I think if you look at the programs that I've initiated when I was a minister, there has never been a big stuff-up in any of them,' she says. For that, she credits the master's, together with her early work in parliament on the Public Accounts and Audit Committee. The combination gave her, she says, 'the ability to spot a trap a mile off and know what protects you from the sorts of mistakes that are commonly made'.

In the first eighteen months of her study, she was a stellar student – scoring nothing less than a B, and mostly As. But in her final year, 1997, her results slipped dramatically. Now Plibersek was doing the minimum necessary to gain a pass. The reason was clear. Tanya Plibersek was suddenly very busy.

She was, by now, deeply embedded in the party, increasingly involved in its processes and its policy development. She was on the women's policy committee and the economics policy committee, and a delegate to the 1998 National Conference. Verity Firth, later a state MP for the inner-Sydney seat of Balmain, and Meredith Burgmann's niece, remembers going to a conference in Hobart with Tanya. Firth was a vice-president of Young Labor. Plibersek was a formal delegate, and therefore got a hotel room, which she offered to share with the younger woman. Watching Plibersek, Firth was impressed. 'She was very knowledgeable and clever and had read everything and understood the policy debate from back to front, whereas at the time, I was much more slapdash about the whole thing.' The two women became firm friends and allies.

About the same time, Rebecca Huntley – academic, social researcher and author – met Plibersek when she was working for Childs. Today, Huntley is one of Plibersek's allies and friends. She believes Plibersek would be an excellent leader of the Australian Labor Party. She has stayed in Plibersek's flat in Canberra, and wrote a chapter in a book Plibersek edited, published in 2020. But at first, she was inclined to dislike Tanya. There were so many good women who had been doing the hard yards for Labor – in staffer positions, in local government, in the union movement – for so long. She saw Plibersek as a blow-in. 'I thought she was a young woman staffer who hadn't done that much in the party. And she was attractive, and bright, and impressive, but I was always thinking, 'Who are you?''

'And the next thing I hear about Tanya, she is running for preselection, for what is the jewel in the crown for the Labor Left, one of its prime seats. The seat of Sydney, which has everything in it, from public housing to the $4-million mansions.' Huntley was not impressed. 'I remember, to my shame, I was confident enough at the time to say to people that it was ridiculous.'

*   *   *

The electorate of Sydney, created in the late 1960s, has always been safe for Labor. Whoever held the seat, at the heart of Australia's largest city, was expected to have the potential to be a minister, perhaps even leader of the party.

The history of the electorate was knitted into the best and the worst of NSW Labor – its corruption, and its capacity for reform. In 1975, a NSW Legislative Council member and left-wing activist, Peter Baldwin, had devoted himself to trying to break the grip of the corrupt Right machine that controlled Labor subdivisions in central Sydney. They were run by 'tough old machine men, some with criminal connections'.[22] He uncovered illegal doctoring of the party's account books in the Enmore branch. In return for his efforts, on 16 July 1980, he was savagely beaten up outside his Marrickville home. The picture of his smashed face was on the front of the Sunday newspapers. Nobody was ever charged with his assault, but the publicity and resulting outrage forced a purge of local branches. It was the beginning of the reform of the quasi-criminal associations of right-wing Labor.

Baldwin moved from state politics to federal parliament as the MP for Sydney. He served as a low-profile but effective minister for employment, then minister for higher education and finally minister for social security from 1993 to the defeat of the Keating government in 1996.

Baldwin was not a clubbable chap. He did not behave in ways that suited the powerbrokers of the party. Some who knew him in those days say he would have been better as a public intellectual than as a politician. Nevertheless, he was one of the Hawke–Keating government's policy thinkers. In 1997, under the leadership of Kim Beazley, the party was licking its wounds after its defeat. It was also examining its policy mix. Baldwin was part of this rethinking. He had written a 50,000-word paper bursting with challenging ideas for a new Labor education policy, including a life-long learning account provided by the government to each school leaver, and a voucher system for post-secondary education. The media was reporting that he was at risk of being expelled from the Left faction because of his market-oriented views. In pushing for root and branch policy rethinking, Baldwin was allied with Mark Latham, who had entered parliament in 1994 as the member for the western suburbs seat of Werriwa. They were influenced by the new Blair government in the United Kingdom and its claim to have moved beyond the old battles between capital and labour and towards a 'third way', synthesising left- and right-wing ideology – supporting the market economy as a creator of wealth, but with government taking a role as a civiliser of the markets and a guardian of public good.

Beazley declared optimistically that the policy-making process in Labor was no longer driven by ideological arguments. The Left were no longer on the outside, throwing grenades. All sections of the party, he claimed, accepted a clearcut social democratic ideology.[23] Beazley promoted Latham to the front bench as minister for education and youth affairs. Latham and Baldwin, in 1996, asked for Beazley's approval to co-write a book on a new policy agenda for Labor. Latham wrote in his diary that Beazley was enthusiastic. 'He reckons that Baldwin and I are the only two Labor MPs thinking on a different plane. Or maybe he says that to all the boys.'[24] But it came to nothing. Soon, both Baldwin and Latham were frustrated and disgusted with Beazley and what they saw as his unwillingness to seriously consider reform. Baldwin, now shadow finance minister, tried to persuade shadow cabinet to consider comprehensive tax-reform options. He got nowhere.

On 18 July 1997, without warning or consideration for party processes or factional niceties, Baldwin announced he would quit parliament at the next election. It was a meltdown that was in some ways a precursor to Latham's departure from parliament seven years later. Baldwin told only a few confidants the day before he made the announcement. He had endorsed no successor.

Normally, a prize seat such as Sydney becoming available would have been telegraphed far in advance. Branches would have been stacked and deals done in advance of the preselection battle. Thanks to the manner of Baldwin's departure, there was no fix and no preparation. It was understood that the electorate of Sydney 'belonged' to the Left. As well, in 1994, the party had adopted an affirmative action rule that committed it to preselecting women for at least 35 per cent of winnable seats by 2002. It was understood that the new candidate for Sydney should be a woman. Within those constraints, the contest for this jewel of a seat was wide open.

The first person to suggest to Tanya Plibersek that she should consider running for preselection was Michael Lee, the member for Dobell on the NSW central coast, who had been a minister in the Keating government. He had met Plibersek at a Labor Party dinner some years before, and they had swapped notes on growing up in the Sutherland Shire – Lee had been raised in North Cronulla. Sometime later, as a former minister for the arts, he had been given free tickets to the opera and had invited Plibersek to join him. This was not a date, he emphasises. Coutts-Trotter was a friend, and Lee knew he and Plibersek were a couple. Lee was in the Right faction – closer to Coutts-Trotter than to Plibersek in his politics. But he thought Plibersek was 'not a typical left-winger. She was quick and smart and frank in discussing things, and a nice human being.' He knew that the seat of Sydney would inevitably go to the Left, and probably to a woman – and he thought Plibersek would be a good choice.

He had a tip that Baldwin was about to announce he would step down a few hours before it became public. His first thought was that he should ring Tanya. 'I just thought she'd be a brilliant Labor Party representative and the federal caucus needed as much talent as it could get. I had no idea if she would be interested in nominating.' Rather, the urgency in his call was that he thought it was important that she did not commit herself to supporting anyone else until she had had time to consider putting herself forward.

After taking Lee's call, Plibersek went straight to see Bruce Childs and asked what he thought. She recalls, 'He said, "It's going to be really hard. You are young, very young. It's a safe seat. Everyone's going to throw everything at you. But what have you got to lose? Why don't you just give it a go?" And I thought, that's kind of exactly the right attitude. I literally had nothing to lose, and the very worst outcome was that I wouldn't win but I would have an interesting experience.'

On the same day those conversations were happening, Anthony Albanese rang Meredith Burgmann. She says he told her the seat was hers if she wanted it, but 'you have to decide within twenty-four hours'. She was thrown into an agony of decision-making. She was the single mother of a young child. She rang friends who were federal MPs and worked out precisely how many nights she would have to spend in Canberra. In the end, she rang Albanese back and turned down the opportunity. Then she heard that Plibersek was nominating. She had great respect for Plibersek's abilities but thought she was too young for the job.

It was soon a crowded field. On 28 July, *The Daily Telegraph* reported that four women had nominated for the preselection, including Plibersek, who was the youngest. The other three were all women who had been prominent in the party for some time. There was a barrister and public defender, Chrissa Loukas; the mayor of Leichhardt, Kris Cruden, and consultant Diane Minnis. All four were from the Left faction. Plibersek was quoted as saying that her relative youth would work in her favour.[25] Most did not agree. The next day, *The Sydney Morning Herald*'s political correspondent, David Humphries, wrote that Plibersek was viewed as a talented future candidate 'but is considered too inexperienced for this contest'.[26]

Plibersek said in interviews for this book that she understood running for Sydney was an audacious move. Previously, she claims – and her friends confirm – she had no thoughts of a political career. But once she was considering the idea, she decided to reject the 'ingrained cultural teaching of women to put their ambition and interests second'.

Nominations continued to roll in. At one point, there were thirteen candidates. Most were women. It was a long and gruelling campaign, partly because the Right-dominated state party organisation, having accepted that the seat would go to the Left, largely surrendered responsibility for managing the contest. Rebecca Huntley remembers, 'Labor feminists used to joke that at state conference, all decisions could be made in the male toilets. So now they decided this was a woman's seat and all these women would be encouraged to fight against each other. It felt like political jelly wrestling. And it went on for a very, very long time.'

There were few ideological differences between the leading candidates. Rather, it was about personality and record. As the months wore on, some of the thirteen candidates peeled off or ran dead. The contest was now between Plibersek, Loukas and Cruden. On paper, Loukas and Cruden were more qualified, and had longer legacies in the party, than Plibersek. Loukas was thirty-six years old and had been a Labor Party member since 1982 – when Plibersek was still in the junior years of high school. She was a promising lawyer and sometimes an acting judge. Cruden was not only the mayor of Leichhardt, a committed long-term unionist and a former president of the Grayndler federal electorate council, but had been on Baldwin's staff, so knew the Sydney electorate intimately.

Cruden was interviewed for this book a few months before she died from cancer on 19 June 2022. She remembered the preselection battle as 'a nasty process because the men didn't care if we fought each other and chewed each other up in the process'. Aged forty-three at the time, she had left high school at fifteen and worked her whole life. She saw Tanya as 'a very different kind of Labor woman to me. She had a degree and she seemed essentially like a middle-class girl. And at the time I resented that.'

All of the candidates wore a path around the meetings of the twenty-one ALP branches in the electorate. Cruden recalled, 'It went on month after month after month. And after a while, we all said the same thing, because you'd listen to someone else's speech and you go, "Oh, that's a good idea. I'll shove that in." It was almost farcical, and the branches were getting sick of us ... By the third speaker, they were all playing games on their mobile phones.'

Nasty rumours circulated about the personal lives of all three of the leading candidates. In the middle of the campaign, the letter that the teenage Tanya had written resigning from the party was dug out of the files and circulated – evidence, it was suggested, that her commitment to Labor was shallow.

The contest famously split the Whitlam family, who were among the Sydney electors. Gough Whitlam backed Loukas and was making phone calls on her behalf right up until the vote. Margaret Whitlam backed Tanya. 'She thought she represented a new generation and a new face for Labor,' remembers the Whitlams' son-in-law, Kim Williams. Tanya's backers also included Childs, Tom Uren, Jeannette McHugh, Ann Symonds, Robert Tickner and Labor senator Kate Lundy.

Meanwhile, Anthony Albanese was friends with several of the candidates, particularly Cruden. He publicly insisted he would not involve himself in the contest and continues to maintain that he did not. Interviewed for his biography by journalist Karen Middleton, Albanese insisted that Tanya had been his contemporary, and that he was not her mentor. He told Middleton that he had not even made a phone call on her behalf during the preselection battle. But although he never formally endorsed her, people in the Labor Left at the time knew beyond a shadow of a doubt that Plibersek was his preferred candidate. Rebecca Huntley remembers, 'At social occasions you would hear people say that she was the candidate he was backing.' Plibersek was quoted in the Middleton book saying Albanese was 'just one of a number of backers. He supported me and there was probably about half a dozen votes from people that he was quite close to.'[27]

In 1997, Albanese and Plibersek were allies and friends, as close as they have ever been – 'in each other's pockets', remembers one Labor Left figure from the time. They were closer than either likes to acknowledge today, when relations between them are cool.

During research for this book, in late 2021 and early 2022, I was told Plibersek was 'in the naughty corner' with Albanese, now leader of the party, and his allies. He was 'looking over his shoulder' at her, it was said – and it is true that in 2021, when Albanese was well behind in the polls, said not to be able to 'cut through', some of her allies were urging her to consider challenging him for the leadership. In 2020 she edited a book, *Upturn*, a compilation of essays by policy thinkers about how to return to 'a better normal' after the Covid-19 pandemic.[28] This, I was told, was seen by the Albanese team as a provocative act.

In the 2022 election campaign, despite being shadow minister for education – an area full of opportunity for Labor after a decade of Coalition neglect – Plibersek was kept largely out of sight, until the media began to comment on her absence. And after the election victory, Albanese surprised her by taking the education and women's portfolios away from her and giving her environment and water instead. The media was full of discussion about whether she had been demoted or not. Environment and water are both important jobs, but the fact that it was a demotion in terms of cabinet ranking is indisputable.

In interviews for this book, I asked Tanya the same question that Middleton asked Albanese. Was he her mentor or her contemporary?

She responded that after their brief acquaintance when she was a teenager, she hadn't had a lot to do with Albanese until she was working for Childs. She is sure Childs would have asked Albanese's opinion before he hired her. After that, they had more to do with each other. They agreed on fundamental values, including feminism, the antinuclear movement and Aboriginal land rights.

So, mentor or contemporary?

'Well, he's not that much older than me. I would say more contemporary. But we have different ways of working. He has always been more interested in and better at the internal politics of the Labor Party. And I've always been more interested in a really broad range of different policy areas. But I don't think of either of those is an advantage or disadvantage ... I don't actually want to be thinking about internal ballots and that stuff, but someone has to.'

How would she describe the current relationship?

'I think we work well together.'

Was it true, as I had been told, that she was in the 'naughty corner'?

'Oh, who cares? I mean, this is schoolyard stuff. That I didn't get invited to someone's birthday party or whatever. Who cares. Really!'

This interview was done in November 2021 – before the election campaign, and before Albanese removed her from the education and women's portfolios.

When Plibersek was running for preselection, Albanese was a relatively new and junior member of parliament – having won the seat of Grayndler in 1996 after Jeannette McHugh's retirement. Plibersek was only an aspirant. Neither of them would have been thinking this way at the time, but the events of 1997 set them up in a way which, twenty-five years later, means that they are almost inevitably rivals.

They are both from the Left, and from the Hard Left, to the extent that that is still an important distinction. They represent neighbouring electorates in Sydney. The logic of factional representation, of the sharing of power, means they can't both be part of the leadership team. If Albanese is leader, Tanya cannot be deputy, and the reverse is also true. If one prospers, the other advances less. In the decades since 1997 they have travelled in the same orbit, each with their chance to be leader, each drawn at times closer to the centre. Back then they were allies and friends. Today they are alternates.

In interviews for this book, Plibersek was particularly testy around the notion that Albanese's support was the deciding factor in her preselection victory. She said it was part of a sexist trope, that women 'can't count, can't do the numbers' and could only succeed with the backing of a man. She says she won preselection on her own.

She is mostly right about that. The Sydney branches were notoriously independent. Albanese could not easily have swung them or instructed them in her favour, and he didn't try. Nevertheless, people who were there at the time say that if he had opposed her, she could not have succeeded. But the deciding factor was her own hard work.

As the race went on, Cruden was aware that Plibersek was outrunning her. Every time she spoke to a branch member, she would discover that Plibersek had been there before her. 'I had a job. I had a child. And no family support. I had so much on. I couldn't get around the electors on that individual basis as well as she did.'

Years later, in 2006, Plibersek's friend Verity Firth decided to run for preselection for the state state seat of Balmain, which overlaps the federal electorate of Sydney. She sought Plibersek's advice. Tanya dug out her files from her own preselection battle. 'It was amazing,' remembers Firth. 'There were lists with notes on everyone she had visited personally or talked to, recording their areas of interest. That is how she won it. She went door to door, person to person, and won the votes across by being so likeable and concerned and convincing. That meant that even when there were pockets of votes that were sewn up by power plays, they were ripped apart, because she had actually gone and talked with individuals at length about their concerns, and nobody else had done that.'

Pip McGuinness remembers times during the battle when Plibersek was not available for social catchups. 'Michael would say she was talking to some wharfie, or at an old person's home, or something. She was everywhere and all over that electorate.'

By October 1997, the contest had narrowed. It was between Plibersek and Loukas. But then Plibersek's world rocked on its axis.

*　*　*

The chocolate-brick house in Oyster Bay where Rose Plibersek lives hasn't changed much since the three children were raised there. When I visited, on a typical weekday morning, the phone rang several times as we talked. The calls were from neighbours wanting a chat or making sure that Rose was okay. One offered to bring her some freshly baked biscuits. 'That is what Oyster Bay is all about,' said Rose. 'It is like a village. Everyone knows everyone.' And in this suburban village, Rose Plibersek has long since become an elder.

But you can feel the sadness as soon as you step into the house.

Rose said that earlier that morning, she had been crying. The calls from her neighbours had cheered her a bit, but still – 'I wonder what I have done wrong in my life to be so punished.' She wishes, almost, that she had not had children. Ray, sitting near her, said, 'But then you wouldn't have me, or Tanya, and your grandchildren. You can't mean that.' She conceded he was right.

But then she talked about Phillip. 'It is a sad life for me. Because I lost my son. I can't get over it. I have a good cry, still, a lot.' And Joe, too, 'could not deal with it'.

In 1997, Phillip Plibersek was working as a senior geologist in Papua New Guinea for a mining company and living in a company-provided apartment in the central business district of Port Moresby. There was an office on the second floor, and the flat was on the fourth floor. In the early hours of Saturday, 4 October, he woke to find an intruder looming over the bed he was sharing with his wife. The man demanded his wallet.

Ray Plibersek says, 'I often wonder what would have happened if the wallet had been by his bed. Perhaps he would still be alive today.' But instead, the wallet was downstairs in the office. Phillip went to get it, followed by the intruder. There was a struggle. He was stabbed to death. Phillip's wife fled the flat, her arms covered in knife wounds. The man who killed Phillip, Haihavu Kore, was a known robber. He had a nick-name, 'Spiderman', because of the way he could climb into flats to steal.

It was early morning on Sunday, 5 October when Ray Plibersek took a call from the police. 'We are at your parents' place,' he was told. 'You need to come here.' When he got there, Joe and Rose 'were crying like I'd never heard them crying'. Tanya was attending an ALP conference that weekend. It was Coutts-Trotter who was dispatched to break the news to her. Straightaway, almost before they had time to absorb the news, Rose, Joe and Ray were on a plane to Port Moresby. They had to iden-tify the body, but they also wanted to try to understand, to make sense of what had happened. Ray remembers, 'My parents were shattered, and it was my job to try and keep them together, and I had my own grief to deal with as well. Mum and Dad were just crying constantly. My mother refused to eat anything. My father was trying to get her to eat. And then he would cry. And I was suddenly like a parent with two children to look after, and I can barely stand myself. And then you see the body and stuff, and it's just horrible. It's just like I can't describe it. It's just beyond awful.'

Tanya stayed in Sydney. She has told journalists since that she didn't think about dropping out of the preselection contest, then in its crucial

final weeks, because she was incapable of thinking about anything. She
was felled by grief. As she described it later, it seemed ridiculous to her
that people weren't talking about his death. 'I understand it's because
they didn't know what to say to me, but my whole world had been split
down the middle and it felt like I was walking around with my heart and
my guts trailing after me on the footpath. I couldn't believe that people
pretended not to notice that.' But she was not immobilised. There was a
candidates' forum in the preselection contest just three weeks after Phillip's death. She was there. She lost a lot of weight in those weeks, and
over the months ahead. But she kept going. 'People were very kind to
me, and I didn't see a point in not doing it,' she has recalled. 'It was just
a matter of whether I could, and I found that I could – so I did.' She told
some people that Phillip would have wanted her to continue.[29]

There are those in the Australian Labor Party who doubt Plibersek's
toughness, and even her commitment. For them, this is an answer. She
may not have thought of a political career just months before, but now
that she was in the contest, she was entirely committed and her stamina
was formidable.

When the preselection vote was held after almost six months of
campaigning, in December 1997, Plibersek beat eight other candidates,
winning 128 primary votes – almost twice as many as Loukas, who got
sixty-five. In the final ballot, after preferences were distributed, she beat
Loukas 197 to 143.

One newspaper commented that 'Ms Plibersek's youth, gender and
political experience help make her a valuable addition to Labor leader
Mr Kim Beazley's reorientation of Labor'. Inevitably, she was compared
to the Australian Democrats senator Natasha Stott Despoja, who was the
same age, had entered the parliament in 1995, and was constantly celebrated by the media as a spunky 'youth' representative. Plibersek told the
media that her priorities were 'attacking unemployment through industry
policy, aircraft noise and the squeeze on housing ahead of the Olym-
pics'.[30] She told *The Daily Telegraph* that she was interested in education
and employment, and that through her experience in the domestic violence field, she understood how government could make a difference in
people's lives.

The paper noted that Plibersek was also 'mindful' of the expectations of the preselectors, and of Baldwin's legacy. 'They want someone who will eventually become a minister as well,' she said.[31]

Today, Chrissa Loukas – now Loukas-Karlson – is a judge of the Australian Capital Territory Supreme Court. As is the convention with judges, she declined to comment on politics – even a political contest more than two decades old – when interviewed for this book. But she said Plibersek did her a favour by winning. At the time she had been asking herself how she could best contribute to a better world. The choice was between law and politics. After the preselection, she went to work in The Hague, met her husband and had a son, and 'none of that would have happened if I'd won the preselection. It was a real sliding doors moment for me. I call it a pyrrhic loss as opposed to a pyrrhic victory.'

Kris Cruden, meanwhile, went on to work for Albanese, becoming his chief of staff and running two of his election campaigns. She was Albanese's close friend. She watched him become prime minister in May 2022 from her hospital bed and died a few weeks later. She remained one of Plibersek's electors until her death. She told me she liked Tanya, but 'we are very different people'. Plibersek, she said, with her university education, 'probably represents the future of the party' more than 'hard-scrabble working-class people like me'.

*   *   *

After the contest was over, Plibersek travelled to Italy with Pip McGuinness and Adam Suckling. She was grieving Phillip and painfully thin. McGuinness recalls that they visited an enormous number of art galleries. It was the first time she realised how knowledgeable her friend was about art, and on this trip Plibersek used it as a solace. They talked about her grief. They agreed she would never get over it. But Tanya Plibersek carried on.

The man who murdered Phillip, Haihavu Kore, pleaded guilty to the murder, but the day before he was to be sentenced, in April 1999, he escaped from jail. It was a further agony for the family – for Rose and Joe in particular. The Department of Foreign Affairs and Trade made inquiries and were told he had returned to his home village, in the remote regions of the Gulf Province. The police apparently had no intention of trying to rearrest him.

Ray Plibersek wrote to Prime Minister John Howard. He asked him to raise the issue at a meeting with the PNG prime minister, Sir Mekere Morauta. Howard acted, and on 27 December 1999 a team of six police travelled by air, truck and boat, then walked four hours to the village to arrest Kore. Years later, he died in jail of AIDS. 'His death was obviously the worst thing that's happened to our family, and I still miss him every day', Tanya says now. 'There's seldom an hour that goes past when I don't think of him. It's not just about losing him, it's also losing the children he never had, and seeing the way it destroyed my parents. I don't often talk about it in public, because I think some things are private – and they are allowed to be private. Phillip was so much fun and so alive. I always think of that quote: "One crowded hour of glorious life is worth an age without a name." So the one comfort is that he lived more in his short time than most people do if they live to an old age. He really did suck the marrow out of life.' On the tenth anniversary of Phillip's death, in 2007, Tanya composed a blog to gather memories of her brother. There were submissions from his schoolmates and his colleagues. 'Phil was a million laughs, some of his jokes endure to today and I tell them to my kids,' said one. 'I will never forget his infectious personality and sense of adventure.'[32]

Phillip Plibersek was thirty-seven years old at the time of his death.

*   *   *

In 1998, Prime Minister Howard called an early election, with the proposed new goods and services tax the central issue. Plibersek's campaign was launched by ALP leader Kim Beazley in Sydney's Chinatown. There were some coy headlines when, as part of a campaign against the GST, she plastered flyers on the back of Campbell's soup cans. There was a snide column in *The Daily Telegraph* comparing Plibersek to the 'the Gen X appeal of the Democrats' Natasha Stott Despoja' and reporting that almost every lamp post in Sydney had a Tanya Plibersek poster 'slapped on it as if she is the ascendant star of a new Hollywood blockbuster, not the Labor Party. The outfits are very Country Road, the look very manicured.'[33]

On 3 October 1998, the Howard government was returned to power – but the result was so close that Labor was celebrating as much as grieving. The first-term Howard government suffered a nationwide swing of about 5 per cent, and the loss of nineteen seats. If the swing had been uniform, Beazley would have won. Nevertheless, it was the single biggest gain by an opposition party in the first election following a defeat. The result in Sydney was never in serious doubt. Plibersek won with a 4.6 per cent swing to Labor, in line with the national trend.

Plibersek was, in a literal sense, Baldwin's successor as the member for Sydney. One of the questions people asked about her then, and have asked ever since, is whether she is his successor in other ways. She is certainly not a wrecker, as Mark Latham became. But what kind of policy thinker is she? Does any part of Baldwin's intellectual legacy reside in her? Does she have the intellectual muscle, and will she have the chance, to help define the party's future?

Labor picked up eighteen seats, meaning Plibersek entered parliament as part of a big influx of new talent. There were nineteen new Labor MPs. They included Kevin Rudd, Julia Gillard and Nicola Roxon. Also re-entering the parliament was Wayne Swan, who had lost his seat in 1996, and Cheryl Kernot, previously the leader of the Australian Democrats, who had defected to Labor in 1997 and resigned her Senate seat. The previous election, in 1996, had seen Anthony Albanese elected. Mark Latham had joined the parliament in 1994. The next election, in 2001, saw a young lawyer from South Australia, Penny Wong, enter the Senate.

This was the generation that would take the party forward and characterise its fortunes in the new century. All of these people were spoken of over the next decade as potential leadership material. Four of them would be leaders, and three of them would become prime minister. Their struggles, achievements and failures would define the new century for the party.

It seemed, in 1998, that Labor could soon expect to be in power. Nobody had any idea how long, difficult and damaging the years ahead would be.

4

WE ARE LABOR

The arc of history is easier to perceive in retrospect. Looking back, Plibersek's time in parliament can be understood as a series of episodes when, if an alternative path had been taken, Labor's and Australia's history might have been very different. What if Labor had kept Kim Beazley as its leader, rather than switching to Mark Latham in 2004? What if, after the trauma of Latham losing the 2004 election, the party had again stuck with Beazley, instead of moving to Kevin Rudd? What if Julia Gillard had not deposed Rudd as prime minister in what he went on to describe as a coup? Perhaps the dysfunction in the government would in any case have led to its downfall – or perhaps the cabinet would have confronted Rudd with the consequences of his management style and the ship of government would have been brought back to an even keel. Perhaps, then, Labor would have won the election of 2010 in its own right, instead of being forced into minority government. Perhaps Labor would then have retained government at the 2013 election, instead of losing to the Coalition, led by Tony Abbott. There might have been no Abbott government, no Turnbull government, and no Prime Minister Scott Morrison. Australia would be a different nation. Within the ALP, leadership would have passed to the new generation in a more orderly, less damaging fashion. But that is not what happened. Instead, Labor's internal dysfunction blighted its six years in government between 2007 and 2013.

The sliding doors moments continue. What if, after the 2013 defeat, when Anthony Albanese and Bill Shorten contested the leadership, Albanese had won? It was a close-run thing. Plibersek played a role in that contest. It fractured her relationship with Albanese. And, more recently still, what if, after the 2019 election defeat, Plibersek had offered herself for the leadership and won it, instead of withdrawing before the ballot? What if she, not Albanese, had led the party to the 2022 election? Would she have presented the same small target? Would she have won? And what kind of prime minister would she have been?

But all that is the alternative history. Instead, we are left with the messy legacy of what actually happened and, in the case of Plibersek, opportunities taken, frustrated and forgone.

Tanya Plibersek gave her first speech in parliament on 11 November 1998, a few weeks before her twenty-ninth birthday and just over a month after being elected. Her parents were there – Joe in his first ever tailor-made suit, organised for him by his daughter for the occasion. Michael Coutts-Trotter flew to Canberra and was sitting beside them. He recalls that Joe and Rose, still grieving Phillip, were on this day 'just vibrating with pride at what their daughter had achieved'.

A new MP's first speech is traditionally a statement of core motivations and bedrock beliefs. Plibersek's contribution met that test – but was also a bit of a mess. In the years since then, she has developed a reputation as a great political communicator. Julia Gillard recalls that even in her earliest years as a parliamentarian, Plibersek was recognised as someone who could be sent out to deal with a difficult media interview. 'She was a great carrier of Labor's message.' But Plibersek's skills are most evident when she is speaking to camera or on radio, in a debate or in impromptu exchanges. Even today, when she gives a set-piece speech, she conspicuously reads from a script, her voice rarely departing from a monotone.

Plibersek credits her journalism degree with helping to form her communication skills. These days television interviews often involve speaking to a robot camera or a computer screen, with no human being in sight. She says she uses a technique taught to her by Wendy Bacon. She imagines there is someone she likes on the other side of the machine – someone intelligent but not necessarily across the issues and needing a clear explanation. 'Often, I imagine it's my mother,' she says. The result is a warm and engaging television presence and a clear, vigorous, yet reasonable-sounding presentation. Nobody in the parliamentary party does it better.

Her speeches, on the other hand, are typically workmanlike rather than inspirational. Here, too, she says she uses a journalistic technique. Reporters struggling to write the first, all-important sentence of an article will often imagine they are talking about the story to a friend. Plibersek says, 'I like to imagine that someone is walking out of the speech after I have given it and runs into a friend who asks them what the speech was about. I think of the first sentence they would say in response. Once I have that idea, that one sentence, then I construct an argument and find the examples and the illustrations. I come up with the concept and build around it.'

But for her first parliamentary speech, she had limited preparation time. Given the big intake of new parliamentarians, she had expected to have to wait her turn, and had done no preparation. In fact, she was one of the first of the newcomers to be scheduled and had only about twenty-four hours' notice. She shut herself away in her office, her head still swimming from the aftermath of the election campaign. She had trouble pulling her thoughts together. Today, she says of that landmark maiden speech, 'It is what it is, it was what it was.'

She rose to her feet in a plain grey suit, her hair at collar length – longer than it is now. She read from a script, only occasionally raising her gaze, and stumbling in places. In the video of the occasion, her fellow new parliamentarians, including Kevin Rudd and Julia Gillard, can be seen watching her attentively, but on the Labor front bench, the manager of opposition business and shadow treasurer, Bob McMullan, appears to have fallen asleep, and the shadow minister for finance, Lindsay Tanner, looks bored. Plibersek describes herself as a nerd, and it was mostly a nerdish speech – just over twenty minutes long and covering a big field of topics, laced with history and literary quotations. Despite a repeating refrain – 'we are Labor because ...' – it lacked a strong overarching idea or structure.[1]

After the conventional thanks to those who had supported her, including Jeanette McHugh, Bruce Childs and Robert Tickner, she began with a history of the activism that characterised her electorate, 'a place where ordinary people have acted collectively to combat injustice and to fight for their rights'.

She talked about the anti-eviction movement that saw the working class confront police in the 1930s, when the terrace houses of Surry Hills, Newtown, Glebe and Redfern were homes to large, working-class families, rather than the wealthy. She talked about the green bans, in which union activism saved the landmark suburbs and buildings of her electorate from demolition and rampant development. This was the tradition that gave birth to the Labor Party, she said. Then, leaping oceans and eras, she quoted Jimmy Carter talking about Leo Tolstoy's novel *War and Peace*:

> The course of human events, even the greatest historical events, is not determined by the leaders of a nation or a state, like presidents or governors or senators. They are controlled by the combined wisdom and courage and commitment and discernment and unselfishness and compassion and love and idealism of the common ordinary people.

She talked about her parents, the sacrifices they had made. Then it was back to world events:

> We are Labor because we have a positive vision for the future. A democratic South Africa, led by one of the twentieth century's greatest men, President Nelson Mandela, ten years ago would have seemed an impossible dream. That General Pinochet would one day be brought to justice for his role in the deaths and disappearances of thousands of Chileans whose only crime was to be democrats must too have seemed an impossible dream.
>
> The hopes that we have for the rest of the world – a referendum on independence in East Timor, the democratically elected government of Burma taking its rightful place with Daw Aung San Suu Kyi at its helm – seem distant and difficult today, but they are possible and we must continue to work as though they are possible. When we lose our dreams for the future, we are defeated.

Then, straining the convention that maiden speeches are not meant to be political attacks, she turned her attention to the Howard government, and what she described as its Thatcher- and Reagan-inspired 'state-led selfishness', typified, in her view, by the GST. She would, she said 'do everything in my power' to defend the people of her electorate 'against the viciousness of this government'.

The next few paragraphs awkwardly wrapped her determination to keep local post offices in her electorate from closing together with quotes from Edmund Burke about the duty of political representatives. Then, reflecting the optimism Labor felt even in defeat, she crowed about the election result, claiming it showed that the Australian people rejected the government's appeal to 'selfishness, racism and fear of change'.

She finished with an adapted quote from Bruce Springsteen's political folk-rock ballad 'The Ghost of Tom Joad', before concluding:

> We will stand beside the most vulnerable and protect them from these ravages – because we are Labor. When in government again, we will build an environment in which they can provide for themselves and their families with dignity – because we are Labor. We will create decent jobs with fair pay – because we are Labor. And if they need a helping hand, we will be there – because we are Labor.[2]

One of the notable things about Plibersek's first decade in parliament is that she did not progress as fast as her fellow newcomers. By the time Labor gained government in 2007, Rudd was the leader, Gillard his deputy. Nicola Roxon was minister for health and later attorney-general. All these people, and many of Plibersek's other contemporaries, were in cabinet, but she was not.

There are several explanations. She was very young – one of the youngest women ever to enter parliament. Despite her time working for Childs, she was less politically experienced than some of her peers and had not done as many hard yards in the party's internal politics as Gillard or Roxon. She had never navigated the factional alliances, corralling support and cutting deals. And it was a crowded field. The incoming talent from New South Wales meant there were many people jockeying for position. The NSW contingent included Albanese and Chris Bowen. There were more candidates for senior positions than there were positions to give.

Gillard says today that Plibersek was 'a much-admired figure' from early on, but that she did not 'get as much opportunity as others to show her policy development capacity'. Wayne Swan, who was made shadow minister for family and community services after the 1998 election, says that he marked her out early, even among the crowded field, as someone to watch. But those recollections have the flavour of retrospective reconstruction. In her first two years in parliament, Plibersek proceeded quietly and carefully. She says today she was overwhelmed just to be there, and – nerdishly – determined to learn the job of an MP and to do it well. She was less concerned with personal advancement.

Meredith Burgmann, watching her progress, approved of her approach. She had feared that Plibersek was too young. The media tended to focus on young women politicians because they were different – still exotic in a parliament dominated by grey-suited men. It was easy for people like Plibersek to get a sugar-hit of media attention, but that was a trap, and a treacherous foundation for a serious political career. Burgmann says today: 'She was very sensible. She did not feed into what could have been a media frenzy all about youth and attractiveness. She didn't really get much attention at all for a couple of years, and by the time she did start getting noticed, she knew what she was doing.'

There was, nevertheless, some early media attention, and it largely demonstrated exactly the kind of trap Burgmann identified. In February 1999, Plibersek was profiled in *The Sydney Morning Herald* by journalist Jenny Tabakoff as 'Sydney's new face in Canberra'. The article likened Plibersek to a high-school head girl and described her as 'cool, committed, left-wing, smart and (let's get it over with) seriously good-looking. "Competent and spunky," as one Canberra observer puts it.'

Interviewed for the article, Plibersek described her family background and talked in a 'trembling voice' about Phillip's murder. The feature quoted Albanese as Plibersek's 'friend and Labor Left colleague'. For the first but not the last time, he denied having any role in her preselection and said she was 'talented and with a big future in the party'. Plibersek herself described her first weeks in parliament as 'really challenging, hectic, exciting, a little scary'.

The feature picked up perceptions about Plibersek that follow her to this day – her opacity, the difficulty of getting behind the polished, head-girl presentation. Tabakoff wrote:

> And then we are in the inner sanctum of her private office which, like its owner, is cool and monochrome and not inclined to be revealing. Plibersek is wearing charcoal trousers with a subtle pin-stripe and a dark boat-neck top with the sleeves pushed up in a businesslike way. She talks in a low voice, smiles occasionally, and becomes agitated only when the photographer takes her to a picturesque house nearby to be snapped. 'But it's not in the electorate,' she says anxiously.[3]

Later in the year, *The Courier-Mail* reported that the new group of young female Labor MPs were 'often stopped by security guards, questioned by airline attendants and ignored by parliamentarians' but were nevertheless 'taking Canberra by storm'. Plibersek was interviewed alongside Senator Kate Lundy, Roxon, Anna Burke and Kirsten Livermore.[4]

Plibersek also featured in a book, *Party Girls*, about Labor women, published in 2000 with a foreword by the former Victorian premier Joan Kirner and co-edited by Kate Deverall and Rebecca Huntley, who had by now reversed her initial opinion of Plibersek and was becoming a friend. Contemporaries say that Kirner was not a Plibersek fan. On the other hand, Plibersek says she received regular messages of support from Kirner.

The purpose of *Party Girls*, the editors wrote, was to explore 'the parameters of the relationship between feminism and labour activism'. Plibersek was interviewed by the journalist Catharine Lumby. This was an opportunity to lay out her credentials and her ideas in a serious fashion to a sympathetic audience. Lumby described Tanya as '[p]oised, charismatic, articulate and warm ... such an impressive package she might have been invented by an advertising agency, hired to sell the Labor Party as the political face of the future'. Plibersek recounted her family history, her reasons for joining, leaving and rejoining the party. She asserted that the factional system benefited women because it gave a structured path to achieving power within the party. 'If all the decisions are being made when people are out drinking, slopping food on their ties in Chinese restaurants, there is no way into that. But if you know that you've got a system of proportional representation ... the situation is vastly improved for women.' The party was still 'blokey', she agreed. Women in politics had to be not only competent and intelligent but also 'a really nice person', whereas men got more leeway for bad behaviour. 'People think, sure he's gruff, sure he just yelled at me and threw an ashtray, but he's under a lot of pressure because he's a leader. And women, as well as doing the job, are expected to nurture the people they represent as well as their colleagues and staff.' In an extended piece of commentary on the interview, Lumby portrayed Plibersek as demonstrating the difficult terrain for female politicians and how they 'find themselves straddling the fault line' of contradictory expectations.[5]

In these early publicity pieces, there are consistent themes – Plibersek's youth, her polish and her charisma – but also questions about whether there was substance behind the presentation. Plibersek told these interviewers that she did not have an ambition mapped out – that she did not aspire to be a minister, for example.

This provoked one of the elders of Australian political feminism, Anne Summers, who had been head of the Office of the Status of Women in the Hawke government. In a book called *The End of Equality*, published in 2003, Summers singled Plibersek out as an exemplar in a chapter titled 'Political Eunuchs'. Plibersek and other progressive female politicians were not vocal or visible or even ambitious enough, said Summers. Plibersek, observed Summers, was one of the youngest members of parliament in one of the safest seats.

> This should be a prime jumping-off point for a stellar career in politics, but the MP told a newspaper interviewer in 2001 that she was not especially ambitious – 'I'm not desperate to be a minister'. Perhaps she was just being modest, which is not really a quality we value in politicians. If she is telling the truth, perhaps she should give up her seat to a more ambitious woman.[6]

Asked today how she explains her failure to progress at the same rate as her peers, Plibersek refuses to engage. Such thinking, she says, 'is so self-defeating. It is a recipe for profound unhappiness in our line of work. You can spend your whole life in the Labor Party and never make it into parliament, despite that being a professional objective. You can spend your whole life in the parliament and never make it onto the front bench or only make it onto the front bench in opposition.'

It is not, she says, that she lacks ambition, but rather that 'you have to be able to be happy where you are and do the best job in the role that you've got without feeling hard done by'. And she refers to 'cautionary tales ... of people who were never satisfied and consequently perpetually unhappy'. She says she had no strategy in those early years in parliament other than to 'learn everything there was to learn from any position I was given'.

She counts herself lucky that when committee positions were divided up among the newcomers, she was allocated the Public Accounts and Audit Committee, which conducts fine-grained examinations of the spending and operations of government, including following up the auditor-general's reports. It was dry material that rarely made headlines, but the experience added to what she had learned from the case studies in her master's degree. It taught her about what could go wrong in government administration. She learned, for example, 'that just because the department says it is going to implement a recommendation of an auditor-general's report doesn't mean it will be done properly or fully. So you always have to test and verify it.'

This set the pattern that she applied once she became a minister, and how she dealt with the public service. She adopted a systematic, careful method of administration. She would speak regularly to public servants, keep lists of the topics discussed and follow up later. 'I'd go back every few weeks and say, "What is the progress on this and show me what progress has been made" ... as a minister, you have to resist the temptation to micromanage the implementation of the things that you're doing, but you have to be confident that the implementation is correct. And the only way to do that is to keep going back to work out where the weaknesses are.'

A new backbencher doesn't get to speak much in parliament. In 1999, Plibersek's first full year, she made brief statements on East Timorese independence, government outsourcing and International Women's Day. The following year, she spoke on the GST and its impact on families, advocated for refugees from the Kosovo conflict to be allowed to apply for protection visas to stay in Australia, and talked about her pride in walking across the Sydney Harbour Bridge to say sorry to the Aboriginal stolen generations of children taken from their families. The Howard government had refused calls to make a formal national apology.

Outside the parliament, she was often called on to represent young, progressive women. At the Sydney Institute in 1999, she debated Liberal backbencher Alan Cadman about the release of the 1997 movie *Lolita*, starring Jeremy Irons and directed by Adrian Lyne. The film was controversial – it was not given a theatrical release in Australia until April 1999, and was then criticised for its soft treatment of paedophilia. Plibersek described it as 'one of the worst films I have ever seen in my life' and said she resented the time she had had to spend viewing it in preparation for the debate. More than this, she resented the fact they were discussing censorship and giving the film free publicity, rather than having 'a real debate about child protection'. They should be talking about teaching children protective behaviours and resourcing child-protection agencies, prosecuting offenders and punishing them.[7]

In the parliament, one of the most politically significant acts in her first eighteen months was to back Albanese in a personal campaign, long before the issue was fashionable, to get legal equality for same-sex couples. Marriage rights were not, at that time, on the agenda. Rather, Albanese wanted same-sex couples treated equally under other areas of federal law. In 1998 he introduced a private member's bill that would have given same-sex couples equal treatment under superannuation law. Many in the senior levels of the party thought his campaign unwise – likely to lose conservative blue-collar votes – but Plibersek was noted by the media as being one of his key supporters.[8]

Cheryl Kernot, recruited to Labor from the Australian Democrats, was having trouble finding her feet in this bigger, combative and often dysfunctional party. She remembers Plibersek offering, after a women's caucus, to explain the Labor Party factions: 'She said she thought it would be useful to give me a bit of a rundown.' Kernot had not understood, for example, that despite all being in the Left, the Fergusons on the one hand and Albanese and Plibersek on the other were opposed. Plibersek carefully explained the fractional battles to Kernot, 'without any emotion or bitterness or nastiness. I thought that was kind of her, because clearly she had noticed that I was saying things that showed I didn't understand. And it was helpful to me.'

Plibersek might have been feeling her way in parliament, but she absolutely threw herself into electorate work. Her enthusiasm and her willingness to get involved in the nitty-gritty of her electors' lives was almost a problem. It was, after all, a safe seat. To the extent there was a threat, it was from the Greens as well as the Liberals. Given the nature of left-wing politics, networks of friendship and enmity bound the two parties in the inner suburbs. Most left-wing Labor members had friends who voted Green, and every time Labor disappointed its left-wing supporters in the inner cities, the Greens gained.

Plibersek appointed Jill Lay, whom she had met through the Sydney–Grayndler women's network, to her electorate staff. Lay had briefly considered contesting the preselection for Sydney herself, but she had dismissed the idea as soon as it occurred – she was a mother of young children. Early in the preselection contest she had told Plibersek that she could rely on her vote, 'and you don't need to ask me again or worry I will switch. It's locked in.' She had decided that Plibersek was the right woman for the job – partly because while Chrissa Loukas was an impressive candidate, 'there are already too many lawyers in Canberra'.

There are, Lay says, layers to Plibersek. 'She is loyal, a nerd, a fighter and a family woman, and she has experienced tragedy and complexity in her life. There is the story of her brother, and Michael's background. So she lives with great complexity, and handles it well.'

Lay was to remain on Plibersek's staff for almost ten years, with most of that time as manager of the electorate office. It was a close partnership, and an example of a pattern that characterises Plibersek, one which is perhaps one of the most revealing parts of her record. She keeps her staff. People stay with her for years, only moving on for personal reasons or better jobs. Some of Plibersek's critics within the parliamentary party distrust her. Suspicious of her calmness and restraint, they some even use words such as 'a bit fake' and even 'passive-aggressive'. The near unanimous testimony of her staff is the best answer to those critics. Passive-aggressive bosses do not run efficient, harmonious offices. Fakes do not retain the loyalty and admiration of the people who have seen them in their worst moments and under pressure. Long before the culture of Parliament House became a media issue, with the 2021 Jenkins report finding that one in three parliamentary staff had been sexually harassed, Tanya Plibersek's office was known as 'functional', 'safe' and 'sane'.[9] There was no bullying, few raised voices and a clear management direction. Mary Wood, who joined Plibersek's staff after the 2004 election and stayed for seven years, including a period as chief of staff, says: 'She's funny, she's smart, she doesn't have tickets on herself, and she was very generous. It was a collaboration working for her, not a command-and-control thing as you get in some political offices, and that is why she has always had good staff.' Rebecca Huntley describes Tanya as having 'retained her humanity in Parliament House, that brutal, horrible, transactional place'.

Of the dozen or so present and former staff interviewed for this book, all testify that Plibersek is a good boss. She also mothers them. There are many stories of her cooking for her staff, bringing in cake, Slovenian snacks or 'really good bread and cheese'. She reminds her younger staff members to ring their parents, or encourages them to buy real estate.

Is she a rescuer? 'That's going a bit far,' says her current chief of staff, Dan Doran. 'It's never intrusive, it's kind.' Another former staffer says, 'There is a bit of that. It's lovely, to be honest. But I'm not sure how you would go with her if you didn't welcome that kind of focused attention.' Another former staffer, while agreeing that Plibersek was an 'excellent' boss, 'someone I admire immensely', also observed that there is a cult of Plibersek – a loyal and almost fawning cohort of 'groupies' within the party membership for whom she can do no wrong. 'I don't buy into that, and I think it is quite unhealthy and distasteful and even dangerous for her.' Others observe that Plibersek's supporters, and the woman herself, might therefore overestimate her popularity in caucus and her ability to swing votes outside of the inner city. On the other hand, her supporters say that her caucus colleagues fail to understand how much she is liked – how taxi drivers, workers, ordinary people across the nation respond to her whenever she appears in their electorates.

In the early days of serving the electorate, her staff had to remind Plibersek that she had people whose job it was to answer the phone or go to the front door and assist constituents on her behalf. She was eager to respond personally. The office was at that time in Crown Street, opposite the Salvation Army youth shelter Oasis. That meant they were often visited by very troubled, often homeless, drug-affected people. The office staff would describe these days euphemistically as 'having a stressful day'. Lay recalls that the federal police were surprised by how reluctant the office was to activate the security provided to all MPs. If there was trouble – someone shouting or distressed – 'we wouldn't immediately call the police or throw them out. We would try to work with them, and that was the culture set by Tanya.'

One Friday evening, Lay left the office at about 6 p.m. and walked down the road to catch a bus, when she was approached by a young man asking for money. She refused him. Then, from the bus stop, she saw Plibersek emerge from the office and get approached by the same youth. 'And even though she was heading home, I saw her take this man back to the office, and I knew there was nobody else there. I thought, "I'm not going to leave you alone"' and went back too. There she found that Plibersek had also refused to give the man money but had promised to find him a bed for the night and other support. She was hitting the phones of the shelters and welfare agencies, with the man sitting across from her and the office in darkness all around them. She found him a bed and drove him over.

Plibersek set a rule for the electorate staff. Nobody should be turned away, when their issue was not federal, until they had been given a name or a number of a relevant contact or some other means of support. Plibersek understood that sometimes a 'complex case' could slow down all the other work of the office, 'and she understood that and allowed for it and encouraged it', says Lay.

Given they represented neighbouring electorates, Albanese's and Plibersek's offices often worked in close cooperation. They also came together in the campaign to save the South Sydney Rabbitohs Rugby League Club when the NRL was determined to cut it from the competition. There were courtroom battles and public rallies, and Souths fought their way back amid a groundswell of public support. The Rabbitohs were the quintessential working-class team. For Albanese, this was a personal passion. He was on the board of the club and on the front line of the campaign. He told journalists he had 'come out of the womb supporting South Sydney'. For Plibersek, it was more about supporting her electorate. She was not into team sport. She told journalists she used to hide at school to avoid it. Her favoured exercise, she said, was 'going for a little run along the cliffs of Bondi',[10] but she was quick to fly the Rabbitohs' flag for her constituents. When, in parliament, Albanese moved a private member's motion of support for the Rabbitohs, Plibersek spoke in support.[11] She later said that 'the most fun work thing' she'd done in her first year as member for Sydney was to join the 50,000-strong rally to save the Rabbitohs. The team won readmission on appeal in 2001 and were brought back into the NRL competition for the 2002 season.

*　*　*

When Plibersek entered parliament, her relationship with Michael Coutts-Trotter was at a turning point. They had been together since that first date in 1991. In 1997, they had bought and moved into an apartment in a converted art deco warehouse in Forbes Street, Woolloomooloo. Together, they were an increasingly important part of Sydney's cultural, political and media networks. Around this time, they contemplated splitting. The crisis was not caused by Plibersek's entry to parliament. She had for years been travelling to Canberra with Bruce Childs during sitting weeks. As Coutts-Trotter puts it, 'patterns of presence and absence were already well established'. He had been prepared for that. He had not, though, been fully prepared for the enormous load of electorate work, which meant that even when she was at home she would be absorbed with the problems and demands of her electorate and would be out several nights a week and on weekends attending events. 'It was all a bit abstract in my mind, until we were in the thick of it,' he says. She had always worked hard. Now, it was all-consuming.

There were other issues as well, too private to merit a place in this book. The result of all this, says Coutts-Trotter, was that although they were still in love, although they still got on well, 'It was a little unclear where the relationship was heading ... we had a really fundamental fork-in-the-road moment of do we take the next step, which is really to cement a commitment to one another, or not, in which case we would probably have gone separate ways.'

They were still discussing the nature of their commitment when events overtook them. In mid-2000, Plibersek fell pregnant. This, as Coutts-Trotter puts it, 'nudged the decision in a direction we were probably going anyway'.

They decided to marry. Coutts-Trotter says, 'It wasn't that we thought having a child out of wedlock would be improper or anything of that nature, but rather, we thought we were suddenly very grown-up, and that we should do everything we could to ensure we stayed together, and making a public commitment was part of that.'

Plibersek's pregnancy became public before the wedding, on 1 November 2000, when, as *The Daily Telegraph*'s gossip column put it, 'after some eagle-eyed speculation from the press gallery', Plibersek confirmed that she was pregnant and planned to marry.[12] She was greatly irritated by the difference her swelling stomach made to her capacity to be taken seriously. She wrote a column for *The Sunday Telegraph* protesting:

> Suddenly, no-one wants to talk to me about economic policy anymore – just babies. (When is it due? Will it be a boy or a girl? Have you chosen names yet?)
>
> People are just being kind, but I'm bored out of my head by baby talk. Especially at work. It's hard to maintain a professional demeanour when colleagues are patting your belly like it's public property and asking how the 'little mother' is doing.

She went on to make a political point, referring to a recent Human Rights and Equal Opportunities Commission report on discrimination against pregnant women. She was better off than many expectant mothers, the report suggested. 'I haven't been sacked, I haven't been demoted and I haven't had my shifts cut. I'll have a couple of weeks' leave if I need it, I'll be able to work flexible hours, and I have a private place to breastfeed or express milk if I want to.'[13]

The couple were married at St Patrick's in Sutherland – the same church Tanya had attended as a child. The priest who married them had buried Phillip and would later baptise Plibersek's three children and bury her father. Her pregnancy was by then obvious to the congregation and the priest – who cracked a joke about it.

In the final days of the pregnancy, the baby was in breach position. Tanya tried everything to persuade it to turn. 'I did yoga. I tried acupuncture. I gave the foetus some stiff lectures,' she recalls. None of it worked. As a result, she gave birth to Anna Coutts-Trotter in February 2001 by caesarean section. That set the pattern for her future pregnancies. Each time she gave birth, it was major surgery. She always found it difficult to recover – not that anyone would have guessed.

She was back at work within two weeks of Anna's birth. Michael, on the other hand, made what he now describes as 'one of the best decisions I ever made' and took six months off to care for the baby, travelling back and forth to Canberra when parliament was sitting so that Tanya could breastfeed. When he returned to work, Rose and Joe Plibersek and Helen Coutts-Trotter, Michael's mother, stepped in to provide the childcare.

Canberra's Parliament House, completed in 1988, had a gym, a bar, a meditation and prayer room, but no childcare centre. Coutts-Trotter says that even with the family support, 'I don't know how she did it ... the expectation was that if you were an MP then you had a wife and they did all the stuff. And Tanya didn't really have a wife.'

Until now, Tanya had stayed in hotels when in Canberra, and sometimes in the hostel she had used when she was Bruce Childs' staffer – basic accommodation with shared bathrooms. Now that became too stressful. There was the strain of carting everything she needed for the baby back and forth to Sydney. Then, when her mother or Michael was travelling, they needed somewhere comfortable to stay.

Lastly, in hotels it could be difficult to get a cot. She remembers sleep-less nights worried that little Anna would suffocate because the only cot that could be found didn't meet Australian standards and was a 'death trap'. She bought a small apartment in Canberra, and it became the baby's second home.

Anna was breastfed for the first year of her life and travelled every-where with her mother. The Tasmanian MP Michelle O'Byrne was also a new mother; Victorian MP Anna Burke had given birth early in 1999 and brought her baby to Parliament House. The old, blokey institution was in the first stages of adjusting to the implications of young, child-bearing feminists among the MPs. These young women were pioneers. Plibersek's office became an exemplar of how it could be done. It was a pattern that persisted for her next two pregnancies and into her period as a minister. Some of her staff also had young children, and she encour-aged them to keep working, if they wanted to. There was a cot in her electorate office and another in her parliamentary office. The conference rooms were used for breastfeeding. Cheryl Kernot remembers going to Tanya's office to discuss something before the party caucus meeting and sitting with the new mother with a door ajar to a darkened room, where Anna was asleep. Jenny Macklin, who was shadow minister for health when Tanya entered parliament, recalls, 'I admired how easily she dealt with it, all without any fuss.' It was lovely, she said, to see the young mothers 'pushing their pushers around the corridors and just expecting to be taken seriously while they were doing it, and managing it all mag-nificently'. Another colleague remembers having a meeting with Tanya in what he describes as 'some sort of windowless box room' because one of the staff members had a sick child who had been brought to work, and Tanya's office, with its widescreen television, had been commandeered for the screening of *Play School*.

Jill Lay says that once the babies were weaned, Tanya and Michael shared parenting, which meant their offices had to work hard at coordi-nating diaries to make sure only one of them was away from home at any one time, if possible. Plibersek tried not to call on her staff for tasks like changing nappies, but as Lay remembers, 'I explained to her, it makes my life easier if you let me do it when you're busy, because it means you keep to your schedule … and people just had to adjust and be comfortable that the MP would have a baby with her.'

Among the earliest memories of Tanya's children are playing in the photocopying room, making pictures of their hands and then drawing faces on each fingertip with pens lent by the staff. Some of those staff became firm family friends and mentors to the children.

Today, Plibersek acknowledges that the juggle of raising young children in politics was tough – and that having children may have been one of the reasons for her relatively slow progression in the parliamentary party. But, she says: 'How lucky am I that I could have this fantastically interesting career and still have my three beautiful children? And hopefully, on my deathbed, they won't hate me, and they'll say it turned out okay.'

As for the decision that Anna 'nudged along', Plibersek and Coutts-Trotter have never again considered splitting. She told *Good Weekend* magazine in 2021, 'Our relationship hasn't always been perfect. There have been tough patches. I have been disappointed and angry at him at times. But I never thought he was at risk of relapsing into drug use. He didn't even take a Panadol for probably the first ten years I knew him.' She described him as 'an extraordinarily disciplined person. He's completely reliable, emotionally available and supportive to me and his children. He's said no to work promotions in the past because of the impact it would have on our family.'[14] In an interview for this book, she said: 'I've been happily married to Michael for twenty-two years, and I feel lucky every day.'

*   *   *

It was from about 2001 – after Anna's birth – that Plibersek began to get noticed in parliament. She was appointed deputy chair of the Public Accounts and Audit Committee, which meant she spoke in parliament – briefly but pointedly – on reports that looked into the government's record on outsourcing and contract management. The media began to talk of her, along with Albanese, as a leader of the Hard Left in caucus,[15] and as the 2001 election approached, she stepped up into that role. On 20 June 2001, in one of her longest parliamentary speeches to date, she spoke in support of equal treatment for same-sex couples, telling the story of one of her constituents who was in a same-sex partnership with a Canadian working in Sydney as a doctor. The Canadian was HIV-positive, which meant his application for permanent residency was likely to be denied, even though he had never had symptoms, and both he and his partner were on retroviral medications that had an established record of keeping people healthy.[16]

The next day, during appropriation bill debates, she talked about government funding for poor non-government schools, using an example from her electorate to criticise the government's new funding model, which was based on the socio-economic status of the postcode of the students' homes. 'If these students are housed, they are often housed in youth refuges – and the relevance that the postcode of the youth refuge has is obviously zero to the needs of these students.'[17] Shortly after, she was on her feet talking about the harm caused by smoking, using some of the figures from her honours thesis and criticising the government's spending of $115 million on an advertising campaign discouraging young people from taking illegal drugs. The campaign, she said, was being ridiculed by young people. She wanted more money for the services dealing with drug abuse, and she named examples from her electorate.[18] A few days later, she was speaking on domestic violence in Aboriginal communities, then again in August on school funding, specifically literacy.[19]

At the same time, she was becoming more outspoken in the party room – an antagonist to the Right, and sometimes to the line taken by the party leader, Kim Beazley. Cheryl Kernot remembers Plibersek, alongside West Australian MP and former premier Carmen Lawrence, as being the most vigorous promoters of debate in a forum that Kernot considered lamentably lacking in lively discussions. 'Caucus was tame,' Kernot recalls. 'Things were not discussed. There wasn't much debate.' Plibersek 'gave the impression, not of someone pushing her way in, but as someone with clear values and a knowledge of where she wanted to go and how to get there'.

The main issue on which Plibersek and Lawrence were outspoken was the treatment of asylum seekers, particularly those who arrived by boat. Beazley was not encouraging the debate. The voters who had drifted to the right-wing, anti-immigration One Nation party were being courted by both sides of politics, and Beazley was pursuing a narrow strategy to carry the ALP to victory – focusing on education, health and taxation. Beazley backed most of the Howard government's policies on asylum seekers, but for an attempt to remove the right of the courts to review immigration decisions. This, said Beazley, was a matter of democratic principle, and decent government.[20]

Having won the popular vote in 1998, Labor was now ahead in the opinion polls, due to dissatisfaction with the government's economic reform program and high petrol prices. Labor had won a series of state and territory elections and scored positive swings in two by-elections. There was every reason for optimism about the forthcoming election, and Plibersek and Lawrence judged there was room for a braver, more compassionate asylum-seeker policy.

On 23 August 2001, Plibersek spoke in parliament on the management of detention centres, and the violence and self-harm that was taking place within them. She argued for detainees to be allowed to live in the community as soon as possible after identity, character and health checks. The government, she said, was using the lives of desperate people in detention to score political points, trying to paint Labor as being soft on refugees. This was 'absolutely aimed at clawing back One Nation voters to the Liberal Party. The minister should be absolutely ashamed of himself for allowing that sort of demonising of refugees for crass political purposes.'[21] Beazley was later to recount that Labor's polling in marginal seats indicated that immigration and refugees would not be big election issues.[22] But just three days after Plibersek spoke on detention centres, everything changed.

On 26 August 2001, about 140 kilometres north of Christmas Island, a Norwegian freighter, the *Tampa*, intercepted an Indonesian fishing boat overloaded with 433 asylum seekers, mainly Hazara people from Afghanistan. Prime Minister Howard used the opportunity to push border security to the centre of the coming election. He refused the *Tampa* permission to land the refugees in Australia. Beazley told parliament that Labor supported the government's actions, but on 28 August, the second day of the *Tampa* crisis, Plibersek was among those reported to have argued in a 'feisty' caucus meeting for Labor to take a different

line. *The Sydney Morning Herald* said that Plibersek, along with Barney
Cooney and Michael Danby, had raised 'serious concerns' about the
ALP's support for Howard's approach.[23]

The next day, the *Tampa*, having made increasingly urgent calls for
medical assistance, entered Australian waters in defiance of government
orders and was boarded by the SAS in a theatre of robust action. The
standoff made headlines across the world. Talkback radio and newspaper
front pages were dominated by the issue – and still Labor supported the
government. Beazley rose in parliament to thank the Australian armed
services, and said that in these circumstances, 'this country and this parliament do not need a carping Opposition'.[24] But later that day, when he
saw the text of legislation Howard was presenting to deal with the crisis,
Beazley discovered a line he was not prepared to cross. If passed, the bill
would have given the government the power to remove any foreign ship
from Australian territorial waters, backdated to give retrospective authority for the boarding of the *Tampa*. The part that troubled Beazley was
that it ensured Australian courts could not review the actions of the Australian military. Without calling a caucus meeting, a decision was made
among the leadership group in Beazley's office that Labor could not support the bill. Howard had forced Labor into opposing the government
on border security. Beazley knew, agonisingly, that with this decision his
chances of an election win had probably vanished.

Under intense pressure, Labor supported other border-protection
legislation, and in the days that followed, the elements of asylum-seeker
policy that have been part of Australia's politics ever since were rapidly
cobbled together – the excision of islands from the Australian migration
zone, detention centres on Manus Island and Nauru, and the use of the
navy to turn back boats.

Plibersek, as a backbencher, had little say in any of this, but in
interviews for this book said she remembered 'most vividly' the caucus
meeting considering how Labor should vote on the excision of parts of
the maritime borders of Australia. She thought that Labor was wrong to
attempt to mitigate the damage by supporting the government. 'There
was nowhere we could go that would satisfy the Howard government
and have them say, "Oh, that's excellent. Labour's now being very, very

productive and cooperative and doing the right thing, and we can take this off the front page."' I always thought that however far we went, they would try and engineer a fight on ground where we couldn't follow them.' She argued in caucus that Labor was like the frog in the heating pot. 'The water gets hotter and hotter and you find yourself in a completely untenable position, that goes against your core values.'

Nevertheless, Labor went on to support the legislation. Party solidarity meant she had to fall into line – or resign. It was a hard lesson for this daughter of refugees on the costs of party solidarity. She recalls, 'I don't think I've ever found it so hard to walk into the chamber and vote for something in my life ... I found it an incredibly difficult time.'

Then, on 11 September 2001, came the attack on the twin towers in New York. Terrorism, racism and border security became conflated in the Australian public's mind – and the polls swung hard in Howard's favour. Parliament considered the twin towers attack on 17 September, and Plibersek was one of many who spoke. Only those who knew about Phillip would have recognised that she was drawing on her own experience: 'When someone is murdered, there is no way to prepare for it. There is no way of understanding it, there is no logic to the act, and it is not something that any human being or any family should have to deal with in a lifetime.'

But she argued for justice, and for compassion:

We must not compound the tragedy of this event by punishing the innocent. When we are talking about pursuing Osama bin Laden perhaps in Afghanistan, we have to remember that the civilians in Afghanistan have suffered perhaps more than any other people on earth. And they are suffering still: from famine, drought and the rule of the Taliban government ... When we seek to punish, we need to be accurate and to be sure of who we are seeking to punish.[25]

Howard called an election for 10 November. He campaigned with the slogan 'We will decide who comes to this country and the circumstances in which they come'. He won easily. The government's vote rose in all states and territories except Tasmania, winning five seats from Labor and one from the National Party.

Plibersek was never at risk of losing her safe seat of Sydney, but she paid a price. There was an 8.5 per cent swing against her in first-preference votes – not to the government, but to the Greens, the only party that had opposed all of the government's border security moves.

The *Tampa* election devastated the Labor Party and its progressive Left faction in particular. It is hard to overstate the trauma. 'It messed with our heads,' says one senior political adviser from the time. It was also destabilising – undermining the party's spirit, its self-belief, and its ability to commit to a leader and a set of policies that could win an election. The party was split internally, between those who couldn't stomach the acquiescence with the government and those who thought, as Mark Latham said at the time, that treatment of asylum seekers was an issue that appealed only to the latte-sippers of Labor's trendier electorates – meaning Plibersek in Sydney and Albanese in Grayndler – but was poison among 'real people', who rightly regarded asylum seekers as lawbreakers. In 2001, Latham and Albanese had a fierce row in a Canberra restaurant on the issue. Latham said that working-class Australians weren't interested in helping people who broke the law. Albanese told Latham not to be ridiculous: 'Working-class people break the law all the time. If you're poor, you have to do it to survive sometimes.'[26]

This was the wedge: Labor was impaled on a spike that drove through the alliance that Whitlam had built a generation before between progressive, university-educated, middle-class people and the traditional support base in the working class. On one side of the metaphorical wedge was Latham, from the aspirational western suburbs of Sydney. On the other was the Hard Left. The party was sandwiched, bleeding votes to the right and the left and internally riven.

Speak to people who were active in the Left of the party at that time and you get tales of tears, near mental breakdowns and sometimes actual mental breakdowns. In 1998, when Plibersek entered parliament, it seemed that Labor might still be seen as the natural party of government, as it was during the long Hawke–Keating years, and that Howard would serve at most two terms. Labor had underestimated him as a colourless, do-nothing prime minister. Now he seemed unbeatable.

Kim Beazley resigned after the 2001 defeat, and his deputy, Simon Crean, a former ACTU president and minister in the Hawke–Keating government, was elected unopposed to replace him, with Jenny Macklin as his deputy. Macklin had entered parliament in 1996 as the member for the Melbourne seat of Jagajaga. She had gone straight into the shadow cabinet, holding portfolios including aged care, social security and the status of women – and now health. She was the first woman to hold a senior leadership position in either major Australian party and was recognised as one of the best thinkers in parliament on social policy. She was to become Tanya Plibersek's mentor. Plibersek says that Jenny Macklin is the best friend she has made in politics. Meanwhile, Crean promoted Latham to the frontbench.

As the party struggled to come to terms with the pain of its defeat, Plibersek continued her activism. In the new year, on 31 January, she was at a demonstration where hundreds of people taped their mouths shut in support of asylum seekers at the immigration detention centre in the Rocks, in her electorate.[27] The following week, Carmen Lawrence spoke at a Perth rally and described Labor's new asylum-seeker policy as 'inhumane' and 'demeaning'. Plibersek was asked by journalists for her views. Compared to Lawrence, she was measured, saying there was a 'strong feeling within the rank-and-file membership of the ALP for a review of our policy in relation to these issues'.

A caucus meeting followed on 11 February with what the media reported as a 'passionate landmark debate'. Plibersek argued for Labor to stop its support for mandatory detention of refugees. She was unsuccessful. Crean told the media that caucus had agreed to review its policy before the election but remained committed to mandatory detention. Hours after the meeting, ten Labor MPs, including Plibersek and Albanese, were at a protest of 3000 people, where Carmen Lawrence told the crowd that the treatment of asylum seekers should be condemned.[28]

At the end of the year, Labor announced its new policy. The party now backed a softer mandatory-detention policy, with women and children to be released into the community after health and security checks, and the appointment of an inspector-general of detention to provide accountability and an independent adjudicator of complaints. But on the essential elements – Christmas Island being excluded from the migration zone, the underlying system of mandatory detention, the use of the navy to deter boats and the 'Pacific solution' of offshore detention of asylum seekers – there was now no difference between Labor and the government. Plibersek and Lawrence had been allies in arguing for a different policy, but now their paths diverged. Lawrence resigned from shadow cabinet, describing its approach as weak, conservative and a pale imitation of the government's.[29] She remained on the backbench until the 2007 federal election, when she did not recontest her seat.

Plibersek chose a different course. She told the media she had tried to persuade Lawrence to stay in the shadow cabinet and that she thought Lawrence had made a mistake by resigning. 'Maybe I'm more cynical than Carmen about politics generally, but I don't expect to get 100 per cent of what I wanted,' she said. 'I like Carmen as a person and for that reason I told her she had made the wrong decision for herself and for the party.' As for the policy that had caused Lawrence to resign, Plibersek was heroically upbeat. It was, she said, 'a vast improvement' and 'a million times better than what the Government's doing'.[30]

In interviews for this book, Plibersek recalled this as 'a depressing period. I think I would have been even more depressed if I'd known how long this was going to be a toxic element of our politics.' Nevertheless, she had made her accommodation with the Australian Labor Party – with the power structures necessary to have a chance of making a difference. She says, 'I never contemplated resigning. There are times when it is difficult to work slowly and methodically through the democratic processes of the party and of parliament. But that's kind of the job, really, isn't it?'

She points to the policy Labor took to the National Conference before the 2016 election, when she was deputy leader of the party. It allowed for a doubling of the refugee intake and a significant increase in the aid budget. 'I think that was a humane, defensible policy ... I don't think it's immodest to say that it was me who was negotiating between the factions and with the various shadow ministers to get to that outcome. And I think that that's what you get if you persist. It's about having some staying power.'

*   *   *

At the same time as they were allied on asylum-seeker policy, Plibersek and Lawrence were also advocating for Labor to oppose any unilateral action in Iraq by the USA and any Australian involvement in an invasion. Lawrence said she might cross the floor if Labor supported the war. Plibersek said she would not support unilateral action unless there was 'clear evidence Iraq had a nuclear weapon loaded and pointed at Tel Aviv ... I would not support a US first strike and I would think twice about even United Nations action.'[31]

When US president George W. Bush argued to the United Nations that Iraq's possession of weapons of mass destruction – chemical and nuclear armaments – made military action inevitable, Plibersek responded in parliament that Iraq was a repressive regime, and she accepted that it was 'probably' developing weapons of mass destruction. The words she said next have haunted her ever since.

She talked about the inevitable humanitarian cost of the war. This was the main reason for opposing armed conflict, she said. But as well:

> I believe that, in this matter as in most others, the US response is governed by self-interest and not by universal principles ... I can think of a rogue state which consistently ignores UN resolutions, whose ruler is a war criminal responsible for the massacres of civilians in refugee camps outside its borders. The US supports and funds this country. This year it gave it a blank cheque to continue its repression of its enemies. It uses US military hardware to bulldoze homes and kill civilians. It is called Israel, and the war criminal is Ariel Sharon.

The reaction was instant. For decades, the so-called 'Israel lobby' – Zionist Jews prominent in law and business – had had an outsized influence on Australian politics and pushed back hard against any criticism of Israel and its foreign policy. Bob Hawke had been a strong supporter of Israel. So were Beazley and Crean. But now this rising member of the parliamentary party was taking a different stance. Her speech made headlines. Even now, more than twenty years later, it is rare to see mention of Plibersek in the Jewish press without some reference to her 2002 speech.

A former Whitlam minister, Barry Cohen, wrote a letter to the Labor leadership, which Crean leaked to the press, in which he said that no Jew with feelings for Israel would support the ALP, and cited Plibersek as the chief culprit. 'For Israel's sins to be attacked without placing it in the context of a 60-year campaign to destroy the state is dishonest and vicious in the extreme,' he wrote.

A year later, Plibersek addressed a group of Jewish students visiting Canberra and was forced to defend herself. She assured them that she did not oppose the existence of Israel. 'What I've opposed is aggressive expansionism, and I think I have every right to say I oppose that,' she said. Had the party leadership told her off for her remarks, she was asked. 'No one told me that I wasn't allowed to say what I believed, but I wouldn't say that I got patted on the back, either.'[32]

But under continuous pressure from the Jewish community, by November 2003, Plibersek was saying she regretted describing Israel as a 'rogue state'. She opposed suicide bombings, she said, and was not an antisemite. She first formally apologised for the comments when she was a minister, in 2011, saying she had spoken injudiciously and that she supported a two-state solution. But her comments were not forgotten. When in 2013 she became deputy leader of the ALP and shadow minister for foreign affairs, the director of the Executive Council of Australian Jewry observed archly that it was 'satisfied' with her elevation because she now held 'much more balanced and better informed' views than she had in 2002.[33] And when, in 2014, Ariel Sharon died, Plibersek recalled him as 'a giant in the history of Israel'[34] – an inarguable assessment. But close listeners would have detected that it was not strictly in contradiction to her earlier statements.

The most cursory glance at Sharon's history lends plenty of support for Plibersek's characterisation of him as a war criminal – yet she has backtracked on describing him that way for twenty years. Interviewed for this book, she restated her regrets:

I think it was intemperate language and it was an irresponsible thing to say for a range of reasons, but most particularly because it allowed people to draw conclusions about my worldview that were not accurate. A bunch of people decided that I was antisemitic and hostile to the State of Israel because of that, and that's actually never been my position.

She should instead have focused on the 'many reasonable arguments' for Australia not getting involved in the war in Iraq, she says. 'Israel was not the problem, it was actually us getting involved in a war that was going to destabilise the region, make it less secure, increase the threat of terrorism, increase the risk to Iraqi civilians, all of these things have come to pass.'

* * *

In early 2003, as war brewed, Labor's position was to oppose any armed conflict that did not have the sanction of the United Nations. Then, in January 2003, Simon Crean declared that Labor might support a war without UN sanction, if the majority of Security Council members voted to invade. It was a confused position. As Latham remarked in his diary at the time, 'try selling that jumble of words in Western Sydney'. It was, said Latham, a 'microcosm of all our woes: personal and factional treachery. Policy confusion and plenty of bullshit. We're a party incapable of governing ourselves let alone the country.'[35]

Plibersek, meanwhile, stated she would oppose war on any terms.

The war in Iraq began in March 2003. Later that year, in October, Bush was visiting Australia and due to address the Australian parliament. Crean ordered Labor MPs to show the American president due respect and to stand at the end of his speech. Plibersek indicated she would defy him. 'I'm going to be polite, but I don't think I can bring myself to participate in a standing ovation,' she said at the time. 'That would be hypocritical after my deep opposition to the war.'[36]

As it turned out, she did stand – but she also handed a dossier of ALP members' speeches against the war, together with a letter signed by forty-one MPs, to the US secretary of state, Condoleezza Rice. Plibersek had meant to give the material to Bush, but seeing the level of security around him concluded she risked being tackled to the ground, or worse.

Once again, she had made an accommodation.

*　　*　　*

There is an odd belief about Tanya Plibersek. People think that, in the Labor Party's leadership travails, she has always been loyal to the leader. Even those closest to her will tell you this. But it isn't true.

The first time Plibersek had to decide how to vote in a leadership challenge was in June 2003. The public opinion polls were dismal for Labor. Crean, as Latham had observed, was failing to deliver a clear, compelling message. Howard was well ahead in the polls as preferred prime minister, with Crean trending down. In April, Kim Beazley did an interview with *The Bulletin* and talked broadly about Australian politics and the changes he would like to see. The magazine promoted it on the cover with the headline 'If I were Prime Minister ...' Beazley said he had not meant this as an attack on Crean, but most people saw it differently.[37]

Crean had made enemies by undertaking internal reforms, such as reducing trade union representation at the Labor National Conference. He had also promoted some of the talented young MPs who had entered parliament at the same time as Plibersek, including Kevin Rudd, Julia Gillard and Nicola Roxon. Plibersek, however, had so far been overlooked – and she had some particular reasons not to favour Crean.

One of the key issues in the inner-suburban electorates of Sydney was the ear-splitting noise from the city's only airport, situated on the edge of Botany Bay. On one side was Albanese's electorate of Grayndler; on the other was Plibersek's seat of Sydney. A new single-issue party, No Aircraft Noise, had been formed and undercut Labor's hold on inner Sydney in the 1995 local government elections. In the state election that year it scored almost a quarter of the vote in some electorates. And when the No Aircraft Noise party ceased to exist, many of its members joined the Greens. By the time Plibersek was contesting the 1998 election, some of the heat had gone out of the issue, thanks to a curfew limiting late-night flights, but the search for long-term solutions was still a frontline issue. In 1986, Hawke had announced that a new airport would be built at Badgerys Creek in Sydney's west, but there was fierce local opposition.

In mid-2003, without consulting Plibersek, Albanese or any other inner-Sydney MP, Crean unilaterally changed the party's approach. Labor would no longer support a new airport at Badgerys Creek, Crean said. He had decided to back the outer western suburbs MPs, including Soft Left leader Laurie Ferguson, over the Hard Left of the inner city.

There was a revolt. Albanese and Leo McLeay, the member for Watson in Sydney's inner south, were the leading voices, but Plibersek was also vocal. She told the media she was 'bitterly disappointed and extremely angry' at the surprise announcement, which was 'a betrayal of my constituents'.[38]

Crean made some attempts to tamp down the controversy, and Plibersek agreed to work within caucus to find an alternative site for a new airport. Meanwhile, Albanese was now allied with his colleagues from the Right – including Wayne Swan and Stephen Smith – in generating support for Kim Beazley to return as leader. Albanese was later to say that he was already a Beazley supporter, but that Crean's handling of the Badgerys Creek issue removed any guilt he might have felt about being disloyal to the leader.[39]

After weeks of destabilisation, on 8 June, Crean announced a leadership ballot for the following week. Beazley said he had only 'one shot in the locker' and gave Crean an undertaking that if he did not win, he would not try again. Beazley said he knew some caucus members expected a series of challenges. 'Forget it,' he said. 'We've got to unite behind this result.'[40]

The media began obsessively counting the numbers and compiling lists of who would vote for each candidate. Plibersek was sometimes said to be supporting Beazley but was more often said to be undecided. She says today that she was in an 'agony of indecision'. She was still a backbencher, not in a position to swing other people's votes or to have much influence on the result. Both Crean and Beazley were well to the right of her own position, but she liked both men. 'I was just a junior nobody in those days, so I was making a decision between two people that I broadly liked and respected.'

She claims – perhaps with the benefit of hindsight – that she fore-saw the damaging effects of leadership contests. 'I thought that knocking off leaders was a bad thing to do, and it would be the beginning of a period of instability.' But on the other hand, she believed that Beazley had a better chance of winning an election. She was torn between loyalty to the leader and the desire to win the next election. 'It was a question about morality versus pragmatism, in a sense,' she recalls. She lost a lot of sleep.

Just four days before the vote, Plibersek's old sparring partner from UTS, Steve Lewis – now a journalist for *The Australian* – reported that Crean was headed for almost certain victory and was under growing pressure to act against Smith and Swan for disloyalty. Albanese had made his backing for Beazley public and was urging others to follow his lead. Mark Latham, on the other hand, was backing Crean and condemning the 'shameful destablisation campaign' being run by the Beazley camp. Lewis had compiled another list of who was supporting whom; he had Plibersek in the 'undecided' camp but likely to vote for Beazley.[41]

When the vote was held, Plibersek did indeed vote for Beazley. She had chosen his perceived electability over loyalty to the incumbent leader. She was on the losing side. Crean beat Beazley by fifty-eight votes to thirty-four. Predictably, Beazley found that perhaps he had more than one shot in the locker after all. The manoeuvring and undermining con-tinued. John Faulkner, leader of the opposition in the Senate, reportedly told Beazley he could have a clear run at the leadership if he would only retain Latham as shadow treasurer. Beazley refused. Latham was a divi-sive figure. Beazley's supporters, including Albanese, had no time for him. Then, in November 2003, when it was clear he would lose another vote, Crean resigned. Not wanting to hand his position to the people who had undermined him, he threw his support behind Mark Latham.

Not a single journalist tipped Latham to win the resulting ballot, but he defeated Beazley with forty-seven votes to forty-five, largely because of a determination among many MPs that disloyalty to the leader should not be rewarded.

Once again, Plibersek was on the losing side. She voted for Beazley. This time, there had been no agonising. The decision was 'easy'. She had drawn firm and unfavourable conclusions about Latham's character long before. Shortly after she entered parliament, they had both attended a National Press Club event at which Plibersek had spoken. At the time, Latham had a column in *The Daily Telegraph*; he attended the event not as a Labor MP but as a journalist and proceeded to prod and provoke her with a series of 'really hostile questions'. She remembers one as: "'The left wing of the Labor Party say they're pro-choice when it comes to abortion, but you are anti the free market and choice when it comes to business." Some ridiculous question like that. It didn't bother me, but it was designed to bother me.' Later, when Latham drew headlines by referring to News Corporation columnist Janet Albrechtsen as a 'skanky ho', Plibersek had criticised him in public.

Latham, Plibersek acknowledges, was an ideas man. She doesn't make the comparison, but in some ways he filled the shoes of her predecessor as MP for Sydney, the prickly and innovative Peter Baldwin. She says, 'I can understand why people who I really like and respect backed Latham and thought he would be a breath of fresh air, and in lots of ways he was that.' But she draws an analogy to describe his failures of character. 'I say to the teenagers in my household, you have just taken it that one step too far. I could cope with all this behaviour, but you put me over the edge now. He was like that. He took it one step too far.' By the time of the 2003 leadership contest, Latham had, in Plibersek's view, 'demonstrated in so many ways he was unfit for leadership'. Beazley, on the other hand, she had come to like and respect, despite their differences. Today, she describes herself as 'very fond' of Beazley and his wife, Susie. They are close friends.

Yet Plibersek feels almost guilty for criticising Latham, despite his later trajectory and his position today – as an upper-house member of the NSW Parliament, representing One Nation.

The truth is, he was good for her. Beazley, and more particularly Crean, had failed to promote Plibersek, passing her over while advancing her contemporaries. Latham, on the other hand, put her in charge of establishing a 'fringe' event at the Labor Party's National Conference. The idea was a forum in which a broader range of policy ideas could be debated, typically including environmental and social-justice issues.

Another aim was to engage with activist groups beyond the ALP. The job drew on Plibersek's natural strengths and her history in social activism outside the party. It also appealed to Latham, with his hunger for new ideas outside the straightjacket of party orthodoxy. In those early months of his leadership, Plibersek even wondered if she had been wrong to oppose him. He seemed to cut through – to have Howard's measure and to have him on the run at last. But Howard was not so easy to beat.

In May 2004, the Howard government introduced a bill to change the *Marriage Act*. The amendment would insert words mandating that marriage be recognised exclusively as a union between 'a man and a woman'. It was a classic wedge for Labor. For some, such as Senator Penny Wong, who was openly gay and in a same-sex relationship, it went to the core of identity. It was also central for Albanese and Plibersek, given they had campaigned for years for the rights of same-sex couples. Latham wanted to avoid the wedge. Without proper caucus consultation, his shadow attorney-general, Nicola Roxon, announced that the party would support the government's amendments.

Plibersek was at her most outspoken in response. She told the *Sydney Star Observer*, 'I think it's terrible ... I've told Nicola in the strongest terms that I feel betrayed by what she said yesterday, and I take very seriously the fact she's not followed proper caucus procedure.'[42]

At a subsequent caucus meeting, Plibersek, Albanese and Wong all argued strongly against supporting the changes. Lawrence argued unsuccessfully for a conscience vote. But Latham and Roxon had effectively decided the matter. Labor would commit to removing all other forms of discrimination against same-sex couples in Commonwealth legislation, should it form government. But it would avoid the wedge and vote in favour of the *Marriage Act* changes.

When the legislation came before parliament, Plibersek spoke about love:

> Surely, with so much hatred, war and division in the world, we would strengthen our community by celebrating love, devotion, kindness and constancy, not by seeking to proscribe it. Which one of us in this place is so morally superior that we have the right to

judge other humans and their love for one another as inferior, second rate or second best? ... As a society we are stronger when we
look for ways to celebrate and increase the sum total of love: not
wall it in, deny it or ignore it because it does not read like a Mills
and Boon novel.[43]

Howard's changes were unnecessary and discriminatory, she said:

> Some time in the not-too-distant future, people will look back on
> this desperate attempt at wedge politics and treat it with the con-
> tempt it deserves. Some time in the not-too-distant future, there
> will be formal recognition of same-sex couples, and the sky will not
> fall in, and we will not be destroyed like Sodom and Gomorrah,
> and life will continue.

It could only be understood as a speech opposing the bill. The amendments to the Marriage Act passed the lower house on 24 June, 2004. No
division was called, meaning parliamentarians didn't have to declare how
they voted. Plibersek says this was a relief: 'I didn't have to vote on it.'

It was yet another painful accommodation.

*   *   *

As the election neared, Latham's initial electoral appeal began to wear
thin. Howard cleverly framed the election campaign around the issue of
trust – highlighting concerns about Latham's character.

On election night, 9 October 2004, the government won easily.
In Plibersek's electorate of Sydney, the first preference vote held steady
on the 2001 figures, but the Greens had another 7 per cent swing in
their favour, closing the gap on the Liberal Party as second place–getter.
Nationwide, the election saw the second consecutive decline in support for the ALP and a further increase in the Coalition's majority. The
ALP's primary vote was at its lowest level in eighty years. The party was
in despair.

In the following days, Latham at first decided to hold on to the leadership. Meanwhile, he spent what he described in his diary as a 'terrible

weekend', trying to decide the allocation of shadow portfolios and 'massage the tender egos and neuroses of 30 Labor frontbenchers'.[44] By now, Plibersek's contemporaries – those who had entered parliament at the same time as her – were being spoken of as potential leaders, particularly Rudd and Gillard. Nicola Roxon was shadow attorney-general. Kevin Rudd was shadow minister for foreign affairs. Gillard was shadow minister for health. Plibersek was still a backbencher.

Turning to his plan for an inner shadow cabinet of about seventeen, Latham reflected that his '[f]irst priority is to promote progressive young women such as Penny Wong and Tanya Plibersek. All the talented Labor women are in the Left, an area where we have a clear advantage over the Coalition. I've given Plibersek the new portfolio of work, family and community.'[45] The man she disliked and regarded as not fit for the leadership, the man she had voted against, had given her her first big break.

A few weeks later, Latham realised his leadership was likely to be challenged. He recorded in his diary that he had told Gillard she should be his successor, and that she 'had better keep buttering up the swinging Caucus voters' in case there was a move against him. Plibersek was on the list of those to be buttered up.[46] He disappeared over summer, uncontactable even by his allies, then suddenly showed up in a Sydney suburban park and resigned from the leadership and from parliament. Kim Beazley was elected unopposed after Rudd and Gillard both withdrew from the contest at the last minute. Neither had the necessary caucus support to seize the leadership.

Plibersek was not in the party room to watch Kim Beazley being elected unopposed on 28 January 2005. She had been pregnant when Latham gave her her first shadow portfolio, and three days before the leadership ballot she gave birth to her second child, Joseph Coutts-Trotter, a brother for Anna, who was now four years old.

Four days after the birth, Kim Beazley visited her at the Royal Women's Hospital in Randwick. She asked him when she should get back to work. He responded, 'Take as long as you need. We've got three years.'

But she was back at her desk within days.

*   *   *

Later in 2005, Mark Latham published his diaries. They were a bitter and vituperative account of his time in parliament. He paid out on many of his colleagues and broke numerous confidences. It was horrible for the party. Quite apart from the bruising defeat, Labor was faced with the shame of having urged the Australian people to regard this bitter, treacherous and unstable man as an alternative prime minister.

Plibersek escaped lightly. Apart from the reference to her as one of the talented left-wing women in the party, the only other mention Latham gave her was at the back, where he detailed the membership of Labor factions. Correctly, he placed Plibersek in the Hard Left – also now known, Latham wrote, as 'The Albanese Left'.

Despite the vitriol, many of Latham's observations about the state of the party were accurate, and even prescient. In his foreword, he wrote of a 'poisonous and opportunistic Labor culture in which the politics of personal destruction is commonplace ... What the powerbrokers cannot control they will destroy.'

When the diaries were released, Plibersek said that 'they tell us more about Mark than about the party. A lot of the bitterness and division that was there while Mark was leader has been resolved.'[47] It was a remark either ridiculously optimistic or disingenuous. Beazley was a twice-defeated leader, Crean's supporters had not forgiven him, and Rudd and Gillard were both ambitious.

5

LEADERS AND TEAMS

Mark Latham's diary did not fully explain the responsibilities he gave Tanya Plibersek after the election defeat in 2004. He said he had put her in charge of a new portfolio called work, family and community. In fact, he gave her the shadow portfolios for youth, work and family, community and early childhood education. She also had the quaintly worded title of shadow minister assisting the leader of the opposition on the status of women – ironic, given Latham's later reputation for misogyny. There is a story among Plibersek's former staff that she had asked Latham to make her shadow minister for the status of women. He is said to have responded that somebody with her abilities and ambition should ask for something with more 'grunt'. He meant, presumably, an economic portfolio. This attitude reveals something about him, but it was also in line with the views of most political hardheads.

Plibersek's responsibilities for work overlapped with another woman promoted to the front bench by Latham – Penny Wong. She was now shadow minister for corporate governance and responsibility, and for employment and workforce participation. Work was at the centre of national debate. With control of the Senate after the election, Howard was pushing through radical changes to industrial relations and welfare. The government's welfare-to-work program, introduced in 2006, broadened the categories of people for whom welfare payments were conditional on mutual obligation: jobseekers were expected to work for the dole, do voluntary work, or undertake training or education. The government's WorkChoices legislation, passed in 2005, removed unfair dismissal laws for companies below a certain size, curtailed the right to strike and privileged individual workplace agreements over union-led collective bargaining. It was Wong, rather than Plibersek, who did the heavy lifting on these areas of policy development – accepting the core idea of mutual obligation but focusing on the weak point of Howard's agenda: the lack of opportunities and the need to invest in the skills of the workforce in general, and of the jobless in particular.[1]

Plibersek took a different route. As she had for all her adult life, she focused on women and their children. On both sides of politics, the women's portfolio was generally given to a junior politician, or else to a very senior minister – even the leader – as an add-on to a raft of other weighty responsibilities. It was rarely placed at the centre of a government's work, nor at the centre of an opposition's grasp for power.

Perhaps one of the measures of Plibersek's success as a politician is that this is no longer the case. In successive elections since her time in the relevant portfolios, first in opposition and then in government, the women's portfolio and issues such as childcare have been central to the political debate. There are many reasons for this, and many women whose work is part of the change, but Plibersek's activism is part of the story.

In these early days on the opposition front bench, she was not working alone. Despite her new raft of responsibilities, Plibersek was still a junior shadow minister, and not in shadow cabinet. In most of her portfolios she was answering to the deputy leader, Jenny Macklin, who was the first woman to achieve a federal leadership position in either of the main political parties. Macklin had been deputy to three ALP leaders: Crean, Latham and now Beazley. As the shadow minister for education, and then for families and community services, she represented Tanya's areas of portfolio responsibility in the shadow cabinet.

Plibersek retained all her portfolio responsibilities when, in January 2005, Kim Beazley succeeded Mark Latham. Then, in a midyear reshuffle, Beazley made some small changes. Plibersek became shadow minister for the status of women in her own right, retained the childcare and youth portfolios, and lost work and family – which were picked up by Penny Wong.

Macklin and Plibersek made a great team. Macklin was greatly respected for her work on social policy and recognised as one of the party's best policy thinkers. 'One of Australia's greatest champions for the marginalised and disadvantaged,' Penny Wong wrote in a tribute when Macklin retired in 2018.[2] Bill Shorten said: 'Every political party in Australia wishes they had a Jenny Macklin, but only Labor has been blessed with her extraordinary mind, her caring heart and her fearless love of the good fight.'[3]

One indication of how toxic Labor Party politics had become, and how much the fear of yet another defeat drove the party, is that the almost universal respect for Macklin's abilities and character were not enough to protect her as part of the Beazley leadership team. The critics did not rate her retail political skills, her appeal to voters or her ability to sell Labor's policies. There was, inevitably, an element of sexism to this assessment – a reflection of the way middle-aged women are too often rendered invisible or are seen as inherently unappealing. As they worked together, it was Plibersek who became increasingly important in the work of communicating the policy agenda – both to the public and internally within the party. Macklin was the main policy thinker, Plibersek the personable and convincing persuader.

The two women had been on friendly terms before Plibersek was given her new portfolios, getting to know each other through the caucus committees on women and social policy. Now they drew closer. They met at least weekly and, Macklin recalls, anything she gave Plibersek to do would be done well. Meanwhile, Tanya describes Macklin as one of the closest friends she has made in politics – along with Wayne Swan, who as shadow treasurer had to be persuaded about any proposals for new spending.

Macklin and Plibersek together achieved a paradigm shift in the political conversation about childcare and parenthood. It was an enormously significant achievement – perceivable, perhaps, only in retrospect given the messiness and noise around Labor Party politics at the time. All discussion of policy tended to be overshadowed in the media by continuing leadership instability.

Before Macklin and Plibersek's work in opposition under Beazley, and then in government under Rudd, childcare and parental leave were seen as part of welfare policy – and therefore in competition with all the other demands on the public purse to care for the most disadvantaged. Any advance on childcare was open to attack as 'middle-class welfare'. By the end of the Labor government, childcare and parental leave were instead an accepted part of economic policy, key to increasing productivity, workforce participation and national prosperity and wellbeing. This paradigm shift was mostly Macklin's achievement – something for which she has never been adequately recognised in the public eye. But in Macklin's own assessment, Plibersek was crucial to the success. She was, says Macklin, 'very helpful in convincing people in the party, in doing the essential political work to get a major policy change adopted. She was a genius at convincing people that it was the right thing to do.'

Initially, most of Plibersek's work was on childcare. She threw herself into the portfolio. Two days before she gave birth to Joe on 25 January 2005, she was touring the press gallery handing out media releases on the shortcomings of the government's childcare policies. She took a few weeks off, but the tide of media releases and speeches on childcare barely slackened pace. From the beginning of 2005 until she lost the portfolio, there were almost weekly statements and, when parliament was sitting, speeches on childcare. She chipped away at the government over poor pay for childcare workers and the complicated system of government regulation and subsidies for childcare. The childcare system was hard to understand and navigate and included everything from private nannies to long daycare and family daycare. There was no coherent policy on quality and standards. Since the Keating government, corporate for-profit childcare centres had been allowed to flourish with little regulatory oversight. They now provided almost 70 per cent of all childcare. Meanwhile, Australia spent less on early childcare education than any other OECD country.

It was an impenetrable system involving all levels of government. The federal government was responsible for funding subsidies and rebates, state governments were mostly responsible for regulation, and local governments often provided the service. Each state and territory had different rules on the ratio of staff to children and the minimum qualifications of carers. Meanwhile, federal government support was delivered through a complex system of multiple payments – a means-tested childcare benefit, usually paid to the provider, and a non-means-tested childcare rebate paid retrospectively through the tax system, together with childcare assistance for those in jobs and education and training. It was a mess. There were shortages in childcare places, but as Plibersek said in early 2006, 'the federal government has no idea where childcare shortages are because it does not collect any data'.[4]

In her first weeks in the portfolio, Plibersek welcomed a successful wage claim in the Australian Industrial Relations Commission for childcare workers in Victoria and the ACT – pointing out they were among the lowest-paid workers in Australia. But the increase, she said, would lead to increased costs, and that would almost cancel out the government's rebate for childcare costs. Five weeks after giving birth, she proposed sweeping workplace reforms. She called for employers to introduce radical family-friendly policies into the workplace, including permanent part-time work, job sharing and work-from-home options. Women should be able to bring their babies to work as a matter of routine if they were breastfeeding, and older children who were off school sick should be allowed to come to the office.

She was modelling the change she wanted to see. Her staff remember visiting her at home in those early months and discussing policy while she breastfed Joe. She would change his nappy on the floor in front of them, a briefing paper or a book on one side. Soon Joe was a presence in the office as well, with a nanny or carer coming and going, toys kept in the reception area and Plibersek sometimes breastfeeding during meetings. She had recruited as her adviser a young Labor university activist, Monika Wheeler, who had been working part-time on Albanese's electoral staff while she finished her degree. Plibersek was her local member and had often turned up at university events Wheeler had organised. Recalls Wheeler: 'I just admired her so much. I approached her one day in a supermarket and said, "Have you any opportunities coming up in your office in the future? I would just really love to work for you."' She joined Plibersek's staff just after the 2004 election defeat. The work, Wheeler recalls, was 'constant advocacy', not only through speeches and women's organisations but also within the party. Wheeler was awed by how Plibersek handled motherhood. Union leaders and business heads, called to meetings to discuss how to retain women in the workforce, were expected just to cope with the presence of the baby. Plibersek also recruited Mary Wood, who had previously worked for Senator Chris Evans, and played a key role in preparing Labor senators for scrutinising government in Senate estimates. Wood stayed on Plibersek's staff, eventually becoming her chief of staff, until 2011.

But while her staff thought Plibersek's juggling of parenthood and politics was 'wonderful', others counted it against her. In May 2005, the Australian Associated Press published an article about affluent, educated, middle-class women who were habitual Liberal voters but who were now deserting the party over concerns about the war in Iraq and the treatment of asylum seekers. The article was littered with sexist terms that were at the time still regarded as an acceptable part of political debate. The liberal women were described as 'desperate housewives' and 'doctors' wives'. Halfway through the piece, the author declared that 'the problem of working women is one that both sides of politics still wrestle with'. The reason they were a 'problem', in the terms of the article, was a lack of childcare. The article recorded that the treasurer, Peter Costello, had announced 80,000 new out-of-school-hours childcare places in the 2005 federal budget. When Plibersek spoke on this plan in parliament, government members jeered at her and called across the chamber, 'Where are your children?' – the implication being that she could not possibly be taken seriously as a mother if she was in the parliament, or in the parliament if she was a mother. The author concluded, with no apparent sense of irony: 'Until the federal parliament can work out its attitude towards working women, the doctors' wives are entitled to feel a little desperate.'[5]

Plibersek recalls that Beazley was easy to persuade on the importance of childcare. 'It wasn't the first thing that would have occurred to him to campaign on, but as soon as I was talking to him about what we wanted to do, he got it immediately.' He was pleasantly surprised, when she invited him to speak at childcare-related events, by the amount of media coverage he received. 'We'd go to a little suburban childcare centre and there'd be five or six TV cameras and print journalists as well, and those journalists were in the age group that had kids in childcare.'

Beazley's own children had grown up, but 'he was reminded of what a large share of the family budget was being chewed up by childcare costs.'

Through constant advocacy, media opportunities and public events, Plibersek succeeded in putting childcare on the national agenda – making it a story that was constantly in the news. 'I don't believe that what happened later in government would have happened if I hadn't proved to all of my colleagues that it was top of mind for people, that it was not just a women's issue, that families saw it as impacting their family budget, the ability for both parents to work.'

First in his budget reply speech in May 2006, then in more detail in July 2006, Beazley outlined the childcare policy Plibersek had worked on, promising to make wholesale changes. This would include 25,000 new places, improved affordability, and a better quality of care, together with a $200-million pledge to create 260 new childcare centres on primary schoolgrounds – the latter being Plibersek's particular contribution to addressing the stress on families created by the morning drop-off of children to multiple locations. The plan also promised that employers who provided childcare would be eligible for fringe-benefits tax exemptions and able to claim business tax deductions, while their employees would be able to salary-sacrifice their fees. Tax rebates for the cost of childcare would be available for older children as well, as was already the case for those under six.

Later, when Kevin Rudd and Julia Gillard took the leadership in 2006, Plibersek lost the childcare portfolio. But when Labor formed government, Plibersek as minister for women, with Kate Ellis as minister for childcare, introduced an even more ambitious policy, including a new national quality framework for childcare and a national early-years-learning framework. As part of Rudd's cooperative federalism, there was a suite of interrelated national partnerships and initiatives and a new regulatory authority, meaning regulation and standards were now uniform.

When Labor lost power in 2013, one of the first actions of the new Coalition government treasurer, Joe Hockey, was to set up a Productivity Commission inquiry into childcare. It recommended the national quality framework be extended, as well as a simplification of government childcare subsidies to a single means-tested payment to the family's choice of approved services. Key components of the policies Plibersek had worked on were now close to bipartisan. Childcare was now understood as central to education, childhood development and national economic wellbeing. It has been central to political contests ever since.

At the same time as they were battling to bring childcare to the forefront of ALP policy, Macklin and Plibersek were advancing another cause – the battle for paid parental leave, or paid maternity leave, as it was called at the time.

Ever since federation, women had been lobbying for the ability to take time off after giving birth and to have a guaranteed job to return to. As with childcare, the issue had been relegated to the edges of welfare policy. Unions, male-dominated for most of their history, had been ambivalent, but since the 1970s women had been increasingly active and senior in the union movement. Between 1979 and 1990, the ACTU made important gains in a series of cases before the Conciliation and Arbitration Commission. Women were granted up to a year of unpaid maternity leave. Then this was extended to adoptive parents, and finally fathers were included, and parents gained the right to request to work part-time for up to two years.

Paid leave was harder to win. The Whitlam government introduced three months' paid maternity leave and one week of paid paternity leave for the Commonwealth Public Service, and in the 1970s most states followed for their public service employees. Later, a few large employers introduced paid maternity leave, but that was little help for most women.[6]

In 2000, Sharan Burrow became president of the Australian Council of Trade Unions and launched a campaign for the introduction of a minimum of fourteen weeks' paid maternity leave. When Macklin became deputy leader of Labor in 2001, the two women joined forces and the push gained momentum. There was support across the political divide. Pru Goward, formerly director of the Office of the Status of Women under the Howard government, and later to be a NSW Liberal MP, was made sex discrimination commissioner at the Human Rights and Equal Opportunity Commission, and immediately started an investigation into options. The inquiry recommended fourteen weeks of paid leave, to be financed at up to the minimum wage and paid for by government. Goward's proposal was backed by the ACTU, the Women's Electoral Lobby and the Australian Industry Group – but not by the Howard government.

Maternity leave was too expensive, Howard said, and would discriminate against women who chose not to work outside the home. Finance minister Nick Minchin described maternity leave as 'middle-class welfare'.[7] Instead, in the 2002 federal budget, treasurer Peter Costello introduced the 'baby bonus' – a $3000 payment for all new mothers with incomes below $75,000, initially paid as a tax refund and then later as a means-tested lump sum. Costello justified the baby bonus as a way to increase the birth rate, which had fallen to the lowest level ever recorded. He famously encouraged Australians to have one child for Mum, one for Dad and one for the country. It resulted in a mini baby boom.

But the baby bonus was not enough for the maternity-leave advocates. The ACTU, the women's movement and Macklin wanted maternity leave recognised as a workplace entitlement – a right. If it was seen as welfare or as part of population policy, it could be reduced or withdrawn at the government's whim.

By the time Plibersek joined Macklin in the fight as shadow minister for women, Australia was one of only two OECD countries that did not have universal paid maternity leave. Almost half of the country's large employers provided paid maternity leave, and it was standard in the public sector – but for most women, and particularly for those in casual employment, it was out of reach. For them, combining motherhood and work was barely possible, unless they had strong family support. Motherhood meant poverty. As the 2007 election approached, the issue was wrapped up with the Howard government's changes to industrial relations laws. Howard argued that the right way to achieve maternity leave was through enterprise bargaining – but it was clear this wasn't working and was even less likely to work if workplace rights were weakened under the government's WorkChoices legislation.

Macklin recalls that when she first began to work on paid parental leave, there was almost no support in shadow cabinet. From the moment

Plibersek got the women's portfolio, she 'just got out talking to every-one. To the unions, to Beazley and then Rudd, to everyone in cabinet, and she really is the most astonishing communicator.'

It remained a tough slog. The battle got even harder as the election approached. Rudd was positioning himself as a safe choice for voters and as a 'fiscal conservative'. Maternity leave would be expensive – a burden on either employers or government or both. Macklin recalls: 'Getting any policy onto the election platform that had money attached to it was very, very difficult.' Wayne Swan was an important supporter, but Wheeler remembers 'everyone was really scared about putting paid maternity leave on the agenda. Jenny and Tanya kept pushing, but they were blocked. And it was fear, really, that blocked it. The fear that this could prevent Labor from winning the election, as it wasn't on the radar at all for the Coalition at this point.'

In mid-2007, paid maternity leave was dropped from the Labor Party's election platform. It was a heavy blow. In public, Plibersek was characteristically restrained. Interviewed on ABC Radio, she commented on a survey that showed 76 per cent of Australians supported paid mater-nity leave, with the cost shared between employers and the government. She was maintaining a public show of party solidarity and not com-mitting Labor, while also trying to keep the policy options alive. 'What this report calls for is a thorough examination of whether there's a cost-effective way of delivering paid maternity leave that doesn't put undue pressure on business either in a financial or administrative sense. We're happy with that call.'[8]

Behind the scenes, Macklin and Plibersek were still pushing. Then, there was a breakthrough – and it came from outside the government. Marie Coleman was a longstanding senior public servant and had been a key figure in the maternity leave campaign for decades. She had been the first woman to head an Australian national statutory authority, the National Social Welfare Commission, under the Whitlam government. Under the Fraser government, she had been director of the Office of Childcare, and she was now chairing the social policy committee of the National Foundation of Australian Women – a lobby group and peak body. Coleman recalls that when the party dropped maternity leave from its election platform she was 'massively pissed off'. She spent a weekend 'pacing and thinking': 'Clearly arguing on the grounds of fairness wasn't getting us anywhere. Arguing on the grounds that women deserved it and that it would be good for mothers and babies wasn't getting us any-where. But the economic mantra of the time was around the fact that the population was ageing and we needed higher productivity. So it seemed to me that the goal was to couch parental leave in terms of productivity and see whether we could argue that way.'

Coleman suggested to Macklin and Plibersek that rather than com-mitting to introducing maternity leave, Labor should instead make an election promise to refer paid parental leave to the Productivity Com-mission for a thorough investigation. The women were familiar with the international research, which demonstrated convincingly that higher female work participation was closely associated with higher national pro-ductivity. As a result, they were confident that a Productivity Commission inquiry would help the case.

This was the paradigm shift – not welfare, not women's policy, but productivity. Macklin and Plibersek grasped the idea with both hands. It became the focus of their lobbying and conversations with their col-leagues. Gillard, as deputy leader, was in Coleman's view hostile to the policy, but Swan and then finally Rudd were persuaded that the com-mitment to the Productivity Commission review was both politically safe and a real advance.

Plibersek says that this experience gave her a 'big lesson in how to advance big changes'. She believes most of her caucus and cabinet col-leagues supported the idea of paid maternity leave in principle, but they saw it as too expensive, too brave and too costly. 'And to be fair, it was going to be billions of dollars at a time when we had made commitments about fiscal responsibility. But Marie's genius with the Productivity Commission inquiry was that it took the issue out of the realms of wel-fare, and into one of economic productivity, and national benefit. It changed the conversation.'

As soon as the 2007 election was announced on 15 October, Cole-man, representing the National Foundation for Australian Women, wrote to both Howard and Rudd seeking a commitment to a Productivity

Commission inquiry. Howard's reply didn't arrive until the day after the election. Rudd replied promptly, committing Labor to the inquiry.

The battle was not yet won. It continued for most of the life of the Rudd government and later became one of the issues that Rudd would use to sabotage Gillard. But today, as a result of this work, Australian parents who are the primary carer of a newborn and who earn less than $156,000 a year are entitled to eighteen weeks' parental leave, paid for by the government at the rate of the weekly national minimum wage. This has transformed the lives of hundreds of thousands of Australian families.

* * *

By the beginning of 2006, Plibersek had moved to a new level within the party and in public awareness. Her work on childcare had increased her profile. So had her continued outspokenness on the rights of same-sex couples. She was well known for speaking up in caucus. In March, the veteran Canberra correspondent for *The Daily Telegraph*, Malcolm Farr, named her in an article about 'a new guard of relatively young Labor women who are certain to dominate the next big changes in the shadow ministry'. Julia Gillard was the 'most prominent', said Farr, but Plibersek was the next named. According to Farr, she was now 'driving much of the social debate within the parliamentary party'.[9]

In the same month, *The Sydney Morning Herald* commissioned her to write a fortnightly column under the title 'Upfront'. Each episode was about 700 words and she could write about anything she wished. The results were classic Plibersek – full of statistics and nerdish detail, leavened with examples and anecdotes. They were well-structured pieces, often referring to the classics of English literature or to recent research, but there was no soaring prose and little rhetorical flourish.

The first column in the series, published in March 2006, was about risk-taking among young people, quoting a recent book by her friend Rebecca Huntley on the importance of peer groups. Plibersek argued that 'cool kids' needed to be recruited as peer educators. Perhaps recalling her own trajectory, she said young people were more likely to be engaged on issues, rather than through political parties. 'We ... have to give young people something bigger than themselves to believe in,' she wrote.[10]

The next column was about fringe-benefits tax and how it encouraged people to use their cars to get to work rather than public transport.[11] Then she wrote about mental illness and how the move to 'deinstitutionalise' the mentally ill had become a way of ignoring government responsibilities and failing to invest in care:

> We can't congratulate ourselves for having saved a psychotic teenager from the hell of a psych ward if our alternative is to allow him to wander lost and lonely until he takes his own life or ends up in jail.[12]

Other topics tackled that year included domestic violence in Indigenous communities, human rights, environmental degradation and poverty in Thailand, the latter in response to a news story about eight endangered Asian elephants from Thailand being offered state-of-the-art enclosures in Australian zoos. Plibersek wrote that there was no point in such measures unless Australia took action to tackle the poverty that led to environmental destruction:

> Some Thai farmers are so poor they sell their children ... In one town, Pa Tek, 70 per cent of families have sold at least one daughter into prostitution. Prices vary from $US114 to $US913 – the latter figure equal to almost six years' wages in Thailand.[13]

In February 2007, she wrote about dental care and how the 'last Labor government had a $100-million-a-year Commonwealth Dental Scheme that treated 1.5 million people. The Howard Government abolished it soon after being elected.' Waiting lists for public dental care had blown out. She shared the story of one of her electors, a single mother who had fled domestic violence and was 'bursting with pride' when her son won a scholarship to attend a North Shore private school.

> But she could not attend his first day of school with him. Her rotting teeth were so bad she did not have the confidence to leave the house ... This is the human cost of government neglect.[14]

In one of the most lyrical of her columns, she used the nineteenth-century English writer Anthony Trollope and his Palliser series of novels as the jumping-off point for reflections on public life. Concluded Plibersek, 'Trollope's last and perhaps most important message is that on your death bed it will be your family and the relationship you had with them that counts, and that whatever you may achieve in public life, your first responsibility is to the people you love.'[15]

Those were to be significant words, given the choices that lay ahead of her.

As Plibersek's profile rose, the ALP was once again preoccupied with leadership destabilisation, with the resulting media reporting overshadowing all the hard work on policy.

Plibersek is among those who believe that Kim Beazley is the good prime minister, perhaps the great prime minister, Australia never had. She describes him as having values and a temperament similar to her own. He is decent, she says. His would have been a quiet kind of leadership. He would have been a team player rather than driven by ego.

He didn't get the chance. By the second half of 2006, Rudd and Gillard had formed an alliance, combining their support. Gillard, as she wrote later, had accepted that she could not at this stage be the leader. Rudd could represent a 'safe change' from Howard for conservative voters, whereas she, as a left-wing unmarried woman, could not make that pitch, so she would settle for deputy. That would mean deposing not only Beazley but also Jenny Macklin. As the challenge approached, Plibersek made it clear to Macklin and Beazley, and within the party more generally, that she was on their side. Her loyalty cemented their friendships.

Gillard was convinced that Beazley did not have the ability to cut through and win against Howard.[16] In parliament in 2005, Howard had made a stinging personal attack on Beazley that encapsulated the doubts about his leadership on both sides of the political aisle. Once, Howard said, he had thought that Beazley would be an effective opposition leader, but he had failed to develop a persona, or to let the Australian people know what he stood for. 'I've watched him over nine and a half years. He does not, Mr Speaker, have the ticker.'[17]

The Coalition had now won three elections in a row. Despite lagging in opinion polls, Howard had, in 2001 and 2004, conjured what political scientist Paul Strangio was to describe as 'Houdini-like escapes' come election time. Labor had been wrongfooted in the *Tampa* election of 2001 and had wrongfooted itself with Latham as leader in 2004.[18] Now Howard, with a majority in both houses of parliament, was pursuing a massively unpopular program of changes to industrial relations that would undermine workers' rights. As Gillard reflected in her memoirs: 'If Labor could not unseat John Howard after eleven years in those circumstances, "When would it ever happen?"'[19] The 2007 election was, it seemed to her and to many political commentators, a make-or-break contest. If Labor couldn't win, it would stop believing that it could. The Hawke–Keating years would be regarded as the exception and Labor's capacity to be a party of government would be permanently damaged.

Meanwhile, Rudd and Gillard were massively popular with the public and the media – dubbed the dream team – which can only look ironic in retrospect. It was their public popularity, as much as anything, that persuaded the party to make the change.

Rudd has argued in his memoirs that rolling Beazley was a necessary precondition to victory in 2007.[20] Gillard, in her book, was more self-critical. She said she might have been wrong in her judgement that, in 2006, Beazley was taking the job of opposition leader too quietly, and that the party was headed for defeat:

> In politics you never get to run the control test. We will never know what would have happened in a John Howard versus Kim Beazley election or what a Beazley Government might have been like. How long Kim would have stayed. Who would have been his successor.

She went on to say that it was her decision to ally with Rudd that made the difference. He could not have attracted sufficient support on his own, without her intervention. 'I bear the responsibility for creating his leadership.' She said she had correctly judged his campaigning capability and electoral popularity, but her 'assessment of how he would perform as leader, in essence what kind of man he was, proved to be dreadfully wrong'.[21]

Plibersek is reluctant to criticise former colleagues, but it is clear there is little in Gillard's reflection with which she would disagree. Beazley would have won in 2007, Plibersek believes, because people were tired of Howard. 'It might not have been the same landslide that Kevin achieved, but a win is a win.' She points out that in the six months prior to Beazley's overthrow, and despite his lukewarm personal approval ratings, Labor was ahead in the polls. And had Beazley won, it would have been a different kind of Labor government.

On Friday, 2 December 2006, Rudd and Gillard confirmed that they would contest the leadership of the party at a meeting the following Monday. The result was a weekend of dread for Plibersek. Nobody was more outspoken in support of Beazley and Macklin than she was. She dropped her customary restraint in talking about internal party matters and condemned the challenge in colourful terms. The leadership challenge was 'heartbreaking ... Because people won't vote for a disunited party.'[22] Rudd and Gillard were talented, she said, but not ready to lead.[23] She compared the Rudd–Gillard challenge to the elevation of Latham, who by this time was universally derided. 'If we persist in repeating the mistakes of our history, then we don't deserve to be in Government ... People will punish us at the ballot box for this.'

The day before the spill, she told *The Daily Telegraph* that the challenge was being driven by a small group of people who were 'waiting like spiders in holes to dart out and spurt their poison'. Beazley backer Senator Steve Hutchins, on hearing this comment, shot a jot of venom at Gillard, saying 'the spider is a redback'.

Plibersek was not alone in speaking out. Wong, too, was one of Beazley and Macklin's most vocal supporters. Macklin had been a mentor to Wong, as well, and she owed her personal loyalty. But the next day, the caucus voted 49 to 39 to replace Beazley with Rudd. Macklin withdrew from the contest, allowing Gillard to be elected as deputy unopposed. Plibersek, the media reported, emerged from the vote 'downcast and stony-faced'.[24] She sarcastically blamed 'the same geniuses who gave us Mark Latham'.[25]

In the short term, Plibersek was wrong about the electorally damaging effect of the Rudd–Gillard move. Rudd led the party to a thumping victory in November 2007. The long Howard reign was over. Labor at last had its chance to govern. But in the longer term, history might judge her prescient. In the words of Paul Strangio, the November 2007 federal election appears like a hinge between two political eras: one stable and marked by executive mastery; the other chaotic and characterised by confounded leadership.[26]

The Labor government of 2007–2013 achieved a lot but squandered many of its opportunities. The most important policy issue of all – action on climate change – was dropped. Gillard deposed Rudd in 2010, claiming 'a good government has lost its way', and Labor was forced into minority government at the subsequent election. Then Rudd replaced Gillard. By 2013 the 'dream team' was clearly unelectable. Labor had failed to manage itself. It had self-sabotaged.

Reflecting on Labor's decades of agony in interviews for this book in late 2021, Plibersek attacked what she described as 'the great man version of history', in which the party and the nation look to a single person as saviour. What matters, she said, is the team, not so much the leader.

Every leader has their strengths and weaknesses, she said. '[They] are not as bad as their enemies think, and they're not as good as their friends think. And the one thing that is absolutely guaranteed to keep a party in opposition is chaos and instability. The view of the public is if you can't govern yourselves, how can you govern the nation? A precondition for any leader's success is a unified party, and a unified caucus behind them ... The leaders who get there by destabilising the previous leader create an environment that guarantees their own eventual demise. Bad behaviour becomes more acceptable because it is more commonplace. And it's a real problem, an institutional problem.'

She believes that if Rudd and Gillard had held their hand in 2006, a victorious Beazley would have served a term or two and then there would have been a 'solid, stable, methodical, process' of succession. Either Rudd or Gillard would have taken over. On balance, she thinks, it would have been Gillard. 'She would have had more time to assert her credentials. If she had had that time, it's possible that Kevin wouldn't have had a chance, and we might have gone straight from Kim to Julia.'

And if that had happened – a peaceful transition to an energised new generation – Labor would be a different kind of party, and Australia would be a different, better country. Perhaps Labor would have won in its own right in 2010, and again in 2013. The Abbott government might never have been.

Needless to say, not everyone shares Plibersek's assessment of Beazley as a potentially good prime minister. They criticise his apparent lack of energy and lack of hunger for the job, and what they see as a lack of policy vision.

Significantly, these are exactly the kinds of shortcomings that some of Plibersek's critics perceive in her. They question whether she has the edge, the ruthlessness, to make a good leader. They question her policy credentials. They don't agree with suggestions from her supporters that she might represent a different kind of leadership – less macho, more team-oriented, with less ego. 'One of the persistent questions in Labor whenever Tanya is discussed as a possible leader is how she would go down, not with the inner-city lefties but with the soccer mums in Penrith and the miners in the Hunter Valley,' says one. 'Views differ.'

This is as good a place as any to say something about Tanya Plibersek and ambition, particularly in light of her comments about the great man version of history, the emphasis of the team over the leader.

In 2021, when she gave the bulk of interviews for this book, Labor was approaching the 2022 election, with Anthony Albanese as leader. Given the tiredness of the Coalition government, Labor was not doing as well in the polls as might be expected. Once again, the dialogue was that the Labor leader could not cut through. Some people were encouraging Plibersek to challenge Albanese for the leadership.

At the last election defeat, in 2019, she had at first intended to contest the leadership, but had withdrawn. Now she was being urged to reconsider. Meanwhile, Plibersek had a fanatical following – almost a cult – within the party membership.

Plibersek's supporters, and those close to her, offered two narratives during this period. They denied she ever counted the numbers in 2021 with a view to a challenge. And they argued that had she taken on Albanese, she would have won, because she had the numbers. I heard stories of her taking soundings of her support. She denies doing this. Bill Shorten, from the Victorian Right, was said to want her to challenge. So did a group within the Socialist Left in Victoria. On the other hand, Albanese's supporters continued to assert that he was not only strategically head and shoulders above Plibersek, but also able to hold a conversation with the Australian people – including those who would not usually vote Labor. Where was the evidence, they asked, that Plibersek could pull votes outside the lefties of the inner city? 'She might have the luvvies on side,' said one senior Labor figure to me. 'She might get people who'd consider voting Green to stick to Labor. But where's the evidence she'd pull blue-collar votes?'

But all this conversation remained subterranean. Plibersek never challenged.

She knew she was being watched. One of her main concerns when the idea of this biography was first raised was that it should be clear she did not seek it to be done: she feared it would be understood as her stalking Albanese.

It is hard to write about ambition in a woman. It is part of the background noise of patriarchy, the landscape of politics and achievement, that ambition accepted and expected in a talented man will be seen as illegitimate and unappealing in a woman.

Plibersek is an interesting case study. As Anne Summers had angrily noted, when Plibersek entered parliament, she denied any ambitions other than to represent her electorate well. In her 2006 columns for *The Sydney Morning Herald*, she used Trollope to argue for the primacy of family and relationships, responsibility to 'the people you love' over ambition in public life.

And yet Plibersek is ambitious, as evidenced by the way she seized the opportunity of preselection for Sydney. She threw herself into that contest with such energy, charm and determination that she won against the odds, and against more obviously qualified candidates. How would that capacity play out in a contest for party leadership?

Those closest to her say it was the experience of watching and living through Labor's leadership contortions, from Beazley to Crean to Latham to Beazley and then to Rudd, that helped Plibersek begin to sense her own leadership ambitions. She watched the manoeuvring and assessed the talent and the judgement of those who circled the leadership race and compared her own abilities to those of the contenders. Nobody was speaking of Plibersek as a leadership contender at that time. She was not even in shadow cabinet.

Rebecca Huntley is one of Plibersek's supporters. She talks about Plibersek's 'conspicuous, extraordinary empathy'. But, says Huntley, 'the Achilles' heel of Tanya's deep and almost poetic humanity is her reticence to make herself into a guru.' She needs, in Huntley's view, to assertively grab an issue and make it her own. 'Has she got the ability to do that? Absolutely. But is there a reticence about doing that? Absolutely.' The idea of a leader having to set out a vision and demand to be followed is a male paradigm, she suggests. Plibersek would represent a more collaborative, less ego-driven model. Huntley draws a comparison with the New Zealand leader Jacinda Ardern.

On this view of things, if Labor were ever to choose Plibersek as its leader, it would be voting for sense over sensibility – for Elinor over Marianne, for calm and good management over vision, emotion and ego. It would be the same kind of choice that Plibersek believes the party should have made in 2006 – a choice for Beazley rather than Rudd. But with the added factor of her undisputed communications abilities.

Meanwhile, the thing that confuses people about Plibersek is that both her reticence and her ambition reside in the same political persona. And this is one of the reasons the Albanese team don't entirely trust her. They see her record – the occasional audacious moves for advancement – and understand her ambition as cloaked, rather than as ambivalent. I think that's wrong. Tanya Plibersek would be a simpler, less layered character if that were true. It is once again that Elinor Dashwood opacity. I think both the reticence and the ambition are real. She has struck a different balance between them at different times. You could call the balance between them unresolved.

*   *   *

In March 2007 the voters of New South Wales returned the state Labor government, now led by Premier Morris Iemma, for its fourth term. Michael Coutts-Trotter had become 'indispensable' to NSW Labor, in the words of his boss, Michael Egan – 'beloved' by Treasury and a confidant of politicians and senior public servants throughout the government.[27] He had risen to be Egan's chief of staff, but after seven years had made a switch to the public service, taking up the position of director-general of the NSW Department of Commerce.

Now, after the election, the new education minister, John Della Bosca, appointed him the director-general of the Department of Education and Training. The appointment triggered another round of publicity over his criminal past. The media could hardly get enough of the story and its implications. Twelve years had passed since Coutts-Trotter had been in the headlines, and for most of the parents whose children were being educated in schools under his supervision, his drug- dealer past came as a shocking revelation. Talkback radio callers pointed out that Coutts-Trotter could probably not be a lollypop man on a school crossing with such a criminal record, and almost certainly not a teacher. Yet now he oversaw the state's schools.

As he had in 1995, Coutts-Trotter took the controversy head on, making himself available to the media, talking again about how he had made his mistakes and 'luckily and remarkably' been given a second chance. This time, though, the right-wing commentators of the Emerald City were not on his side. Tanya Plibersek was mentioned in almost every news story. The ABC Radio program *The World Today* declared that while his talents were undisputed, 'there is little question his impeccable relationships with the Labor Party, including his wife, Federal Labor MP Tanya Plibersek, have been critical to his success'.[28] The NSW opposition described him as a 'Labor mate' who would never have been appointed to the job – which was not advertised – without his connections.[29] Gerard Henderson, the director of the Sydney Institute and conservative columnist for News Corporation papers, said that while everyone was entitled to make good on their youthful mistakes, it was 'most unwise' to make Coutts-Trotter head of education. 'I mean, Alan Bond has done his time, but I don't think anyone would make Alan Bond head of the Treasury Department.' The head of the Public Schools Principals Forum, Cheryl McBride, asked whether he was 'really the model we want for our young people ... do we want young people to think it is OK to be a drug addict and to be a trader, and to recover from that?'[30]

As he had twelve years before, Egan spoke in Coutts-Trotter's favour – how he had redeemed and rehabilitated himself, how indispensable he had become. 'People who work with him swear by him and all of his detractors today, particularly those who will be working with him, will soon find that he's a first-class human being and they will regret ever having any doubts about him.' Della Bosca declared that Coutts-Trotter had the government's 'absolute confidence' and that he was a 'stellar example of someone who has learnt from the mistakes he made as a young man. I think he is exactly what we need to provide reinvigorated organisational leadership for public education.'[31]

Tanya and Michael had known that the appointment was likely to renew the controversy. This time, navigating the consequences was more complicated. They had their children to consider. Anna, now six years old and in primary school, was old enough to know something was going on. There had to be a family conversation.

Anna Coutts-Trotter remembers that the family talk came in the car, after they had been out for a meal. She was mostly preoccupied with the fact that she had been promised an ice cream for dessert. Her parents told her there was something they had to tell her. She listened and then, the family folklore goes, continued to lobby for the ice cream. It was only years later, as she grew older, that she came to a deeper understanding of what her father had done, and what he had been through – the police brutality, the violence witnessed in jail, being 'banged up' with the killers of Anita Cobby. And the social media posts in which her mother would be described as a drug whore.

But at this time, the private family conversation was soon played back to the public as part of the media management. Coutts-Trotter told *The Sunday Telegraph*:

I had to sit her down and explain to her that her dad's been to jail. As a six-year-old, you understand things in pretty black-and-white terms, you know: people who go to jail are bad, and people who don't are good. I've got to tell her no, it's a bit more complicated than that. I felt a bit heartsick about it. I worry that it might get raised with her in the playground, but I really wanted this job.[32]

Plibersek and Coutts-Trotter told *The Daily Telegraph* their message was pitched at a level they hoped their daughter could accept. They had used the example of a friend who was a smoker, and used that to tell her there were other kinds of addiction. Coutts-Trotter added, 'She's a bright girl. I think she'll be asking the next set of questions far too soon.'[33]

Meanwhile, Plibersek leapt into the media herself, to frame the story. She said that whenever she was confronted by drug-blighted kids in her electorate, she thought of her husband. He was a 'beacon of hope', she said, and 'an inspiration'. He showed that change was possible for everyone. 'If there's any good to come out of his past being dredged up again by the Opposition it's that it might give hope to other families struggling with having a teenage child in similar circumstances,' she said.[34]

It was great media fodder and a welter of profiles, interviews and opinion columns followed. For the month of April 2007, Michael Coutts-Trotter, Tanya Plibersek and their story of redemption were at the centre of public debate in Sydney and even nationally. Coutts-Trotter was, as usual, almost embarrassingly frank. He was asked about redemption and said, 'Redemption ... well, I'm not sure how you can tackle life without the belief that redemption is real, is possible, is a factor. I'm a lapsed Catholic but I'm culturally Catholic. When I think of redemption it is notions of Christian redemption I think about.' He talked about achieving a 'state of grace' through the recovery process, particularly through attending Narcotics Anonymous meetings. 'I felt as if I did better than I could have on my own. So you draw strength from human fellowship.'[35]

Then, as such things do, the issue faded away. By the end of April, Plibersek was in the media being asked, as part of a lifestyle feature, what made her happy. She answered that it was exercise. She had hated sport at school. But now, 'Feeling fit and strong is something that makes me very happy. I swim, go the gym, do yoga, bushwalk and run.' She was swimming about a kilometre each day in the harbour, and being a mother had transformed her attitude to exercise. She wanted her children to see her as strong and physically competent. Joe, she said, was now two years old and fearless. When swimming, 'He sticks his head right under water and comes up laughing with the water dripping off his eyelashes.'[36]

And the Emerald City moved on.

* * *

Despite her outspoken opposition to the Rudd and Gillard leadership coup, Tanya Plibersek was not penalised. Rudd did not punish any of the Beazley backers. Instead, she was promoted – losing childcare, but gaining the shadow portfolios of human services and housing to add to her existing responsibilities for the status of women and youth.

Housing was central to the Rudd agenda as the election approached, which made it all the more remarkable that Plibersek still wasn't in cabinet when, on 24 November 2007, after a thirty-nine-day campaign, the Rudd–Gillard team achieved a stunning election victory. Labor won 83 of the 150 seats in the House of Representatives. This represented a twenty-three-seat swing to Labor. In the electorate of Sydney there was a 3.92 per cent swing towards Plibersek; the Greens went backwards, scoring only 21 per cent of the vote. The Howard years had at last come to an end, and a talented Labor front bench were more than ready to make change. The 'dream team' was in charge, and the air was full of hope.

6

HOMES

On election night 2007, Tanya Plibersek was on Channel Seven's panel of political commentators as the results came in. Early on, it was clear that the Rudd government would be elected in a landslide. Plibersek was flushed with joy. She told the anchor, David Koch, she was 'very excited about what we can do'.

'So you'll hit the ground running?' he asked.

'Absolutely.'

Then Koch turned to Plibersek's counterpart from the Coalition ranks, the minister for employment, Joe Hockey. He had been responsible for the workplace reforms that were now the chief reason for the government's defeat, and the personal cost of the political reckoning was clear. Hockey was choking up. He said he was devastated. Plibersek, sitting at his elbow, wiped the smile from her face and briefly reached out to him, a hand on his shoulder, as he talked about having to sack twenty staff, and how hard that would be. But she couldn't restrain her smile for long. 'I wish nobody any ill, but there are some very, very happy people around Australia right now,' she said. Told that foreign minister Alexander Downer was refusing to talk to the media, she said, 'Well, he's always been a bit of a sook, hasn't he?' Later she said, 'You really see a person's soul in defeat.'

In his victory speech a short while later, Rudd promised 'a new consensus'; a putting aside of 'old arguments' between state and federal governments, between business and government and private and public. He promised 'energy, determination and vigour' in prosecuting a new agenda and 'a new page' for the nation.

The election had been fought, mainly, on the Howard government's WorkChoices legislation, but as well the government was looking tired. There had been regular talk of a challenge to Howard's leadership, although none emerged.

Rudd's motto going into the election was 'new leadership, fresh ideas'. The program he took to the people was cautious, almost conservative. As Gillard later outlined in her memoirs, the intention was for Rudd to represent a safe change from Howard.[1] The main points of difference from the government, apart from industrial relations, were action on climate change, including a pledge to ratify the Kyoto protocol and a renewed federal involvement in housing policy – and the latter was Plibersek's job. She was sworn in as minister for housing, and minister for the status of women – the main two portfolios she had previously held in opposition.

There had been no dedicated housing minister under the Howard government. Rather, housing had been one of the responsibilities held by successive family and community service ministers. When Plibersek took the reins, it had been a long time since anyone in the federal government had conceived of this complex web of local, state and federal government responsibilities, of individual welfare and national aspiration, as a single area of policy deserving of systemic attention from the Commonwealth.[2]

The Hawke–Keating government's interest in urban design and building better cities was a distant memory. The prevailing philosophy of the Howard government had been to leave housing to the market. Public service responsibility for housing policy under Howard had at first been a small part of the giant Department of Social Security and then, after the 1998 election, a branch within the Department of Families and Community Services. No senior federal public servants were involved directly in housing the Australian population.

Now Plibersek was responsible for one of the most complex, powerful and emotive areas of public policy, although she was still not in cabinet. At one end of the spectrum of advantage were the homeless. At the other end, property investors and developers, national aspiration and the building of wealth. A safe and decent home is basic to every other kind of human welfare. Health, employment, the nurturing of family, the ability to get an education, to acquire possessions and to feel safe – all depend on a decent place to return to, and to sleep.

Federal government involvement in housing had been central to nation-building after the Second World War. The first Commonwealth State Housing Agreement, started by Labor, ran from 1945 to 1955. Under this, the federal government lent money to the states for a big public house building program. The Menzies government reoriented this to home ownership – a central concern of the 'forgotten people' of the aspirational middle classes. Home ownership was promoted as the bedrock to participation in society, a stake in the common purpose of the nation. But from the 1980s, a neoliberal consensus across the political parties had seen federal governments retreat from spending on housing. The Hawke–Keating government had made drastic cuts to funding for public housing. Now, the Commonwealth's main contribution was paying rent assistance to social security recipients. Urban planning and public housing were chiefly state responsibilities, with money funnelled from the federal government in tied grants. The rest was left to market forces – but not free market forces, largely because property investors had the advantage of generous and market-distorting capital-gains and negative-gearing tax concessions, which put pressure on prices. To make things worse, the Howard government cut grants to the states for social housing, while the cost of buying and maintaining homes rose.

Housing was a political problem for Howard. From the middle of his period in power, homes had been becoming less affordable for first homebuyers. The Productivity Commission had argued that capital-gains tax concessions be reviewed, and releases of land and planning approval processes improved. It also called for a more tightly targeted system of grants for first homeowners. The Howard government ignored most of the proposals.[3] Howard famously responded to the issue by saying he had never had anyone 'shake their fist at me and say ... "I'm angry with you for letting the value of my house increase"'.[4]

Meanwhile, the housing policy vacuum was being filled by people from outside the government. By early in the new century, an informal coalition had formed between welfare groups and academics to influence policy development. In the words of two of the leading academics, housing had become 'arguably the most fundamental cross-cutting policy issue confronting Australian governments.'[5] It was central to almost every other area of national aspiration. It was not only a welfare issue, but an economic and environmental issue. Housing affordability in the private market could not be divorced from a profound lack of public and social housing. The big public housing estates that had been built in the 1950s and 1960s were now falling into disrepair. Many were becoming uninhabitable, and decades of underinvestment meant that secure housing was increasingly unachievable for the poorest Australians. At the next level up, there wasn't enough affordable housing for low-income earners close to areas where there were jobs.

State governments were not providing enough public housing, and in response there was a nascent community-housing sector made up of charitable organisations and not-for-profits. This sector was in its infancy when Labor took power, but its potential was beginning to become clear. Community-housing tenants, unlike public housing tenants, could still claim the Commonwealth rent assistance, which meant there was more money in the social housing sector overall. Community-housing associations could be more flexible than governments, building innovative projects using a mix of private and government money. Surveys of tenants suggested that the community-housing organisations were better landlords than governments, more responsive to their tenants' needs. A new term – 'social housing' – had begun to take hold, describing not only the public housing provided by state governments, but also low-cost homes built and managed by these community-housing organisations. But despite the benefits, community-housing organisations were controversial even within the welfare sector. Some saw them as a privatisation of what should rightly be a government responsibility.

Plibersek remembers she was disappointed when Rudd first gave her the shadow housing portfolio and took away her childcare responsibilities. She had loved working in childcare and given it her all. But she recalls, 'I had housing for about five minutes and just fell in love with it too.'

She had the advantage of a strong interest from the leader. Rudd had suffered from homelessness as a child. That experience was a fundamental part of his self-image and his political motivation. As the election year of 2007 dawned, action on housing became an increasingly important point of difference between Labor and the government. Rudd described housing affordability as a 'barbecue stopper' – using Howard's pet phrase for issues that people cared about.

But Plibersek soon discovered, as the election approached, that while Rudd was determined to do something about housing, he had no developed strategic policy. As the election promises were crafted, the process within the opposition resembled an episode of the ABC satirical drama *The Hollowmen*.

Plibersek recalls: 'It was, "Okay, we're writing a budget thing, and so can we work out how big the number should be? So how big? If I say this number, how do you respond to this number?" And they kind of came up with the numbers before they came up with the policy ... Kevin knew he wanted to do something, and it was for me to construct what that thing would be.'

Already, the numbers being thrown around in the policy-making program made it clear that it would be the largest single social program in Labor's election offerings, but in early 2007, nobody realised just how large it would become.

*   *   *

Plibersek was lucky that the housing policy community was more than ready to welcome her to its policy development circles. In 2004, the Housing Industry Association, the ACTU and Australian Council of Social Service had together taken the lead to convene the National Affordable Housing Summit under the leadership of Professor Julian Disney, a respected policy consultant, academic and social justice advocate. The summit group advocated for a six-point plan of action from the Commonwealth government, including a five-year national housing plan, a national affordable housing agreement between the states and federal government, more public money spent on affordable housing, tax reform, and a strategy for land and infrastructure planning.

These ideas were backed by research and in some cases sophisticated modelling.

Plibersek began her engagement with the portfolio in a way that was, in her own words, 'typical of how I've worked in each of my portfolios'. She found the people who knew the area and sat down to listen to them. While still in opposition, she became a regular presence at academic conferences and roundtables. Between the summit group and the academic community, she found the bricks of an innovative housing policy were already there, ready to be used. What was needed was a government prepared to act – and the necessary talent for implementation.

Adrian Pisarski, the chairperson of the peak housing lobby group, National Shelter, met Plibersek when she was shadow minister and remembers her as having a 'generous mind and a clear interest in good policy'. She was also, in those early days, clearly inexperienced and feeling her way. The summit group knew that Labor's response to its call for action would depend heavily on the views of Swan, Rudd and perhaps Macklin.

The summit group had developed an innovative program it called the National Affordable Rental Incentive (NARI). It was designed to boost the resources available for affordable housing and the range of people who could benefit from it. After years in the welfare sector, Disney had accepted that no government was likely to address the growing need for housing using only taxpayer money. 'I like the concept of public housing. I'm not keen on privatising things without very good cause. But the size of the problem is way beyond what even the most crazy spendthrift government could possibly address sufficiently through public housing.'

The NARI would be aimed at providing housing not only for people on very low incomes, but also for those just above that – people who were a low priority on public housing waiting lists, but who were struggling to afford market rents, let alone to save and buy a home. The idea was to offer a subsidy to commercial or non-profit organisations to build housing for rent, on condition that rents were set at least 20 per cent below market level for at least ten years. This would reduce the pressure on public housing waiting lists, as well as on the lower end of the rental market. It was a way of using a comparatively modest amount of taxpayer money to make providing affordable housing attractive to the property industry and financiers – a market-led solution to what had traditionally been seen as a welfare problem. In the Australian context, it was a new idea, but similar schemes were already operating successfully in the USA and Europe.

From 2004 onwards, the summit group had been pitching this idea to both sides of politics. Disney recalls, 'We had the Liberals at least as much in mind as Labor, because we knew that if this was to work, it needed bipartisan support to survive ... but we thought that it should attract the Liberals because, after all, it was using private enterprise.' But the Howard government showed little interest.

The summit group knew the NARI would run into opposition both from those on the left who opposed private-sector involvement in expanding social housing, and from those on the right who thought the private rental market should be left to its own devices. As well, the Australian property-investment industry was not used to the idea of building specifically for low-income renters. The summit group wanted the program to be carefully managed, and to start small, with expertly managed tenders leading to a small tranche of large developments. There would need to be careful marketing to large institutional investors. Many in the group wanted the projects to be managed and tenants selected by the not-for-profit community sector, to remove any chance of rorting – for example, by developers renting discount properties to friends and relations.

Pisarski recalls that the summit group had achieved a 'rare thing': business, unions and the welfare sector were all arguing for the same thing. He got the impression that John Howard was interested in the NARI, but 'we could never get it past the treasurer, Peter Costello. All we ever got back from him was that housing was a market problem, and the market would fix it. Plainly ignoring that the market hadn't fixed it and wasn't fixing it, and here was a market-led solution.'

By early 2007, with the government failing to follow up the idea, the summit group was talking to Plibersek and Swan. Swan, as the senior of the two, took the lead. Disney remembers Plibersek was chiefly concerned with homelessness, and housing as a welfare issue. 'She seemed more comfortable with the traditional thinking of the social-welfare and community-housing sectors than with the business sector and more innovative programs to boost affordable housing ... the NARI concept probably would have been alien to her at that stage.' Swan, on the other hand, was enthusiastic. His chief adviser, Chris Barrett, was already familiar with similar schemes operating in the USA.

By now, the summit group had done detailed modelling and costing on the NARI in cooperation with the Housing Industry Association and the investment funds. The summit group advised Swan that the maximum appropriate target for the first four years of the scheme was to build 28,000 affordable homes. Disney emphasised to Rudd, Swan and Plibersek that the program should build progressively from a modest base, not be expected to boom from the beginning. He recalls telling Plibersek that it was a new kind of incentive and a new kind of product in the market. It would take time to consult with major financial developers and financial institutions, especially superannuation funds. Meanwhile, Plibersek's policy thinking, and the impact of the housing policy community on her views, were reflected in her *Sydney Morning Herald* column. In February 2007, she wrote that homes were increasingly unaffordable. Federal government spending on public housing had been slashed and the states were struggling to maintain decaying public housing stock. Crisis accommodation was at crisis point, with 78 per cent of families seeking emergency accommodation turned away each night.

> Our approach to housing affordability has been muddled and contradictory for too long. Each price lever is pulled or pushed in isolation. We need to include all types of housing – emergency accommodation, public and private rental, community housing and home purchase – in our thinking; and we need an agreement between the three levels of government that will end the blame game.[6]

Three important summit meetings were held in 2007 as the election approached. The first, convened by Plibersek and Rudd, was in March and focused on homelessness. The second, convened by the summit group, reiterated its call for action, including the NARI proposal. The third, convened by Labor, was immediately before the election. Ideas discussed at these forums would later become policies Labor took to the election, 'including helping would-be homebuyers to save through superannuation-style savings accounts. Entwined with the housing agenda, and the acceptance of a role for national leadership, was Rudd's preoccupation with a 'new federalism'. Aided by coast-to-coast Labor state governments, he wanted to transform the relations between the Commonwealth and the states through a new series of national agreements. Accountability for grant spending – including on public housing – would be tied to agreed outcomes.

By the middle of the year, Plibersek was echoing the views of the housing policy community – that so-called 'demand-side' innovations, or policies to help people buy or rent houses – were not enough:

> At the end of the day we won't solve the affordability crisis in Australia without building more houses. Higher immigration and more people living alone and living longer mean we need more homes every year than we are building.
>
> Those new homes must include affordable rental accommodation, affordable first homes and social housing. However, this won't happen unless all three levels of government co-operate to drive reforms, and unless innovative ideas about how to pay for the expansion of available housing through public and private investment are implemented.[7]

As the year wore on and Rudd rose in the polls, Plibersek's fortnightly column became increasingly optimistic. In April she wrote about *Star Trek*.

> Why do people love *Star Trek*? Because it speaks of a future for humanity where poverty, racism and sexism no longer exist; where we deal with our neighbours (unless they are the evil Borg) with respect; where our basic needs are met; and where exploration, learning and the life of the mind are more important than Victoria Beckham's new haircut.[8]

She went on to attack Howard for failing to invest the proceeds of the mining boom in a better future – including through housing.

It was Wayne Swan who first told Disney that the NARI would be part of Labor's policy platform for the election, but when the policy was announced by the troika of Rudd, Swan and Plibersek in August 2007, the NARI had had a name change, and a change of ambition. It was now the National Rental Affordability Scheme, or NRAS. The summit group was worried by the change of title. The word 'incentive' had been carefully chosen to emphasise that the scheme was aimed at bringing in new players and new resources – not just another government welfare program. Another worry was that rather than starting modestly and building slowly, Rudd announced that 50,000 houses would be built in the first four years. That would be an immense challenge. Disney was told that the 50,000 figure was 'purely because Rudd said 28,000 is not big enough for a major policy announcement'. The 'pick a number, is it big enough?' approach to policy formation had apparently won out. The summit tried to get more realistic targets adopted but with no success. The unrealistic targets were, in Disney's view, very damaging to perceptions of the scheme, and gave the Abbott government a convenient excuse to dump it.

When, in Brisbane ten days out from the election, Rudd delivered his policy speech on 14 November 2007, housing and WorkChoices were part of a pitch that depicted Howard as having lost touch with ordinary working Australians. Labor would implement an affordability strategy that would 'keep alive the great Australian dream of one day owning your own home'.[9] There was a suite of measures: the special savers' accounts for home buyers, more houses to be built under a special housing affordability fund and, most innovative of all, the NRAS. Each new house built would be life-changing for the occupants but would also provide jobs for tradespeople and a massive kick-on economic effect, Rudd said. All of this was to be underpinned by a new agreement with the states – the National Affordable Housing Agreement, or NAHA – as part of a new cooperative federalism.

In a column the week after the election win, Plibersek reflected: 'Winning elections is one thing, governing another. The challenge of winning is nothing to the weight of responsibility that comes with deserving the faith the Australian people have placed in Labor. The new Labor government will, in the minds of many, be defined by its first achievements.' She wrote that Rudd was off to the climate change conference in Kyoto, and as a result his deputy, Julia Gillard, would be acting prime minister – the first time the nation had been headed by a woman. She finished by quoting US president John F. Kennedy's inauguration speech. 'With good conscience our only sure reward, with history the final judge of our deeds, let us go forth to lead the land we love . . .'[10]

This was her penultimate column. Her final, on 12 December, was about Jane Austen and one of her lesser-read works, *Northanger Abbey*. Plibersek made a case for reading novels, and for English literacy. She talked about Austen's heroines and what could be learned from considering their faults.

> Jane Austen's heroines are appealing (except, perhaps, the insipid Fanny Price) but they are mostly flawed. Emma Woodhouse thinks too highly of her own understanding; Elizabeth Bennet jumps to false conclusions; Anne Elliot has to learn proper balance between respecting the wishes of her family and being true to herself. No one can help reading these novels without asking, 'Am I guilty of the same failing?'[11]

Perhaps it was just a matter of available word length. Perhaps she did not see a newspaper column as an appropriate forum for self-revelation. But Plibersek did not reflect on the Austen heroine closest to her sense of self: the well-behaved, sensible, outwardly controlled and inwardly passionate Elinor Dashwood, and her beloved sister, Marianne, with her incapacity to self-manage.

* * *

Over the summer of 2007–2008, recovering from the election, Plibersek and Coutts-Trotter took the children for a holiday to the most remote part of her electorate – Lord Howe Island, a thin, crescent-shaped volcanic remnant only eleven kilometres long, a two-hour plane flight across the Tasman Sea and home to about 400 people. By some historical quirk, this island, together with some of the islands in Sydney Harbour, is part of her electorate. There have been many family holidays there over the years – paid for by the family, Plibersek emphasises – as well as regular trips for work.

Then she was back on the mainland and in the thick of things. The media were all over her. Channel Seven's *Sunrise* program was looking for a replacement for the team of Kevin Rudd and Joe Hockey, who had done a double-act on the program for years – helping to build Rudd's profile and political career. The plan was to pair Plibersek with the Liberal Party's Greg Hunt, who was then shadow minister for the environment. The segment didn't last. The pair were judged to lack the requisite chemistry.

But on her own, Plibersek had begun to be a media darling. In May 2008, she appeared on the first episode of the ABC's new program *Q&A*, in which a panel of participants answer questions from the audience. She became a regular panellist – after Malcolm Turnbull, the second-most frequent participant. She was also the subject of a long profile in *The Daily Telegraph*, in which she talked about the juggle of family, with Anna now seven and Joe just three. The author noted that in her Crown Street electorate office, pictures of the children were pinned next to policy notes, draft speeches and memos. 'Below one family happy snap are two small blue hand-prints – Anna's.' Plibersek told the author that her parents looked after the children every Friday, followed by family dinner. She said she had gone on holidays exhausted but had returned feeling like she had changed batteries. 'But in an area like housing, anything you do takes some time to make an impact. You don't build houses overnight, so I was very keen to get started as quickly as possible.'[12]

Plibersek set about establishing her ministerial office. She kept Monika Wheeler, who mainly helped with the women's portfolio. Another senior adviser was Pia van de Zandt, who had joined her staff shortly after the 2004 election defeat, when Plibersek was shadow minister for women. Van de Zandt had first met Plibersek at the NSW Ministry for the Status and Advancement of Women, where they had briefly overlapped – van de Zandt's first week was Plibersek's last. They met again early in Plibersek's days in parliament, when van de Zandt was working as a solicitor at the

NSW Women's Legal Service, and Plibersek asked to come along and meet the agency's Aboriginal women's advisory board. Van de Zandt was cynical, at that stage, about politicians, but Plibersek had stayed for three hours and had barely spoken, instead listening to the women and taking notes. 'She was desperately curious and culturally competent, and all of those things just really struck me. And I thought, Yeah, I just want to work for you.' They met again when Pia gave evidence to a parliamentary committee considering reforms to family law, and Plibersek approached her afterwards, inviting her group of law-reform colleagues to continue the discussion in her office – and provided them with an impromptu morning tea.

The chance to join Plibersek's staff came after the birth of van de Zandt's child and the 2004 election defeat. No vacancy was advertised, but van de Zandt wrote to Plibersek 'cold', offering to work for her, and was hired, initially part-time.

Van de Zandt is a Plibersek fan. She says she is often asked if Plibersek is as good in person as she seems in the media. 'I reply that she is better.' She admired the way Plibersek handled Joe, breastfeeding as she was briefed. And later, when Plibersek was a minister and van de Zandt's own four-year-old child was sick and had to be brought into the office, Tanya 'whipped a blanket out of somewhere and suspended it between two chairs to make a cubby and switched on the office television and held all her meetings that day somewhere else'.

Van de Zandt became one of the main members of Tanya's staff handling housing policy, focusing on homelessness. Another staff member (later chief of staff), Mary Wood, focused on first homebuyers and the housing market. Van de Zandt remembers discussions within the parliamentary party about why Plibersek was not in cabinet, but Plibersek herself was 'just was completely uninterested in those conversations. Friends of hers would talk about it. Sometimes political operatives in and around the office would be talking about it. And she just wouldn't engage. She was just interested in what she could get done in her portfolio.'

As her first chief of staff, Plibersek recruited a former public servant, Michael Woodhouse. It was a slightly unconventional appointment, because other than a brief period working for Labor in the lead-up to the election, he had no experience as a political staffer. His career had been in hospitals and in health policy. She made her expectations clear at their first encounter, Woodhouse recalls: 'she told me she didn't want a political operative. She wanted a bureaucrat ... Tanya was looking for a chief of staff who could help her develop a positive relationship with the bureaucracy.'

Plibersek put effort into the office culture. She hung a laminated sheet in the ministerial office tearoom. It was a copy of the poem 'If—' by Rudyard Kipling. Written in about 1895 as a form of paternal advice to the poet's son, the poem is another explication of the virtues of grace under pressure. Kipling, in line with the values of his time, saw them as quintessentially male virtues, but Tanya said to her staff that, leaving aside the gender-specific language, 'If—' summed up both how she wanted to behave herself, and how she wanted them to behave. No melodrama, no histrionics, no vainglorious ambition or ego.

> If you can keep your head when all about you
>   Are losing theirs and blaming it on you;
> If you can trust yourself when all men doubt you,
>   But make allowance for their doubting too:
> If you can wait and not be tired by waiting,
>   Or being lied about, don't deal in lies,
> Or being hated don't give way to hating,
>   And yet don't look too good, nor talk too wise ...
> Yours is the Earth and everything that's in it,
>   And – which is more – you'll be a Man, my son!

Her staff remember a lot of energy being spent on correspondence. Given her twin portfolios of women and housing, Plibersek was often getting letters from desperate people – women on the run from violence and at risk of homelessness. She would get 'really grumpy' reading the draft responses written by the public service. She would stand at the door of her office, swearing: 'How the fuck can anyone write this stuff?' Recalls Woodhouse, 'If someone wrote to her, she wanted the response to be empathetic, and directly address the situation.' Her ideal response was that someone should call the letter writer and make sure they were safe. Then, the written response should contain useful referrals to services. There should be a minimum of bureaucratic language.

Meanwhile, she fed her staff. Every few days she would bring in good bread from an artisan bakery, or lovely cheeses, or home-cooked Slovenian snacks. She would cut up vegetables and make soup in a pressure cooker. There were always cakes and pastries in the kitchen.

Moving into the ministerial wing, recalls van de Zandt, was like 'going from being a pauper to a king or queen overnight'. She had worked with Plibersek for years, but sketching out ideas in community halls, the Qantas Club, or after hurried phone conversations with Pisarski or Disney or one of the other members of the housing policy community. Now there was a cultural shift. She remembers being told by the public servants charged with assisting the transition to government that from now on, she must always address Plibersek as 'Minister', and never as Tanya, when they were in front of the public or stakeholders. It took some getting used to.

Housing-industry people who had had direct access to Plibersek's phone number when she was shadow minister suddenly had to observe proper process and make appointments if they wanted to speak to her. It was no longer good enough for passionate advocates for the homeless to accost her and shout at her about Labor's perceived inadequacies – as some of them had been in the habit of doing. Now, she had a whole department – the grandly named Department of Families, Housing, Community Services and Indigenous Affairs, which in theory was there to serve them and to help them implement policy.

Van de Zandt remembers being 'desperate' to see the incoming government brief on housing. She expected to learn things that had not been apparent to them in opposition. But when it came, the brief could hardly have been more disappointing. It was only four pages long. It was apparent that the incoming minister and her staff knew more about housing policy than the department on which they would now rely for implementation. Woodhouse recalls, 'We had to say to them, "We don't think you guys really know much about housing or the people involved."' In those first few months, much of the work involved transferring the relationships Plibersek had developed with the housing policy community to the relevant people in the department.

There have been reviews of Plibersek's time as housing minister both by the auditor-general and by academics in the housing community. Lack of public service capacity is a persistent theme. One academic review found that the public service had a 'basic lack of generic skills' in housing and that the culture was characterised by 'defensiveness and insularity'.[13] Staff turnover was high, there was no senior deputy secretary managing the area, and the department lacked both the culture and the skills to effectively roll out the highly innovative National Rental Affordability Scheme.[14]

Nevertheless, the Rudd government had a head of steam. In January 2008, cabinet approved the first home saver account pledged during the election campaign. In February, with interest rates rising, Plibersek and treasurer Wayne Swan 'improved' their offer of assistance to first home-buyers by announcing there would be a 15 per cent government contribution for low-income couples. A few weeks later, Plibersek met her state counterparts to begin work on what was to become the National Affordable Housing Agreement – part of Rudd's aspirations for a 'new federalism'.

In March 2008, the *Australian Financial Review* reported that the government had been in office less than three months but had already announced nearly $2 billion worth of initiatives to make housing more affordable.[15] Meanwhile, Plibersek and Rudd had announced there would be a white paper on the problem of homelessness, with the aim of developing a comprehensive, long-term plan.

The development of a white paper is a slightly old-school approach to policy formation. It is a systematic process, starting with a draft, or green paper, which provides an authoritative guide to a dilemma facing government, canvasses solutions and is designed to stimulate debate. A white paper usually follows – a statement of government policy. It's a process that can be driven from inside the bureaucracy or by specially picked experts and outsiders.

Plibersek chose the latter approach. She recalls she wanted a careful and deliberate process of policy formation because, with Rudd as prime minister, she had a particular kind of opportunity. He was personally committed to tackling homelessness. 'I didn't want to stuff up that opportunity by doing something gimmicky ... if complex problems had simple answers, someone would have done it already. Complex problems often have complex answers that have to be explained in a simple way, and that's what the white paper process allows you to do.'

She appointed a steering committee. Her choice as its head was no surprise. Tony Nicholson had been the executive director of the Brotherhood of St Laurence, and centrally involved in welfare and housing policy for years. Less predictable were the two other appointments. Heather Nancarrow represented a link between Plibersek's two portfolios of women and housing. She was the director of the Queensland Centre for Domestic and Family Violence. Plibersek was acknowledging and responding to the fact that a key cause of homelessness among women was the need to escape domestic violence and abuse.

The final appointment was Anna Buduls – a company director and philanthropist at that time unknown outside a small business community. Buduls had been propelled by grief into an involvement with homelessness. In 2006 she had been pestering her long-term partner, a tech entrepreneur, to write a will. He never got round to it, but he told her that if he died first, she should give his fortune to homeless old men. 'Give them rods to fish with,' he said. In other words, focus on ways to bring people out of poverty.

Three months after that conversation, he died suddenly. Buduls inherited a software company she barely understood and a considerable fortune. Hollowed out with grief, she began to act on his wishes, partnering with Mission Australia to fund the Michael Project, named after her partner. It was to provide long-term stable accommodation for men, while giving them intensive support to help them build better lives.

Plibersek agreed to launch the Michael Project. Buduls recalls an audience of homeless men, 'all in their Sunday best', waiting for Plibersek to arrive. Van de Zandt came early. Buduls approached her and asked that Plibersek not talk about her. It was only twelve months since her partner had died and she feared she would break down. 'I was still very raw,' she recalls. 'I wanted the launch to be only about the homeless guys. I didn't want it to be about this broad who happened to have money to spend.' Plibersek, tipped off, gave a speech that acknowledged Buduls, but did not focus on her.

Days later, Pia took Buduls aside and told her what Plibersek had been planning to say. She had been going to tell the story of the Mausoleum of Mausolus, built in the fourth century at Halicarnassus by Artemisia, who was both wife and sister to Mausolus. Plibersek had learned about the site from Diana Lewis all those years ago at Jannali Girls' High, and had visited it during her gap year travels. It was one of the seven wonders of the ancient world. Artemisia, Plibersek had planned to say, was broken-hearted when Mausolus died and built the mausoleum as a tribute, to help her survive her grief. Plibersek had been going to say that this was what Buduls was doing – building homes for the homeless out of love, grief and memory.

Telling this story for this book, Buduls tears up. She had no idea that Plibersek had engaged so deeply with her story. She has never forgotten it. Says van de Zandt: 'That sums up why it was hard to stop working for Tanya.'

The white paper process underway, the National Rental Affordability Scheme was launched in July 2008, with Rudd's ambitious target for 50,000 homes. Rudd expanded it further, saying that if the first tranche of homes attracted financing, there would be another 50,000 on top of that.

Already the problems with the department's lack of capacity were emerging. Even in those early weeks, it was clear that the cultural gap in the department was too large. The department lacked enthusiasm for the scheme and an understanding of how to implement it. The summit group pushed for stronger commitment from the top of the department and for more staff, rather than the handful of lower-level officers. It wanted vigorous promotion of the program to the business sector rather than waiting passively for applications from small welfare organisations. 'They were still thinking of it as a welfare program,' recalls Disney. Of Plibersek, he says: 'She was greatly hampered by stubborn resistance from key officers in her department. They and the all-powerful Treasury resented the fact that NRAS had been adopted by Labor when in opposition, before they could get their hands on it ... Their strong preference was to boost the Commonwealth Rent Allowance despite the fact that, unlike NRAS, it neither guaranteed any new dwellings nor any improvement in affordability. Instead, it encourages landlords to charge higher rents.' Disney says that external advice and monitoring was 'strongly resisted ... Despite repeated attempts, we seemed unable to get action on the key problems we raised, but it often wasn't clear whether our concerns had been brought properly to Tanya's attention.'

If the department was proving disappointing, Plibersek had other sources of help. The prime minister's wife, Therese Rein, a successful businesswoman, had made it clear that she wanted to help the new government with its agenda. Most senior ministers – already suffering from Rudd's tendency to micromanage – didn't want her involved, but Plibersek grabbed the opportunity. She recalls: 'Why wouldn't I want her involved, given her contacts in the private sector?' Soon, Rein was sitting in the office eating a cake baked by Plibersek, holding one of the staff member's babies on her lap and discussing how she could help. She went on to organise and host a series of private lunchtime policy discussions, including at the Lodge, bringing together the finance and building industry with the housing policy community. Academics would be invited to give summaries of their latest research. Senior people from Treasury would answer questions. Recalls van de Zandt, 'It got to the point where the state housing ministers started ringing us, saying, "Hey, I understand Tanya is doing these policy discussions. Can we please come to them?"'

Rein was also appointed patron of one of the burgeoning community-housing organisations, Common Ground, which specialised in housing rough sleepers using regular rental agreements, but with individualised health, support and employment training services on site – a model similar to that pioneered by Buduls with the Michael Project. Now, Rein had been brought in to be centrally involved in housing policy.

* * *

Amid all this frenetic activity, Plibersek's own housing situation had changed. She and Coutts-Trotter had bought a double-fronted, three-bedroom house in Rosebery – at the southern extremity of her electorate – in 2005. Now, their flat in Woolloomooloo was on the market, and when it sold in mid-2008 the proceeds were used for renovations and extensions at the new house. This was to become the family home and remains so today. The park up the road – only minutes from her front door – is the regular backdrop for Plibersek's weekend media conferences, announcements and photos. The back garden has a swimming pool surrounded by a square of lawn, and in pots outside the back door Tanya grows orchids, celebrating each flower. When they bought the house, it had an open metal fence. Today it hides behind a thick, high hedge.

And she cooks. Many people told me this biography would not be adequate if it omitted to mention her dinner parties. The living area that overlooks the garden has the furniture shoved to the sides so that extra tables and chairs can be brought in, and the food rolls out from the kitchen. The conversation is about literature, families, books – rarely about politics, other than the occasional comment on one of Tanya's media appearances. 'It is a generous place,' says Pip McGuinness, 'and extraordinary that she can do it when sometimes she is meant to be on a plane to Canberra early the next day.' The Plibersek–Coutts-Trotter family has help, of course – a nanny when the children were young, and a cleaner twice a week. But the dinner parties are Tanya's. On Fridays, she tries to get home in time to pick up her youngest child from school and cook a family meal. She says cooking is one of the ways she assuages guilt for being a 'bad friend' – so often away and too busy for catchups. Anna Coutts-Trotter rates her mother 'the best cook in the world'. The family and their friends come together around her meals.

* * *

Throughout 2008, the white paper on homelessness was underway. A green paper was drafted and put out for consultation. The draft, according to those involved, suffered from intervention by Rudd's office. But the steering committee regained control through the extensive consultation process that followed. There were dozens of meetings around the nation – over kitchen tables in remote Indigenous communities, and in homeless centres in the inner city, including in Plibersek's electorate. Plibersek attended many of the consultation sessions.

Nicholson remembers Plibersek as being unusually at ease with homeless people. 'There was none of the awkwardness or condescension that I've

seen with other politicians or senior public servants in the same circumstances ... she really showed great courtesy and respect for them.' He recalls
a meeting at a homeless shelter. 'One man was very agitated and worked up
and started flailing around and yelling. And Tanya just took his hand and
sat down alongside him and just de-escalated the whole situation by letting
him tell her about his life and his concerns. I thought that was quite skilful.'

The white paper, titled 'The Road Home: A National Approach to
Reducing Homelessness', was released in December 2008, a little more
than a year after the Rudd government came to power. As the introduction stated, it was the first comprehensive national strategy to tackle
homelessness. Homelessness was not only a housing problem, the report
said. There were many drivers and causes, including a shortage of affordable housing, long-term unemployment, mental health issues, substance
abuse, and family and relationship breakdown. The white paper's vision
was to foster a sustained, long-term effort from all levels of government,
with a view to halving homelessness by 2020.

'The Road Home' drew on the initiatives that the government had
already put in place, including the National Affordable Housing Agreement with the states and the NRAS. It proposed interlinked strategies to
prevent homelessness and the cycle of disadvantage, including bringing
together mainstream services such as Centrelink and health and employment services so that vulnerable people did not need to deal with each
organisation separately. There was to be a research capacity so that interventions could be measured against performance indicators. Lastly, a
new Council on Homelessness would monitor the program, reporting
to the prime minister annually.

Van de Zandt remembers the white paper being delivered – the culmi-
nation of a huge effort – just before the Christmas holidays. 'We all had a
rest at Christmas, and I got back in mid-January, and there was a phone
call saying, "Oh we need to stimulate the economy ..." And that changed
everything.'

The housing portfolio, already big and complex, already moving at
speed, was about to become enormous – the home of the biggest social
program of the Rudd government, and one of the biggest ever under-
taken in Australia.

*   *   *

On 15 September 2008, when the Rudd government was less than a year old and the homelessness white paper was nearing its final draft, the global financial services firm Lehman Brothers imploded in the United States. It was, as treasurer Wayne Swan put it later, 'a day that redefined the way we think about financial safety. It felt like the global financial system was ripping apart at the seams.' Credit markets froze. Investors ran for cover. What became known as the subprime mortgage crisis in the USA – in which the national government had to bail out big banks after mortgages went bad – had started a couple of weeks previously, but the collapse of Lehman was the day on which it became clear, in Swan's words, that the global financial crisis had gone from being 'a big deal to truly frightening ... Lehman's collapse downright terrified us.'[16] The world economy seemed headed for recession. The only question was how bad it would be, and what the Australian government could do to ameliorate it.

Rudd and Swan acted boldly. First, they guaranteed savings deposits in the banks, preventing any chance of a run. Then, with Treasury secretary Ken Henry, they decided on an immense stimulus to ward off recession – or even depression. 'Go early, go hard, go households,' was the motto. In October, money was sent directly to households' bank accounts.

Then, as the homelessness white paper was released, a second stimulus package was worked up. This one would be about infrastructure – government funding for building projects that could be done quickly, creating jobs for the tradespeople at risk of unemployment, and putting more money into the economy. Grants were available for schools to build facilities. The first homeowners' grant got a boost, with a subsidy of $7000 for existing properties and $14,000 for new builds. There were other schemes – such as the infamous pink batts insulation scheme, in which the government subsidised households to insulate their homes, inadvertently encouraging an unregulated industry to scale up quickly. That led to dangerous work, and deaths.

In the months and years that followed, all these schemes were controversial. When government tries to get money out the door quickly, mistakes and waste are almost inevitable. Every misstep made media headlines. But few remember that the biggest part of the second stimulus package was a national jobs plan centred around an enormous $6.4-billion spend on new social housing, as well as refurbishment of 2500 public housing homes that were becoming uninhabitable. The housing stimulus was boosted by land grants and more subsidies from the states. In scale, it was beyond the highest hopes of the white paper. The sector had almost stopped believing that government would ever again put serious money into building new social housing. The stimulus proved that it was possible. It was the largest single investment in social housing in a quarter of a century.

The reason few outside the housing sector remember the scale and importance of this program is because there was no controversy and few headlines. There were no stuff-ups and no waste. That was largely Plibersek's achievement – aided by capable people in the state governments' housing agencies.

It had to be done quickly. Unemployment was already rising. The near certainty of recession loomed. In just four years, nearly 20,000 new social housing properties were built, another 12,000 uninhabitable properties were refurbished, and over 80,000 tenants' homes were upgraded. This involved cooperative work with state and territory governments, multiple community-housing associations and numerous builders and tradespeople.

Wayne Swan comments that Plibersek's development of an 'erudite' policy platform was part of the reason that he and Rudd felt confident injecting so much cash into her portfolio so quickly. The rollout of the national housing stimulus was not a miracle, but rather the legacy of the hard work of the previous year. It is the element of Tanya Plibersek's time as housing minister that everyone agrees went well. Pisarski describes it as 'working brilliantly – the best program in all that stimulus spending'.

Verity Firth, Plibersek's friend from the NSW Left, was the NSW minister for education at the time. She was dealing with the state's role in the $16.2-billion Building the Education Revolution program, which involved constructing new halls, libraries and classrooms in schools.

The newspapers were full of headlines about rorting, inflated quotes and buildings that were next to useless for the target schools. Part of the problem, Firth says, was that the federal department was not listening to feedback from the states. Says Firth, 'The problem at the time was that there was a certain arrogance coming out of the federal government, but not from Tanya. She was always prepared to sit and listen to what the states were saying.'

Meanwhile, Plibersek recalls: 'It's hard to think of the global financial crisis as a stroke of good luck, but for me in that portfolio, it was. We had shown that there was an incredibly strong case to build and to repair public housing. And so we did it. We did it really well. We did it ahead of time and on budget. And there's a lasting legacy that I will, to my dying day, be proud of.'

Managing the rollout was a huge task. Plibersek tackled it systematically and calmly. She reported regularly to Swan and to Macklin. She kept big spreadsheets that told her on a weekly basis which housing projects were at planning approval status, or had had the slabs poured, or the walls up and the roof on. 'It was cooperative,' she recalls, 'but I had some pretty clear expectations of what was to be achieved, the time frame and so on. I think that was a very good way of working.'

Plibersek made a crucial decision in the first days after the stimulus announcement. She negotiated with state governments that three-quarters of the completed homes should be managed, and in some cases owned, by the nascent community-housing sector. As a result of that and the NRAS boost, over the four years of the stimulus build, community housing went from a cottage industry of modest projects to a substantial and maturing sector.

Adrian Pisarski considers this one of the best legacies of Plibersek's time as housing minister. Community housing in Australia today includes dozens of larger not-for-profit companies with sophisticated management, able to take on major development projects. In this lies the future of improving social housing, he says.

In 2012, a KPMG review gave the social-housing initiative a glowing report card. For every dollar that had been spent on construction, about $1.30 was generated in the economy. The program led to an estimated ten-basis-point increase in Australian GDP, and about 14,000 new full-time jobs. The program had been run so efficiently, KPMG found, that the number of homes built exceeded the targets by about 13 per cent. The homes, according to KPMG, were of high quality, 'with no discernible difference between private and social housing'.[17] It is the social-housing initiative that Plibersek prefers to remember when asked about her time in the portfolio. It was, she says, 'a really beautiful thing'. When she visits Melbourne, on her way from and to the airport she passes a development that provides supported housing to home-less people, built during her time as minister. There is another, similar development in Camperdown, Sydney. 'I know people who actually lived there,' she says. 'I have such incredibly vivid memories of the peo-ple that I met, who moved into places that we built ... People who had been rough sleeping.'

She recalls being in Adelaide with Therese Rein and meeting a man who showed them 'his beautiful little new unit'. He had baked a cake for them – a vanilla sponge – in his new oven. He took them to his bal-cony and pointed to the abandoned service station across the road and told them that he had slept there every night for seven years, until he was given his new home. She remembers the first family in New South Wales to move into a home built with the stimulus spending. They had a son who was profoundly disabled and had been carrying him up and down the stairs to a third-floor apartment and lifting him in and out of the bath. Now they had a new home, purpose-built, with lifting equip-ment and a bathroom designed to fit a wheelchair. She met a father in Melbourne who had been refused permission to have his daughters stay overnight because he had nowhere for them to sleep. Now he had an apartment with a second bedroom, and he could have time with his chil-dren again. Plibersek tears up telling these stories. There are plenty more of them. 'There's so many stories of lives changed,' she says.

The new homes – 32,000 of them, including the refurbished public-housing units – were a long-term addition to Australia's stock of social housing. Since they were built, tens of thousands of lives have been quietly but dramatically transformed because of the simple expedient of a secure home. Tens of thousands more people will live in them in the future.

The Social Housing Initiative was one of the big successes of the
Rudd government, and that was largely Plibersek's achievement – through
her preparation of a coherent policy framework, and through her sheer
competence in a complex job of management. It says something about
the nature of our national conversation, and of our politics, that today
almost nobody outside the housing sector remembers that it was done –
because there were no problems. That's how we value competence.

But not everything in housing during Plibersek's time was as successful. The social-housing stimulus diverted the focus of government
and housing providers from the NRAS, which was delayed in its development. The hoped-for big tranches of housing run by consortiums
with professional management never emerged. Instead, there were
small projects. Universities got involved, using the subsidy scheme to
build student housing. In principle, there was nothing wrong with that.
Students needed cheap housing too, and the summit group thought it
might help get some larger projects underway. But when up to half of
those units were occupied by international students,[18] it opened the
NRAS to attack from the opposition, aided by a pile-on in the pages
of Rupert Murdoch's *Australian* newspaper. The NRAS, in Disney's
view, wasn't rolled out along the lines proposed by the summit group
due to the inadequate encouragement of state and local governments,
a lack of high-level brokerage and tenders to attract major funders and
developers, and poorly designed rules about the selection and management of tenants.

Disney and Pisarski both attribute the fact that the NRAS failed to
reach its targets partly to a lack of capacity in the department, but also
to Plibersek's junior status and her lack of experience as a minister. Had
she been more senior and more experienced, they believe, she might
have been prepared to take external advice on the design of the program, rather than allowing the department to dominate. If the NRAS
had been better managed, Disney is confident it would have provided a
much larger and longer-term boost in affordable housing, to follow on
from the one-off of the Social Housing Initiative.

Plibersek at least partly agrees. She says that, given her time again, she
would work even harder to build the capacity of the community-housing

sector, so that it could have taken on larger-scale projects using the NRAS. She thinks the scheme was ahead of its time: 'I think if you came up with a new program like this today, it would be easier to explain to people, because big superannuation companies in Australia and overseas have worked out that residential property is an increasingly significant investment class to big investors.'

Of the 50,000 NRAS homes promised by Rudd, about 35,000 were built before the program was terminated after Labor lost government. That matched the pace which the summit group had predicted to Swan at the outset. When the NRAS was terminated, the number of applications for funding was growing and was already more than enough to achieve the 50,000 target. Plibersek says that if Labor had retained government, 'we would have built an additional 50,000. We were on track for 100,000.'

When Labor lost power in 2013, Disney wrote to the new housing minister advocating a redesign of the scheme to match the original idea more closely. He failed. Abbott abolished the NRAS in the first budget of his new government. Disney and Pisarski say that the finance industry was just beginning to 'get NRAS' – assisted by the new maturity of the community-housing sector – when it was cancelled. In 2019, when Tanya Plibersek was deputy leader of the party, Labor made an election promise to reinstate the NRAS, but Labor lost that election.

The Grattan Institute released an analysis that concluded the NRAS was 'expensive, inefficient and mainly helped those not in greatest need'. Instead, the Grattan Institute advocated simply building more social housing and lifting Commonwealth rent assistance. But plenty of experts disagree. Marcus Luigi Spiller, an associate professor in urban planning at the University of Melbourne, has said, 'There may have been problems with the NRAS, but the idea behind it – a scheme to leverage private sector investment – remains one of three key policy legs on which a strategy to address rental affordability rests.'[19] Disney says the Grattan report misrepresented the NRAS's goals and performance. 'It was a very regrettable departure from Grattan's usual standards of rigour. And by contrast with NRAS, its recommendations would have inflated rents, aggravated poverty traps, helped far fewer people in need and wasted government

Joe and Rose Plibersek on their wedding day in Sydney in 1957, and with Tanya in the 1970s.

The Plibersek family circa 1980: Rose, Ray, Tanya, Joe and (seated in front) Phillip.

In Turkey during her gap year, 1989.

With her parents, Rose and Joe, on her swearing-in to federal parliament in 1998.

Life as a backbencher and new mother: with baby Anna in 2001.

Tanya and Anna at a rally for the Sydney Rabbitohs rugby league team, 2001.

In Sydney with Tom Uren, luminary of the Labor Left and former deputy party leader.

With Julia Gillard and Jenny Macklin, 2013. ALAN PORRITT / AAP

With her mother, Rose, in 2013. ROSS SCHULZ / NEWSPIX

Behind the scenes at the 2016 ALP campaign launch. Left to right:
Tanya Plibersek, Paul Keating, Bob Hawke, Julia Gillard, Blanche D'Alpuget
and Chris Bowen. DAN DORAN

Campaigning with Bill Shorten in Sydney, 2016 – rescuing a rat delivered by
The Chaser team. JASON EDWARDS / NEWSPIX

Celebrating the 'yes' vote for same-sex marriage, 2017, with Penny Wong, Magda Szubanski and Bill Shorten. KYM SMITH / NEWSPIX

With Anthony Albanese at the Sydney Mardi Gras, 2018. DAN HIMBRECHTS / AAP

An impromptu debate with Craig Kelly in the corridors of Parliament House, February 2021. SAM MOOY / GETTY

In neon yellow at the 2022 swearing-in of the Labor government's cabinet, with husband Michael Coutts-Trotter and children Anna, Louis and Joseph.
AUSPIC / DPS

money.' Nevertheless, the NRAS experience influenced state government initiatives, particularly in New South Wales – and these kept the idea alive. Most of the independent reviews of the NRAS have endorsed the concept but faulted its implementation.

During the 2022 election campaign, Labor leader Anthony Albanese promised 30,000 new social and affordable homes to be built over six years, financed by a new $10-billion Housing Australia Future Fund. The houses would be built in partnership with institutional investors and community-housing providers. It appears that, as with the NRAS, the social housing will have subsidised, regulated rents. The scheme was included in the government's first budget. Disney says the Future Fund program will be 'potentially very useful' but that it will be a 'tragically lost opportunity' if it is not used to bring in new sources of funding, as proposed by the original NARI. Treasurer Jim Chalmers has made it clear he wants to harness the $3.4 trillion superannuation industry to the cause, and has claimed some of the biggest funds are 'excited' by the opportunities.[20] While this book was under preparation, Australia was once again in the middle of a homelessness and housing affordability crisis. One element of this was that the ten-year contracts under which low-income earners were able to rent NRAS properties at a discount were ending. Thousands of families who had been paying below market rent were being forced out. Some were at risk of homelessness.

In interviews for this book, Plibersek compared the NRAS to Medicare. 'Medicare didn't spring fully formed from the sea like Botticelli's Venus,' she says. It took time for it to become established as an unassailable part of Australian life. She believes that if the NRAS had had more time, it would have succeeded and become an accepted way of providing decent housing for low-income earners.

But the NRAS did not get more time, because the Labor government ran out of time. The move on Kevin Rudd by Julia Gillard and her supporters in June 2010 blew up fast, out of a groundswell of panic and personal animosity, fuelled by factional powerbrokers and made possible by Rudd's reduced standing – partly because of the relentless media focus on the aspects of the stimulus spending that had not gone smoothly. Largely to blame was Rudd's chaotic leadership style. Asked about this in interviews for this book, Plibersek declined to comment. She said she always got on well with Rudd. But her staff from the time and her colleagues say she was more than aware of the problems. Extraordinary pressures were placed on staff, with demands for briefings, then more briefings. Sometimes office staff worked through the night in response to requests from the PM's office, only to see their work ignored. There were extraordinary levels of stress in the days leading up to each housing announcement.

As a junior minister, and not a factional player, Plibersek played no part in the ferment that led up to the move to depose Rudd. Despite her close relationship with Wayne Swan, who was centrally involved, she was taken by surprise. 'I know it sounds weird, but I didn't see it coming,' she says.

On the day the challenge emerged, 23 June 2010, she was locked in a meeting room in the ministerial wing with her staff. She heard rumours that there was to be a challenge that evening. She commented to her staff that the rumours did not sound right. 'And several hours later, it became apparent that it was on. And I remember just thinking, "Well, that's it. We've lost the next election. Who's going to vote for a party that knocks off a democratically elected prime minister?" If you had asked me, "Should the challenge go ahead?" I would have said emphatically, "No, absolutely not."'

The media reported that Plibersek would back Rudd in the challenge the following day. But that changed.

Plibersek spent much of the night before the challenge talking to Jenny Macklin. They were both sick at heart. As the evening wore on, and both sides hit the phones and counted the numbers, it became clear that the result would be close. Macklin and Plibersek thought the worst result would be for Rudd to score only a narrow win, with Gillard moving to the back bench and continuing to agitate. By the morning, Plibersek had decided that, although she was against the challenge, she would vote for Gillard in the hope of making a quick and decisive change. Many others were coming to the same conclusion. Rudd records in his memoirs that at about this time, Albanese, who had been trying to shore up Rudd's numbers, visited him in his office and told him, 'You're fucked. And I don't think you should run.'[21]

There was no vote. Tears streaming down his face, Kevin Rudd announced at the party meeting on 24 June that he would not put Labor through the trauma of a caucus ballot. He resigned as leader in Julia Gillard's favour. Plibersek later discovered that Gillard had always assumed that if it had gone to a vote, Plibersek would have backed Rudd. Long after it was all over, when the two women were growing closer, Plibersek confided that it wasn't so. But mostly, Plibersek remembers, 'I just wanted it to be over and for us to focus on governing ... It was never the right thing to destabilise the leader. No leader, no matter how good, can win if they're being destabilised. I genuinely can't think of a time when [leadership destabilisation] has left us in a better, stronger position.'

Gillard's victory had immediate and long-term consequences for Plibersek and the housing portfolio, which, by now, Plibersek had come to love. Under Gillard's leadership, Labor lost its focus on housing policy. Gillard removed Plibersek from the portfolio and instead made her minister for human services and social inclusion. Housing was wrapped into Jenny Macklin's vast portfolio responsibilities. Over the remaining three years of the Labor government, housing had a quick succession of five different ministers, as Gillard reconfigured her cabinet and then, in the final months, Rudd returned as leader. Within the public service, responsibility for housing was repeatedly realigned and fragmented. By the final years of the Labor government, social housing and homelessness programs were in one ministerial portfolio, remote Indigenous housing and Indigenous housing policy in another, affordable housing in a third, and aged housing in a fourth. The capacity within the public service, never satisfactory, was atomised.[22]

Meanwhile, Rudd's new federalism also failed. By the time Plibersek was moved on from the housing portfolio, key aspects of the agreement, such as how to measure agreed outcomes, had yet to be agreed. That work was never done. When Abbott was elected, the attempt ended. The legacy, according to Pisarski, is that the states have been able to reduce their commitment to public housing. He says: 'The intent of having a broader agreement on housing affordability rather than a narrow "welfare housing" agreement was right in concept but in practice produced worse results.' He blames 'Rudd's insistence on broad outcome-based agreements with states and poor and rushed drafting'. In October 2022, the Productivity Commission released a report describing the agreement as 'ineffective', describing it as 'a funding contract, not a blueprint for reform' that did not 'foster collaboration between governments or hold governments to account'.[23]

There was one area of housing policy that the Rudd government never addressed, and that remains unfinished business to this day: tax reform, and in particular the Howard government's tax concession for capital gains and the ability for landlords to negatively gear investment properties against other income. Repeated reviews of the tax system, and Grattan Institute research, confirm that these tax concessions distort investment decisions, make housing markets more volatile and reduce access to home ownership for first homebuyers. Like most tax concessions, they benefit the wealthy at the cost of the poor.

People who dealt with Plibersek during her time as housing minister remember raising tax reform with her. She never encouraged them. She said there wasn't enough support in the party for taking the issue on. And yet without tax reform, government attempts to address housing affordability are like driving a car with one foot on the accelerator and the other on the brake.

Nine years after Plibersek left the housing portfolio, when she was deputy to the then leader, Bill Shorten, Labor took to the 2019 election an ambitious set of policies that included pegging back negative gearing and halving the capital-gains tax concession. In the recriminations that followed the 2019 election defeat, those policies were often blamed, and by the 2022 election the policy had disappeared. Labor instead presented a small target.

Was Plibersek influential in including those policies in the 2019 election platform? What is her share of responsibility for the ambition of the Shorten agenda, and therefore for the 2019 defeat? In the lead-up to the 2022 election, Plibersek was reluctant to be drawn. Facing my questions, she shifted in her chair, clearly uncomfortable. Tax policy, she agreed, is 'part of the equation' on housing affordability and homelessness. 'And we are going to have to work out how we balance the needs of the next generation of homeowners against the desire of their parents to own investment properties.'

So did she support the 2016 and 2019 election policies on tax concessions? And did she support the decision to drop them in 2022? 'I don't really want to talk about it,' she said. Pressed, she added: 'I recognised even then that it was a bold move to mess with the great Australian human right to own an investment property.' But, she says, largely due to her experience in the housing portfolio, 'I was prepared to campaign for policies that reduce the generosity of tax concessions in this area.'

Rudd and Plibersek aimed to halve homelessness by 2020. They wanted to make housing more affordable for both tenants and owners. Judged against those targets, they failed. When they came to government, it was estimated that there were about 100,000 homeless people. In the 2016 census, that figure was 116,247. Both figures are almost certainly underestimates. When this book was being written, housing had never been harder to afford.

A report by the Real Estate Institute of Australia found that housing affordability in 2022 was the worst it had been in ten years. Tony Nicholson, reflecting on his work on the white paper for Plibersek, says it is just as relevant now as it was in 2008. The long-term, strategic approach to tackle homelessness never happened. 'Any side of government could still pick it up, and you'd hardly have to change a comma,' he says.

Plibersek was one junior minister in a flawed government. Her work on the housing stimulus is one of the main reasons she is regarded today, even by those who don't like her, as 'competent' and a good manager. But critics of her time in the portfolio say she was more of a social worker than a policy innovator – a success in delivering a scaled-up traditional program like the social-housing stimulus, but less successful with an innovative program like the NRAS.

In Plibersek's career, she has repeatedly had responsibility for policy areas where the work is never done – where it is never possible to announce victory, or to declare a problem solved.

Ending homelessness was one she was given.

Ending violence against women is one she chose for herself.

7

WOMEN AND THEIR CHILDREN

Many of Tanya Plibersek's colleagues do not rate her as a deep or innovative policy thinker. The Plibersek-sceptics – the ones who say she is better liked among the 'luvvies' of left-wing Labor voters than among her parliamentary colleagues – make this point most forcefully. But even her supporters in the parliamentary party, those who say they would vote for her to be leader, given the opportunity, tend not to nominate policy innovation when listing her main strengths.

Asked for her weaknesses, the Plibersek-sceptics suggest that she can be 'prickly' with those she disagrees with, including the current leadership team. They point out that she has spent her career in portfolios that involve spending taxpayers' money, rather than managing the economy or growing national wealth. The criticism the Morrison government made of Anthony Albanese in the lead-up to the 2022 election – that he had never held an economic portfolio – could be made with even more force against Plibersek, should she ever be leader.

All acknowledge her empathy, her hard work and her communication skills. Her colleagues note the qualities she displayed in the housing portfolio, particularly after the injection of stimulus spending. They see her organised, systematic mind – dealing well with multiple levels of government, with business and the public service – and her ability to get the best from the people around her. But they also say she is not a big-picture thinker. After all, they say, the innovative policy thinking in housing had been mostly done by others – the housing policy community – before

Labor came to government. The work on childcare and paid parental leave was done in partnership with Macklin.

Plibersek is, in the words of one of her colleagues a 'bring people together, have a good listen, enable and persuade kind of person' rather than a 'big-picture, follow-me kind of person'. This does not mean she is not a potential leader. Some argue that the time for flights of oratory – for visionary, follow-me leadership – is over. We live in more sceptical times. 'To quote the great Tina Turner,' said one senior Labor figure interviewed for this book, 'We don't need another hero.' The same person pointed out that one of Labor's most successful prime ministers, Bob Hawke, was best known for managing a strong team, communicating to the electorate and retaining public support, rather than devising visionary policy on his own.

All of this commentary on Plibersek's policy credentials – largely delivered by men – tends to overlook her longest-lasting and most profound policy contributions, which were in her work affecting women and children. In particular there is her work on domestic violence and violence against women.

Plibersek says she can't remember a time when she wasn't aware that domestic violence was an enormous issue. She has a childhood memory from when she was very young. It was the middle of the night. Little Tanya was awakened by one of her mother's friends arriving in distress, in fear for her life. She can't remember the specifics of what happened that night, or how old she was, or how the situation was resolved, but young children sop up atmospheres like sponges. She remembers her mother supporting her friend. She realised that night that not all homes were as safe and loving as her own, and that some women had good reason to fear their husbands. It had a profound impact.

She recalls: 'I found it really shocking, because my parents had a very loving and equal relationship. It was traditional in some ways, because my dad was the breadwinner and my mum was the homemaker, but they loved and respected each other and all the important decisions they made together.' She recalls arguments between her parents as being 'lopsided' because her father would keep his temper, and her mother would get heated and emotional. 'But they really loved and respected one another.' They never belittled each other. The arguments were two equals disagreeing, and the conflicts were healthily resolved.

As she grew older, she watched her mother's friendship circle. There were other cases – women with violent, sometimes alcoholic husbands who seesawed between trying to care for their partners and running away to keep themselves and their children safe. There were few places to turn. The police were mostly not helpful and this migrant community did not necessarily trust the agencies of government. Rose, Tanya's mother, took the women into her home, and tried to help over many years. In one case, the death of a woman's husband was acknowledged as a relief for everyone and a liberation for her. In other cases, the women's lives, and those of their children, were blighted by decades of fear, physical abuse and coercive control.

Tanya draws a continuous line between her growing awareness of her mother's attempts to help her friends and her own time as women's officer at the University of Technology, Sydney. Some women felt pressured into having sex, sometimes with members of the teaching staff. As we have seen, on the remote Ku-ring-gai campus, nursing students feared walking to their cars after evening classes. One of her wins as women's officer was organising for security guards to be available to accompany women to the carpark on request. She had been assaulted herself, on the street and at social occasions. And, as her article for *Vertigo* revealed, in her late-teenage years she had a personal conviction that she would die from sexual violence. As a frustrated junior research assistant at the NSW Office of the Status of Women, she had tried to make a difference to the lives of women at risk of violence and left because she concluded it was not possible under the state Liberal government.

This, then, was the work of her entire adult life – the area she knew best and felt most deeply about. As minister for women in the Rudd and Gillard governments, she got her chance to make a difference, and she used it.

Julia Gillard observes that in government, politicians often find themselves working on things that have nothing to do with the reasons they went into politics, even if they are happy and proud to do them. But sometimes 'your position and your heart align, and your power in that moment is absolutely alive'. For Plibersek, Gillard says, that moment came when she conceived and brought into being the National Plan to Reduce Violence Against Women and Their Children – one of the biggest, most complex and systematic policy interventions in Australian history, and unique in the world. Twelve years after its creation, it has touched every life in Australia. At the time of writing, a new Labor government is devising a second plan, to cover twelve years from 2022.

Plibersek held the portfolio for the status of women at the same time as she was minister for housing. In other hands, 'women's issues' might have been relegated to second priority. Plibersek feared that outcome herself. She had at her disposal a small public service team, the Office of the Status of Women, which comprised about three dozen staff. The portfolio had languished under the Howard government. Morale, remembers Monika Wheeler, was low. In those early days, Plibersek addressed the office several times on the standards she expected. There was her preoccupation with correspondence, which she was also emphasising with the housing bureaucracy. And she pulled the public servants up for other errors, such as spelling mistakes in briefings and draft cabinet submissions. She was tough and demanding but rarely raised her voice.

In her first year in the portfolio, a new head of department was recruited. Sally Moyle had worked for the Australian Human Rights Commission and had known Plibersek for years. She arrived to find an office that 'had been run into the ground for so long'. Yet women's policy stretched across government. There was an infinite number of things the office could, and probably should, involve itself in, but not enough resources to do it all. There were also outreach activities with the broad women's movement and managing Australia's international obligations, including under United Nations conventions.

Moyle recalls that Plibersek was worried that the women's portfolio was everywhere and nowhere, that it lacked focus and risked slipping from the government's priorities, not least because of her own workload as minister for housing and her status as a junior minister. Says Moyle: 'She was keen to have an identified gender equality agenda. She wanted to bring structure and coherence to the work. To have some strategy and framing around it.'

Work began on a strategic agenda. The focus was a keynote speech, to be delivered at the Sydney Institute. From mid-2008, drafts of the speech passed back and forth between Moyle, Wheeler and Plibersek, with the framework becoming clearer with each draft. The result was finally delivered on 6 November 2008 – a little less than a year since the Rudd government had come to power, and the day after Barack Obama was elected as the next president of the United States. Titled 'Women and Men: A New Conversation About Equality', the speech began with a personal anecdote. Plibersek's son, Joe, now nearly four years old, had been watching a movie about the Second World War with his father.

> My husband said Joe was pretty interested in the tanks, but what really struck him was something quite different. 'Where are all the women, Dad?'
>
> Joe's view of the world is that men and women are essentially equal. He is used to seeing women as both carers and earners. He expects women to be everywhere – equal partners in all of life's joys and sorrows, including war.

She talked about the advances women had made

> The days when all women were ... automatically disadvantaged are behind us, thanks to the enormous effort over generations of many inspirational women, feminists, here in Australia and around the world.
>
> But just as Barack Obama's wonderful win yesterday does not spell the end of African American disadvantage overnight, the fact remains we cannot yet say that equality has been won.

She laid out her priorities for the portfolio as a series of challenges. The first was to improve economic outcomes for women – closing the pay gap, improving women's retirement incomes and achieving fairer sharing of unpaid work. Paid parental leave – not yet committed to by the new Labor government – was mentioned as part of this economic agenda. The second challenge was reducing violence against women. The third was to ensure women's equal place in society – improving women's representation in government and business, including through board membership. Lastly, she called for 'a conversation between Australian men and women' about caring for children.[1]

Much of the work on these priorities was already underway. The fight to get paid parental leave funded in the 2009 budget was being fought even as she spoke. After the 2007 election victory, one of Jenny Macklin's first actions, as the new minister for families, housing, community services and Indigenous affairs, had been to organise the drafting of a cabinet submission to set up the Productivity Commission inquiry that Labor had committed to in opposition. The inquiry started almost immediately and received hundreds of formal submissions, including many from families forced into poverty, or forced to delay parenthood, because of the lack of paid maternity leave.

When the report was released in February 2009, it was an emphatic endorsement of the case that Macklin and Plibersek had been making. Paid parental leave was justified not only to address the wellbeing of families and children, but on hard economic grounds. The commission recommended a taxpayer-funded scheme under which parents could take eighteen weeks' leave and be paid at the rate of the adult minimum wage. This, the commission said, would make it clear that 'taking time out for family reasons is viewed by the community as part of the usual course of work and life for parents in the paid workforce'. It would also 'counter some of the incentives against working posed by the tax and welfare system – potentially contributing around six months of net additional employment for the average woman over her lifetime', as well as increasing employee retention rates and reducing employers' training and recruitment costs. There would be huge benefits for families – better health outcomes for children and mothers, more breastfeeding with all the well-established health benefits that came with it, and happier and healthier families. All this was expected to cost just $310 million annually, once reduced social-welfare payments and the removal of the baby bonus were offset.

But the battle was not won. By the time the Productivity Commission report was released, the government was preoccupied with trying to return the budget to surplus after the big stimulus spending during the global financial crisis. At the same time, Macklin was also arguing in cabinet for an increase to pensions, after years of inaction had left many older Australians in poverty. The paid parental leave scheme that went before cabinet was a minimalist, means-tested version of what the Productivity Commission had recommended. Primary carers earning less than $150,000 per year would get payments at the weekly rate of the federal minimum wage for eighteen weeks after the birth of a baby. The proposal was to introduce the scheme from 1 January 2011.

The final cabinet debate on pensions and paid parental leave is now one of the most disputed moments in the history of the Rudd–Gillard governments. Both measures were hotly contested. Rudd recalls in his memoirs that there were 'acrimonious debates within the Cabinet about so-called middle-class welfare' when the paid parental leave scheme was discussed. He claims Gillard was 'the most voluble opponent' of the changes and that 'most of us in the cabinet room that day were stunned by the force of her objection'. According to Rudd, Julia 'couldn't understand why we were about to indulge a bunch of middle-class yuppies with a paid parental leave scheme courtesy of the general taxpayer. Why did they need this sort of support when there were a whole bunch of other groups in the community who needed it more?' He says that, on the other hand, he saw it as a 'necessary measure' to support families and encourage the birth rate.[2]

After Gillard replaced Rudd in June 2010, and when she was in the middle of the 2010 election campaign, she was blindsided by a leak to political journalist Laurie Oakes, who said his sources claimed she had vehemently opposed both the pension increases and paid parental leave. It was a damaging allegation, playing into the misogynistic view of Gillard as a hard-hearted, childless single woman. In her memoirs she alleged that the leak was sabotage from Rudd and his supporters. It was, she wrote, 'the worst bastardry at the outset of an election campaign that Labor has ever known'. She blames it for the fact that Labor failed to win government in its own right.[3]

Interviewed for this book, Gillard says she was and remains 'a huge, huge fan of the paid parental leave policy'. Macklin and Plibersek, she says, had done many years of thoughtful policy work and community advocacy, 'and it needed that lift to get it across the line. Tanya was central to that.' She says she was not opposing the scheme in cabinet but questioning it, as was her duty as deputy leader and a senior minister, particularly after a period of high government spending and the need to return to surplus.

Wayne Swan supports Gillard's account. He and Macklin had pushed 'most aggressively' for the measures, assisted by Plibersek. They were convinced that such important reforms should not be abandoned just because of the global financial crisis and its aftermath.[4] In an interview for this book, Swan said: 'There was this real question as to how many of these policies we could deal with coming out of the GFC. Can we do both pensions and paid parental leave, or not? Can we eat two big pieces of policy, in the middle of what was until recently the biggest deficit seen in a long time?' Gillard, he says, was only testing the arguments, 'as should a senior minister'. On the other hand, Marie Coleman suspects that Rudd's view of events is at least partly right. She had met Gillard during the long battle for paid parental leave. 'She clearly didn't warm to it. She might say she was just questioning it, but the only question she ever asked me was: how are we going to pay for it?'

Plibersek was still not in cabinet, let alone on the key, four-member Strategic Priorities Budget Committee, or so-called 'gang of four', comprising Rudd, Gillard, finance minister Lindsay Tanner and Swan, which was effectively making the big spending decisions. It was Macklin who argued the case in cabinet, and to the committee. Paid parental leave, Macklin says today, could easily not have happened. 'In a way, it is a miracle that it did.' Again, she credits Plibersek with much of the work of persuasion. The scheme came into effect, as planned, on 1 January 2011, after the 2010 election that had taken Labor into minority government. Later, in 2013, the scheme was extended to include pay for fathers and partners. In 2014, after Labor had lost power to the Abbott government, the Department of Social Services conducted a review of the scheme. It found paid parental leave had lengthened the time that women – particularly low-paid women – took off work after a child was born, but increased employee retention. Mothers felt better – less rushed and stressed – and were happier with their work–life balance and their increased income security. The review found that the scheme had improved health and wellbeing, particularly for the disadvantaged.

Many of the achievements of the Rudd–Gillard government were dismantled by the Abbott government, but paid parental leave was not among them. Indeed, at one stage in the lead-up to the 2013 election, Abbott suggested a more generous scheme of twenty-six weeks' of leave at the woman's full wage, with a levy on big business to pay for it. Plibersek opposed that on the grounds of cost, and because it would clearly bene-fit higher-income mothers the most. The Productivity Commission, asked to assess the idea, concluded against it and the idea was dropped. Later, in 2015, the Abbott government proposed making changes to pre-vent what treasurer Joe Hockey described as 'double dipping', by which some women claimed paid leave both from their employer and from the government. That idea was also dropped after it became clear it would not pass the Senate. Key crossbenchers described it as mean and stupid.

In the first leaders' debate during the 2022 election campaign, Anthony Albanese described paid parental leave as an example of the kind of 'big reform', along with Medicare and the National Disability Insurance Scheme, that only Labor could be trusted to deliver. The bat-tles that had to be fought within the party to achieve the reform have sunk into history. Paid parental leave has now become an accepted part of Australian life and is seen as an economic measure and workplace enti-tlement – not welfare. It could easily have been otherwise. Gillard counts this as one of the main achievements of Labor's time in power. Swan says he is also 'immensely proud … it was a big, big breakthrough and long overdue. We did the minimal scheme, but it sure as hell was better than nothing. It's a credit to Jenny and a credit to Tanya. It was bloody diffi-cult to do, but we got it done.'

Many women can take credit for that change. Plibersek is one of them. Macklin had been engaged, one way or another, in this battle for most of her public life. From her, Plibersek says she learnt the limits of passion and conviction, and the importance of patience and persistence. 'You can't just push and push. You have to chip away at the resistance, and that can be a lifetime of work.'

When Albanese convened the jobs summit in September 2022, there was resounding support for increasing paid parental leave to twenty-six weeks. The ACTU advocated making it easier for parents to share the leave between them, so fathers could also be intimately involved in their children's early years. A few weeks later, the government announced that increased entitlements would be gradually introduced. By 2026 parents will be entitled to twenty-six weeks of leave, with the right to decide how to share the time between them.

This is an example of the long, incremental path to reform – studded with half-measures and less-than-perfect schemes, rarely allowing for moral vanity or declarations of victory, but eventually becoming an accepted part of how the nation works.

*　*　*

At the same time as she was fighting for paid parental leave and implementing housing policy, Plibersek was trying to set up systems to carry women's policy forward. She emphasised to Moyle that she wanted to make a real difference. Whatever idea the office put on her desk, she would ask for a briefing on the practical differences it would make to women's lives. She told the staff she did not want to just 'tick bureaucratic boxes', and she didn't want them doing that either. Moyle appreciated the emphasis, but also urged Plibersek to pay attention to systemic issues, including bureaucratic processes, because they were essential if the office were to be able to fulfil its function as a catalyst of lasting change across government, making sure that gender considerations were factored into all areas of government responsibility. It was a continuing tension. Plibersek's instincts were always for practical examples and impact.

One issue highlighted this tension between real-world outcomes and systemic forms and protocols. The government was due to adopt the United Nations' Protocol to the Convention on the Elimination of Discrimination Against Women. As is the way with United Nations documents, the protocol was heavy with worthy language. Getting it signed was, Wheeler remembers, 'a very big deal' for the government. Howard, in keeping with his general scepticism towards the United Nations on human rights matters, had refused to endorse the protocol when it came into force in 2000.[5] The Rudd government's adoption was an important signal of a change of attitude to international forums – consistent with Rudd's signing of the Kyoto protocol and his emphasis on working as part of the international community. Moreover, signing the protocol would signal an acceptance that safeguarding and promoting women's equality was a key human rights obligation.

But Plibersek initially delayed. She pushed the office to provide her with briefings on the practical effects on women's lives. The first attempts to do this failed to satisfy her. She pushed harder. By this time, her attitude was causing consternation across the government. Senior public servants were pulled in from the Department of Foreign Affairs and the Attorney-General's Department to provide her with briefings. Her question to all of them was: 'What practical difference will this make to women?' The result was a detailed reflection on that question from across the bureaucracy. Finally, she was satisfied. The Rudd government acceded to the protocol in January 2009, after a parliamentary inquiry. Three months later, Plibersek went to New York to deliver Australia's country statement to the United Nations Commission on the Status of Women. It was the first time an Australian minister for women had attended the event. The job was usually left to senior bureaucrats.

Plibersek did more than attend. For the first time, Aboriginal women were included in Australia's delegation – notably June Oscar, now Australia's Aboriginal and Torres Strait Islander Social Justice Commissioner. Oscar and other leaders had founded the Fitzroy Women's Resource in the Fitzroy Valley, 2500 kilometres north of Perth in the remote west Kimberley. Plibersek hosted a screening of a documentary, *Yajilarra*, about their work addressing suicide and alcohol abuse. Elizabeth Broderick, Australia's sex discrimination commissioner, remembers the room being packed with First Nations women from around the world. She remembers, 'It was quite a moment in my professional career. Very moving. But also quite a moment for Australia. It felt enormously significant.' Oscar, meanwhile, thought Plibersek 'very genuine, very approachable and a good listener'. Because of her attendance at the UN forum, Oscar was able to lead side events, such as discussions on the impact of alcohol on unborn children in First Nations communities, which had little profile at the time.

Plibersek was also chipping away at the third challenge identified in her Sydney Institute speech – women's equal place in society. There was plenty to be done. When she became minister, women made up 57 per cent of the Commonwealth Public Service, but only 35 per cent of the membership of government boards. She set about correcting that. Her office maintained a list of qualified women who might otherwise be overlooked. As a result, Anna Buduls, who had almost no public profile before Plibersek had recruited her to the housing white paper, was placed on a list of recommended candidates for the Foreign Investment Review Board, and was ultimately appointed.

The situation in corporate Australia was even more dismal. The government had been collecting data on women in leadership positions in the private sector since 2002, but when Plibersek took the portfolio, only 8 per cent of corporate board positions were held by women, and more than half of the top 200 companies on the Australian Stock Exchange had no female directors. Progress was achingly slow. Broderick, as sex discrimination commissioner, was calling for mandatory quotas to be set for the private sector, with penalties for non-compliance. Plibersek took a different path. She used threats and public pressure. She reviewed the *Equal Opportunity and Workplace Act* so that it required companies with 100 or more employees to report annually on gender equality indicators, and made it clear that if they didn't improve, she might take further action. The annual reports were made public. Since then, there has been a steady increase in the number of women on boards. At the time of writing, 34 per cent of board members on ASX200 companies are women, and women made up 42 per cent of new appointments. There are now no ASX200 boards that do not include women.

Plibersek made other structural changes that helped to bring power and coherence to the many groups that were working on women's issues. She established $3.6 million in funding for six National Women's Alliances, each with a specific focus, including on economic security, immigrant and refugee women, and rural and Indigenous women.[6] It was a unification and coordination of the sector. Plibersek recalls: 'I wanted to make sure that women's groups were able to speak to government effectively, to tell us what we weren't doing well.'

Plibersek made advances in all the areas she outlined in her Sydney Institute speech – some incremental, some more substantial. But her single biggest contribution, and her greatest piece of policy intervention, was on action to reduce violence against women.

In housing, thanks to the work of the policy community, there had been a framework of action ready to be picked up and implemented by the new Labor government. Violence against women was different. For years, overworked, often traumatised women in fragmented and under-funded groups had been battling to help the victims of violence in a system that for most of history had failed even to recognise violence against women as a social problem. They worked in women's refuges, in legal services, in police forces, in hospitals and public health – but there was little coordination and no coherent government narrative. Different groups were often forced into competition with each other for scarce funding. They were ground down, often resentful and preoccupied with dealing with their small bit of this enormous social problem.

For centuries, domestic violence had been regarded as a private matter. The first public battles, in the 1970s, had been to establish women's refuges. In the 1990s and early 2000s, it was still common to hear conservatives suggest that these modest, chronically under-resourced havens were undermining family values, and that women were either to blame for or should simply leave abusive relationships. The women who worked in domestic violence were effectively engaged on the front-line of a never-ending battle – dealing with trauma, disadvantage, injury and death.

Properly conceived, domestic violence was the biggest health, human rights and law enforcement issue in the nation – and one of the biggest economic issues – but it was hard for the women at the coalface to lift above the all-consuming work to think about how violence might be combated in a systematic way – and how it might be prevented. Government action tended to focus on law enforcement, and that, together with the funding of refuges, was mostly a matter for the states.

Plibersek was clear from the outset that what was needed was a conceptual shift – for violence against women to be accepted as a national crisis hiding in plain sight, needing sustained attention at every level of government. She brought to the task the networks and perspectives she had formed throughout her adult life. As she puts it: 'I was very familiar with the people and organisations that had been lobbying for improvements. They didn't have to try and reach me through the media, they already knew me and I knew them, with some of those friendships dating from my time as women's officer at university. I had people that I could go to to test ideas, and I had been part of the relevant conversations for decades.'

In opposition, she had added to her networks. Wheeler remembers that whenever Plibersek and her office travelled for any reason, they would add an event that allowed them to visit and talk to local women's groups. There were plenty of ideas, but no neatly packaged set of policy proposals. Plibersek recalls: 'I knew that we needed to have both attitudinal change and legal change.' She had no doubt that this was a role for the federal government.

Beazley, prompted by Macklin, had in opposition committed a future Labor government to developing a long-term plan to combat violence against women, as well as to establishing a national council on violence against women and their children that would report to cabinet. In August, Plibersek gave a speech at the NSW Legal Aid Conference in which she addressed the view that it was for the states and territories to provide services to women and children at risk, and that the Commonwealth's role was merely 'informing policy programs and practice'.

'I think we can go a bit beyond that,' she said. The federal government had four key roles: education, 'so that each generation will be less likely to commit or be victims of violence as adults'; leadership, encouraging cooperation between governments; financial support through social security; and law reform, 'to ensure federal laws prioritise the safety of victims of violence and the best interests of children'. A Rudd Labor government, she announced, would create a National Plan to Prevent Violence Against Women and Their Children, developing 'a coherent national vision' to address 'domestic and family violence, sexual assault, child sexual assault and other forms of violence against children'. The plan, she said, 'will be long term. It will be accountable. It will allocate responsibility and set out timelines for change.'[7]

A week before the 2007 election, Plibersek gave more detail, announcing that the national plan would have as key elements education about
respect and investment in crisis accommodation.[8] The commitment got
little attention in the shadow of the looming poll, but these policy statements were anchors for an ambitious agenda.

Rudd, in turn, had a personal commitment to the issue of domestic violence, and Plibersek used that, too. In 2008 Rudd gave a keynote
speech at a White Ribbon fundraising event. It was unusual for an Australian prime minister to speak on this topic, and Rudd brought passion
to the subject. He said that responsibility for violence lay with the perpetrators – mostly men. He rejected victim-blaming and the idea that
violence against women was just part of the way the world worked:

> We often prefer silence to the confronting truth that nearly half
> a million Australian women have experienced violence from their
> partner or former partner. Well, we can be silent no longer. Because
> for too long, silence has been seen as tolerance. This is just plain
> wrong.

It was time, he declared, to have a national conversation and turn the
terrible statistics around. 'Because each of these statistics is a human
face. And it is my gender – it is our gender – Australian men – that are
responsible.'[9] International research had established conclusively that the
chief underlying cause of violence against women was gender inequality. But for a prime minister to state this in such rousing terms was new,
and a landmark.

White Ribbon was in theory composed of men who wanted to
combat domestic and family violence. In fact, much of the organising
was being done by women, notably the co-founder, Libby Lloyd. Three
months before, Plibersek had handpicked Lloyd to chair the promised
National Council to Reduce Violence Against Women and Their Children, which had been reconceived as much more than a small agency
reporting to cabinet, but rather as an engine of fundamental change.

Lloyd had worked with the United Nations High Commission for
Refugees in Indonesia and Iraq, and in Australia as a Commonwealth

public servant, mostly in refugee policy, before helping to restart the White Ribbon campaign in Australia. She had first met Plibersek when she was a new parliamentarian, and recalls Anna being changed on the floor of the office as they discussed how to get violence against women on the national agenda. She encountered Plibersek again at a Labor women's caucus meetings and remembers Tanya arriving fresh from the parliamentary gym in her activewear, 'all huffing and puffing and looking absolutely fabulous'.

The other members of the new council, handpicked by Plibersek and Lloyd, included frontline domestic violence workers, journalists, public servants and academics and survivors of violence from across the country. It was an extraordinary group – mostly women who rarely hit the headlines or gained public attention, all of them toiling away in their respective areas, but all part of Plibersek's professional network. Lloyd remembers it as a 'fantastic group ... the chemistry was brilliant'. Plibersek charged them with devising a comprehensive, ambitious and systemic long-term national plan. Remembers Lloyd: 'Tanya was always the one with the policy vision here, but Rudd certainly wanted to act. With her as the minister and Rudd as prime minister, the feeling was that anything was possible, and we couldn't let the opportunity drop.'

Lloyd recalls her work on the council as one of the most extraordinary times of her career. 'I've never experienced anything like it before or since. How often does a minister bring together a group of people with expertise and trust them to get on and do the job, and give them all the resources and liberty to do it? Many of us were working full-time jobs as well, but we found a way to incorporate this very hard work around the rest of our lives. We knew this was a moment in time, an opportunity that might not be repeated, and we had to seize it.'

Plibersek says today that she never doubted that government action could, and should, reduce violence against women. She regarded it as a problem analogous to getting smoking rates down, or stopping people from drink-driving. It was not only a matter of personal responsibility. There needed to be strong laws, properly enforced, but also an attitudinal change. 'I can't remember a time when I didn't think that those two things had to go together.'

The national plan would have to involve all levels of government and touch on almost every portfolio – from law enforcement to health. It would involve an agreement between local, state and Commonwealth governments. As the plan developed, Lloyd worked with the Standing Committee of Attorneys-General, which included all the states and territories. She thought it essential that the plan should outlast any particular government and asked for the opposition to be brought into the conversation. Plibersek told her, 'I can't do that work,' but she gave Lloyd her blessing to start conversations across party lines. Gradually, the vision – the idea that something big and ambitious and long-term could and should be done – began to permeate the national conversation.

The council released its report, titled *Time for Action*, in April 2009. It proposed that Australian governments should commit to a twelve-year plan, including a target for 'a significant and sustained reduction in violence against women and their children'. The plan outlined was immense and ambitious, spanning every level of government and almost every area of government responsibility. It was ahead of its time in its understanding of intersectionality – the way in which men's violence overlapped with other forms of discrimination and marginalisation caused by gender, ethnicity, Indigeneity and poverty.

The twelve years of the plan were broken down into four three-year action plans, and it outlined six key aims: communities to be safe and free from violence; respectful relationships; strengthened Indigenous communities; improved services for women and children who were experiencing violence; effective action from the justice system; and the need for perpetrators to stop their violence and be held to account. There was a focus on prevention by changing community attitudes. Central was the still politically radical assertion that the core cause of violence against women was gender inequality.[10]

The Commonwealth released its response to the council's report almost straightaway, with a commitment of $42 million to address urgent recommendations. These included the establishment of a new national domestic violence and sexual assault telephone and online counselling service (now known as 1800 Respect), the implementation of respectful relationships programs in schools, and the development of a social marketing campaign targeted at young people and parents. The report was referred to the Council of Australian Governments and formed the basis of a national agreement.

Australia formally adopted the National Plan to Reduce Violence Against Women and Their Children in March 2011. Its scope, ambition and foundations were unprecedented in Australia and unique in the world. It represented a national commitment to a long-term strategy to address a wicked, multi-faceted problem. Total expenditure by the Commonwealth across the life of the National Plan was around $723 million, accompanied by additional spending by state and local governments. But by the time the plan was adopted, Plibersek was no longer minister for women. She had announced the launch of 1800 Respect on 19 July 2010, just two days after Gillard had called an election for 21 August. The Labor government had begun its painful final chapter.

While drama, tragedy and misogyny engulfed the Labor government, the National Plan was implemented. New agencies were created and new programs developed and rolled out. As well as the national telephone service, there was a new dedicated research organisation, Australia's National Research Organisation for Women's Safety, or ANROWS, charged with producing evidence to support actions to reduce violence. Another organisation, Our Watch, was established to oversee prevention work, including working with media and providing training to employers and community organisations. Respectful relationship curriculum was developed and piloted in schools. A national community attitudes survey was established to assess whether community intolerance of violence was increasing.

By the time Labor was defeated at the 2013 election, the first three-year action plan – which was focused on building the evidence base and devising strategies for attitudinal and behavioural change – was coming to its end, and the second, meant to build on those foundations, was about to begin. Although the Abbott government dismantled much of Labor's legacy, the National Plan survived – or at least, the framework remained in place.

Under the new Coalition government, the women's advocacy networks were caught up in an attempt to prevent charities from undertaking advocacy work and they became risk-averse. The telephone counselling service 1800 Respect had at first been staffed and managed by the Rape and Domestic Violence Services Australia, an expert agency. But the Coalition's social services minister, Christian Porter, limited its funding and then attacked it for supposedly not answering enough calls. This was used as a reason to hand the service to Medibank Health Solutions, part of the insurance company Medibank Private. Calls were taken by non-specialists who would triage the callers, referring them on to domestic violence services. This added an extra step for women in crisis to negotiate before they could reach qualified counsellors.

In 2019 Our Watch was forced to take down a website offering materials about consent and respectful relationship for use in schools. Instead, the Morrison Coalition government funded an advertising campaign that resulted in ludicrous videos that failed to mention sex or rape and instead used metaphors of milkshakes and sharks to allude, confusingly, to issues of consent. Journalist Jane Gilmore – a specialist in the area – wrote in 2022 that Our Watch had become unable to criticise the government because it depended on it for funding. 'When Our Watch is being used as political cover for the government's ongoing failure to act on preventing men's violence against women, silence becomes collusion.'[11]

Interviewed for this book, Plibersek argued that while the Coalition government had maintained the framework of the plan, it had undermined 'the intention that we started with'. She talked about refuges that had been left wondering if their funding would be renewed, just so the government could make an announcement of money that was in fact already committed. An auditor-general's report into implementation of the plan, released in 2019, found that attention to planning and performance measurement had declined and was now 'not sufficient to provide assurance that governments are on track to achieve the National Plan's overarching target and outcomes'.

Nevertheless, much was achieved. The plan began a national conversation that remains underway. A national attitudes survey in 2021 found that Australians were more likely to recognise that preventing a partner from seeing their family and friends, controlling them through finances or harassing them via text message were forms of domestic violence. Australians are now less likely to excuse domestic violence as a loss of control due to anger or alcohol, and less likely to believe that women have a duty to stay in violent relationships for the sake of the family.

Social change of this scale and ambition is the work of ages. In the years since the National Plan was launched, the prevalence of intimate partner violence has remained relatively stable, and sexual violence has become even more common. But to use that as evidence of failure is to misunderstand the scale of the challenge, the nature of far-reaching reform, and the patient persistence needed to achieve social change. You could say that Rudd and Gillard failed to tackle homelessness, because there are still homeless people – more than ever. You could say Plibersek failed with the National Plan. But that critique, while it points up the urgency of the work, would be unfair. These are problems that span governments and whole societies. They are part of the work of reform that seems never to be done – which does not mean it is wrong to try.

Today Plibersek regrets that she didn't move faster, so that the plan could have been further underway before Labor lost government. Once again, Labor simply did not have the time. And that, she acknowledges, was largely Labor's fault – the cost of leadership destabilisation. But she points out that today, nobody suggests that a national plan is not needed. The debates about the importance of national action on violence against women, and the central role of gender inequality as a cause of violence, are over and have been won, she says. 'Support for these types of measures is much broader across the political spectrum ... I think most people now accept that this is a legitimate and even important area of activity for the federal government.' That was not the case when she started her work.

Thanks partly to the work done under the plan, there are now specific Law Reform Commission recommendations and reports from parliamentary inquiries that 'give us a really strong blueprint ... Much more is known about what drives attitudinal change among young people,' she says.

At the same time, new problems have cropped up. She worries about the 'saturation level' of violent pornography. 'That really was not a big feature of the initial National Plan because the internet just wasn't what it has now become.' She thinks such pornography is so all-pervasive that 'if we're not careful, there's going to be a generation of young people that can't experience sexual pleasure without violence or degradation attached'.

In opposition, Plibersek had been the shadow minister for women, as well as shadow minister for education. She and most of her colleagues expected her to keep both those portfolios in government, in which case she would have had the job of driving the implementation of the new plan and addressing the shortcomings. To everyone's surprise, including her own, Prime Minister Albanese took these portfolios away from her. Instead, she was made minister for environment and water. At the time of writing, Katy Gallagher is minister for women and shares responsibility for the National Plan with the minister for social services, Amanda Rishworth.

The government released the new ten-year plan on 17 October 2022. It declared an aim to end gender-based violence within a single generation – expressing confidence that this can be done through targeted action and social change. The new plan began with a powerful statement from a coalition of survivors: 'It is time to transform our pain into action. There can be no more excuses – that it is too hard, we don't know what to do, it's too complex. It is everyone's responsibility to end the perpetration of violence against women and children, and all victims of gendered violence.'

There was a commitment to a dedicated plan for First Nations people, and an emphasis on prevention, early intervention, response and recovery. The new plan also called for men to develop 'healthy masculinities'. In many ways, the new plan was world-leading. But at the time of writing, targets and measurements have not been provided.[12] Two five-year action plans, which will presumably contain more detail, have yet to be released. How will we know the plan is working?

Plibersek remains convinced that Australia can 'massively reduce the incidence and severity' of violence against women, but it will take a sustained effort over decades. 'It cannot be done in a stop-start fashion and it can't be done unless we are prepared to admit that gender inequality is the most significant factor in violence against women. And it requires bravery and leadership because as soon as you talk about gender inequality, there'll be someone pushing back and saying, "What about men?" How much worse would it be, she says, if it were not for the National Plan? This is the patience and persistence Plibersek says she learned from Jenny Macklin – understanding that policy innovation can be the work of a lifetime. Sometimes, it takes longer than that.

In her work on women's policy, we can see the fundaments of Tanya Plibersek as a politician. First, there is her empathy – her instinct, on seeing people in distress, to help. Second, and equally important, she believes in the efficacy and duty of government. Faced with a social problem, even or perhaps particularly one as intractable, complex and culturally embedded as gender-based violence, she believes that government has both the power and the imperative to fix it. In Plibersek's worldview, there are few areas where government should step back. You might even describe her work here as benign social engineering.

Despite all the problems, the National Plan has now touched the lives of almost every Australian. Respectful relationships curriculum is now compulsory in government schools in Victoria and New South Wales. Other states have also begun to include it. The media has begun its own conversation. Stories that once would have been written off as 'just a domestic' are now reported. Police can no longer expect to get off lightly if they suggest that women are to blame for becoming victims of violence because of how they dress or where they go.

The paradigm shift that Plibersek achieved was to move violence against women from the sidelines of public policy to the centre. This is perhaps her single biggest contribution to public policy so far. Much has been done, but the full story of this policy intervention has only just begun. The breadth of the innovation, its systemic nature and its impact were, unquestionably, Plibersek's contribution – and the main answer to those who don't rate her as a policy thinker. In this area at least – closest to her heart and aligned with her lifelong experience – the criticism doesn't hold up.

8

BIRTH RIGHT

The five-week 2010 election campaign was, in Julia Gillard's words, 'the election campaign from hell ... the political equivalent of one of those horror movies in which, right when you think things are as bad as they can possibly be, there is another shocking burst of guts and gore'.[1] When Gillard deposed Kevin Rudd in June 2010, Plibersek had predicted that the move would mean Labor would lose the next election. For most of the campaign that seemed more than likely. Tony Abbott was now the leader of the opposition, having replaced Malcolm Turnbull in December 2009, largely because of Turnbull's support for a carbon pollution reduction scheme. Gillard was Australia's first female prime minister, but any goodwill resulting from that was overshadowed by confusion and anger over Rudd's downfall. Labor had failed adequately to explain why he had been deposed. In the election campaign the party had not only to reinforce Labor's policy messages, but also establish Gillard's credentials. And all the time, she was being undermined by Rudd and a campaign of leaks.

If all this wasn't enough to deal with, Plibersek was pregnant. She and Coutts-Trotter had not planned to have another child, at least not during an election campaign, but the pregnancy was nevertheless welcome. She told the media the coming baby was 'a lovely surprise' and she and Michael had always wanted three children – a mirror to her own family of origin.[2] The child was due in October.

Plibersek was also facing sexist commentary about her pregnancy. Businessman and politician Clive Palmer was later nominated in the Ernie Awards – a satirical annual prize for misogyny – for remarking to a heavily pregnant Plibersek on the campaign trail that she could not get 'too excited in your fragile condition', and ABC Radio presenter Genevieve Jacobs got an award for services least useful to the sisterhood for asking her, 'Do you feel bad other people are raising your children?'[3]

Plibersek had not been a particular ally of Gillard in the past. She had been distressed by her unseating Jenny Macklin as deputy leader in 2006 and horrified by her deposing of Rudd. Despite this, in government she had come to appreciate Gillard's calm efficiency as deputy leader during the chaotic Rudd period. They had developed a good working relationship. Gillard recalls: 'People had a range of feelings about me and Kevin replacing Kim and Jenny, but I don't recall ever having a cross word with Tanya in any of that period.'

Now the rampant misogyny aimed at Australia's first female prime minister bound the women of the Labor Party together. Both the media and Gillard's political opponents made frequent reference to her hair, her clothes, her bum, her voice, her de facto relationship and her child-free status. Plibersek was 'furious' about the sexism Gillard was facing. Personal loyalty to Macklin meant her relationship with Gillard had not been close, even as they worked well together. Now that began to change. Partly, it was an acceptance by all concerned that Macklin was never likely to return to the leadership team and it was time to move on. But it was also a response to the sexism.

Gillard later told *Marie Claire* magazine:

When the sexist remarks started flying at me, I wondered if I was reading something into it and making it about gender when it wasn't. It was very reassuring to have Tanya alongside me saying, 'No, you are reading it right, it *is* about you being the first woman to lead Australia. She was terrific at that.'

In an interview for this book, Gillard said, 'Tanya is a very active, thoughtful feminist. She was very knowing about and very critical of the treatment of me and very conscious of the personal support that I would need. And she played a role in giving me that personal support, right through the time I was prime minister, and I will never forget it.' Macklin was also 'hugely supportive', Gillard said, putting aside their past bad feelings. Plibersek says she regrets not publicly calling out the sexism more at the time. She thought it would fade away and that Gillard's talents would silence the critics. Instead, over the course of the prime minister-ship, it got worse.

Gillard had believed for some time that Plibersek should be in cab-inet. She thought it a mistake and an injustice that she had not already been included. If she won the election, she planned to correct that. But as the women crisscrossed the nation on the campaign trail, Plibersek was wondering if she could cope with both a cabinet position and a new baby. The campaign was particularly gruelling. One day, she flew from campaigning in Hobart to Townsville. She was dressed for the southern capital in boots and warm clothes. In the heat of Townsville, she stood behind Gillard at a media conference and felt her vision swim. She real-ised she was fainting. Through sheer force of will she managed to stay upright until the cameras had been turned off, then sat down hard on the nearest chair.

Plibersek knew it was likely she would need a caesarean, as she had with her two previous children. She had always found recovery from the surgery difficult – and now she was forty years old. She was committed to breastfeeding the new baby for at least a year, as she had with Anna and Joe. During the campaign, she told Gillard that the timing for a pro-motion wasn't right. She would welcome a portfolio, but not a cabinet position. But it was understood between them that as soon as Tanya was ready, she would be promoted to cabinet.

Interviewed for this book, Plibersek was almost apologetic for this voluntary delay in her career. She doesn't want other mothers to think that they can't 'do it all'. But a cabinet position would have meant weekly trips to Canberra even when parliament wasn't sitting. 'It just seemed like a tip over the edge of what I could handle at the time or what I wanted to have, but I don't want the next generation of political women to think you can't have kids and have a career in parliament. I have done it for more than twenty years and it is manageable, but it is tough at times.'

Plibersek's earlier prediction that Labor would lose the 2010 elec-tion proved only partially correct. Labor and the Liberal–National Party

Coalition won an equal number of seats. The parliament was hung. The balance of power was held by the newly elected Greens MP for Melbourne, Adam Bandt, and independents Tony Windsor, Rob Oakeshott, Bob Katter and Andrew Wilkie. Plibersek's own seat was never seriously under threat, but she suffered a 5.91 per cent swing against her, ending with 43.29 per cent of primary votes; the Greens won just over 28 per cent of the primary vote, a 3 per cent increase on the 2007 result, closing in on the Liberal Party, which was in second place.

For seventeen days the nation was in limbo as Abbott and Gillard wooed the crossbenchers. Ultimately, Gillard struck a deal that allowed Labor to form government. The deal included commitments to reform in parliamentary processes, the establishment of a Parliamentary Budget Office and, as part of the Greens' agenda, improving Australians' access to dental care. The outcome was optimistically referred to by Gillard as a 'new paradigm' for the parliament.

Being able to form government was a relief, but the election result was a shocking comedown from the exhilaration and hope of the Rudd landslide in 2007. It was clear that Labor would have to perform a miracle to win another election. Meanwhile, the previous July, treasurer Wayne Swan had committed to achieving a $3.1-billion budget surplus within three years. This commitment to a surplus and the discipline it demanded set the character of the last sad years of the Labor government. Every new spending program had to be scrutinised, and most were rejected. Those that got through had to be accompanied by an offset to the new spending. The paid parental leave scheme was introduced, as promised. The National Disability Insurance Scheme was introduced – a big reform, one of the biggest that Labor would deliver. There was also a new model for school funding. But all proposals had to run the gauntlet of the Expenditure Review Committee meetings and searing cross-examination by the new finance minister, Penny Wong.

Despite the discipline, the surplus became a retreating chimera and was never achieved. The commitment had been based on a Treasury forecast that turned out to be wrong – predicated on an optimistic prediction of how tax revenues would rebound as the country recovered from the global financial crisis. Nevertheless, the government had harnessed its economic credentials to the promise of a return to surplus, and even as figures flowed in suggesting a surplus was unachievable, Gillard and her cabinet continued to talk about it in absolute terms. 'Failure is not an option,' Gillard said.[4]

The last term of the Labor government was a heartbreaking time as the consequences of the party's dysfunction came home to roost, and the likelihood of defeat in 2013 became a certainty.

During all this time, Plibersek grew closer to Gillard and to Swan. Albanese, on the other hand, performed an extraordinary job of gaining trust with the crossbench. As leader of the government in the House, it was his patient work that helped hold the minority government together, day by day and bill by bill. In particular, he negotiated with Windsor and Oakeshott to bring about parliamentary reforms. There were times when staying in government played out tactically on the floor of the parliament as an hour-by-hour proposition, and it was Albanese, drawing on his experience of strategic factional politics, who held it together. 'He was the absolute glue in the machinery,' Tony Windsor later recalled.[5] Meanwhile, Gillard, Swan and others were dealing with strategy and policy.

At the same time, although he says he admired the job Gillard did as prime minister, Albanese continued to believe that she had been wrong to depose Rudd, and that the result would be a disaster at the next election. There was some history to this. Gillard had been aligned with the Victorian Soft Left, back in the days of the factional wars. Albanese and Gillard had been antagonists since student politics, but this was well in the past. He recognised her talents. At the time of the Gillard coup, he had tried to persuade his colleagues to prevent it, saying, 'If this happens, we will be killing two Labor prime ministers.'[6]

As the months went by, he was one of those who did the numbers for Kevin Rudd, calculating the chances of his return. He has claimed he wasn't much involved at first – never leaked, never undermined Gillard.[7] Others dispute this. Some Plibersek supporters believed that Albanese was always undermining, and even suspect a succession deal between Albanese and Rudd. Eventually, Albanese declared his support for Rudd. He was open about this, offering Gillard his resignation. She kept him in his role for the sake of stability in the government, but in the final days, as she later observed, 'It got to the stage where it was not really possible for him to be completely transparent and truthful with me, as well as playing the role for Kevin that Kevin wanted him to play.'[8]

During this period, Plibersek's relationship with Albanese, the man to whom she had been so close, began to fracture. In the view of several of their colleagues, Plibersek was moving out of his shadow. In Rebecca Huntley's view, Plibersek was now more confident in her own judgement. She and Albanese had been on the same side in all the leadership agonies since Latham replaced Crean. Now they were increasingly on different sides. Plibersek was in a deepening alliance with Gillard. Albanese remained allied to Rudd.

Plibersek's role in the unrolling tragedy of the final three years of the Labor government can be divided into two brief periods. She held the portfolios of human services and social inclusion for sixteen months, during the period when Louis was born and breastfeeding. She then became minister for health – and finally entered the cabinet – in December 2011, holding that job for the final eighteen months of the government. Against the backdrop of a government on the way out, her personal profile continued to rise. By the time the government was defeated, Tanya Plibersek was being spoken of as a possible future prime minister.

On 9 September 2010, two days after the deal that saw Labor form minority government was announced, Plibersek wrote an upbeat article for *The Sydney Morning Herald* quoting Edmund Burke on the virtue and importance of compromise. The article was a marker of how far Plibersek had travelled away from the radical teenager who had resigned from the Labor Party rather than tolerate its compromises on her ideals. Now, she said, the deals with the Greens and independents may lead to 'a golden age of Australian democracy'. She celebrated pragmatism. Rather than leading to more timid government, she said, 'the contrary may be true: the government will need to be ever-mindful of strongly and consistently making our arguments in the community as well as the Parliament'. Gillard, she said, had a proven record as a consensus politician. As for the hope for a kinder and gentler parliament, that was up to the opposition.[9]

The hope was soon dashed. Abbott was determined to test the government's numbers on the floor of parliament at every step, and at the beginning of the new parliament, Plibersek was at the centre of that battle.

She was sworn in as minister for human services and social inclusion on 14 September, her baby due in three weeks' time. Under longstanding convention, the two major parties would grant a 'pair' to an MP who had to be away from parliament for health reasons, meaning that an MP from the other side would also agree to be absent. Plibersek had asked for a pair to cover the period in which she was due give birth. Abbott refused to grant the pair. Plibersek was forced to attend parliament in late September. She carried a towel with her into the chamber in case her waters broke. 'I was very, very pregnant and pretty uncomfortable,' she remembers. She told the media. 'Of course it makes me and any other woman thinking of having a baby anxious ... It will be very serious and very counterproductive if women [MPs] can't consider having a child.'[10]

Ultimately, and after public outcry, Abbott granted the pair – but only until her formal maternity leave ended on 31 October. As the political journalist Malcolm Farr wrote, the fate of the national government was so fragile that once Plibersek's baby was born, 'a bout of colic could mean the difference between bills being passed or rejected'. Plibersek had her final day in parliament on Wednesday, 30 September, went home that evening and gave birth to Louis Paul Coutts-Trotter on the Friday. She told the media: 'We are very lucky. He is a placid baby who is just adorable. He is like a little koala at the moment. Hardly cries.'[11]

That was only part of the story. Plibersek had had a virus that affected her placenta, meaning her 'little koala' was underweight. And, even more than after her previous births, she found the recovery hard. Nevertheless, days after giving birth she was receiving briefs at home. She had said she would only take three weeks of maternity leave, but it ended up being eight weeks before she was physically back in the office. Her staff remember her arriving in a welter of cribs, toys and prams, cradling Louis. Parliament by now had a childcare centre, with limited places, but Plibersek and Coutts-Trotter juggled the care of the new arrival as they had their previous children – with a combination of paid care, family support, and Tanya and her staff setting an expectation that if people wanted to deal with the minister, they would have to cope with the presence of a breastfeeding infant.

The human services portfolio was an operational job, rather than a policy role. It involved overseeing the operations of Centrelink, the government's social-welfare agency, Medicare and the Child Support Agency. Once again, Plibersek was reporting to Jenny Macklin, who as minister for community services represented the portfolio in cabinet. In the first few weeks in the job, while she was still at home recovering, Plibersek had to oversee the rollout of disaster recovery payments and emergency relief after a series of floods in Queensland forced the evacuation of thousands of people. She had Louis on her breast and the phone cradled against her shoulder as she 'micromanaged' the response, including insisting that all the government workers on site wear an identifying T-shirt, partly so that residents felt supported, but also so that workers from different agencies felt part of a single team, dedicated to the relief effort.

Human services is the kind of portfolio that only makes headlines when something goes wrong. The fact that the payments were rolled out quickly, and without problems or controversy, was barely remarked upon at the time but stands out now – after a very differently handled response by the Coalition government during the devastating floods of 2021 and 2022. Plibersek brought her management style to bear – setting clear expectations, checking public service work, and encouraging and demanding the best.

Plibersek's other ministerial job – social inclusion – had more scope for policy work. She inherited an existing agenda largely crafted by Gillard, who had held the portfolio before becoming prime minister. The portfolio was a Labor government invention – there had been no equivalent under the Howard government. The idea of social inclusion had been defined by the United Nations as 'the process by which efforts are made to ensure equal opportunities'. Gillard had established a social inclusion board that had produced recommendations, and this formed the agenda Plibersek inherited.

Gillard's status as deputy leader had been a signal that social inclusion was a major priority of government. Now its relegation to the outer ministry under Plibersek was seized upon by critics. Former leader Mark

Latham wrote that social inclusion was an example of a 'technocratic' model for alleviating poverty. The social inclusion board had had negligible impact on poverty, he wrote.

> Very few disadvantaged citizens in Australia would know it existed. Yet this could have been a policy area that animated the Labor faithful, implementing bold new solutions to social exclusion. At least under Rudd, the board had cabinet status, answering to Gillard as the minister for social inclusion. In the minority government, however, it has been downgraded to the outer ministry, one of the responsibilities of the ineffective Tanya Plibersek. Such a mournful reflection of modern Labor's priorities: Gillard spent three years supposedly working on social inclusion, only to sideline it as an issue under the so-called new paradigm of politics. Perhaps privately her conclusion is the same as mine – technocracy does not work.[12]

Technocracy, in Latham's use of the word, meant control of society by government. It was a hit at that core belief of Plibersek, and of most progressive Labor politicians – that government could and should intervene, both broadly and minutely, to improve people's lives.

Three days before she gave birth to Louis, Plibersek laid out her own definition of social inclusion in a speech to the Sydney Institute. She started by talking about Edward 'Weary' Dunlop, the famous surgeon who had inspired Australian prisoners of war on the Burma–Thailand Railway. 'Dunlop led by example,' she said. 'He insisted that the strong take care of the weak.' She spoke of Mary MacKillop, who was about to be elevated as Australia's first saint. 'MacKillop and the Sisters of St Joseph of the Sacred Heart … dedicated their lives to educating poor and orphaned children and caring for the aged poor and incurably ill.' MacKillop and Dunlop were universally admired, she said, because they worked to alleviate poverty and improve the human condition. But:

> Even people who admire these great Australians sometimes believe that similar efforts to alleviate poverty today are beyond us. They see efforts to make Australia stronger and fairer as naive or 'bleeding

heart'. So how do we apply these traditions of Australians looking after one another to the challenges that face us today?

Social inclusion, she said, aimed to reduce entrenched forms of disadvantage – 'kids growing up in jobless families, homelessness, people locked out of paid work because of mental illness or disability – by getting services across government and the non-government sector to work efficiently together'.

Social justice, she said, was not a charity, but a right: 'Education, a job, good healthcare and shelter should be the birthright of every Australian.' But with rights came responsibilities:

> [to] make the most of the education you're offered; to do paid or unpaid work as you can; to take seriously our laws and democracy, and our responsibilities to our families and neighbours ... We should think of social inclusion as mateship; egalitarianism; self-reliance coupled with the ability to give and accept help; our mutual responsibility one to another – the bedrock of our great nation.

Plibersek also defended income management, the scheme under which disadvantaged people were given a proportion of welfare in the form of direct payments for essentials, rather than having the freedom to spend the money as they saw fit:

> I make no apologies for this approach. Standing by and allowing people to blow their money instead of feeding their kids or paying the rent is not doing anyone any favours. Critics say this is not a long-term solution and that we must empower people. And I agree that the best solution in the long term is for these Australians to get a job, to learn to manage their money and to overcome the complex issues that have led to their chaotic life circumstances. But in the short term, the kids need feeding and the rent needs paying.[13]

The portfolio was the kind of job in which it was almost impossible to satisfy everyone, particularly when government spending was so constrained. Veteran feminist Eva Cox attacked Plibersek's work because it did not increase income-support payments. When social security was inadequate, it was 'indulgent' and 'abstract' to talk about other forms of disadvantage, Cox said, or to suppose that it was the government's role to engineer the details of people's lives.

Macklin recalls social inclusion was 'a really, really hard job' because it involved areas of public policy that were largely the responsibility of the states, and of local government. The federal government's main lever for poverty alleviation was the social-security system, but evidence from numerous studies, and the work of the social inclusion board, had shown that this alone did not improve entrenched disadvantage. There were regions, suburbs and towns where joblessness, poor education, poverty and substance abuse overlapped. Plibersek's main contribution, according to Macklin, was to 'think seriously about how the Commonwealth could most usefully get involved'.

The social inclusion board had recommended a tailored approach for locations with a population of 5000 inhabitants or less. The idea of place-based initiatives wasn't new. There were already such programs at state level. Now it was suggested the federal government broker agreements with all levels of government, with a single public servant in each location with the power to lead the effort across governments, with case workers assigned to understand the details of people's lives and help them find appropriate services.

Implementing this work fell to Plibersek. The result was a program called Better Futures, Local Solutions, piloted in ten areas across the country. The idea was to break the cycles of long-term social security dependence. If it worked, it would save the Commonwealth money in the long term, as well as improving people's lives. But Better Futures barely had enough time to get off the ground, let alone for its success or otherwise to be assessed. The work continued under her successor, Mark Butler, but the government was now in its last days. The Brotherhood of St Laurence reviewed the program in 2015 and noted that, as with so many of Labor's initiatives, the scheme was 'prematurely cut short following the election of the Abbott Government'. Today, few remember the program, and details about its impact are hard to find. There had been signs the approach was working, but there simply had not been enough time for the program to develop.[14]

A more lasting program aimed at lowering the barriers faced by disadvantaged people crossed Plibersek's two portfolios. She began the process of co-locating federal government services, combining Medicare, the Child Support Agency and Centrelink in single one-stop-shop offices. Counter staff were retrained to handle queries concerning all the services, rather than specialising in those of a single agency. It was a modest change for government – cost-neutral, and therefore possible even under the government's self-imposed financial discipline – but it was logistically complex. The change endures and over the years has made a big differences in the lives of people who would otherwise have spent time trekking between multiple offices.

As Plibersek juggled her new portfolios and her new baby, there were changes in the Coutts-Trotter–Plibersek household at the intersection of their personal and professional lives. In March 2011, there was a state government election in New South Wales. After sixteen years in office, the Labor Party, led by Premier Kristina Keneally, was defeated in a landslide by the Liberal–National Coalition, led by Barry O'Farrell. The new government was reported to have a hitlist of senior public servants, and initially it appeared Coutts-Trotter was on it. One of the first actions of the new government was to remove him from his job as director-general of education. But within weeks the media was reporting that despite his background as a Labor appointee, and despite his marriage to Plibersek, Coutts-Trotter had impressed the new regime. He was to be given a job running the Department of Finance and Services. Shortly afterwards he was moved again, to become director-general of the family and community services department, tasked with devising the government's child protection reform agenda and organising disability services for the NDIS. So began a pattern that continues in Plibersek's home to this day. The household contains a senior public servant for a state Liberal government and a senior federal Labor minister, with their areas of responsibility often overlapping. It involves a juggle and a high level of trust.

During the research for this book, I sat at the dining table while Coutts-Trotter scooped up NSW government documents from among the breakfast dishes, and Plibersek dashed behind him to feed Louis a breakfast of boiled eggs, tomatoes and toast. Says Plibersek, 'He has to know, and his bosses have to know, that even if he left some document or submission on the breakfast table, I am not going to look at it. And I have to know the same thing.' They claim they rarely discuss the detail of politics and policy. 'Our time at home is focused on family,' says Coutts-Trotter. They discuss the broad issues, but not at the level of what each government plans.

They were now, in the words of *The Australian* newspaper, 'one of the highest profile power couples in Sydney', alongside Albanese and his then wife, Carmel Tebbutt, who until the change of government had been deputy premier of New South Wales, and Malcolm and Lucy Turnbull.[15] They say they argue less these days about politics. Coutts-Trotter says they have each moved closer to the other in their views. Meanwhile, he gets satisfaction from the classic public servant role: giving frank advice and guarding the administration of government. Plibersek, he jokes, still wants to change the world. Yet compared to the young woman he first dated back in 1998, who wanted to get out of the car on the Anzac Bridge because he argued in favour of electricity privatisation, these days she has a pragmatic understanding of reform, and of the difficulties involved.

Other people think they can see Coutts-Trotter's influence in Plibersek's detailed, systematic approach to issues, and her concern with the on-the-ground detail of how things are implemented, over and above ideology. 'She approaches government more like a public servant than a minister,' says one. 'And she understands better than most ministers what a well-functioning public service should look like.'

*   *   *

As 2011 drew to a close, clashing loyalties and the legacy of betrayals continued to tear the parliamentary Labor Party apart.

There were some things on which Plibersek and Albanese were still united. The issue of same-sex marriage, which had been a festering sore in the party since Mark Latham committed the ALP to backing Howard's changes to the *Marriage Act* in 2004, was about to erupt. A lot of work had gone on behind the scenes by Labor figures including Plibersek, Albanese and Penny Wong. Now they judged the time was right to push for a change in the party platform, against the reservations of socially conservative trade unions, and against the views of the prime minister herself.

Before Howard's changes to the *Marriage Act*, same-sex marriage was barely on the political agenda. Albanese recalls that in all his years of activism on the issue of gay rights, 'nobody had ever rung me saying they wanted to get married and asking for the law to change. It just wasn't an issue.'[16] Howard's attempt to wedge the Labor Party had changed that for good. After 2004, twenty-three bills dealing with marriage equality or the recognition of same-sex marriages were introduced into the federal parliament, most of them sponsored by minor parties. Four came to a vote, three in the Senate. Ironically, Howard's attempt at wedge politics had made same-sex marriage a federal parliamentary issue. It was before the parliament almost constantly until marriage equality was finally achieved in 2017.

In government, Labor had kept the promise it made in 2004 to remove all other forms of discrimination against same-sex couples in federal legislation. More than eighty laws had been changed. But party solidarity demanded that Plibersek, Albanese, Wong and the rest voted in accord with the party platform, and against same-sex marriage, whenever the issue came before the parliament.

Plibersek was absent – still on maternity leave – in November 2010 when the newly elected Greens MP for Melbourne, Adam Bandt, successfully put forward a motion calling on all MPs to gauge their constituents' views on the issue of marriage equality. Labor supported that motion.

Gillard had declared herself opposed to same-sex marriage. This was widely understood as a condition of her alliance with Don Farrell, the socially conservative leader of the South Australian Right faction, and one of the so-called 'faceless men' who had engineered her challenge against Rudd. In late 2010 the issue became part of the campaign of leaks that undermined Gillard's leadership. One revealed that Rudd had agreed privately with 'key Left faction leaders' to back same-sex civil unions, and that he had also intended to grant Labor MPs a conscience vote on same-sex marriage. The next day, under pressure, Gillard announced that the Labor Party National Conference scheduled for 2012 would be brought forward by more than six months, to December 2011, to allow for a full-blown debate over the party's policy differences on the issue.

Meanwhile, Wong for the first time went public supporting a change to the party platform at the South Australian Labor convention in late 2010. The South Australian conference became the first state Labor conference to vote to change the platform to support for same-sex marriage. Other states and territories followed.

Shortly after returning from maternity leave in February 2011, Plibersek told parliament that she had complied with the Bandt motion and conducted a formal consultation in her electorate on same-sex marriage. She had received more than 2500 submissions, 89 per cent of which favoured recognition for same-sex couples. 'The prime minister has indicated that this issue will be debated at the Labor Party's national conference later this year. I believe that that is the right time to renew Labor's program to deliver this final measure for full equality for same-sex couples, and I will be making a case for change at that conference.'[17]

At the NSW Labor conference a few months later, same-sex marriage was up for debate, but no vote was taken – this was a strategic move to avoid a brawl with the conservative unions. Instead, the issue was referred to the National Conference, which Plibersek described as 'a vital step in the inevitable path of supporting marriage equality in this country'.[18]

In her memoir, Julia Gillard described same-sex marriage as 'the most explosive' issue at the 2011 national party conference. She argued that her position was not that same-sex marriage was too radical, but rather that marriage itself was an archaic institution. 'While my own reasoning and position were undoubtedly idiosyncratic, I nevertheless created the space for Labor to have the debate and resolve it.' This is indisputable. By bringing the National Conference forward, Gillard had allowed a genuine debate and airing of divisions rather than the stage-managed display of unity that would have been necessary had it been held closer to the 2013 election.

But, as the conference approached, it became clear she was likely to face a humiliating defeat on the issue. The party's two most prominent gay politicians – Penny Wong from the Left and Andrew Barr, the ACT deputy chief minister, from the Right – were to move and second the motion that the party policy on same-sex marriage be changed. Veteran political reporter Michelle Grattan described it as a 'pincer movement', with Gillard in its grip.[19]

Gillard staged a tactical retreat. Realising she would likely lose the substantive motion, she appealed for a compromise to allow Labor MPs a conscience vote rather than binding them to vote in line with the new party platform. Commented Grattan: 'Losing the conscience vote would be a disaster for Ms Gillard, who has put her authority on the line over it.' On the Friday before the key vote, Gillard appealed to factional leaders and senior cabinet ministers, including Anthony Albanese. They agreed to help her save face by backing a conscience vote.

The motion came before conference on 3 December, a Saturday, and the second day of the gathering. Ardent speeches were given on both sides. Plibersek told the conference: 'Every great change has a time and the time for this great change has come ... We must not say to gay and lesbian Australians, "You're almost equal and that's good enough." Almost equal is not good enough.'[20]

She knew, by the time she spoke, that they had won. They had the numbers. On 3 December 2011, the Australian Labor Party voted on the voices to change the party platform in favour of legalising same-sex marriage. While the numbers were not counted, it was clearly an overwhelming victory. Along with the core of Left support were dozens of Right delegates who thought the time for change had come. The long work of background talks, of persuasion and communication, had succeeded.

But then, in the compromise negotiated behind closed doors, a motion was passed 208 to 184 allowing MPs a conscience vote. Apart from saving the dignity of the prime minister, many – including Albanese – were convinced to back this policy because they knew some Labor parliamentarians would cross the floor in any case, meaning they would then be expelled from the party unless they were allowed a conscience vote. Plibersek was of a different view. She said in interviews for this book that she understands the need for a conscience vote on abortion and euthanasia – matters of life and death. But when it comes to same-sex marriage, 'It is a slightly different relationship with faith. Nobody was ever asking the Catholic Church, for example, to solemnise same-sex marriages, or for any religious organisation to change anything they were doing ... so I thought that the essential argument about equality before the law meant that the Labor Party should commit to this, and expect its MPs to vote the platform. Do we have a conscience vote about whether we allow racism in our community? Do we have a conscience vote on whether we allow sexism or ageism? We don't.' But for now, the giant advance in changing the party platform was qualified.

Gillard was saved from an embarrassing defeat, but the limits of her authority were exposed. She now led a party with a policy on gay marriage that she did not support. Although Plibersek was against the conscience vote, she fell into line and applauded the result, telling the ABC's *Insiders* program: 'This is a huge step forward from where we were at the last ALP national conference, where even the idea of civil unions or a conscience vote on civil unions seemed beyond our reach.'

There were other issues at the conference that demonstrated how Plibersek, who had once resigned from the party rather than compromise her ideals, had matured into compromise. The conference had debated the offshore processing of asylum seekers and the sale of uranium to India – both of which Plibersek opposed, and on which she was defeated. But, she told *Insiders*, all this was a sign of the health of the Australian Labor Party – not a reason to retreat, but rather to step forward. 'I think it shows what a strong, vibrant, thoughtful party culture we have,' she said. 'It also shows, frankly, that if you want to influence what Labor governments do, you should join the Labor Party. And the victory that branch members had yesterday on the issue of marriage equality is just one example where campaigning within the Labor Party has made all the difference to what will happen in public.'[21]

The change to the party platform freed Plibersek to vote with her personal convictions. In February 2012, when Labor MP Stephen Jones brought a private member's bill to legalise same-sex marriage before the parliament, she voted in favour, together with thirty-seven of her fellow Labor parliamentarians. The bill was defeated. Tony Abbott, vehemently opposed, had refused to grant his party a conscience vote and together with twenty-six Labor parliamentarians, including Gillard, their votes were enough to defeat it. Other attempts followed throughout 2012, with similar results. It was a deadlock. Either the Liberal Party had to grant a conscience vote to its MPs, or Labor had to disallow one. Until then, same-sex marriage would not exist in Australian law.

Weeks after her near humiliation at the national conference, Gillard reshuffled her ministry. This was widely reported as an attempt to shore up her position as Rudd continued to agitate, and the polls showed the Labor government's support had tanked. Gillard had given poor polling as one of the reasons for her move on Rudd in 2010, but now her numbers were far worse than his had been. Abbott had reclaimed his lead as preferred prime minister.

In the reshuffle, Plibersek at last entered cabinet. It was, the commentators agreed, long overdue. Plibersek was 'seen as a very capable pair of hands, someone who's calm and very measured'.[22] She was noted as being one of the government's best communicators. Plibersek had indicated to Gillard that with Louis now more than a year old and weaned, she was ready for a cabinet role. She remembers her conversation with Gillard as being 'very simple. She offered me the health portfolio and I said, "Yes, please. Thank you very much."' Plibersek replaced Nicola Roxon, who was now to be attorney-general. Health was, as Gillard puts it, 'together with education, the lifeblood of Labor ... I thought she was the perfect person to carry that forward.' It was a big promotion. In terms of seniority, Plibersek was now on an equal footing to Albanese, who was minister for infrastructure. It was, in the words of one of their colleagues, 'the sorcerer's apprentice becoming the sorcerer ... he probably always had in his mind a relationship where he was the senior figure and she was doing well, but one rung below him. Now she was on the same rung.' Her rise meant the old structural problem – the fact that they came from the same faction and the same area of Sydney – began to rub. In any future contest over the ALP's leadership team, only one of them could prosper.

The year 2012 was a continuing nightmare for the Gillard government, even as it continued to pass legislation and introduce reforms. But against the backdrop of that dysfunction, Plibersek's personal profile continued to grow. In March, she featured in the first series of a new program on the ABC, *Kitchen Cabinet*, anchored by journalist Annabel Crabb. The format was for a federal politician to cook a meal for Crabb in the politician's home, while she provided dessert. As the cooking and eating proceeded, Crabb would quiz them about their personal history and their politics. When the format worked, it was revealing. When it failed, it was because of its stagey nature, and sometimes the suspicion that the politician never cooked in real life.

Plibersek the accomplished cook didn't have to fake it. She greeted Crabb at the door of the Rosebery family home and served an entrée of olives cooked in a cheesy short pastry. Plibersek explained she always made the pastry in double quantities, freezing half. Then freshly baked snacks could be provided at short notice simply by defrosting balls of the pastry in the hand and wrapping them around the olives before baking.

Also on the menu were zucchini flowers stuffed with breadcrumbs, ricotta, Manchego cheese, anchovies and fresh herbs from the garden. Over a main course of pasta with ocean trout – the fish tossed raw through the steaming noodles with ginger and chilli – Plibersek talked about her frequent trips back to Slovenia. She was more famous there than she was in Australia, she said, because Slovenians celebrated the achievements of the expatriate community.

Crabb quizzed Plibersek about the Labor Party's factions. How could it be that Rudd had been rolled by the Right, even though he was of the Right? And that Gillard was supported by the Right, even though she was of the Left? Plibesek said she thought the factions were of less consequence now. When she had entered parliament, they had been driven by a mix of ideology, but also by personalities. Now there was more 'enquiry and flexibility on policy issues'. She was referring to the party's trajectory, but she could equally have been describing her own.

Then the two women moved on to Crabb's dessert – a roasted strawberry cheesecake with a gingernut crust.

*   *   *

A few weeks after *Kitchen Cabinet*, on 11 April 2012, Joe Plibersek, Tanya's father, died in hospital, after being nursed for months in the house he had built at Oyster Bay. A few years before, he had been diagnosed with an aggressive form of prostate cancer. It had already spread to his blood and bones when he was diagnosed. It was a death sentence. There was, Plibersek recalls, lots of time to say goodbye. In that way, it was not as traumatic as the loss of Phillip had been, twenty-four years before. But the grief was sharp. In his last days, her father cried because he realised he would never know his youngest grandson, Louis. 'It was possible to see what kind of people Anna and Joe were going to be,' she says. 'He had a sense of that. But he realised he would never know what kind of person Louis was.'

Later, in 2015, Plibersek wrote an article for the online women's magazine *Mamamia* about her father's death. She said he had been a strong advocate of euthanasia, and in his final days had refused treatment that might have prolonged his life.

> I wasn't ready to lose my dad. I don't think I ever would have been. But I was able to respect his decision to refuse further treatment. I could see how weak he was physically, how difficult the blood transfusions had become, and how he hated not being able to walk to the bathroom. I could respect his decision because he had told me so clearly that when the time came, I had to let him go … My beautiful father fought cancer bravely … he didn't, in the end, reach for the large bottle of morphine he'd been given to manage his pain. It sat at home in the refrigerator, used sparingly, a drop at a time, as he traded off pain for the lucidity he wanted as he said his good-byes.[23]

Joseph Plibersek's memorial service was held at St Patrick's – the same church in which Tanya had been married and Phillip memorialised. He was cremated, and his ashes buried alongside those of Phillip in the Roman Catholic section of Woronora Memorial Park in the Sutherland Shire, in the heart of quintessential Australian suburbia. The park overlooks the Woronora River, its name drawn from the Dharug language of the traditional owners. It is about as far as it is possible to imagine from the mountains of Slovenia.

Joseph Plibersek had arrived in Australia with nothing. He had lived long enough to see the infant who had fallen asleep on his lap as they

watched the news sworn in as a senior cabinet minister and talked of
as a potential future prime minister. His death notice listed five grand-
children – Tanya's three plus her brother Ray's two. Raised in trauma,
with little love or opportunity and no security, he had delivered all those
things and more to his children and grandchildren.

I asked someone close to Tanya Plibersek if there was anything I was
missing about her. They replied that this book would be at fault if it did
not talk about her patriotism – her belief in the Australian dream, as
exemplified by her parents' story. She is not nationalistic, they said, let
alone jingoistic. She believes in talking about the dark parts of Australia's past. But she tears up when talking about the idea of the nation – its
promise. She believes in our obligations to it, and the need for loyalty.

In her Sydney Institute speech outlining her agenda for the social
inclusion portfolio, Plibersek advocated for Australian schoolchildren
being taught to recite the citizenship pledge. She said she loved going to
citizenship ceremonies because of the 'bravery and optimism' of new citizens. Moving to a new country was, she said, like having a second child.

> When you have your first child, you think it's impossible to love
> another child as much as this first one. And yet when that second
> child is born, your heart expands and your love is doubled.
>
> I tear up when I see new citizens take the oath or the pledge,
> and I tear up when I have that opportunity during citizenship cer-
> emonies to repeat the pledge myself.[24]

And she recited it: 'From this time forward, I pledge my loyalty to
Australia and its people, whose democratic beliefs I share, whose rights
and liberties I respect, and whose laws I will uphold and obey.'

Australians, she said, should know it by heart, and say it often.

9

END OF GOVERNMENT

f it was true that Plibersek was more famous in Slovenia than in Australia when Crabb ate her pasta and ocean trout, it didn't remain true
for long. At intervals throughout 2012, surveys showed she was one
of the most recognised political names in Australia. She appeared frequently on the ABC's late-night news program *Lateline*, using her human
touch to defuse situations. When, in February, a video was leaked showing Rudd swearing like a trooper – part of the ongoing fights between
Gillard and Rudd supporters – Plibersek tackled the moment with a
quip: 'I'm glad there's no camera on me when I am driving.'[1]

That year there were several lengthy newspaper profiles, including a cover story in *Good Weekend* magazine by Anne Summers, under
the headline 'Cool, calm, elected'. Summers noted Plibersek's frequent
appearances on the ABC's *Q&A* program and extracted a confession –
despite her calm articulateness, Plibersek found *Q&A* a nerve-racking
experience. 'On Monday nights, "I hear the music and I feel sick and
nervous in the same way as when I am on,"' Plibersek told Summers.
But '[s]he continues to do it, not because it's enjoyable – it isn't – but "it
is a great opportunity to talk about what we are doing." Summers noted
that Plibersek had a passionate following, that people used the words like
'adore' and 'love' when describing her, but that she had been described by
others as 'a complete fake', 'a show pony', 'completely lazy', as having 'no
personal loyalty' and as 'totally nutty – there's nothing she wouldn't do'.[2]

Earlier in the year, veteran Canberra political observer Richard
Farmer had praised Plibersek's 'soft-spoken forcefulness' on television
and described her appearances on *Lateline* as 'a first-rate performance
by a politician of increasing stature'. Even the government's critics were

giving backhanded compliments. *The Australian*'s right-wing columnist Janet Albrechtsen wrote in September 2012 that Plibersek 'has a
gift for sounding wonderfully articulate and perfectly measured even
when saying the most ridiculous things'. She was commenting on one
of Plibersek's appearances on *Insiders*, in which she had promised to cut
waste from the health budget.

> Either the Health Minister believes in Utopia and a federal Fairy
> Godmother or she is taking voters for fools. Either way, it's surely
> time for a refresher course in first principles when it comes to the
> fate of taxpayer dollars.[3]

But Albrechtsen arguably did Plibersek a disservice.

It is true that the bulk of Plibersek's ministerial experience has been
in big-spending, interventionist portfolios of government, but in her
short time in the health portfolio she showed a capacity to nip and tuck,
to take on vested interests and to save government money, as well as
spending it on important reform.

As the new health minister, Plibersek entered a field littered with
the remnants of Rudd's ambitious attempts to stop blame-shifting and
cost-shifting between state and federal governments. He had promised,
during the 2007 election campaign, to 'fix' this within two years. If it
didn't improve, he said he'd hold a referendum to allow the federal government to take responsibility for public hospitals. From then on, health
had been at the centre of Rudd's reformist zeal. But the history of health
reform is another contested area in the recollections of Rudd and Gillard.

Rudd envisaged fundamental reform by which the Commonwealth
would become the majority funder of Australian public hospitals, and
hospital management would devolve to local networks that would work
closely with GPs and other services to overcome the fracture between
Medicare-funded healthcare and state-funded hospitals. Hospitals would
be funded not with block grants delivered through state government, but
directly by the Commonwealth, on the basis of a nationally set price for
each service they provided. The 'glue' holding all this together was to be a
system of patient-controlled electronic health records, so that the various

parts of the system had access to common data, allowing patients to be navigated through the system with maximum efficiency.[4] There was to be a new agency, the National Preventative Health Agency, to tackle this arguably most important but historically neglected area of care. All this was to be introduced alongside an agreement with state governments to return some of their GST revenue to the Commonwealth.

In his memoir, Rudd describes these measures as the biggest social-policy reform of Labor's first term of government, but after Gillard deposed Rudd, and state elections led to new Liberal governments in Victoria and New South Wales, the states walked away from the agreements. Gillard as prime minister, with Roxon, had to renegotiate. There was to be no takeover by the Commonwealth, no role for the Commonwealth in state and territory hospital planning, and, crucially, no redirection of GST revenue. What remained was an extra $16 million in health funding from the Commonwealth, the Preventative Health Agency, and a new funding model for hospitals based on the services they provided.

Rudd was furious at the compromises. He walked out of the cabinet meeting at which they were announced. He recalled: 'When push came to shove neither Julia nor Nicola had a reformist bone in their bodies. What we fought for for more than three years had been given away in an instant. I could have wept. Privately, in fact, I did.'[5] Gillard, on the other hand, wrote about Rudd's reform effort as an example of the 'nightmare' of his chaotic management style. Rudd's agreements with the states were 'never going to last', even if there hadn't been a change of government in New South Wales and Victoria, she said.[6]

It was a grim prehistory to Plibersek's time in the portfolio. She had the job of implementing the remaining elements of the reforms, which were by themselves significant and important – the activity-based funding for hospitals, and the new agencies that would oversee those arrangements, as well as preventative health. Asked to adjudicate between Rudd's and Gillard's accounts, she declined. 'I'm never into talking about the personality stuff between Kevin and Julia. I found her very easy to work with, and I found it very easy to respect Kevin.' As for the ambition of Rudd's reform agenda, she says, it should not count against him that not all of it succeeded. 'It's an example of a leader with a huge vision and appetite for change. Say they achieve 50 per cent or 10 per cent of what they set out to achieve. To attack that is so wrong, because we go forward through that attempt.' When she took on the health portfolio, she thought the achievements of the government had been undersold. 'For the first time, the Commonwealth was taking a real leadership position on health reform. We were spending all this extra money, and I thought we could do an even better job of telling the story of the reforms.'

By the time she got her feet under the desk, the agreements were in place, and the new agencies were being set up. Stephen Duckett, now director of the health program at the Grattan Institute, had been a key figure in designing the arrangements, and watched the rollout with interest. He recalls it all went 'extraordinarily well', and he credits Plibersek with that achievement. 'She showed an organised mind, a systemic approach and a good communications style, combined with an element of toughness.'

Another of the big reforms during Roxon's time as health minister had been the introduction of legislation mandating plain packaging for cigarettes, and the tobacco companies were challenging the government in the High Court. Roxon, now attorney-general, handled the details of the legal action – in which the government was eventually victorious – but Plibersek oversaw the detailed implementation, including the choice of a deliberately unappealing khaki colour for the packaging.

The implementation of electronic health records was anything but smooth. E-health seemed to hold great promise, but in fact governments worldwide were finding it was more complicated than they had first thought. There were conceptual problems with a system intended to be used by both consumers and health professionals, with one side entering information that could not be understood by the other. Doctors resented the extra work involved in data entry. Patients didn't see the point. Uptake was slow. But as well as these systemic problems – which were being experienced worldwide and continue to the present day – Plibersek found herself struggling with her department.

She was not a fan of the department secretary, Jane Halton. Halton was a Howard-government appointment who had been in the role since 2002. Before that, she had been best known as the deputy secretary in the Department of Prime Minister and Cabinet who had ruthlessly and efficiently executed the Howard government's agenda during the *Tampa* affair and later as convener of the People Smuggling Taskforce. Today, opinions on Halton are divided within the Labor government. Some admire her dedication and focus. Others would prefer to keep her at arm's length.

Rudd had made it part of his election pitch in 2007 that there would be no mass sacking of Howard-government appointees. It was a principled decision, but in the case of health, some thought change was needed. Other senior health bureaucrats at the time recall that the department was exhausted after the Rudd reform agenda. They were aware that the secretary and the minister had failed to establish a relationship of trust. They are reluctant to attribute blame for that. Plibersek thought that despite many excellent public servants in the department, it was being run with cynicism. 'It's hard to be a minister when the department's not functioning at its optimum level.' She responded by making a particular effort to talk to people in the middle-management levels of the agency, and to insist that Halton include these people in their meetings. 'I used to ring people who wrote me a particularly good brief and say, "This is really good work. Keep it up." And sometimes they were so shocked that they didn't believe it was me. They thought someone was having a lend of them.' There was also a lack of trust. As it became clear that the government was in its last months, there were a series of leaks from the health department to the opposition.

Plibersek had recruited to her staff Dan Doran, who today is her chief of staff. He had previously worked for Verity Firth during her time as NSW education minister, before joining the prime minister's department. One of his first jobs was to try to work out what was going on with the implementation of electronic health records. He recalls, 'No one could give me a timeline about when things needed to be delivered to make sure we were ready to go live. Either the timeline didn't exist or they wouldn't give it to me. So I constructed one myself and actually went down to the department with it and said, "This is what the minister needs to be sure that this thing is on track." It's not a stretch to say that implementation is a bit of an obsession for Tanya – that's one of the reasons she gets so much done. But it was always a battle to get things we needed. The department regarded the politicians as superfluous a lot of the time, but Tanya didn't tolerate that.'

The consensus in the media when Plibersek became minister for health was that the big reforms had been done – and that there was now no money, and no time, for the government to attempt more. Plibersek did not agree, but if she wanted to do more, under the government's rigid self-imposed fiscal discipline, she had to find offsets – cuts and savings.

At her first press conference as health minister, Plibersek identified improving access to dental services as one of her top priorities.[7] This had been one of the conditions for the Greens' support of the minority government, and today, the Greens regularly claim credit for the advances made in dental care under the Gillard government. It's a claim, says Plibersek, that 'just drives me crazy ... Adam Bandt has these big posters saying "Kids' dental, brought to you by the Greens," and it's not true. We did it. Labor did it. I did it.' Macklin says that the Greens might have pushed for the reform, but 'it wouldn't have happened without Tanya'.

Plibersek had to find a way forward on dental care before the May 2012 budget – and with no new spending, unless it was offset by other savings.[8] The first option for saving money was obvious – introducing means testing to the rebate the government paid to lower the cost of private health insurance. This was longstanding Labor Party policy. Roxon had tried to get it done but failed to get the support of the crossbench. The Greens wanted the subsidy completely removed and the savings put into public health. The private health industry argued that any means testing would see an exodus from private insurance, leading to a greater burden on the public system. Trying to untie this knot and find a way through took weeks of Plibersek's time in early 2012. She told parliament: 'I don't want a situation where the people who sit on this frontbench or that frontbench have their private health insurance subsidised by the people who clean this chamber at night.'[9] But most of the talking took place behind closed doors. In February, she secured the three votes she needed – from independents Andrew Wilkie and Rob Oakeshott, and Greens MP Adam Bandt.

Plibersek also had other ambitions. The Gardasil vaccine against cervical cancer had been approved in 2006, and a government-funded vaccination program had been rolled out for girls. Boys were not included. They couldn't get cervical cancer, but there was evidence that they could transmit the virus that caused it. To Plibersek, making the vaccine available free to boys made total sense – but there was a cost, which meant there had to be an offset.

It was that way for everything she wanted to do in the portfolio. She remembers: 'When I was really confident something was the right thing to do, I would go to the department and ask for a list of possible offsets. Then I would spend hours and hours examining every option and thinking, "How would this work in practice?" And I would call people who worked in the area – doctors or pharmacists or whoever. And I would call the patient advocacy groups. So I'd be really confident when I decided on which option I was pursuing.

'Then I would take it to cabinet and say, "I want to do this thing. This is the offset." And then there'd be more questioning. Is this really worth it? Who will be affected? How many people? What are they likely to say? What is the impact? What are the politics? I never went with ambits, but I made sure I knew my material and was able to give them alternatives.

'So I'd be saying stuff like, "If you don't want to do this, we can do this instead. It's smaller. It won't help as much, but it'll get some of the way there. Or we'll save less if we do this thing, but it'll be less controversial."

'And it was only after a long period of thinking about it and evaluating the alternatives, then selling the decision to my colleagues, that I would then be talking to the crossbench or to the media. So it was a long process.'

Wayne Swan remembers Plibersek taking her proposals to the ruthlessly dry Expenditure Review Committee. 'Health ministers are always walking through the door saying, "We want a lot more money." It's perennial. She got a good grilling, just as Nicola Roxon did before her. But she was always up to the mark. She knew she had to be reasonable. She knew that compromises had to be made and she had to order her priorities. But if you've got a minister who's done their homework, and has the evidence and has prepared the ground well, you can still get some things up.' Every minister wanting to spend money, says Swan, went through 'the equivalent of an economics PhD' to make their case. He offers this as an answer to those who say Plibersek lacks experience in financial portfolios.

In the last days of the Gillard government, the Gardasil vaccine became available free of charge for teenage boys. Largely thanks to that, Australia is today a leader in the elimination of cervical cancer, and likely to eliminate the disease within the next few decades.

So what was the offset?

One of the staff she had recruited to her office, Paul Nicolarakis, observes that Plibersek is an 'aesthete, both in a policy sense and a literal sense. She likes things to be balanced, fair and if possible deliver a positive sum result. She sees beauty in her policy role when she can kill two birds with one stone, and have an elegant solution that saves money and allows spending that makes good things happen.'

In this case, the money-saving solution was work on the Pharmaceutical Benefits Scheme – under which the Commonwealth government subsidises many drugs to keep them affordable for the public.

Getting a medicine listed on the PBS is a long undertaking. First, the drug must be approved, and then an independent panel of experts has to be convinced that it is both effective and the best solution for the relevant complaint.

Duckett, a former health department secretary, had found that the price the Australian government was paying for many medicines was several times higher than that paid by other countries. This was costing taxpayers billions of dollars – $1.3 billion in 2012–13 alone. Since 2007, drug companies had been required to report on the price they charged pharmacies for generic medicines. Often, this included big discounts. This information was used to calculate the average price being paid and, months later, the government subsidy would fall in line with those disclosures.

The price disclosure system had been startlingly effective. About 150 medicines had fallen in price, some by more than 50 per cent, saving millions of taxpayer dollars – but the whole process from disclosure to the drop in the subsidy took eighteen months. During that time, drug companies and chemists gamed the system. Drug companies would offer specials during the data-collection period and pharmacists would buy months' worth of medicine, knowing their profit margin would be protected when the price fell later. Pharmacists were also receiving in-kind gifts instead of direct discounts, such as shop fit-outs, flights or conference tickets, and these effective discounts didn't show up in price disclosure. Duckett wanted Plibersek to introduce a new scheme, based on benchmarking against prices paid overseas. He had meetings with her and pressed his case. She gave him a good hearing, he remembers, but in the end decided to go a different route. Rather than introducing a new system, she simply sped up the existing one – taking the eighteen months from price disclosure to subsidy adjustment to just twelve months.

Plibersek says she chose that approach because the drug companies were resistant to revealing the prices being paid in other countries, and the government lacked the power to make them do so. Also, there were good reasons for price variability. 'If you're a company making HIV medicine and you're selling it to South Africa for a fraction of the price that Australia pays for it, is that really the worst thing in the world? So benchmarking would have failed to make an allowance for a country's capacity to pay.'

The legislation to simplify the price disclosure regime was announced right at the end of the Labor government on 2 August – only hours before the start of the caretaker period after the calling of the 2013 federal election. When the legislation came before parliament, in November 2013, Peter Dutton was health minister and took the opportunity to have a go at Labor. He described the measures as Labor making 'a desperate last-minute attempt to raise revenue after six years of waste and mismanagement'.

But the real story lay in the fact that he introduced the new scheme without amendment.[10] It saved the federal budget an estimated $835 million. And, in the offsets Plibersek had presented to cabinet, it was this money that paid for the Gardasil vaccine to be given free to boys, as well as for an expansion of the National Bowel Cancer Screening Program. Both programs remain in place today, keystones in preventative health.

Plibersek says that one of the 'great things' about being a minister was being able to ring up experts in the field and ask them questions about their research. 'Like "I see you got this NHMRC grant for your research. Can you explain to me how this might make a difference in people's lives?"' In 2012, Adam Elshaug was a recently graduated PhD candidate on a Harkness Fellowship in the USA when he took a call from Plibersek's office. His PhD, which she had read, was about how Australia assesses which items should be included in the Medicare Benefits Schedule, and therefore eligible for Medicare rebates. Now Plibersek wanted him to fly back to Australia and brief her.

Elshaug had argued that Australian had good, robust and evidence-based procedures for listing new treatments – but almost no procedure for taking old treatments off the schedule when they had either been made redundant or when there was no evidence for their efficacy. An example was knee arthroscopy – a surgery for those with knee pain to 'clean up' cartilage. It was frequently performed, and paid for under Medicare, but the evidence suggested it didn't improve patient outcomes. Another issue was blood testing for vitamin D, which went through a fashionable moment and became a standard test for GPs to order – even though there was little clinical evidence tying vitamin D levels to health outcomes.

Nicola Roxon had made a start on reassessing old treatments. It was immensely politically costly. Ophthalmologists, for example, were still being paid top dollar for cataract surgery, which when it was introduced had required an overnight hospital stay and a high level of skill. Now, improvements in technology and methodology meant it was a day procedure that could be performed largely by nurses. Surgeons were raking in millions of dollars from the government, still charging the old prices. When Roxon tried to lower the Medicare rebate, the ophthalmologists took out full-page advertisements suggesting that under Labor, grandma wouldn't be able to get her cataract surgery.

But despite the political cost, Plibersek, looking for offsets, was determined to beef up the effort. Elshaug remembers: 'I literally turned up in Canberra and went into a meeting with her and her advisers. I was nervous. I had had some bad advice about how to present to her, and as soon as I got in the room, my heart sank because I felt like I was not going to present what she was interested in hearing. I remember to this day her leaning forward on the desk and saying, "This is an incredibly exciting area. What can we do? Where can we make some really big wins?" And it was a very human interaction. It wasn't wonky. It wasn't political. It was her wanting to do good. She was incredibly down-to-earth. And she was very excited by the prospect of these savings.'

Plibersek established a comprehensive management framework for the Medical Benefits Schedule, overseen by a committee of experts. Elshaug sat on the committee. It was not, in his view, an unqualified success. A shortcoming was that the membership was predominantly vested interests, who saw their role as resisting changes that affected their areas, rather than safeguarding the public interest.

In her previous portfolios, Plibersek had relied on experts, pulling together people from diverse fields and drawing a policy agenda from them. When it came to dealing with vested interests in healthcare, it didn't work ideally. Says Elshaug: 'It was quite a contrast to go from a meeting with Tanya, where she was all enthusiasm and energy, into a meeting of the committee, which was not quite so enthusiastic, shall we say, and blocking all the way.'

There were some wins. The committee made changes to the guidelines for when vitamin D blood tests should be ordered, and significantly lowered. There were other examples of progress. Elshaug thinks more would have been done had Plibersek remained minister. The structural problems could have been fixed.

But then Labor lost the 2013 election. Elshaug assumed the work of the expert committee would continue. 'We had meeting dates set up, we were expecting just to carry on.' The first sign of trouble was when, after the election, all the material about the MBS disappeared from the health department website. The committee was disbanded; its work stopped dead.

That was not the end of the story. When Sussan Ley took over from Dutton as health minister in 2014, she revived the process and the committee, giving it a new name. Elshaug, by now a professor at Sydney University, was once again recruited. Asked to advise on processes and structures, he recommended that it be made clear to the members of the committee that they were there as individuals, rather than representatives of their profession, and that their brief was to advise in the

public interest. Today, in Elshaug's view, Australia has 'reasonable' processes in place for assessing items on the MBS. The process that led to
that result began under Roxon, was advanced under Plibersek and is now
bipartisan. It could have happened sooner, but as with so much of the
Labor agenda, it fell victim to the voters' verdict on the dysfunction of
the government.

*   *   *

Those who had concluded that the Rudd–Gillard government was out of
money and out of time for major health reform were taken by surprise
when, on 29 August 2012 and without apparent warning, Plibersek and
the Greens' health spokesperson, Richard Di Natale, announced a plan
to provide free dental services to 3.4 million children and 1.4 million
adults on low incomes, at a cost of $2.7 billion. Labor would also spend
$1.3 billion on treatments for pensioners, concession card holders and
people with special needs. Asked where the funding was coming from,
Plibersek assured the journalists that it would not affect Labor's ongoing commitment to a surplus, which was, she said 'rock solid'. So how
was it to be done?

Ever since Medibank (later known as Medicare) had been introduced
by the Whitlam government, dental had been the missing element –
the gap between the claim that Australia has a universal health care
scheme and the reality. Whitlam couldn't take on the enormous cost,
nor a dispute with dentists, when he was already burning political capital battling doctors and the private health insurance industry over the
rest of Medibank.

Ever since, including dental work in Medicare has been a step too far
for successive governments. This is all about money and politics – not
health. There is no medical difference between the mouth and the rest
of the body, and the consequences of dental work not being covered by
Medicare play out in the health of poorer Australians. About a quarter
of Australian adults say they avoid some foods because of the condition
of their teeth. For low-income people, it's about a third. Low-income
people are more likely to have periodontal disease, untreated tooth decay
or missing teeth. That, in turn, leads to other health problems, such as

diabetes and heart disease. Low-income adults have fewer teeth, on average, than people with higher incomes.

The reason no government has been willing to include dental health in Medicare is the enormous cost – estimated to be at least $5.6 billion in extra spending a year. Because of that cost, any scheme would have to be means-tested. For Labor, that represents a risk. Including a means-tested scheme in Medicare would set a precedent that might be used by a future conservative government to undermine the whole of Medicare, making other parts of it means-tested as well. That would turn Medicare from a universal health system into a residual scheme only for the very poor.

When Plibersek turned her mind to making advances on the affordability of dental care, there were a variety of building blocks in place. The states ran public dental schemes aimed at the poor, with varying eligibility criteria. The system was underfunded. Some people could wait years for attention. Meanwhile, the Commonwealth government's main contribution was the subsidy for private health insurance – which many Australians paid primarily to help with the costs of dental 'extras'.

The Howard government had in 2004 introduced a limited scheme as part of a focus on chronic disease. It covered dental services for people with chronic and complex conditions. When Plibersek took on the portfolio, she decided that the scheme was poorly targeted, because it wasn't means tested. She recalls being told by dentists that they were often providing people with dentures and bridges on the taxpayer purse. 'And they would have people in the dentist's chair saying they had to hurry up and complete the work because they needed to catch a business-class flight to go on holiday on a certain date.' More than half the expenditure on the scheme was on crown, bridge and implant services and removable prostheses – restorative work, rather than preventative.

This, Plibersek decided, was to be her source of savings. She got costings from the department on subsidising dental care for kids and pensioners. 'I couldn't afford to do both, so I did kids first. And I would have done pensioners next ... kids had to come first, because if you get their teeth right when they're little, you get the lifetime benefits.' She first convinced the Greens, and then cabinet, that to provide dental care for kids, the chronic disease scheme had to go. Eliminating that, together with the means-testing of private health insurance rebates, was the offset for providing better dental care for children.

The Commonwealth Child Dental Benefits Schedule began in January 2014 – after Labor had lost power. Today it provides children up to the age of seventeen whose families receive any government payments with up to $1000 of dental work in a two-year period. The scheme is underused. After the change of government from Labor to the Abbott-led Coalition, it was not promoted. A 2019 Grattan Institute report found that it was used by less than half of those who were eligible. This, Stephen Duckett has written, is 'an astonishing public administration failure. Parliament passed legislation for the scheme in the expectation that it would be used as proposed – and allocated funds accordingly.' Plibersek says today that had she remained as health minister, the scheme would have been better advertised and implemented. Then she would have done more. Extending dental care to children was a first step. Her next step would have been to find a way to extend it to pensioners.

But the government's time was up.

In the 2019 election campaign, when Plibersek was deputy to Bill Shorten, Labor's policies included $2.4 billion for a pensioner dental plan, which would have given free dental care to three million Australian seniors up to a value of $1000 a year. In 2022, with Albanese as leader, this policy had disappeared. Instead, Labor said it was committed to a long-term goal of expanding Medicare to dental health services, but not specifying any time frame. The Greens are the only political party promising free dental care – having taken a $77.6-billion pledge over ten years to the 2022 federal election.

*   *   *

During her hectic months as health minister, Tanya Plibersek dealt, once again, with the legacy of Michael Coutts-Trotter's past as a drug addict. A friend of his from those times, someone who had also managed to quit drugs and establish himself in a professional career, wants this story to be told. He doesn't want his name used. I'll call him Peter.

Peter had been off drugs for twenty years when, in 2010, he was in an accident that required major surgery. The doctors gave him the opioid oxycodone for the pain and he had trouble getting off the drug. He ended up in rehabilitation.

He came out, believing himself cured – then, as he puts it, 'busted after about six months. It was a confronting, terrifying time.' On the line was his career, and perhaps more fundamentally the self-respect and self-image he had painstakingly constructed since his first recovery from addiction.

On the night before he was to enter rehabilitation for the second time, 'I had this real mental breakdown.' He rang Michael, but Tanya picked up instead. Peter talked things through with her. 'She was in a pretty demanding position, and there was a lot happening in health, but she got up and came over to my place, driving right across town, and she sat down with her arm around me, telling me how she and Michael loved me, and she stayed with me for hours through that night before I had to go back in. I'll never forget it. That generosity, that kindness, is how you measure people.'

Peter recovered in rehabilitation, has not relapsed, and remains a close friend of Plibersek and Coutts-Trotter.

* * *

In February 2012, Rudd launched a leadership challenge. Gillard called a ballot for 27 February. In the lead-up, many senior ministers who had previously held their tongues on their reasons for moving against Rudd in 2010 decided the time for restraint was gone. They launched stinging attacks.

Wayne Swan, then deputy prime minister, lambasted Rudd as a 'dysfunctional' cabinet colleague. Tony Burke said of Rudd's term in office that 'the stories that were around of the chaos, of the temperament, of the inability to have decisions made, they are not stories'. Nicola Roxon declared she could not work with Rudd again. Stephen Conroy said that Rudd had had 'contempt' for his colleagues, the parliament and the public. Albanese, meanwhile, tearfully called on his colleagues to stop attacking each other. 'I have despaired in recent days as I have watched Labor's legacy in government devalued,' he said. 'We have been a good government since 2007, under Prime Minister

Rudd we advanced a great deal … we should be proud of our record and not undermine it,' he said. Pleading for an end to the infighting, he said he wanted to get back to 'fighting Tories … that's what I do'. He was in tears. And, ultimately, he was declaring his loyalty both to the Labor Party and to Kevin Rudd. He offered Gillard his resignation. She declined it.[11]

Plibersek did not join in the denigration of Rudd, but she was by now firmly on Gillard's side – both because of her belief in supporting the leader, but also out of personal regard. She went on ABC TV's *7.30* in the lead-up to the spill and pleaded for an end to leadership crisis. 'We must sort this out on Monday. That must be the end of it, because our record is not getting out, our successes are not making an impact on people, and, more importantly, our plans for the future are being lost in these internal discussions.' She was invited by Chris Uhlmann to reflect on the criticisms being made of Rudd. 'I'm not going to pass judgement on people. I have plenty of my own personal failings, and what I do every day is get up and go to work and do the best job I can for the people that I care about, that I want to serve. And I think a majority of my colleagues feel that way.'[12]

In her memoirs, Gillard gave tacit recognition to the widening rift between Plibersek and Albanese, and the political cost. 'Tanya's bravery in continuing to support me when many of her closest allies would not was spectacular.'[13] Gillard defeated Rudd in the leadership ballot by seventy-one votes to thirty-one, but, contrary to the appeal Plibersek had made, that wasn't the end of it. The destabilisation continued.

Late in 2012, Gillard had arguably her finest moment in parliament when she rose to deliver what has become known as 'the misogyny speech' – an angry response to the relentless sexism she had faced from the media and from opposition leader Tony Abbott:

> I will not be lectured about sexism and misogyny by this man; I will
> not … If he [Abbott] wants to know what misogyny looks like in
> modern Australia, he doesn't need a motion in the House of Repre-
> sentatives, he needs a mirror. That's what he needs.

Within minutes of its delivery, the speech had travelled around the world on social media. It remains the thing Gillard is best known for.

Plibersek was sitting on the front bench, just out of the camera's view. She features in the video once – legs crossed, dressed in one of her trademark suits, her face raised to the leader, and her eyebrows sky high.

There was another spill, sparked by Simon Crean, in March 2013 as the government tanked in the polls. Rudd did not contest it, and Gillard was re-elected unopposed. By now, the government looked like a rabble, its achievements overshadowed by its dramas and dysfunction. It was unelectable. The only question was the size of the loss.

Finally, on 26 June 2013, Gillard called another leadership spill in the face of mounting speculation about Rudd's intentions. Rudd won the ballot fifty-seven to forty-five and was sworn in as prime minister the following day. 'Rudd wins the game of thrones', said one headline. 'Rudd's revenge' and 'The Rudd resurrection', proclaimed others. Albanese was elected deputy leader, along with a new Senate leadership combination: Penny Wong with Jacinta Collins as her deputy.

Six cabinet ministers immediately quit the frontbench: Wayne Swan, Greg Combet, Stephen Conroy, Peter Garrett, Craig Emerson and Joe Ludwig. But Plibersek, despite her personal support for Gillard, did not resign.

The day Rudd was re-elected leader, Plibersek returned from the party room and went quietly to her office. Her staff were watching, hearts in their boots. They suspected she was crying.

Then she came out and spoke. She apologised to them. She said that the Labor government had let them all down, and disrespected their hard work and dedication, through its inability to govern itself.

Then she cooked them lunch.

Most of them knew they would be out of a job within weeks.

*   *   *

The Gillard government passed 561 bills through the parliament before Gillard was deposed on 27 June 2013, including a number of significant policies, and legislation reflecting Plibersek's work. But when it came to the election on 7 September, it was not enough. The Coalition had a decisive win, with a two-party preferred vote of 53.41 per cent to Labor's 46.59 per cent. Labor's primary vote fell to 33.38 per cent, its lowest in over 100 years. The Coalition won ninety seats and Labor fifty-five, with the remainder going to small parties and independents. All the great promise of six years before had dissipated. Labor was out of government, and there was no reason to expect its fortunes would be restored anytime soon.

Three weeks after the election, Gillard made her first major public appearance at a packed event held at the Sydney Opera House, organised by Anne Summers. Plibersek was in the audience.

Summers talked about how Australia's first female prime minister had been 'ruthlessly stalked and denigrated'. Gillard talked about her 'murderous rage' at the sexism – the cartoons drawn with her with a dildo, Alan Jones calling for her to be dumped at sea in a chaff bag. Gillard mentioned Plibersek several times – as 'one of the most gifted communicators in Australian politics'. The audience erupted in applause that went on for a minute. Plibersek was caught on camera – mouth closed, smiling eyes.

Later, an audience member asked Gillard what advice she would give the new prime minister, Tony Abbott, who had made himself minister for women. Gillard replied: 'Please reach across the partisan divide and ask Tanya.' She was asked later which of the people sitting in parliament she would name as the next female prime minister. 'I think I have already indicated who is a very talented female member of parliament,' she responded. Again, the audience erupted in applause.

From this time forward, Plibersek's name was mentioned every time there was speculation on Labor's leadership. Gillard's comments put it on the record that she had to be considered a future prime minister.

On election night in 2013, Plibersek was on the ABC panel of commentators as the results rolled in. She was asked to reflect on the defeat. She insisted that the party could no longer tolerate division – that Beazley would have won in 2007. That it should not be about the leadership alone, but about the team – every MP, and every Labor member, pulling together if the party was to be rebuilt. She said she would give Labor nine out of ten for governing the country – and 'zero out of ten for governing ourselves'.

She was perhaps overgenerous with the nine out of ten. There had been important failures, including the dropping of the Carbon Pollution Reduction Scheme and, in her own portfolio, the only qualified success of the NRAS. But it was true that the government's successes and reforms – including avoiding recession after the GFC, the housing stimulus, the National Disability Insurance Scheme, paid parental leave, dental care for kids, and the National Plan for the Prevention of Violence Against Women and Their Children – were overshadowed by internal dysfunction.

Her words became one of the most frequently quoted epitaphs on the tragedy and dashed promises of Labor's six years in government.

10

AMBITION AND DEFEAT

Tanya Plibersek took up boxing. She really went for it – attacking the punching bag with a strength and ferocity that her coach, personal trainer Eleanor McCarthy, attributed to her farm-worker genes.

It was about halfway through Plibersek's first term in opposition after the election defeat. Michael Coutts-Trotter, aware that ten-year-old Joe was outgrowing his classmates, decided that some father–son boxing sessions might benefit his confidence as he entered adolescence. They went to the famous Tony Mundine Gym at the heart of The Block, Redfern – part of Plibersek's electorate, and an important centre for Sydney's First Nations communities.

The gym was, Michael Coutts-Trotter recalls, the kind of place where people fresh from jail would come to reconnect with community, and where Indigenous sportsmen would train youths from all backgrounds. It had 'the smell of a million people's DNA wafting out of the floorboards', he recalls. It was 'a real blood, sweat and tears gym' – a tough and atmospheric place, providing great social support. He and Joe began to train – going at the pads and the punching bags under McCarthy's direction, and absorbing the poise, discipline and skill of the sport without, as Coutts-Trotter puts it, 'actually getting punched in the face'.

Then Anna started training, then Louis, and finally Tanya came too. Today, McCarthy still trains the entire family, though they have switched from boxing to weights training and attend a different gym. McCarthy, an Indigenous woman, became a close family friend and mentor to the children.

Plibersek had always been fit – running, swimming and, with Michael, a 'gym junkie'. McCarthy was impressed by both her toughness and her humility – the way she and Michael, 'these important people you see on TV', took instruction and strove to improve. Early on, McCarthy told Tanya that her young son had just had a dental check-up at his day-care – part of the youth dental scheme Plibersek had introduced in her final days in government. Tanya surprised McCarthy by bursting into tears. 'She said this is why she did what she did, and this is why Labor should be in government, to help families like mine,' says McCarthy. 'She got really emotional about it.' And then she went at the boxing again, holding nothing back.

Tanya hated being in opposition. Like most of her colleagues who survived the election, she had absorbed the lessons about the cost of leadership instability. For her, at least, these were not new insights. She had always believed Beazley and Macklin should not have been deposed by Rudd and Gillard in 2006, and that the party would still have won government and been stronger as a result. But in what was to turn into almost a decade in opposition, as Labor twice failed to regain government despite a divided and lacklustre government, Plibersek was tested. Should she do what she had criticised others for doing? What some of her closest friends in the party were urging her to do? Should she have the self-belief, the arrogance, the conviction of her own abilities to seek the leadership for herself? Should she, even, consider tearing down an incumbent leader?

In opposition, Plibersek was continuously named in the media as a potential Labor leader. She was included in many of the polls in which the public was asked to nominate a preferred opposition leader. Some-times, in those early days, she outranked both Bill Shorten and Anthony Albanese. Then, as the years went by and Shorten became increasingly unpopular, it was between her and Albanese, with Shorten a distant third.

In the first few weeks after the 2013 election defeat, Plibersek made a crucial decision. In interviews for this book, she minimised its impor-tance – suggesting it was unremarkable, and that it would be childish for anyone to continue to hold it against her. Yet it continues to influence, perhaps even determine, her political trajectory.

After the defeat there was an automatic spill of the Labor leadership. Under the rules introduced by Rudd, the new leader was to be decided by a ballot equally weighted between rank-and-file party members and the parliamentary caucus. Several names, including Tanya's, were mentioned in the media as potential contenders. She says 'a few people' rang her to urge her to run. One of them was former prime minister Bob Hawke. 'He had always been a great friend and a great supporter,' she says. She told him that her children were too young – Louis was about to turn three. Hawke repeated those words in a media interview on election eve, ruling her out of contention because of her children, at the same time as saying she was 'very impressive, intelligent, a capable minister' and that she might be interested in being deputy leader.[1]

There was a social media campaign advocating a Plibersek run, complete with hashtag – #Plibersek16 – and Hawke was excoriated on Twitter and Facebook for supposed sexism. The feminist group Destroy the Joint pointed out that Shorten also had a three-year-old and did not see that as a barrier.[2] But Plibersek says today, 'Bob was just repeating what I had told him.' She says she did not seriously consider running in 2013 and a few days after the election publicly ruled herself out.

Would she have succeeded if she had made a different decision? 'I don't know,' she says today. Media commentary suggested she might have had the numbers among the party membership, but not in caucus. Her weaknesses were said to be being insufficiently combative, and possibly not wanting the job enough.[3] But public opinion polls continued to suggest that Plibersek was more popular than Shorten, and only narrowly behind Albanese.[4] She was mentioned, along with Jason Clare, as 'the face of the future' by Rudd's former strategist Bruce Hawker.[5]

Her withdrawal left two contenders: Albanese and Shorten. With the party's recent self-sabotage so much in mind, they ran an outwardly civilised campaign over the weeks following the election, touring the branches and conducting public debates, with each taking pains to declare their respect for the other. But this was the Labor Party. Behind the scenes, it was fierce, and toxic.

Shorten was from the Right and had the faction's support. Albanese, seeking support from his own Left faction, carried the burden of the old battles between Hard Left and Soft Left. His old enemies the Fergusons were against him. So, too, elements of the Victorian Left, led by Senator Kim Carr. The antipathy between Albanese and Carr is notorious to this day, even though nobody close to them seems to completely understand its origins.

As Albanese's factional ally, Plibersek was expected to vote for him and to campaign on his behalf – and she did. Verity Firth remembers going to a big meeting of the Sydney membership, where Plibersek introduced Albanese and urged her supporters to back him. Says Firth: 'Her people hit the phones and mobilised support for him. They did everything loyal factional colleagues should do.'

Then Bill Shorten turned a clever trick.

In an interview for this book, Shorten said he hadn't dealt with Plibersek closely before the 2013 leadership contest, but he regarded her as 'the most talented woman in the caucus ... I respected her integrity. I also understood that to run the Labor Party, you've got to have the Right and the Left in lockstep. If you have a leader from the Right, then the deputy has to be from the Left. I thought she was a future leader, and I thought I could work with her.' In the lead-up to the ballot, 'I spoke to her once or twice. She was going to vote for Anthony because they were on the Left. But she said she could work with me if I won. And I said, "That's all we need." There were no deals or any other understandings beyond that.'

It isn't clear if Tanya Plibersek understood that Shorten might use her name in public. Jeannette McHugh says she believes Plibersek thought he had made a promise not to do so. But on 12 September, just two days after Plibersek had ruled herself out of the leadership contest, Shorten told the media it would be a 'positive thing' if she was deputy leader – and he would be happy to have her in that position if he was successful in the ballot. Firth remembers thinking, 'Oh, you clever man.' Tanya could not be deputy to Albanese, because they were from the same faction and the same part of inner Sydney. If people wanted Plibersek in the leadership team – and many did – they would have to vote for Shorten.

In early October, days out from the ballot, the political journalist Patricia Karvelas, then working for *The Australian*, rang Plibersek's office and asked her if she would indeed be willing to serve as Shorten's deputy. Plibersek's current chief of staff, Dan Doran, was working as her press secretary at the time. He remembers taking the call. There was a discussion in the office. Should she rule it out?

She decided not to. It turned out to be, he acknowledges, a consequential decision – perhaps bigger than they realised at the time. There had been no internal plotting, he says, no briefing of journalists behind the scenes or manoeuvring to Albanese's disadvantage. 'It was simply an answer to a question from a journalist, not something we were putting about.'

The resulting story was published on 4 October. The lead paragraph said that Plibersek had confirmed she would willingly serve as deputy to whoever won – either Shorten or Albanese. Karvelas quoted 'senior Labor sources' as saying that Shorten had done 'great damage' to the Albanese campaign by nominating Plibersek as his deputy, because 'many members, particularly women, want her in the leadership team'.

> While the popular Ms Plibersek will not put herself forward as part of a ticket with Mr Shorten, the fact she has confirmed she would stand as deputy even if the right-wing Mr Shorten wins could sway many left-wing voters and feminists who back her strongly.[6]

Plibersek's decision not to rule herself out for the deputy position did not determine the result of the leadership ballot. The Fergusons and Carr mobilising against Albanese were almost certainly the deciding factor. But it is equally certain that she turned at least some votes in Shorten's favour. Albanese saw it as betrayal.

There are two ways of viewing Plibersek's decision not to rule herself out. On one hand, it might be seen as a betrayal of Albanese, a choosing of her own career aspirations over the fortunes of her faction and its leader. It was a leapfrogging over Albanese into the leadership team. On the other hand, why should she have put aside her own ambition? One of those close to Plibersek says she had reached the stage of her career, and the level of esteem within the party, where 'not to step up would have been too self-effacing.' 'There comes a time in political careers where you have to step up, or not,' this person says. 'The alternative would have been to accept a position permanently in Albanese's shadow.'

Jeannette McHugh, the woman who had held on to the seat of Grayndler for Albanese until he was ready to enter parliament, says, accurately, 'Nobody is a bigger supporter of Albo than me.' Yet she supported Plibersek in her right to run. 'It was her perfect right to make it clear she was available for the deputy leadership.' Few men, McHugh says, including Albanese himself, would have ruled themselves out if they had been in the same situation. 'You can either say, "Isn't she ruthless?", or you can say, "Why the hell shouldn't she?"'

Wayne Swan, who is now the national president of the Labor Party, said in an interview for this book: 'Why should she have stood aside if she wanted to be deputy? I think what she did shows that she's got a bit of steel. She was entitled to run, and the party was entitled to have the choice.' And Julia Gillard says: 'She was factionally and personally obligated to vote for and campaign for Albo, and she did. But she was also right to conceive of herself as the best person to serve alongside Shorten.'

There were what McHugh describes as 'unfortunately inevitable' consequences for Plibersek in the Left faction. 'A lot of people in the Left got upset with her. People that she adored. And I stood by her. She had every right to be deputy, and of course, she did it wonderfully. But in doing it, she was many, many, many times seen to be supportive of Shorten. She'd be standing beside him, or sitting behind him in parliament, and she'd be smiling up at him. And people who disliked Shorten with a passion found that hard to comprehend.'

In interviews, Plibersek dismissed any suggestion that her decision was one of the reasons for the coolness between her and Albanese. Indeed, she denied that there was any such coolness, at least on her side. How childish it would be, she said, if a decision like that were still held against her.

She said these things in mid-2021, before the 2022 election campaign that made Albanese prime minister. If she truly believes her 2013 decision doesn't still rankle with Albanese, then she is entirely alone in that belief. And, judging from the things she has said to friends and colleagues, the claim that there is no coolness on her side is disingenuous, if politically prudent. Albanese was approached to be interviewed for this book. After not receiving a response for months, in August 2022 I was told to expect a phone call from him for 'a ten-minute chat'. The phone call never came. Attempts to follow up were not responded to.

In the 2013 leadership ballot, Shorten won 64 per cent of the votes in the parliamentary caucus. Despite Albanese's stronger showing in the rank-and-file ballot, this was enough to secure Shorten a 52 per cent majority in the combined vote, and for him to become leader. Nine members of the Left faction had voted for Shorten. They were a mix of the Ferguson Soft Left and members of the Victorian Left who were aligned with Kim Carr (although Carr himself had voted for Albanese).[7] One of the nine, Senator Kate Lundy, had initially told Albanese she would vote for him but changed sides. Members of her faction were angry about her decision. She retired at the 2016 federal election.

Plibersek became deputy leader unopposed. She gave an emotional speech, recalling that her parents had arrived in Australia as migrants with just one suitcase each. Gillard tweeted her congratulations to 'a woman of achievement & vision, wit & warmth'.[8]

Crikey indulged in an editorial prediction – that Plibersek would become Labor leader after Shorten lost the 2016 election, and that she would win and become prime minister in 2019.

> She's smart and politically savvy. She's wildly popular among the left-wing faithful, and sensible enough to win over the Right rump. She's an effective and believable communicator – something Shorten and the previous two Labor leaders all struggled with – with as clean a hand as any after Labor's bloody internal battles. She's a woman, at a time when plenty want revenge for the way Julia Gillard was treated. In three years' time she'll be ready to lead. In six, it could be the Lodge. Albanese might have had a shot in 2016. Now it's Plibersek best positioned to be the next Labor prime minister of Australia.[9]

That prediction seemed reasonable at the time. Most thought that Albanese had missed his chance and that Plibersek had vaulted over him. But the prediction would prove completely wrong.

*   *   *

Throughout Shorten's leadership, Albanese was in the wings as the alternative leader. The last chapter of his biography, published in 2016, was titled 'Never Say Never'. Asked by the author, journalist Karen Middleton, if he would ever challenge Shorten, he didn't give a clear answer.[10] At various times between 2013 and 2019, when the polls were bad and as Shorten became more unpoular, Albanese was said to be doing the numbers. When he was threatening Shorten, he was also effectively threatening Plibersek. Most of this happened behind the scenes, only occasionally breaking through into media reporting. A review of the 2019 election later commented that Shorten's period as leader was 'characterised by stability, as a result of the collective decision of the federal caucus to prioritise unity'.[11] To the public, the ALP presented a mostly united face, and it was the Coalition government that was engaged in seemingly endless leadership rivalries and instability.

Meanwhile, Plibersek was a loyal deputy to Shorten. He recalls, 'First, she had my back. Secondly, she was a straight shooter with me. If something didn't feel right to her, she'd tell me. So she was honest. She was loyal. She built up a really excellent education policy. She never leaked. She was constructive. She was excellent.' He said Plibersek sorted out some 'immensely difficult and complicated personal issues' during her time as deputy. 'She was great at that.'

Plibersek saw the job of deputy leader as being largely about 'human resources'. She consciously set about trying to change the culture of the parliamentary party – to make it more collaborative and consultative, less brutal, and to make sure all voices were heard. She had watched how Macklin handled being deputy to Crean, Latham and Beazley. 'I tried to emulate the way she did it. That meant picking up when people were having a hard time and trying to help them. Sometimes that's personal. Sometimes it's issues in the office. Sometimes it's a policy thing ... Things like making sure that people feel valued and included. Staying in touch with candidates, making sure that they were getting what they needed to do their campaigning well. And trying to sort out policy differences and playing a role in reaching healthy compromises.'

The #MeToo movement was taking off in the United States, with women speaking out about sexual harassment and assault. 'I was looking at that and thinking, well, that's going to happen here too, so let's get ahead of it.' She went looking for the federal Labor Party's sexual harassment policy and complaints procedure and found there wasn't one. She looked at what the state branches of the party had done and used this material to update the federal policies and procedures.

Convention dictates that a deputy leader can choose their portfolio. Plibersek chose to be shadow minister for foreign affairs. She has given different explanations for this decision over the years. In interviews for this book, she said she welcomed the intellectual challenge. In previous interviews, she has said that she wanted a big change, because it would have been too painful to have to watch closely as the Abbott government dismantled her achievements in women's policy, housing, social inclusion and health.[12] In February 2016, she told the National Press Club that it was because of her interest in history. 'I don't think you'll be shocked to hear that I've never been a fan of the "great man" theory of history ... The history that interests me is the more complex story. The ebb and flow of events, the spark and slow burn of resurgence and decline. The shifts in power and influence that see nations rise and fall. Reading about this is one thing, living through it is another ... In this job, loving history helps when you are witnessing it firsthand.'[13]

All these reasons are true, she says. There was also another reason, although she doesn't nominate it. If she were to be a potential future leader, it was desirable to broaden her credentials beyond the social policy portfolios in which she had built her reputation.

As with her previous jobs, she began by reaching out to the experts – including the man generally credited with being Australia's most successful foreign minister, Gareth Evans. During the Hawke–Keating governments, Evans had articulated Australia's role as a middle power in the region, and in particular the idea of 'good international citizenship', not only as the morally right approach but also as an essential component of enlightened national interest. Evans initiated the United Nations peace plan for Cambodia. Other successes included Australia's role in the establishment of the International Chemical Weapons Convention and founding the Asia-Pacific Economic Cooperation forum (APEC), as well as the Association of South East Asian Nations (ASEAN) Regional Forum.

Evans had known Plibersek since she entered parliament but had not had much to do with her until now. When she took the portfolio, he offered to help and she took him up on it. Over her time in foreign affairs they met regularly for lunches and dinners. She sent drafts of some of her key speeches to him for comment – in particular a scene-setter she gave to the Lowy Institute in her early days in the job. Evans made only minor suggested changes and comments. She had, he was delighted to see, adopted the language he had pioneered – of good international citizenship. Today, he counts Plibersek as a friend.

At first, Plibersek was a 'fish out of water' in foreign affairs, says Evans. 'She was unfamiliar with conceptualising about foreign policy and with the legwork of meeting and talking to senior representatives of other countries.' None of this dismayed him. 'This is not rocket science for someone who's highly intelligent and highly motivated and works hard and reads well. And she's all of those things.' She was a 'sponge', he says, rapidly absorbing facts and ideas. In his view, her 'intelligence, application and decency' made up for her lack of detailed foreign policy knowledge and experience.

Plibersek also consulted Hugh White, Professor of Strategic Studies at the Australian National University in Canberra. There were a number of close and detailed discussions between them from 2013 to 2016, all initiated by her office. White, too, got the impression she was in the portfolio to build her credentials, rather than because of a passion for the area. She approached foreign policy as an 'extremely professional policy thinker', and in some ways more like a public servant than a minister, he says. 'She would think through the issues in a systematic way. It was a sober approach, rather than a bubbling up of policy enthusiasm. Not that she didn't have interests and ideals and commitments. She did, but she approached the issues that we talked about in a way that you could almost call dour.'

White has often been on the outside of foreign policy convention. In recent years, this has been largely about how Australia should handle its relationship with China as its principal trading partner, and the USA as its most powerful ally. White has argued that Australia needs to adjust to a future in the region in which China will be dominant. White found that Plibersek's lack of ideology about foreign affairs meant that she was relatively unconstrained by the politics, and 'more willing to think radically about policy directions than most other people in the foreign policy space ... I think she's quite politically courageous and more politically courageous than we're used to from the modern Labor Party.'

In her early days in opposition, Plibersek had to contend with maintaining a principled position on foreign policy, while also dealing with its impact on domestic politics. In January 2015, the Abbott government decided to send troops to Iraq to help train that country's army in the fight against Daesh, or Islamic State, as it tried to establish a new caliphate across the Middle East. Later, the issue was whether Australia should support the bombing of Daesh positions in Syria. (During an interview on ABC TV's *7.30* program, Plibersek told the interviewer that 'your own reporter', Matt Brown, was covering the conflict – Brown also being, of course, her former high-school boyfriend.[14]) Abbott was trying to wedge Labor on the issue – conscious of the party's previous opposition to the Iraq War, and Plibersek's role in particular as one of its most outspoken opponents.

Plibersek consulted both Evans and White. Both supported her in the view that Australian involvement in the battle against Daesh was correct on both principled and pragmatic grounds, and Labor moved quickly to support the government's actions. Plibersek argued that failing to help the US to liberate territory from Daesh 'could condemn innocent Iraqis to the same fate as the 800,000 Rwandans brutally murdered in just 100 days, two decades ago'. It was quite different from the Iraq War, she said. First, this time the Iraqi government had requested help. Second, there was a moral basis in the responsibility to protect.[15]

One of her achievements as shadow minister was to advocate for Australia to provide more help during the West African Ebola outbreak in 2014. She argued prominently and consistently for the government to expand its aid by sending health workers. Recalls Evans, Plibersek as a former health minister was well aware that Australia had a lot to offer. When, in November 2014, the Abbott government finally yielded to pressure and moved to make a modest contribution, most observers credited Plibersek's consistent pressure.

Plibersek's speeches as shadow foreign minister contained few departures from foreign policy orthodoxy. Typical is one she gave at the Lowy Institute in June 2016 in the lead-up to the election. She laid out the fundamentals: 'The US alliance, our region, global engagement.' She mentioned Evans and said that good international citizenship 'aligned with enduring Labor values of solidarity, fairness, equality, justice and inclusion'. Like many foreign policy thinkers at the time, she was optimistic about what the rise of China would mean for Australia, predicting it would bring 'tremendous opportunities and benefits'. If she were foreign minister after the election, she said, she would travel to Timor-Leste as part of intensified efforts to resolve the dispute over maritime boundaries.[16] After this announcement, the government moved on the border issue.

She was conservative in other areas. Former US computer intelligence consultant Edward Snowden made world headlines in May 2013 by blowing the whistle on the extent of US surveillance of its citizens. Plibersek said the revelations were not in the public interest and should never have been made.[17] She took the same attitude to WikiLeaks founder Julian Assange. Neither deserved special consideration as journalists, she said. In interviews for this book, conducted as Assange faced possible extradition to the US, she said he was 'not a journalist, any more than I am'. She had, at least, done a journalism degree, I remarked. 'Yes, but I am a politician, not a journalist, and he is an activist or something, but not a journalist. Nevertheless, I think he has effectively been in jail long enough and should be allowed to return to Australia. The punishment is excessive.'

Given the need for bipartisanship on foreign policy, ministers for foreign affairs and their shadows sometimes develop a mutual respect. This was not the case with Plibersek and the Coalition's foreign minister, Julie Bishop. The two women did not get on, and the antipathy was both personal and political. Plibersek was furious about successive cuts in the foreign aid budget. She now believes Bishop had no warning of the worst of the cuts. 'That's horrendous. If I were a minister in that position, I'd be furious.' Another source of tension was their different attitudes to feminism. In a 2014 address to the National Press Club, Bishop, then the most senior woman in the Abbott government, refused to describe herself as a feminist, and denied that Gillard had been the victim of misogyny. It is an attitude Plibersek regards with contempt.

When Plibersek was appointed foreign minister, Bishop brought up her 2002 description of Israel as a 'rogue state' and said Plibersek should once more publicly recant. Then, in 2014, Bishop described Plibersek as a lightweight compared to Labor's previous foreign minister, Kevin Rudd. Bishop said she had become friends with Rudd and often consulted him, but not Plibersek.[18] Many in the foreign policy community thought it a case of the pot calling the kettle black. Bishop was a presentable face for Australia, but was not herself seen as a deep policy thinker.

On one matter, the two women were united. When, in 2015, the 'ringleaders' of the Bali Nine – a group of nine young Australians caught trying to smuggle heroin from Indonesia to Australia – Andrew Chan and Myuran Sukumaran, were facing the death penalty, Bishop and Plibersek both made emotional pleas for their lives in parliament. Bishop was close to tears, but it was Plibersek's speech that most stuck in people's minds. She spoke about her husband, and how he might well have ended on death row if his crime had been committed in Thailand. She talked of her brother, Phillip, and how if she had had to decide the punishment for his murderer, 'I couldn't have thought of a punishment bad enough ... that is why we don't make decisions about punishment on the basis of how we feel, but on the basis of universal, consistently applied rules'.[19]

Bishop's jibes against Plibersek did not land well. The Jewish community was by now barely exercised by Plibersek's previous criticisms of Israel. ALP identity and businessman Michael Easson, of the Australia–Israel–UK Dialogue Forum, said Plibersek was better disposed towards Israel than former foreign minister Bob Carr, who was regarded as pro-Palestinian. Rather patronisingly, Easson said: 'Tanya is a very good person for the role. She will grow and develop.'[20]

He had no reason to be disappointed. In November 2013, as the new Abbott government voted against condemning Israeli settlements on the West Bank, Plibersek was muted in response, saying only that 'the unlimited building of settlements in land that is considered Palestinian land is not helping with the peace process'.[21] In 2014, she offered her condolences over the death of Ariel Sharon, the man she had once described as a war criminal, saying he had made a 'courageous stand' for a 'two-state solution in the peace process' – a statement that was, to put it very mildly, contentious.[22]

The question of whether Australia should recognise Palestine as a state was a sore point for Labor at the time. Bob Carr argued for immediate recognition, and several state ALP conferences in 2014 and 2015 backed that view. Plibersek responded: 'State conferences don't make Labor's foreign policy.' The national conference in 2015 – the last before the 2016 election and thus a key policy-setting forum – instead determined that the party would not discuss recognising a Palestinian state unless there was a prolonged period with no progress on peace talks. It was only in 2018, after Plibersek had left the portfolio, that the National Conference called on the next Labor government to recognise Palestine as an 'important priority' and as part of a two-state solution.[23]

In 2018, at the Byron Bay Writers' Festival, Plibersek played a word-association game with an interviewer. She was asked to respond to the words 'Julie Bishop'. There was a significant pause before she said 'fashionable'. The crowd laughed. But in interviews for this book, Plibersek said she now got on 'quite well' with Bishop, following Bishop's departure from politics in 2019. When, in 2018, Malcolm Turnbull was forced to resign as prime minister and the Liberal Party elected Scott Morrison instead of Bishop as leader, Plibersek texted Bishop with commiserations. 'She was a much more popular person than Scott Morrison. It says something about the Liberal Party that they couldn't bring themselves to elect her as leader,' Plibersek observes. And she sees the irony – perhaps the poetic justice – in Bishop's previous failure to acknowledge the sexism faced by female politicians.

I first asked Plibersek to talk about her time in the shadow foreign affairs portfolio in an interview in late 2021. She was oddly reluctant, in a way out of character with our previous interactions. We had been talking freely and expansively, in the same interview, about the health portfolio, but when it came to foreign affairs she said she was unwilling to answer questions because 'the portfolio is held by someone else'.

The someone else, of course, was Senator Penny Wong – Anthony Albanese's close political friend and ally, and, after the 2022 election, Australia's foreign minister. Plibersek declined to answer questions on how Australia should be navigating its relationship with the USA and China, or the growing importance of Indonesia, or the Quad arrangements with India, Japan, USA and Australia. A few weeks later, I asked Gareth Evans what he thought was the reason for this reluctance. 'She wouldn't want to be treading on Penny Wong's toes,' he said.

When Plibersek was shadow foreign minister, Wong was shadow minister for trade, but it was already clear that Wong aspired to the foreign affairs job, which she took after the 2016 election. Evans has dealt with and advised both women. Wong, he says, is a more 'self-conscious intellectual' than Plibersek, and used her time in opposition to craft a conceptual foreign policy framework around Australia's interests and values. But, he says, had Labor won in 2016, Plibersek would have been 'absolutely fine, more than fine' as the country's foreign minister.

In a later interview, after the 2022 election, I tried again to get Plibersek talking about foreign policy, telling her she had shut me down earlier. 'Perhaps you asked the wrong questions,' she said at first, prickly, before adding that she couldn't remember the details of our earlier exchange. Asked if she was reluctant to trespass on Wong's territory, she denied it. 'Foreign policy is sensitive, and it's a sensitive time,' she said. 'It's consequential. And having a bunch of people with a bunch of different opinions is really not helpful to the national interest.' But, she said, 'We can talk about China if you want. We could talk about it for three hours. What do you want to know?'

I asked if she thought, as Hugh White has argued, that we need to get used to Chinese dominance in our region, and that we can't rely on the US. She responded that Australia's alliance with the US was 'really important, particularly at a time when democracy, human rights and the international rules-based order were under attack'.

She is less optimistic about China now than when she was shadow minister for foreign affairs, but 'I still think we should be looking for areas of cooperation'. She was particularly troubled when China dropped its commitment to negotiate on climate change in the wake of US speaker Nancy Pelosi's visit to Taiwan in August 2022. It should be possible to identify areas of common interest, even at a time of tension, she said. The relationship is improving, she thinks. She hopes for cooperation on climate change, and the type of aid that China is prepared to invest in the Pacific, 'because they do have a big aid budget and the quality of the investment has not always been terrific. I think if we could find some projects to cooperate on, like reef restoration or mangrove restoration, that would be great. There are many areas of potential cooperation.' But, she added, 'I really do think if anyone can sort it, Penny can.'

Another issue combining domestic and international politics during Plibersek's time as shadow foreign minister was refugee policy. Shorten wanted to alter the party's opposition to turning back boats carrying asylum seekers. The Left faction, led by Albanese, opposed him. The issue erupted at the ALP National Conference in July 2015. Shorten was staking his leadership, then considered to be on shaky ground, on the issue. It was described by the media as 'the riskiest moment of his twenty-one months as federal leader'. Albanese gave an impassioned speech to the Left caucus. He could not himself turn back a boat at sea, he said. Therefore, he could not vote for others to do so. Newspaper reports described Plibersek as being in a 'bind' because of her need to show loyalty to Shorten while following personal conviction and factional solidarity.[24] In fact, however, Plibersek supported Shorten on turning boats back, and had spoken in support of changing the policy in shadow cabinet and Left caucus.

She said in interviews for this book: 'I was part of the leadership group and I thought it was important that there was a solid position from the leadership group ... I thought it would be politically impossible to go to the next election without a strong policy on offshore processing and turn-backs.' The compromise – which she takes credit for negotiating – was a commitment to doubling the humanitarian intake of refugees arriving through regular means, together with a funding boost for the UNHCR and its processing of refugee applications offshore. 'I thought that was a fair balance to try to discourage people from making a really dangerous journey on boats.'

Shorten won on the issue at conference, and the policy was adopted. Plibersek, together with Wong, avoided voting on the change in person, instead lodging their votes by proxy. Plibersek gave her vote to Terri Butler, who voted against Shorten's position. It was an awkward contortion – to have backed her leader in her internal statements, and then allowed her proxy to vote against him. *The Australian* commented that Plibersek had been left 'dangling from a trip wire like Wile E. Coyote'. The debate, *The Australian* said, had served as 'shadow boxing' between Albanese and Plibersek over future leadership ambitions.[25]

Ever since that 2015 conference, Albanese has backed ALP policy on boat turn-backs – whether out of a change in his personal convictions or political pragmatics. In the 2022 election campaign, debating Prime Minister Scott Morrison, Albanese said that turn-backs had worked. 'The truth is that the Labor Party have been very clear about supporting boat turn-backs. I support it. Everyone in my team supports it. We'll implement it.'[26] I asked Plibersek if she thought Albanese had changed his view. 'That is a question for him,' she said.

Another key issue at the 2015 conference was the conscience vote on same-sex marriage. On this, Plibersek was both outspoken and visible – and on the opposite side to both Shorten and Albanese. In the lead-up to the conference, she had announced she would be pushing for an end to the conscience vote on same-sex marriage, meaning that all Labor parliamentarians would be bound to vote for any future marriage equality bills before parliament. Shorten and Albanese were in favour of same-sex marriage rights but against forcing Labor MPs to vote against their conscience.

The Left faction was split. It met privately on the morning of the vote, 26 July, in a final push to reach agreement. Albanese spoke emphatically in favour of a conscience vote. Plibersek and Wong argued that freedom from discrimination on the basis of sexuality is a right, and the party should vote as one.

They negotiated a compromise. The conscience vote would stay in place for the rest of the parliamentary term, and for the one after that, but from 2019 all Labor MPs would be obliged to vote for same-sex marriage, in line with the party platform. It was an intellectually inconsistent compromise, suggesting that same-sex marriage was a matter of conscience for now but in four years' time would suddenly become an inalienable human right. But there was a payoff. In return, Shorten made a public promise that he would introduce legislation to legalise same-sex marriage within the first hundred days of a Labor government. The compromise motion was successful and became party policy; this was the position Labor took to the 2016 election.

Two weeks after the Labor Party conference, the Coalition party room met to try to solve its own impasse over same sex marriage. Abbott emerged after six hours to tell the media that the current term of parliament would be the last in which Liberal and National MPs would be bound to vote against same-sex marriage. After that, there would be a conscience vote. But, right at the end of a long address, he said that in the next parliamentary term, the matter would be put to a public vote – a plebiscite.

Both sides of politics had moved. Labor would enforce a pro–marriage equality vote after 2019, and the Liberals would allow a conscience vote after the next election. It was now next to inevitable that same-sex marriage would be achieved in Australia. The only question was when, and how.

One month later, Malcom Turnbull deposed Abbott as leader of the Liberal Party. To get the job, he had to pledge to the National Party that despite his own preference for a parliamentary vote to establish marriage equality, he would stick to the plebiscite plan.

On Turnbull's first day as prime minister, 15 September 2015, Plibersek asked him a question about a marriage equality bill then before the house. 'It would take half an hour of parliamentary time to allow this bill to be voted on. It could be done tomorrow. Will the prime minister allow a vote on this bill and allow members of his party a free vote as he has publicly called for previously?'[27] Turnbull recommitted to the plebiscite. Plibersek dismissed his position as 'ridiculous'.

The 2016 federal election was a double dissolution, called by Turnbull on the grounds that the Senate had twice rejected government legislation to establish the Australian Building and Construction Commission. But that issue soon faded away in a campaign dominated by jobs, the economy and the future of Medicare.

Plibersek campaigned hard, both on her own behalf and by Shorten's side. Turnbull and Shorten were both being pursued by the ABC satirical program *The Chaser*, which was trying to deliver each man a live rat, as a reference to their respective histories in undermining party leaders. Plibersek and Shorten were touring the Sydney Fish Markets when *The Chaser* finally caught up with them, delivering the rat at their feet in a Tupperware box. As Annabel Crabb commented: 'The viewer could sense – in Shorten's preparedness to touch his rat only with a tentative fingernail – his lightning-fast and almost certainly accurate judgement that a man who has knocked over two Labor leaders should not tarry over-long in any broadcast situation involving *rattus rattus*.'[28] He handed the rat to Tanya – who lifted it out of its container, cradled it, and eventually took it home as a family pet. She invited her followers on Twitter to suggest a name, and later reported the rat was 'safe at home now with some nuts, zucchini and banana to snack on'.

Meanwhile, two weeks before the poll, Plibersek gave a speech that serves as a marker in her career – an articulation of how this woman who had once resigned from the Labor Party, disappointed at its compromises, this once-firebrand member of the Left, now understood the party and her role within it.

Delivered to the progressive think-tank the McKell Institute, the speech was framed as an attack on the Greens, and an argument for left-wing voters to stick with Labor. But it was more than that. The speech came as close as Plibersek ever has, in a set-piece address, to high oratory. Yet she was not advocating for high emotion, or extremes, or radical ideas, but rather speaking in favour of incremental reform – the sense, sensibility and discipline involved in being a party of government. This was Plibersek as a mature politician, a leadership contender and a veteran of managing difficult portfolios in government. She referred to the archetypal symbol of Labor ideals, Ben Chifley's light on the hill, but qualified it:

> The reason the light on the hill is an image we return to so often
> is that it reflects the two essential elements of our party. We are

idealists ... But we are also realists – we know that our ambitions for our nation are not easily achieved. The road of the real reformer often takes the steeper face, the harder climb and the more unforgiving ground. Idealistic and pragmatic – we can be both ... We accept that incremental progress is part of our great journey.

She went on to talk about Medicare, and how the path to universal healthcare began under Chifley, was unwound by Menzies, introduced by Whitlam, unwound again by Fraser, and reinstated by Hawke.

That's the long version of the story of Medicare – and that's the point ... this took forty years of struggle ... The creation of Medicare took more than a hollow principled stand, it took more than just wishful thinking, it took more than slogans, it took more than protests. It took real, tough politics. It took idealists who were prepared to fight to win government. The creation of Medicare reminds me why participation in mainstream politics is so important and why, to borrow from Teddy Roosevelt, I'd rather be in the arena, 'face marred by dust and sweat and blood', on that rough path, than retreat to the comfortable distance of commentator or critic. I'd rather spend myself in a worthy cause.

She took the customary shot at the Greens – characterising them as cynically robbing votes from Labor by positioning themselves as more 'pure', knowing they would never have to take on the discipline and responsibility of government. 'Voters should rightly ask where are the actions, and the sustained effort, the achievements by which Greens have delivered real progressive change?'

The Greens, she said, were 'intellectually shallow and politically naive'. She hit back at the Greens taking credit for the children's dental scheme she had ushered in as health minister:

Kids' dental care as part of Medicare wasn't brought to you by the Greens, it was brought to you by a Labor government when I was health minister, building on the health policy gains made by

previous Labor governments, hard won through negotiation with
the crossbench in a minority government. And I had to work out
how to structure the system responsibly and how pay for it too.

The path to the light on the hill was 'slow and rocky', she said. The party
had been walking it for more than a century. 'That whole time we have
had to take a majority of Australians with us, but that's our strength and
our success too. And that's why progressives should vote Labor.'

The federal election was held on 2 July 2016. The result was much
closer than anyone had expected – the closest election since 1961. Labor
had come within a whisker of being the first opposition in eighty-five
years to oust a government after just one term in office. The result
wasn't clear for days. In the week-long interregnum before a result could
be announced, it seemed possible that Labor might be able to form a
minority government.

Yet at the same time, the media speculated about what might hap-
pen if Labor lost. Under party rules, the leadership would be vacated.
Both Albanese and Plibersek were considered possible contenders.
Today, Plibersek says she never seriously considered running at the time.
Shorten had won at least fourteen seats. 'It would have been pretty harsh
to knock him off after a result like that.'

Albanese, on the other hand, was said by the media to be manoeuvring for a run, but to have been told that he would get no support, in
light of the result.[29] He later denied to his biographer that this was so.
'I wasn't running. I knew that from the result,' he said.[30] Shorten was
re-elected as leader unopposed and started on the closest thing a loser
could have to a victory lap. The Liberal Party, under Malcolm Turnbull,
was wobbly, and now locked in its own mire of leadership instability.

Victory for Labor in 2019 seemed a certainty.

*   *   *

With the 2016 election behind them, the Turnbull government pushed
ahead with the plan for a plebiscite on same-sex marriage.

Plibersek wrote an article for *Mamamia*, taking as her focus an
eleven-year-old called Eddie who had visited her office, arguing for his

mums to be able to get married, without the need for 'a $7.5-million campaign' that would allow people he had never met to judge the worth of his family.

She wrote about her own marriage. Nobody got to vote on whether she and Michael Coutts-Trotter should marry. She recapped the changing attitudes to marriage – how once Aboriginal people had to seek permission to marry a non-Aboriginal person. How soldiers who fell in love with Japanese women were not allowed to marry, and could not return to Australia if they did, until 1952. 'My mother-in-law was forbidden from marrying her first love because she was Catholic and he was Protestant – that seems absurd and cruel to us today.' But times had changed, and rightly so, she said. 'We already know the majority of Australians support marriage equality. It's time for the Parliament to make marriage equality a reality – it could be done next sitting week, without a damaging and divisive $170-million plebiscite.'[31]

In parliament, she spoke passionately on her opposition to the plebiscite:

> For the same-sex couples who hear their relationships are second-rate, I will not, and Labor will not, support this plebiscite. For the children of same-sex couples who hear there's something wrong with their family, I will not, and Labor will not, support this plebiscite. For young gay and lesbian people who might be struggling with their sexuality, or are just thinking about coming out, I will not, and Labor will not, support this plebiscite.[32]

Legislation to conduct the plebiscite was twice defeated in the Senate. On 9 August, the government announced that instead there would be a postal survey. This could be done without the need for a parliamentary vote. A High Court challenge to disallow the survey failed, and on 12 September over 16 million survey forms were mailed out, with a date of return of 7 November. Labor hadn't wanted a public vote, but once it was inevitable, everything was thrown into winning it.

On 15 November, the Australian Marriage Law Postal Survey result was revealed. Of the 12.7 million Australians who voted, 61.6 per cent voted yes and 38.4 per cent voted no. Legislation for same-sex marriage was now inevitable. On 7 December, it passed the parliament with only four votes in dissent. Plibersek told parliament: 'By the end of today, Australia will be a better, kinder, fairer place for all of us.'[33]

That evening, Plibersek was with Shorten, Wong, the comedian Magda Szubanski and a welter of others at a party held at Parliament House. It was a joyous occasion, a marker of real national change. The mood was euphoric. Shorten was talking to his children via FaceTime and handed the phone to Tanya. The whole exchange was caught on video, posted to YouTube and then picked up by the Channel Seven news. 'Oh sweetheart, I am so proud of you too,' said Tanya to Shorten's kids. 'I'm proud of your daddy ... he did such a good job ... It wouldn't have happened without your daddy.' And Shorten laughed. The warmth between Plibersek and Shorten was unmistakeable. But in a sign of things to come, on social media Plibersek's popularity was overshadowed by the reaction to Shorten. There were lots of green-face vomiting emojis.[34]

*   *   *

After the election, Shorten asked Plibersek to give up foreign affairs and instead take on education, as well as becoming shadow minister for women. Plibersek was reported to have been reluctant at first, but she was lobbied hard. Shorten told the media: 'This is about putting a great policy thinker on the political frontline.' Education was one of the most important areas of policy for any government, and for Labor governments in particular.

It was rich and complicated territory for Labor. The Rudd–Gillard governments had adopted the recommendations of a 2011 report by David Gonski, which laid out a way to clean up Australia's convoluted and opaque school-funding system. Under the Gonski reforms, there would be a needs-based funding model, under which every school – whether private or public – would receive a base level of funding, known as the Schooling Resource Standard (SRS). This was to be based on student numbers, with loadings for categories of disadvantage, including disability, low socio-economic status and Aboriginal and Torres Strait Islander students.

The Gonski report was hailed as the answer to Australia's educational woes – a roadmap to creating an equitable school funding system. But, under political pressure in the last months of her government, Gillard made key concessions that undercut the reform, promising that no school would lose money. By definition, needs-based funding meant that some schools would receive more funding and some – particularly wealthy private schools – would receive less. Then the Abbott government had cut funding to education and health.

In the May 2017 budget, Turnbull reversed, announcing extra funding for schools under the Gonski model. He committed the government to meeting 20 per cent of the SRS for government schools, and 80 per cent for non-government schools, with the aim of reaching at least 95 per cent of the SRS for all schools by 2023. State and territory governments were meant to fill the gaps. Plibersek responded by announcing Labor would oppose it because its structure effectively locked in underfunding for public schools.

As for higher education, Gillard as education minister had introduced a demand-driven system for university education in which universities could take as many students as they wished, and receive the Commonwealth subsidy for each of them. As a result, since 2008 enrolments of undergraduate students from poorer backgrounds had risen 66 per cent, Indigenous enrolments had more than doubled, and there had also been big increases in disabled and rural and regional students. A Productivity Commission report, however, judged the results as mixed. The demand-driven system had made progress in improving equity of access, but many students were entering university ill-prepared and struggling academically, with high dropout rates.[35]

After the 2016 election, the Turnbull government suspended the demand-driven system, capping funding for enrolments at 2017 levels for three years, with increases from 2020 to be tied to universities meeting performance measures. It was for Labor, expected to win the next election, to outline an alternative approach. On 16 November 2016, Plibersek gave her first major speech as shadow education minister. She recounted her parents' story.

Both my parents had been torn from education too young by war and poverty. Both of them smart, life-long learners, multi-lingual, curious about the world. Like most parents, they wanted for their children what they missed out on. And even in a world where technology, automation, the mass movement of people, climate change, and other factors are making workforce predictions heroic, parents are right to want a great education for their children.

She declared it 'appropriate' that university students paid fees, given the private benefits that came from university education, but said that cost should never be a barrier, because an educated population was one of the best ways to sustain strong economic growth. Labor, she promised, would deliver a more seamless higher education system and invest 'billions of dollars extra' in universities and schools.

It wasn't long before she was giving more detail. Education was among the first of Labor's big spending commitments in the lead-up to the 2019 election. On 11 May 2017, just after the Turnbull government's budget, the ALP committed to a full level of funding to public schools under the Gonski formulae, as well as more money for Catholic and independent schools. Every school would achieve its SRS within ten years. This was to cost $22 billion – an immense and costly reform.

As the election approached, there were more big spending promises. Labor committed to permanent funding for preschool and to extend it to three-year-olds, at a cost of $9.8 billion over three years. Childcare would be free for most low-income households, at a cost of $4 billion over four years. Labor also committed to return to the demand-driven system for universities, which it said would give 200,000 more Australians the chance to go to university, at a cost of $10 billion over a decade, plus $300 million to upgrade buildings and equipment. On top of that there was a $1-billion vocational education package, including $380 million for 100,000 free TAFE places, $224 million for 150,000 extra apprentice incentives, $200 million for TAFE building upgrades, and $10 million for the creation of 1300 new scholarships for Indigenous people to study at TAFE if they lived outside the big cities.

On 28 July 2018, on a day dubbed 'Super Saturday', there was a raft of by-elections caused by the forced resignations of MPs when they were found to be ineligible because they held dual citizenship. Plibersek had at first been the subject of media speculation about her eligibility but was quickly able to clear the record by providing a letter from the Slovenian embassy confirming she had never been a Slovenian citizen.

The by-elections were crucial for both Shorten and Turnbull. If Labor performed badly, the media commentary suggested, a challenge to Shorten from Albanese would surely follow. But, against most expectations, Labor won all five by-elections. It was an excellent result for the party. The Albanese speculation faded, and once again there was every reason to expect that Labor would shortly be returned to government.

Just after Super Saturday, Plibersek appeared on stage at the Byron Bay Writers' Festival. She was asked if she would someday be prime minister. The audience cheered the question – applauding so long and so loud that Plibersek had to wait some minutes before she could answer. She replied: 'The honest truth is I would rather be a backbencher in a Labor government than do anything to ever harm our chances. In my heart I believe that working people and vulnerable people rely on Labor governments to make their lives better. That's honestly the most important thing.'

The Super Saturday results cemented Shorten's leadership but were bad for Turnbull. On 21 August, he survived a challenge from Peter Dutton. Plibersek was in grand oratorical form, characterising his administration as 'a Frankenstein's monster of a government: it has the face of the member for Wentworth [Turnbull], the policies of the member for Warringah [Tony Abbott] and ... the cold, shrivelled soul of the member for Dickson [Dutton]'. On the same day, she switched to personal abuse of Dutton, characterising him as 'a 21st-century Chucky doll'.[36]

A few days later, having declared that if Dutton had the numbers to win a motion calling for a leadership spill he would not stand for re-election, Turnbull lost the spill motion forty-five to forty. Dutton, Scott Morrison and Julie Bishop were the candidates for the leadership. Bishop was eliminated first. Dutton and Morrison proceed to a second round, and Scott Morrison was elected forty-five to forty as leader and prime minister.

The by-election results, the leadership chaos on the Coalition side, the tiredness of the government and the close result in 2016 all made a Labor victory seem inevitable. On top of that, there were the public opinion polls. By the end of 2018 there had been fifty-six consecutive Newspolls predicting a Labor win – despite Bill Shorten remaining unpopular.

Tanya Plibersek took it upon herself to begin the work of preparing for government. She was urged on in this by Gareth Evans, who had done similar work for previous incoming Labor administrations. As well, she considered that one of the main weaknesses of the Abbott government had been a 'terrible start' because it had no agenda, other than unpicking as much as possible of what Labor had done. She tried to involve Bill Shorten in the work, but he pushed back, saying – reasonably enough, she says – that his main job was winning the election, rather than thinking about what came afterwards.

She pressed on. Starting the project a year out from the 2019 election, she compiled what she describes as 'a big fat folder' of work. There was 'a plan for the first day, the first week, the first 100 days'. She revised the cabinet handbook and put together a list of people who would make good senior appointments to the public service. She recalls, 'I had a list of what cabinet needed to do, what caucus needed to do, what ministers needed to do. We had some machinery of government changes prepared … it was all ready.'

On Thursday, 11 April, Scott Morrison announced that the election would be held on 18 May. Just four days before, there had been another announcement of great significance to the Coutts-Trotter–Plibersek family. The NSW government announced that Coutts-Trotter would be the new secretary for the Department of Justice. The former inmate was now to be in charge of Australia's largest court and prison system.

Predictably, there was another round of publicity and commentary, particularly when an email Coutts-Trotter wrote to the department's 40,000 employees became public. Coutts-Trotter was continuing his policy of openness about his past. 'There's one thing I want to tell you about myself,' the email said. 'You may know it already. But, if not, I want you to hear it from me first. As a teenager I used and supplied drugs. In 1984

I was imprisoned for conspiracy to import heroin. I spent nearly three years in jail and then around 18 months on parole.' He asserted that his background would be an asset rather than a liability.

By now, Coutts-Trotter's past was well known. Some commentators pointed out that he would have trouble getting a job as a cop or a prison guard with a record like that, but for the most part his frankness was described as inspirational – the reverse of the usual bureaucratic obfuscation. Coutts-Trotter made himself available for multiple media interviews. The resulting stories referred to the fact that if Labor won the coming election, as everyone expected it to do, Coutts-Trotter would soon be married to the deputy prime minister.

Betting agencies had Labor ahead in twenty Coalition-held seats. Closer to polling day, they had Labor at extremely short odds – predicting an 86 per cent probability of a Labor win. One betting agency was so confident of the result it paid out backers of Labor two days ahead of polling day.[37]

But the polls – all of them – were wrong.

Interviewed for this book, Plibersek said that, unlike most of the Labor movement, she was never confident of victory in 2019. 'I was hopeful, obviously. And I was working very hard for Labor to win, but I thought there were a few weaknesses in the campaign, and I thought the change to Scott Morrison at the last minute was very beneficial for the Liberal Party because he was an unknown quantity, and he ran a very disciplined campaign.

'Because people assumed we were going to win, we had kind of become the government. So our policies were under extraordinary scrutiny and Bill was getting all sorts of questions of detail every day and the actual government was kind of skating along on the surface without any real analysis of their record or any challenge to what they wanted to do in the next term ... It was a very superficial campaign.

'We got bogged down in all sorts of complex detail and held to account for what we were going to do on the assumption that we were winning. And so I was nervous the whole way along ... And then on election night, the early exit polls had a 3 per cent swing to us, and I was relieved. I thought, "If that's consistent across the night, we'll get there."'

On election night, Plibersek was on the panel of commentators for Channel Nine news, sitting next to Anthony Albanese. Julie Bishop was representing the other side of politics. Early in the broadcast, Plibersek and Bishop sparred over which party had the worst leadership instability.

Then, Plibersek and Albanese both began to frown over their laptop screens, their shoulders slumped, their faces ashen. They didn't look at each other. Here were two Labor true believers, both talented, sharing core Labor values, representing similar people in neighbouring seats. Yet in that moment each of them seemed alone, hunched in personal misery, unable to offer the other any comfort – adjacent, yet far apart. All over Australia, election parties held by Labor supporters started with champagne on ice, ready to be cracked open. By 9.30 p.m. the parties had turned into wakes.

The Morrison government had been returned to power.

11

THE COUNTRY
THAT WE MAKE

There was so much blame to go around after the 2019 election defeat – so much shock and pain and depression in the Labor team. Senior shadow ministers had to consider if they had enough motivation to go on – to suffer another three years with no certainty that they would ever be able to use their talents in government. Were the coalition parties now the natural government of the nation? How, after hanging together, suppressing their internal tensions, and advancing a bold social justice agenda, had Labor failed again?

Tanya Plibersek did not doubt her ability to keep going. She still loved her job – the electorate work perhaps most of all, and that did not rely on being in government. And, she says, she was less shocked by the defeat than some of her colleagues. Yet she had to face their anger and their disappointment. In the agony of unexpected defeat, there were plenty of people prepared to blame Shorten and her. Some of them briefed journalists. She was said, by unnamed sources, to have been responsible for 'dragging Shorten too far to the left'.[1] Until now, while the party's fortunes had waxed and waned, her reputation had been only burnished. The 2019 defeat was the first big hit to her personal standing. The big-spending election promises, journalists were told, had been in the areas closest to her heart. Spending on her portfolio of education – pursuing the Gonski reforms – had been the most expensive single item on the agenda and one of the first announced election commitments. Other big-spending promises included $15 billion on childcare and childcare subsidies, $9 billion to provide old-age pensioners free dental care, another $9 billon for affordable housing, $10 billion for TAFE and universities and $8 billion on preschool and kindergarten. The agenda Labor had taken to the election could easily be read as a summary of the issues Plibersek had pursued throughout her parliamentary career.

Late in the year, the party published its own review of the reasons for the defeat. Chaired by former minister Craig Emerson and the recently defeated Labor premier of South Australia, Jay Weatherill, the review was based on interviews with more than 120 MPs, candidates and party members. It found no single reason for Labor's loss, but rather a constellation of issues.

Labor lost because of a weak strategy, a failure to adapt to the change in Liberal leadership when Scott Morrison replaced Malcolm Turnbull, a 'cluttered policy agenda' and an unpopular leader in Bill Shorten, the review said. 'No one of these shortcomings was decisive but in combination they explain the result.'

The review found, extraordinarily, that there had been no formal campaign committee, meaning there was no forum for devising effective strategy, assessing the campaign as it proceeded and correcting the course. There were many policies, but no narrative to unify them. 'We could not find any documented strategy that had been discussed, contested and agreed across the campaign organisation, the leadership and the wider Labor Party,' the review said.

> New spending policies appear to have been decided by a combination of the leader and his office, a shadow expenditure review committee and an augmented leadership group ... These decisions were not informed by an overarching strategy. Indeed, the National Secretary seems to have been taken by surprise by the number and size of the policy offerings that were announced during the campaign.

Scott Morrison, meanwhile, was an unknown quantity, and had successfully established himself as a likeable 'daggy dad' figure. Shorten had continued to use language such as 'the big end of town' to attack the Liberals. That had been potent against the wealthy Turnbull but fell flat when used against Morrison. 'Bill Shorten's unpopularity contributed to the election loss,' the review said.

Another key factor, the review found, was that Labor's natural support base of unions and progressive organisations had already 'banked the win'. Rather than campaigning for a change in government, the emphasis had been on lobbying for Labor to commit to the groups' favoured policy agendas. Said the review: 'Labor's policy formulation process lacked coherence and was driven by multiple demands rather than a compelling story of why Labor should be elected to government.' Meanwhile, the media was so convinced Labor would win that it had treated it as the government in waiting, scrutinising its polices minutely, while the government escaped with less examination. Another issue identified was changes in demographics – a new cohort of voters, many of them insecure casual workers in the outer suburbs and regions, who were vulnerable to scare campaigns. It was these voters who had been frightened by Labor's reform ambitions and tax changes. The wealthier investors who would have lost money had Labor been elected had largely supported the changes, despite their self-interest.

The review recommended that Labor should not be less ambitious about policy in future campaigns, 'but its policy agenda should be less complex ... The nature, size and breadth of pre-election policies should be carefully considered ahead of the 2022 election.' It was this insight, together with his own strategic judgement, that was to drive Albanese's 'small target' approach to the 2022 election campaign.

The Emerson and Weatherill review echoed and legitimised the view being expressed by many in the party, and by the political journalists who took their briefings – that it was the ambitious spending agenda that 'drove' the tax policy. Early on, a decision was made that Labor had to present a better bottom line to the budget than the government. Therefore spending had to be matched by new revenue-raising measures. The welter of spending announcements – almost daily – and the proposed tax changes spooked voters, the review found, playing into the government's scare campaign that Labor could not be trusted with the economy.[2]

The two main tax policies were a withdrawal of franking credit refunds, and restrictions on the negative gearing of rental properties.

The idea that the spending promises drove the tax measures is disputed by people close to Shorten and Plibersek. Rather, they say, it was the other way round. They point out that the negative gearing changes had also been part of the policy agenda in 2016 – when Labor did better than expected. According to this account, it was shadow treasurer Chris Bowen who wanted to attempt ambitious tax reform. Tax reform came first, and the spending promises followed. As is the way with internal disputes in the Labor Party, each camp argues its side with total conviction and as a simple binary. Either tax drove spending (that is, Bowen is to blame), or spending drove tax (Shorten and Plibersek are to blame).

But of course it is not so simple as accounts given out by rivals and the self-interested tend to suggest. Tax and spending programs are arrived at in a more complex, iterative fashion. In 2016, nobody expected Labor to win. Therefore the tax policy was 'an entirely different equation' for the voting public, said one senior party source. In 2016 Labor had been facing Turnbull, who was a poor campaigner. 'In some ways the land-mines that cost us the 2019 election were there in 2016, it's just that they were prosecuted more effectively by Morrison than by Turnbull,' said this source. 'As Bill kept making more promises, the spending bill kept growing and growing and growing ... there was no sense in which we started the 2019 process with a blank sheet of paper. Everything in 2016 was locked and loaded and we built on it.'

Hindsight is a wonderful thing. In retrospect, the party hardheads argue, the big education commitments, including the Gonski reforms, should have forced a consideration of what else a new Labor government could afford to do. Plibersek should not be blamed, they say. Of course she was going to argue for her portfolio. Said the senior source: 'It was for the leader and the shadow treasurer to assess it all. It was for them to say to Tanya either "We can't do this" or "We can't do all of this" or "If we do this we can't do anything else". None of those things were said to her.' Perhaps, if just the Gonski reforms had been pursued, and the tax reforms limited to negative gearing, the election outcome would have been different. We will never know.

So what does Plibersek say about all this – the excoriation of the policy mix, the damning comments about strategy, and the balance of blame? In interviews for this book, Plibersek said she took 'complete responsibility' for the loss. 'I'm responsible, and I am more sorry than anyone else.' More responsible than Shorten? 'No, I'm not more responsible than Bill, but I just feel the weight of it. Three more years of a Liberal government were terrible for the country and I don't think anybody regrets it more than I do. I really feel sick about it. Every day of the last term of the Coalition government, whenever they did something that I didn't agree with, I reproached myself for being part of giving them that extra term they shouldn't have had.'

If she had doubts, as she claims, about the campaign, why was she not able to act? She was, after all, deputy leader. 'I do feel like I was pretty frank about my concerns the whole way through the campaign. Sometimes I was able to change the way we were doing things, and sometimes I wasn't. A campaign is a lot of people working together. I'm sorry that I wasn't able to change some of the weaknesses that I identified, but I don't run away from taking responsibility for it.'

She acknowledges that many of the big spending promises were issues close to her heart and political history, but it wasn't just her. Shorten and the rest of the leadership team were 'entirely on board ... Bill and I had an excellent working relationship. We had a lot of similar views about what a Labor government should look like ... It's a fair criticism to say we were fighting on too many fronts, there was too much content in the policy offering. But am I ever going to apologise for wanting to properly fund public schools? No, not ever.'

She says she agrees with many of the findings of the Emerson and Weatherill review, but not the claim that there was no campaign committee. 'I don't see it that way. We had a leadership group meeting every morning at 6.30. We had regular meetings of the parliamentary leadership and the national secretary and other advisers, including Bill, Penny Wong, Don Farrell and national secretary Noah Carroll. What we didn't have is regular meetings with all of the state secretaries, for example, in one room, which some campaigns in the past have done.'

She prefers to emphasise the scrutiny Labor was subjected to, because of the expectation it would win. 'I still think if you look back on the 2019 election and ask, "What was Scott Morrison's plan for the country, for his prime ministership?", you would really struggle to identify a single new policy ... It was a very superficial campaign. And I was nervous the whole way along.'

*   *   *

The day after the election, the Labor team entered a collective depression. It took the party at least six months to rally. Yet, straightaway, there was to be another contest. Shorten stood down from the leadership on election night. A new leader had to be chosen under the rules that divide the vote, if there was more than one contender, between Labor parliamentarians and the broad ALP membership.

To nobody's surprise, Albanese announced his candidacy the day after the election. Plibersek was expected to follow. On the ABC *Insiders* program on Sunday, she confirmed she was considering running.

Shorten threw his support behind her. Julia Gillard made her first intervention in politics since she lost the prime ministership and endorsed Tanya Plibersek.[3] Other candidates were expected to include shadow treasurer Chris Bowen and shadow finance minister Jim Chalmers – although, as the press noted, both were closely associated with the spending and tax package so recently rejected at the election. This was expected to count against them, and potentially against Plibersek too.

The media were expecting that Plibersek would declare her candidacy on Monday afternoon. It came as a shock when, instead, she issued a statement ruling herself out. She said she had support from across the party, but 'now is not my time ... At this point, I cannot reconcile the important responsibilities I have to my family with the additional responsibilities of the Labor leadership.'

In the following days Penny Wong, leader in the Senate and a key figure in the left of the party, backed Albanese. Bowen and Chalmers stepped back, and Albanese became leader of the Australian Labor Party unopposed.

In the months that followed, Plibersek gave a few interviews reflecting on her decision. In a podcast hosted by Gillard, she said she was put off by the amount of time on the road, and the impact on her family. She said she was worried that other women might draw from her decision a message about the inability to have children and take leadership positions. She felt bad about that, but: 'To other women, I say, "You are not responsible for the life and fate and opportunities of every woman. You need to make the decision that is best for you" ... If you've got no kids you get criticised for not understanding what families are going through. If you've got kids, you get criticised for neglecting them. There's basically no right answer. And so, what can you do but please yourself? You have to do the thing that's best for you in your life and for your family.'

Gillard remarked that she had been criticised for not having kids. How did Plibersek cope?

'I cook in batches and freeze food. I get my clothes out each night that I'm going to wear the next day, because I don't want to be making decisions under pressure at five o'clock in the morning in the dark as I'm rushing off to work,' she said. 'You try and reduce the pressure by being super-organised and balance that at the same time with being present when you're with your kids.'[4]

Plibersek's supporters were shocked and disappointed by her decision. Jenna Price, a columnist for *The Sydney Morning Herald*, speculated that some dastardly internal Labor politicking was at work. Or had Plibersek had an unaccountable attack of imposter syndrome? As for the kids – Price had telephoned Plibersek's office offering to give up her own career to help care for them.

> I live in her seat. I think she's fabulous ... Unkindly, the young man who took my call laughed at me. Then, I'm pretty sure he put it on loudspeaker and asked me to repeat my generous offer. The entire Plibersek office was laughing at me. He promised to pass my message on to Tanya. I still haven't heard anything, but Tanya, if you are reading this, the offer still stands.[5]

On social media, Price's call was quickly shared, liked and taken up. Within hours, Plibersek could have had an army of child carers at her disposal. But none of them knew the full story. None of them knew there was a scar here, a trauma they could not soothe.

Tanya Plibersek told the media and some friends a few more stories about what had happened on that Monday morning. Louis – nine years old – had crawled into his parents' bed and been surprised to find his mother there. She had hardly been at home during the campaign – or for the previous gruelling six years of deputy leadership.

Another story Tanya told friends was about being in the playground with Louis. He had spent fifteen minutes or so on the equipment and then announced he was ready to go home, because he assumed his mother had no more time to give. That hurt.

These anecdotes were true, but not the whole story.

Meanwhile, the media was taking background briefings from within the parliamentary party, and as a result reported the real reason she had withdrawn was because she didn't have the numbers in caucus.

This was a continuation of consistent claims about Plibersek, briefed out by Plibersek-sceptics and her rivals. They acknowledge her popularity with the public and the party membership, but say she is less admired by her parliamentary colleagues. The political journalists reported that the left in caucus, faced with two candidates from their faction, backed Albanese over her.

When I was researching this book, that account was repeated to me. I put this to Tanya in one of our early interviews. She remarked, acidly, 'There seems to be this presumption among some that women can't count.'

Members of the Plibersek camp urged me not to 'fall for' the line. They believe that had she contested the leadership at any time between the 2019 defeat and the final months of 2021, she would have won. And some of them were urging her to try.

In my last interview with Plibersek, I asked her again about the claim that she didn't have the numbers in 2019. 'That's absolutely what people who like to background against me would say. We'll never know. It's history. But I am pretty confident that if I had run, I would have won.'

So why did she withdraw?

The full story of that decision was not Tanya's to tell. It belonged to her daughter, Anna, who was eighteen years old at the time of the 2019 election. Her story appears here for the first time.

* * *

When I first contacted Plibersek's office in March 2021, seeking cooperation with this biography, I asked to interview her, Michael Coutts-Trotter and her brother and mother. Almost as an afterthought I asked if Anna, then 20, and Joe, 16, would also like to speak to me.

The suggestion caused an obvious frisson of anxiety among Plibersek's staff, which puzzled me. I was asked if I had a particular set of questions for Anna and Joe. I replied that I had no agenda, but given I would be speaking to many people who knew their mother it seemed reasonable to give them the opportunity as well. For over a year, there was no firm answer to my request. Anna might speak to me. She might not. There were things happening. It had to be her decision.

When I interviewed Jeannette McHugh, she impressed on me that Plibersek had been telling the truth when she said the family was the reason for her withdrawal from the leadership contest. There was more to it, she said, but it was up to the family whether or not they shared the story. I asked Jenny Macklin if she believed that family was the reason. She responded, with great emphasis, that she *knew* it to be true. She would give no further details.

And when I interviewed Michael Coutts-Trotter, he said there had been 'a number of things' behind the decision, 'but fundamentally, with the three children, each one of them had something going on at that point that needed a bit more parental attention than usual, particularly for our daughter'. He said that Tanya had been exhausted after the election campaign and 'nine years of grinding work'. They had discussed her decision, and he had told her he would support her no matter what she decided to do.

'To the extent that I could be a fair observer, she absolutely had a coalition of support from left and right factions. So it was absolutely obtainable. But basically, what our kids needed was the deciding factor.'

Anna eventually decided to speak to me. She did so because, like her mother before her, she wants to make a difference. She has already been brave. She has already stood up, before a court of law, to try to make what happened to her matter. She wants to tell her story to help others.

It is a hard story to tell – heartbreaking, soul-crushing – and it will be hard to read.

I met Anna on a Friday afternoon in August 2022, over the dining table in the open-plan living area of the family home. She was now twenty-one years old. She resembles both her parents – Michael's tall, thin physique and her mother's blonde hair, silky and long, parted in the centre.

She remembers what it was like growing up around her mother. Photocopying her hands on the office machine, then drawing little faces on the images of her fingers. Raiding the biscuit jar in the office. Playing with her mother's staff. She talks about her early childhood and the birth of her brothers. 'I was obsessed with Joe when he was a baby. I wouldn't let him go out of my sight. And I used to say to Mum, "I have to give him twenty kisses before I go to preschool. And Mum would say, "He's asleep." And I would say, "Well, I need to give him twenty kisses," so she would have to let me give him kisses before I went.'

Tanya told the children from an early age that she wanted them to be many things – brave and bold – but if she could choose just one character trait, it would be kindness. In the case of Anna there was no need for urging. From her earliest years it was clear that she had in common with her mother the gift, or the curse, of conspicuous empathy. At the time of our interview she was studying at the University of Sydney to be a social worker – the career her mother had once considered. She said it had been clear since her childhood that she was destined for 'the caring professions'. While still at Randwick Girls' High School, she featured in the local paper because she had won an award for volunteering as a visitor to the Montefiore home for aged people. That work had begun when her history teacher urged the students to interview Holocaust survivors. Anna was so moved that she kept going back.

'It was difficult hearing those stories, it was very confronting,' she told the newspaper. 'But very important and everyone was so kind.' Where had the urge to help people come from, the reporter asked? 'I think my parents, they are both social justice advocates and have been my whole life. Since a baby I've been going to Mum's events and meetings. So from a young age I've known I need to do the right thing.'[6]

On the day of her interview with me, she had spent an hour on the phone to a survivor of sexual abuse who was due to appear in court the next day. Anna was able to help. It drains her, but 'this is what I do now. This is what I do with what happened to me. I try to use it.'

Anna believes that she was more vulnerable because of this empathy and compassion. She didn't use the word 'boundaries', but it occurred to me, as I listened to her. She said: 'There's a lot of evidence that shows people in caring professions are more targeted by abusers. People who care are vulnerable. You kind of think you can fix them or you make excuses for them. So, I was like, "Oh, he's just doing his exams now. He'll be better after that." Or, "Oh, he's just trying to get into university. He'll be better after that." Or then, "He's just doing his university exams. He'll be better after that." And it's never-ending. There's always excuses that they make for their behaviour. And I wanted to look after him, to be good for him.'

Tanya and Anna are close. Anna asserts that despite her job, her mother is 'more available to me than many of my friends' mothers are to them. I call my mum for, like, everything. I'm always texting her and calling her. If I'm going for a job interview and I'm thinking about what I want to wear, I'll send her six photos of options. That's if she's not home. If she's home, then I'll get her to come and watch me try them all on and help me decide, because she always gives really good advice about things like that. I'm always asking her questions and I tell her about everything that's going on with my life and my friends. I've always been really, really open with her. I've never been shy to tell her things.'

But there was a period, when Anna was in her mid-teens, when she didn't tell Tanya everything that was going on. During this time, Anna's personality changed. Already thin, she lost weight. She lost friends. She withdrew from her family and became moody and hard to reach. This was during the years when Tanya was deputy leader of the Australian Labor Party and working to improve its culture.

Over this time, Anna was being abused by her then boyfriend. The abuse began at the start of the relationship and the violence and controlling behaviour gradually got worse, escalating to serious sexual assault. Anna's abuser was eventually convicted of assault because of what he did to her. He has also been convicted of serious crimes committed against other girls, but has never gone to jail. There are legal reasons why few details can be published.

Anna recalls: 'I experienced pretty much every kind of abuse you can think of. It was emotional, it was physical. It was even financial, as much as you can be financially abused as a teenager. He tried to stop me talking to my friends. I lost so many friends.' She tried to appease him. She made excuses. She loved him. 'I was so manipulated. I wasn't myself. I lost myself.' She didn't want to go into further details for this book. The court process was traumatic. Anna was in the witness box for four days, three of them under cross-examination. Her friends and her parents also gave evidence about what they had seen and heard of her boyfriend's behaviour, and its impact on her.

Anna is recovering. Part of that recovery has been to use her experience to help others. In 2021 she and some others founded a not-for-profit group, The Survivor Hub. Through social media, a website and in-person meetings, it provides support for survivors. Anna is telling some of her story now as part of that effort. She wants people to understand that the court system retraumatises survivors and fails to hold perpetrators to account. She wants people to know that in this area, the justice system is broken. And she hopes to help people understand how perpetrators manipulate you – how they use your best features against you. How you can end up scarcely knowing your own mind, and how insidious it is. And then, if you have the courage to go to court, the things you said to yourself to try to minimise the trauma – the excuses you made, the kindness you showed – will be used to attack your credibility. You felt sorry for him? Then you must be lying. And so the abuse goes on – not only individual, but systemic. Not only a personal tragedy, but a society-wide one. An ongoing, in-plain-sight nightmare that touches just about everyone's life.

Anna has often asked herself why these things happened to her, given all her advantages. And, in particular, the daughter of a feminist mother who has spent a large part of her career advocating on gender violence issues – the woman who is chiefly responsible for the National Plan for the Prevention of Violence Against Women and Their Children. But now Anna knows the central lesson. Her own story is proof. It can happen to anyone. She emphasises the word. '*Anyone.*' She went to court with the full support of her family, excellent counselling – all of her advantages and privileges. Yet the experience nearly destroyed her – even more than the abuse had done. Today, she does not necessarily advise the survivors she meets to go to court. It is a big decision. She understands why they might choose not to do so.

At the time Tanya had to make the decision whether to seek the Labor leadership in May 2019, she knew that her daughter would soon have to face being a witness against her abuser in court, although the date the case would begin was not yet known. 'And the thought of not being able to be there for her through that was just too much.' In the lead-up to the start of the case, Anna was finding it hard to face the days. She either slept around the clock or was woken by nightmares. She wandered the house in the middle of the night, desperately seeking distraction. She leant on her friends and her family, and yet, because they were to be witnesses, they could not discuss the detail of what had happened to her. It was during this time that Anna saw her father cry for the first time in her life. Her mother, she says – with just a hint of an eyeroll – 'Cries all the time. Happy, sad, she cries. Mum crying doesn't mean anything special, but Dad doesn't cry.' But at this time, having his daughter hurt, being unable to fully support her, Michael Coutts-Trotter, jail bird, senior public servant, living evidence of the capacity for human redemption, broke down and wept.

* * *

Anna had finished telling me her story. We were sitting at the family dining table. It was a Friday afternoon. Tanya had told me earlier in the day that on Fridays she tries to pick up Louis from school, and to cook the family dinner. Now she was at the door, and came into the kitchen. Would it bother Anna if she pottered around while we talked? Anna told her that it would, and asked her to go away.

She wanted to use the remaining minutes of our interview to tell me nice stories about her mother, and she knew that if she did it while she was listening, 'She will cry. She always cries.' Tanya dashed around making Louis a toasted sandwich and putting a pork roast in the oven, then moved out to the study.

So how did Anna feel when her mother decided not to run for the leadership of the Labor Party?

They hadn't really talked about it much. They don't talk about politics at home – or at least not the internal machinations of the Labor Party. Rather, 'We talk about values.'

'If something's going on in the news and Joe and Louis and I don't know how we feel about it, we might bring it up to Mum and Dad or ask them what they think about it, because obviously they have more information than we do. They know what's going on. And then Mum and Dad might explain how they feel about something. We don't often disagree. I think I'm a little bit more woke with identity politics than Mum, but she's more woke than all of my friends' parents. It's a generational thing.'

The day in 2019 that Tanya announced she would not be a candidate for the Labor leadership, she took Anna out to lunch. 'We celebrated, Mum and me. I remember how nice it was. Just going out for lunch in the middle of the day.'

Now Joe was home from school, and joined us at the table, listening to the conversation. He volunteered that he regretted that his mother did not contest the leadership. 'We support her values.'

Anna agreed: 'I believe she would have been really, really good at it. There are a lot of politicians who aren't in it for the people, but she's in it for the people. It is just so obvious she cares about people and she wants to make Australia better for everybody. I'm not saying anyone else, or Albo, doesn't feel that way. I'm just talking about Mum.'

Sadly, too many parents will not have to imagine what Tanya felt when she learned her daughter had been the victim of sexual and domestic violence. It is a disturbingly common story. Most daughters, most mothers in this situation never go public, and never go to court. But for Tanya there was the extra burden of knowing so much about men's violence against women, and yet not having been able to protect her daughter.

Two months after speaking to Anna, I sat at the same dining table with Plibersek for our final interview. What did she want to say about Anna's story? It had been, she said, 'devastating'. 'You ask yourself whether you could have or should have done more to protect your child. It's not an easy question to ask yourself.'

She thinks Anna is recovering as well as anyone could, and 'I'm really proud that she is using her experience to help other people. But it has just been awful. Listening to Anna give her victim impact statement to the court was the hardest hour I've experienced as a parent – but I was so proud of her too.' She agrees with Anna that part of the mix was her empathy. 'I think she's absolutely right about that. Her empathy and compassion were used against her by someone in a phenomenally manipulative way.'

As for her own experience giving evidence, it was 'awful ... but I was more upset that she was subjected to all the same kind of questions that I thought we stopped asking victims of crime in the seventies. What were you wearing? What had you been drinking? It enraged me to see up close how broken the system is and how much it adds to the trauma.'

As for how this could happen to her daughter: 'I've always known that it can happen to anyone. The way that men like that behave is very calculating. They take someone away from their support networks, their friends, their family. They destroy their self-confidence so they can't behave in the way they normally do. So what happened to Anna all fits in exactly with everything I know academically about this issue, and have known since I was her age, and everything I've ever said.' There are tears in her eyes. She says: 'But knowing this stuff doesn't alleviate the guilt of not protecting her.'

What role did Anna's trauma play in Plibersek's decision not to run for leader? She says it played a crucial part, but was not the only factor. 'I couldn't imagine saying, "Sorry, I can't be with you today. I've got to fly somewhere for a conference."'

But she doesn't want Anna to think it was only her. It was broader than that. 'I've been close enough to all of the leaders of the Labor Party. I've had a front-row seat for a long time. I know what it entails to do the job properly. Louis was nine when we lost the 2019 election. Joe had his HSC this year. And I miss them when I travel. I miss them a lot ... I love my job. But I had to make that decision on what was right for us, what kind of parent I want to be.'

Tanya Plibersek was carrying Anna's story with her throughout the last term of the Morrison government. It was on her mind in March

2021, when historical rape allegations surfaced against the then attorney-general, Christian Porter. (He has always denied the allegations.) It was with her when former Liberal staffer Brittany Higgins alleged she had been raped by colleague Bruce Lehrmann in Parliament House. As this book went to print, the court case against Lehrmann was dropped because of its effect on the mental health of Higgins, whose life was said to be at risk as a result. That, too, had its impact on Anna and her mother.

And, years earlier, there had been another set of allegations. After Bill Shorten became leader, Plibersek, like many others, was contacted by a woman who claims to have been raped by Bill Shorten in the 1980s, when he was nineteen. Plibersek had no knowledge of this until it was aired in the media. In 2014, the allegations were investigated by the police, and dismissed. The police said there was no evidence capable of securing a conviction. Shorten went public, describing the allegations as 'abhorrent and untrue'. Plibersek told the media that the investigation had been thorough, 'and that should be an end to the matter'.[7]

*   *   *

Meanwhile, the merciless, potent business of politics moved on. In the first Albanese shadow cabinet, Tanya Plibersek lost the women's portfolio to Julie Collins, but retained education and training. She was, of course, no longer deputy leader. The fact that she and Albanese were from the same faction, and the same few square kilometres of Sydney, ruled out that possibility, even if there had been no rivalry between them. Instead, Richard Marles from the Victorian Right succeeded her. Albanese, Marles and Penny Wong as leader in the Senate, and Kristina Keneally as her deputy, now made up the leadership of the parliamentary party. Plibersek regained the women's portfolio in a January 2021 reshuffle. She lost training. So why these shifts in responsibility? In our final interview, Plibersek would not be drawn. 'Those are questions for the leader.'

For most of the period between the election defeat of 2019 and the 2022 election, there were constant doubts about Albanese's leadership. Plibersek was continuously mentioned in speculation. In March 2020 – just a few months before Anna had to appear in court, and just as the

Covid pandemic began to change the world – the media was suggesting that she was positioning herself for a challenge. She was reported to have made appearances at backbench meetings she normally wouldn't have attended.[8] In November, political journalists reported that Labor MPs were increasingly concerned their seats were at risk because of Albanese's failure to make an impact in the opinion polls. Shorten praised Plibersek in a couple of interviews, while stressing there was no vacancy for the leadership.[9]

In late 2020, Plibersek released a book. *Upturn: A Better Normal after Covid* was a collection of thirty essays by her friends and the policy thinkers she admired. ACTU secretary Sally McManus wrote on economics. June Oscar had a chapter on First Nations and remote communities. Cate Blanchett and Kim Williams wrote about cultural policy, Adrian Pisarski wrote on housing policy and Gareth Evans on foreign affairs. Plibersek edited the collection, and contributed a brief introduction and a chapter on education policy, anchored in her personal story. 'We didn't have much money growing up, but all I had to say was "It's for school" and my parents would find a way to pay for the excursion, or the book, or the art supplies … they knew education was a ticket to freedom and choice.' The rest of her chapter was an elegantly structured argument for ALP policy.[10]

Writing books is common thing to do for those who aspire to be prime minister. Mark Latham wrote several before he became Labor leader. Tony Abbott wrote *Battlelines*, laying out his values and personal political history. Jim Chalmers wrote *Glory Daze*. But *Upturn* was a different kind of book. Rather than presenting her own ideas, Plibersek was curating and promoting others. Launching the book at the Sydney Institute, she riffed on John Howard's famous aspiration that Australians should be 'relaxed and comfortable'. She wanted to 'aim a bit higher' and have them be 'relaxed and confident' about the country's future. 'What's the return to our citizens for the enormous discipline and compassion and patience and goodwill that the vast majority have shown? Well, the return has to be a better country on the other side,' she said.

I asked Plibersek why she had published this kind of book, rather than one filled with her own policy ideas. 'What inference do you draw from this?' she asked me. I said there were a couple. One was that it said something about the character of her leadership, should she ever be prime minister. We might conclude that she would be a collaborator, a facilitator, rather than the kind of leader who lays out a vision and demands to be followed. 'Okay, and is there another possible inference?' The other inference, I said, was that she didn't have enough ideas of her own to fill a book.

She replied: 'I think being able to listen to people who are experts in their field and draw the best out of them to inform your own thinking and decision-making is a really important skill in politics. And there are people who listen to others and plagiarise their ideas and pass them off as their own. I think it's much better to be open to it – to enable the contest of ideas and also give credit to people who know what they're talking about.' Had she ever thought about writing a Tanya Plibersek book, laying out her vision? 'No.' Why not? 'Because I'm busy doing my day job. I have so many opportunities to share my ideas and values – every speech, every interview and more importantly the policies I implement. I don't think what I believe would be a mystery to anyone.'

Reviews of *Upturn* were generally, but not exclusively, favourable. It was a difficult book to sum up – in some parts merely a list of asserted imperatives: Australia should do this and must do that. The most critical review came from two academics who wrote: 'Readers of *Upturn* are invited to wander through a maze of ideas with no coherent, well signposted ways to the future. This book had rich promise but is a missed opportunity.'[11]

The release of *Upturn* was noted by the Albanese camp. There, at least, it was taken as a piece of political positioning.

By January 2021, Sportsbet was wagering that Albanese would not make it to the next election. Plibersek was favourite, ahead of Chalmers and Marles, to replace him.[12] *The Australian* described Plibersek, Bowen and Chalmers as 'sharks' circling Albanese. They were ready to strike, the article asserted, but did not want to be seen as wreckers. Albanese was said to be 'strategically inept and policy-barren ... he just doesn't have what it takes'. Meanwhile, Plibersek's profile was 'skyrocketing'.[13] Another article in *The Australian* asked: 'Could it be any coincidence that the meteoric rise in Plibersek's presence has come just as Labor leadership speculation surrounding Albo has never been louder, because of his poor personal Newspoll ratings? ... the bemused Albo camp have clocked Plibersek's increased media profile lately, and are more than a little curious about its timing.'[14]

And so it went on. By this time, the worst of Anna's trauma before the courts was over.

Plibersek was not encouraging the speculation. She told the media Labor needed to focus on the main game rather than talk endlessly about itself.[15] But when I was researching this book, I was told by two sources that in early 2021, she had been taking soundings about her support. She was not, I was told, doing the numbers in a systemic way. Rather, in the atmosphere of an expected challenge to Albanese, probably to be brought on by either Bowen or Chalmers, she was assessing whether she would be a competitive contender.

In our last interview, I asked Tanya Plibersek if she had considered a leadership challenge against Albanese in 2021. She said: 'I've never been involved in leadership destabilisation in all my years in parliament. It's not how I behave and anybody who knows me knows that.' Had she sounded out her support? 'Well, what does that mean? It's a fuzzy term ... I am not going to comment on rumours from unnamed sources.' When I pressed her, she said, 'That's just not right. I've worked my guts out to support every leader we've had.' Later, she said that after the 2019 election many colleagues had rung her, some urging her to contest the leadership. And it was normal and to be expected that she spoke to colleagues as well. 'But despite having a strong level of support, I ultimately decided not to run, for the reasons I have already shared with you.' But she was talking, in these remarks, about the post-election context in 2019. She would not be drawn further on her actions in early 2021, other than to deny she had sounded out support.

On 2 February 2021, amid all the speculation regarding her profile and her prospects, Tanya Plibersek went viral. Craig Kelly, the maverick Liberal member for Hughes, had been spreading misinformation about the pandemic, including scepticism about vaccines and promotion of ineffective treatments. Plibersek was addressing the media in a corridor of Parliament House, saying that Scott Morrison should pull him into line, when Kelly walked out of the Sky News studio and crashed into the scrum of journalists and cameras.

She smiled at him, briefly reached out to touch his elbow, as though to soften the blow, and then told him she had been arguing that 'the PM has to stop you from spreading these crazy conspiracy theories'.

Kelly raised his hand at her, two fingers pointing and cutting at the air. He quoted a professor who had appeared in that morning's newspapers giving him qualified support and insisted she 'Read him. Read him. He says Craig Kelly is exactly right.' Plibersek asked if that meant that the prime minister was wrong when he encouraged vaccination. 'The prime minister is exactly right,' said Kelly, caught in his own contradictions.

It was a striking image – the poised, smiling Plibersek, assertive but not aggressive, and the angry, red-faced man, stabbing at her with his fingers. *Crikey*'s Guy Rundle commented later: 'Kelly had the demeanour of a wombat pulled from its hole by scientists to have its arse microchipped.'[16]

Plibersek said to Kelly: 'My mum lives in your electorate and I don't want her exposed to Covid because of these crazy conspiracy theories of yours.' That grab made all the television news bulletins that night, but the exchange was appearing on social media almost before it was over. The tone of the response was clear. Albanese was for most voters relatively unknown – a grey, unexciting figure. Here was this extraordinary woman. Why wasn't she the leader?

There were immediate consequences to the exchange. Within minutes of the interaction, Kelly was summoned to Scott Morrison's office and, it emerged later, told to 'shut up' on his Covid activism or face deselection.[17] A few days later, Kelly quit the Liberal Party and moved to the crossbench, reducing the government's majority to one. In August, he joined and became the leader of Clive Palmer's United Australia Party. He went on to lose his seat to the Liberals in the 2022 federal election.

Meanwhile, on the afternoon of the encounter, Plibersek rang the old family home in Oyster Bay and warned her mother not to take calls from journalists. She feared Rose might be targeted by anti-vaccination activists. To her relief, she found Rose was having a peaceful day – entirely unaware her daughter was leading the news.

A few weeks after the Kelly episode, with Plibersek's profile at an all-time high, I made the first approach to her office seeking cooperation with this book. She made it clear she didn't want it written – but knowing that a book would be written with or without her cooperation, she calculated it was better to cooperate and have some agency. The Covid pandemic disrupted the project. I was locked down in Melbourne for much of the period of my research, unable to travel, and several interviews were conducted by Zoom. Plibersek got Covid.

I watched from Melbourne as NSW Liberal premier Gladys Berejiklian was forced to resign because of an ICAC investigation and was replaced by her former treasurer, Dominic Perrottet – a committed and socially conservative Catholic. One of his first acts, on 7 October 2021, was to move aside the previously appointed head of the NSW public service and install Michael Coutts-Trotter as his personal choice to head the Department of Premier and Cabinet. In a statement, Perrottet said: 'Michael's dedication to serving the people of NSW is something I have long admired, he will bring tremendous experience, humility and energy to what is a very important and challenging position.'[18] The media described Coutts-Trotter as 'highly respected, hard-headed and a professional public servant'.[19]

The Coutts-Trotter story of redemption was again in the headlines, and the media pointed out that his wife might soon be a senior minister in an Albanese Labor government. Even though the election was now just months away, so talk of a challenge to Albanese had abated, some didn't discount the possibility that Plibersek might be a future Labor prime minister. How would that work out over the breakfast table?

Meanwhile, Anna Coutts-Trotter tweeted the stories, writing simply: 'So proud of my dad.'

* * *

On 18 November 2021, I was due to interview Tanya in her Sydney electorate office – the first time we had been able to schedule a face-to-face meeting since the lockdowns. Some were predicting there could be an election as early as January. The party had locked in behind Albanese as leader. The time for a challenge, if it was ever seriously contemplated, had passed.

At the last minute, there were changes to the timing of our interview. Tanya had been called at short notice to take part in an announcement about providing free broadband internet for kids who didn't have it at home – part of Labor's plan to improve the NBN. She had to travel out to a school in the western suburbs to appear with Albanese and the shadow minister for communications, Michelle Rowland. I was left with hours to wait and stooged around in the cafes closest to her office in the inner suburb of Redfern. I chatted to her electors and her supporters.

They feared Albanese was being too cautious, presenting too small a target. 'We only win government when we give people something to vote for,' said one of Plibersek's supporters. 'When we offer a vision.' For months Albanese had been telling his team that the strategy was to have a careful, deliberate campaign, with a few big points of difference from the Coalition but not too crowded with policy announcements. Then, 'We will kick with the wind in the final quarter.'

Gone were the big education spending commitments that had been part of the mix in 2019. Plibersek's education portfolio barely got a mention in the campaign. Gone were the negative gearing and franking credits tax changes. The previous month, political commentator Sean Kelly had published a column noting Albanese had some policy promises on climate change, housing and childcare, and a theme – 'build back stronger' – but for the most part, his strategy was 'make sure there is nothing for the other side to hit'. Said Kelly: 'I think Albanese is running out of time to make an impression, and I tend towards thinking that is a problem for Labor.' The headline on the piece read: 'Albanese says he's in the final quarter, so when is he going to start kicking goals?'[20]

Labor's big point of difference from the government had been signalled the previous May, and the detail was announced two weeks after my day in Redfern. Labor would commit to reducing carbon emissions by 43 per cent by 2030 – a slightly less ambitious target than Bill Shorten's 45 per cent, but much more ambitious than the Coalition, and accompanied by plans for upgrades to the electricity grid, community batteries and renewables manufacturing.[21]

I met Plibersek again on 7 December. I was to spend some of the day following her around. She rose early and, as is their habit, she and

Michael went on a twenty-minute walk with their two small dogs to a local cafe. A quick coffee, then a fast walk back to the family home, and Plibersek disappeared to shower and dress.

Most serious female politicians try to adopt a uniform these days, ever since Julia Gillard had to put up with constant comments about her clothes. The aim is to wear something neat, flattering and unremarkable – the equivalent of a man's suit. In theory, if you wear more or less the same thing each day, it will never be worth remarking on. Plibersek's uniform is a boat-necked blouse and a succession of simple trouser suits made of a light material that drapes well but doesn't crease or stain. For public appearances, she will put on heels, but on this day, and most of the time – even in parliament – she wears runners.

On this day, the suit was powder blue. As soon as she was ready, we were in her car rushing through city traffic, her press secretary in the back seat helping her rehearse lines for an appearance on Sky News. We parked and dashed through the streets to the tiny studio just off Martin Place – a room containing a robot camera and not much else. For the few seconds before she went live, Tanya closed her eyes. She was frowning and looked tired. Then, on cue, she opened her eyes, smiled and was aglow. I remembered what she had told me about her interview technique: was she imaging that inside that camera, her mother was listening?

Later that day, she put on heels and gave an oration at NSW Parliament House to memorialise the Holocaust scholar and historian Colin Tatz. She used it to rebut suggestions by the federal education minister, Alan Tudge, that students should be taught a positive version of Australian history. This was an authoritarian-style deleting of the past, she said. 'We face the past with courage because we're confident as a people that the truth won't break us. I love my children more than life itself, but I don't think they're perfect. I draw their attention to how they can do better, precisely because I love them. Some parents never pull their kids up. And could anyone honestly say those kids are better off for it?' She was using her children as an analogy for the nation.

Later, I read that passage to Joe and Anna. They hadn't been aware she had mentioned them. 'Oh, that's funny,' said Anna. They agreed it made her sound much stricter than she really is.

*   *   *

For most of the mainstream media, the main theme of the campaign for
Tanya Plibersek was her absence.

One month before election day, *The Sydney Morning Herald* ran a
story under the headline 'The chosen and the frozen: Plibersek, Shorten
benched during Labor's campaign'. It was based on a leaked internal
memo from the campaign headquarters telling candidates that the media
would be given transcripts of media appearances only for Albanese and
a few selected shadow ministers. 'Experienced frontbenchers including
Plibersek, Shorten, Ed Husic, Clare O'Neil and even Brendan O'Connor
have, in comparison, been largely side-lined.'[22] When Albanese held the
campaign launch on 1 May, the media noted that Plibersek wasn't there.

Gareth Evans was watching the campaign and read the media reports.
He was relieved that the polls were looking better for Labor but was still
worried. Evans tries to stay out of the details of political campaigning.
He knows interference from 'old soldiers' like him is not always welcomed, but he dashed off an email to his friend Penny Wong, saying
that if what the media said was true it was 'just totally and depressingly
nuts ... everywhere I go [Plibersek] is regarded – like yourself – as a huge,
enormously attractive and articulate, asset for the party. With things so
delicately poised the leadership team just can't afford to be playing these
games. Please do something.'[23]

Ninety minutes after pressing send on that email, he got a phone
call from Tim Gartrell, Antony Albanese's chief of staff, and was assured
that Tanya was not being frozen out and was being fully used. After
that, whether because of his intervention or for other reasons, Evans
noticed Tanya was getting more visibility. He wrote to Gartrell again
on 9 May:

> Good that things are looking a bit more comfortable with latest
> polls, and to see Tanya P getting more visibility, as discussed: she's
> a safe and attractive pair of hands. One of our greatest compara-
> tive strengths is our whole shadow cabinet team, and great to have
> a number of them on regular show, including beside the leader:

whatever some of the media cretins are saying, it doesn't diminish
him in the slightest to occasionally defer to them on detail.[24]

Evans was alluding to a growing perception in the party that Albanese
was now showing his considerable strengths to the electorate, but that
his weakness – a tribalism in which perceived enemies and rivals were
frozen out – was also on display.

I was assured by some of those involved in the campaign that the
media was wrong in its reporting about Plibersek's role in the campaign.
She had not been sidelined. Plibersek agrees: 'I was travelling every day.
I did dozens of major interviews. I launched I don't know how many
campaigns. I did a lot of state visits. I don't feel like I was under-utilised.
I worked really hard. I was everywhere. I was on the tarmac before dawn
most days and travelling sometimes to two or three states in a day. And
I was delighted to do it. I really love campaigning.' Her office provided
a list of more than seventy media appearances Plibersek made during the
campaign, and more than thirty-nine electorate visits.

As for her absence from the campaign launch, it had been decided
there was no point in 'a whole bunch of shadow ministers being there.
She had been representing Albanese at a May Day rally with 'I don't
know how many thousands present'. 'If journalists want to cover an
event, it's really up to them to go,' she said. 'They could do that rather
than pretend there is some great internal party significance to the fact
they didn't cover it.' Meanwhile, the media were mainly focused on supposed gaffes by Albanese – stumbling over the unemployment figures,
and then emphasising with a single word, 'absolutely', that he was in
favour of lifting the minimum wage.

But the media had it wrong. Scott Morrison was unpopular with
Australian voters, and Anthony Albanese had indeed kicked with the
wind in the final quarter. He had done enough to convince the population of his own strengths, and those of his team. On 21 May, the
Australian Labor Party won the federal election. It was clear early in the
evening, as the votes were counted, that the Coalition couldn't win. It
had lost to so-called 'teal' independents, running on climate change and
integrity issues in traditionally safe Liberal seats. Every state and territory

except Tasmania swung to Labor on the two-party-preferred vote. The Coalition won only fifty-eight seats, its lowest share in the House of Representatives since 1946.

Yet it was not a landslide victory for Labor. Only a third of voters gave their first preference to the ALP. The crossbench swelled to sixteen, including independents and Greens. The combined major-party vote for Labor and the Coalition was the lowest on record, at 68 per cent. Plibersek was on the ABC television panel of commentators as the results rolled in. Journalist Leigh Sales asked her: 'What has Labor done wrong that it hasn't been a landslide?' Plibersek responded: 'A win is a win is a win.' But behind the scenes, Plibersek supporters saw, in the low primary vote, confirmation of their previous view: that the small-target approach was not the way for Labor to go forward. It was a win, but a narrow one.

In our last interview, I asked Tanya what she thought about Albanese's small-target strategy. She said: 'We won. So it was plainly the right decision to take. To be constrained. To focus on a few key areas. I don't regret most of the policies that we took to the people in 2019. I think they were good policies, perhaps not all exactly right, but by and large. And I think there was a lot of energy and enthusiasm from party members in support of what they saw as a good, strong, idealistic platform. But the downside was we didn't become the government ... So I think the more targeted focus did help us in the election campaign.'

As this book went to print, the media was judging the Albanese government a success. In December 2022, the ALP released its review of the election campaign, and laid out a plan to make this a long-term government. There was no room for complacency, the review said. Morrison's unpopularity had been the main reason for the win. That was the context in which the Albanese strategy had worked.

Now, Labor has a once-in-a-generation opportunity to establish a long-term government and change Australia for the better. Taking advantage of that opportunity starts with a candid assessment of the 2022 election result and the lessons it holds for the future ... The election victory conclusively affirmed the Labor campaign's strategic

judgment to maintain focus on the Morrison government's nega-
tives, and to present a more targeted set of policies, even if it may
have moderated the primary vote.

But more was needed if the vision of a long-term Labor government was
to be realised. Mostly, it was about being competent:

> By governing well, placing a high value on internal unity and
> stability, and drawing together voting constituencies around well-
> designed policies that attend to peoples' needs, concerns and
> Australia's national interest, the opportunity to establish a long-term
> Labor Government can be realised. Competent, trustworthy gov-
> ernment, and Parliamentarians actively and consistently engaging
> their constituents, will be rewarded by voters.[25]

Twenty-seven recommendations laid out the detail of the plan, including addressing disaffection in outer-suburban electorates, and a constant
clear articulation of policies and values, together with the importance of
keeping to campaign promises to retain and build the trust of the people.

After the election victory, for the most part Albanese allowed those
who had held shadow portfolios to keep them. Plibersek was fully expecting to be minister for education and minister for women – portfolios
she had held for a long time and that were close to her heart. Instead,
Jason Clare was promoted to the education portfolio, and the women's
portfolio went to Katy Gallagher, who was also minister for finance.
Plibersek was made minister for the environment and water. It came as
a complete surprise.

Predictably, the media said she had been demoted. It was true. In
public, she pointed out how important the environment portfolio was to
voters, and how excited she was to get to grips with it. But she was now
junior to Chris Bowen, who had been given the climate change and energy
portfolio. I asked her if Albanese had given her any reason for the change.
'Well, you have to ask the leader that. I'm not going to talk about conversations we had.' I told her I had tried to speak to Albanese, without success.
There was a suggestion of a shrug in reply.

Meanwhile, the line from the inner circle of government is that environment is complex and powerful, and Plibersek's administrative competence and systematic mind will be important to the competent, careful, considered kind of government Labor was intent on providing. Others point out that environment and water are both very difficult and complex portfolios. They both involve making hard decisions that will often please nobody. Plibersek would find it hard to maintain her high popularity and her profile.

But if the intention was to bury her in difficulty and complexity and to reduce her visibility, Plibersek had other ideas. When the ministry was sworn in on 1 June 2022 and gathered on the steps of Government House for the customary photo, Albanese was central in a front row full of women – Wong immediately to his left and Katy Gallagher to his right. Tanya was on one side, wearing a trouser suit in neon yellow. The eye was automatically drawn to her smiling face. Sally Rugg, a political campaigner, tweeted: 'Stop commenting on women's outfits etc but also I loooove @tanya_plibersek's neon yellow suit.' 'The yellow is to frighten off the greens,' replied another. Since then, Plibersek's suits – which previously tended pastel – have often been in primary colours. On budget night, sitting on the front benches as Treasurer Chalmers gave his speech, she was in bright red. Once again, you couldn't help but look at her.

As for the substance, Plibersek took every opportunity to draw attention to the issues in her portfolio. Less than four weeks after being sworn in, she flew to the United Nations Oceans Conference in Lisbon and declared in a keynote address that 'under the new Australian government, the environment is back – front and centre'. She announced that Australia would endorse the Joint Declaration on the Creation of a Global Coalition for Blue Carbon – the term for carbon captured by marine ecosystems. In a media interview she said she wanted Australia to take a global leadership role in ocean protection.

In July, she released the *State of the Environment Report*, which by law is completed every five years by a group of independent experts, including the country's most respected scientists. The report had been delivered before Christmas 2021 to the previous minister for the environment, Sussan Ley, who had not released it. As Plibersek said in a major National Press Club address: 'When you read it, you'll know why.' It was grim. 'Since the last report, marine heatwaves have caused mass coral bleaching in the Great Barrier Reef. Warming temperatures have reduced kelp beds along the southeast coast, as well as threatening reef habitats and the abalone and lobster industries they support. At the same time, Australia has experienced a plague of marine plastics.' She excoriated the Coalition government for its lack of action. Two years before, the *Environmental Protection and Biodiversity Conservation Act* – the key piece of legislation under which the Commonwealth exercises its environmental powers – had been reviewed by the former head of the Australian Competition and Consumer Commission, respected businessman Graeme Samuel. He had declared the act was outdated and needed fundamental reform. The Morrison government had done nothing.

Plibersek told the Press Club: 'This is the situation I'm inheriting as minister for the environment and water. Years of warnings that were ignored or kept secret. Promises made, but not delivered. Dodgy behaviour, undermining public confidence. Brutal funding cuts. Wilful neglect. Laws that don't work to protect the environment or smooth the way for sensible development. All against the backdrop of accelerating environmental destruction. It's time to change that.' It is this job – a fundamental reform of the national environmental laws – that she has declared to be her chief priority.

Plibersek released the government's response to the Samuel Review on 8 December 2022, as this book was going to print. She committed the government to establishing a new environment protection agency with powers to decide whether or not developments proceed and to enforce laws designed to protect and restore nature. She confirmed the government would introduce new national environmental standards against which conservation, protection and major development applications will be measured. There was to be a new three-tier 'traffic light' system for determining when development could occur, either relatively freely, with caution or barely at all. This, she said, would give business certainty and speed up the process – a 'win–win' for developers and the environment. But, disappointing some, there was no 'climate trigger' allowing for development to be ruled out because of its effect on climate change. And, at the time of writing, there is no detail on additional government funding to meet its aims of environmental restoration and zero new extinctions.

With this package – to be legislated in 2023 – Plibersek gave up many powers previously held by the minister to the new EPA. She will still have the power to 'call in' some projects. Early responses from the environment movement were positive. The World Wildlife Fund welcomed the emphasis on the new EPA to enforce environmental laws. Also welcome was the traffic light system, to prevent most development in environmentally sensitive areas. But, said the WWF spokesperson, the proposed timeline to introduce legislation in late 2023 was concerning because any real change would be unlikely to occur until 2024. 'Our wildlife and wild places cannot afford to wait this long for action.'[26]

It is a typical Plibersek agenda – systemic, rather than emotional, with a public servant's concern for proper process. As she had told the Press Club earlier in the year: 'I understand that campaigns to stop individual projects will motivate and energise some people. Others will want to focus on individual species, or a particularly beautiful place. I know these campaigns can capture the public imagination. But in my judgement, what our environment really needs is a changed system … Without structural reform, we'll be resigning ourselves to another decade of failure; without the tools we need to arrest our decline.'

Systemic reform does not make easy headlines. Plibersek was repeatedly being asked to rule out new coal and gas projects. In August, in one of the first uses of her considerable powers, she decided to disallow Clive Palmer's proposed open-cut coalmine adjacent to the Great Barrier Reef, but she told journalists that other projects would be decided on a case-by-case basis.

Plibersek is bringing her systematic mind to policy areas that are often messy and emotional. She is muting her passion. She is, as environment minister, more Elinor Dashwood than Marianne.

If the environment portfolio is difficult, water is even harder. The main issue in the portfolio is the Murray–Darling Basin, and the core problem is that water has been overallocated for decades. The Murray–Darling Basin

Plan, legislated in 2012, failed to account for climate change, and the problem will only get worse. Penny Wong was the first water minister after the plan was legislated. She simply bought back water from willing sellers. Ever since, rural communities have argued that the buybacks had a devastating effect on the social fabric – yet Wong's period as minister remains the most successful in achieving water returns to the environment, and the Productivity Commission has endorsed the approach. Under the Coalition government, buybacks of water were capped and largely stopped, and the emphasis shifted to dubious efficiency schemes and engineering works that were meant to result in equivalent water savings. The plan is now coming to an end. It has achieved a great deal. Recent droughts would have hit harder had it not existed. But overall, it is at risk of failing. The targets set were always inadequate, even more so if climate change is factored in, and only a tiny fraction of the promised 450 gigalitres of water savings for the environment, which were part of the deal agreed between the states, have been achieved. Plibersek has already made it clear that she will consider more buybacks, and money was set aside for this in the budget.

In our final interview, Plibersek said she was nevertheless optimistic about the plan. The money in the budget was not only for buybacks, but for any water-saving measures. She was open to all ideas. 'I'm optimistic because I feel like there's someone in charge now who actually wants to deliver that plan, as opposed to the last nine years, where successive water ministers have said that they are committed to delivering the Murray–Darling Basin Plan but haven't done anything really to do that ... I think it will get a lot further in the next couple of years than we have in the last nine.'

If Plibersek manages to deliver more water savings, then manages to get the states to sign up to a new plan with ambitions that account for the impact of climate change, it will be one of the most significant policy achievements in the history of the nation. But because water policy is so complex, contested and neglected, she could do a brilliant job and only a few would understand her achievement.

I asked Plibersek about her ambitions for the future. 'I want to be a really good environment minister, and leave a better environment when I'm gone than the one I inherited.'

Can she imagine retiring? She joked that she admired the record of the queen, who was still performing official duties a few days before her death. 'I couldn't really overstate how much I love my job. I really like the local member part of it. And it still feels like a privilege every day to do this work.' You can do some things from opposition, she said, but in government 'every day you can change the world in a better direction, a little bit or a lot. There are things that I do with a signature that I would spend months or years fighting for if I were an activist outside of government. And it still gives me chills that I get to do that.'

Against that, I suggested, were the compromises she had had to make to remain effective within the Labor Party. 'I don't think that's a high price to pay, to be honest. I think that sometimes things take a little longer because you're a party of government, but when you do them, you actually do them. You don't just talk about them. And that's why I'm there not to make a speech and feel smug about it, but to actually change people's lives. And the methodical, painstaking work of government is the only way that that gets done.'

Some still ask whether Tanya Plibersek could be a future prime minister. Politics is unpredictable, but with Albanese having won an election, and at the time of writing increasingly popular with the public and favourably regarded by the political class, her chance may have passed her by. After the 2019 election was her chief moment of opportunity. She could have forced the issue in late 2020 or early 2021, had she been prepared to tear a leader down. Who knows what the outcome would have been? Would she have won? Would she now be prime minister? But ultimately, she is not that kind of person. I believe she was restless in early 2021, concerned by Albanese's weakness in the polls. Plenty of people were urging her to make a move, and she must have considered it. But she stayed true to her longstanding view that the party – and the team – matters more than individual ambition, and that leadership destabilisation always leaves the party weaker.

As I write this, Tanya Plibersek is a few weeks away from her fifty-third birthday – not so old. If we assume that Albanese serves two terms and then makes way for a replacement, Plibersek would be around sixty-one. Perhaps she would be a contender, but by then the next generation of potential leaders will be pressing their claims. Jim Chalmers, nearly ten years younger than Plibersek, is considered a possibility. Some mention Clare O'Neil, born in 1980 and presently minister for home affairs, as the most likely woman to lead the party in the future. Barring unforeseen events, when the leadership falls vacant again the party is likely to look to the next generation.

On one of the days I was following Plibersek around, she said she wanted to show me her favourite place from which to view her electorate. She ran out of time, and we didn't get there. But one morning, the month before the 2022 election, I went there on my own. It is Mrs Macquarie's Chair – a ledge carved out of the rock by convicts in 1810 at the command of Governor Lachlan Macquarie for his wife, Elizabeth, who had travelled with him to the colony on the edge of the known world.

Elizabeth Macquarie, the history books tell us, took a kindly interest in the welfare of female convicts and Aboriginal people. She was interested in gardening and agriculture and planned the road that today runs around the inside of the Domain parklands to this point, where she used to sit and watch the harbour. Sitting on her chair, I imagined that Macquarie and Plibersek might find a lot to talk about, if time were collapsed and they could share that seat.

But the chair does not give a complete view of the seat of Sydney. It looks over the northern border of the electorate, which runs through the middle of Sydney Harbour. Straight ahead, you can see the North Shore electorates of Warringah and North Sydney, both traditionally held by the Liberal Party but now both in the hands of independents, who may or may not signal a fundamental change in Australian politics – a shift away from the major political parties.

Look left from Mrs Macquarie's Chair and you have the picture-postcard view of the Sydney Opera House and the Harbour Bridge. You have to walk westward down the road and along the foreshore to see the glass towers of the CBD, or in the other direction to take in Woolloomooloo and the millionaires' mansions of Potts Point. Well out of sight are the public housing towers and the new, tackily built apartment complexes springing up in the south of the electorate, near

Plibersek's home in Rosebery. Also out of sight is the rapidly gentrifying suburb of Redfern, the heart of Sydney's Indigenous community.

Meredith Burgmann told me she thought Labor would eventually lose the electorate of Sydney, and all the inner suburbs, to the Liberals – because increasingly only the wealthy could live there. Others told me that when Tanya Plibersek retires, it will be the Greens who take her electorate, as they have already taken the corresponding seat of Melbourne in Victoria. It is her personal following that is holding them off.

I sat on Mrs Macquarie's chair thinking about the election contest to come, about small targets and big pictures and how the nation changes. And about Josef Plibersek, and his spider, and all the hopes he had for his own future in this strange nation. I thought about the history of the place, from the first inhabitants to Mrs Macquarie and forwards to Plibersek's irascible predecessor as MP for Sydney, Peter Baldwin, his campaign against the corruption in his own party, and his largely unsuccessful bid to encourage it to tackle big, transformational policy reform. And so to the current situation, a constant balance between the need for reform and the need to gain and retain the trust of a cautious, conservative population.

Plibersek says that her electorate is beautiful, and it is. Almost anything could have been built on that harbour and been beautiful. But the Emerald City is also ugly. On that day, for example, my travels in pursuit of Tanya Plibersek's story had taken in the homeless camping out in the train stations and under the bridges, and the ice addicts swaying through the streets near her electorate office in Redfern, past the potted plants and window boxes of the houses of the wealthy. I had seen homeless women, many of whom would be on the run from domestic violence. My interview with Anna was ahead of me. So much to celebrate. So much to mourn and regret.

This is where we live, I thought. The tangible result of what is politically possible, and the country that we make.

ACKNOWLEDGEMENTS

It takes a village to write a book of this sort. I would like to thank all the people who agreed to be interviewed or who provided information. For the most part, their identities will be clear from the text, but there were another nine people who provided information and perspectives but did not wish to be identified.

I thank Tanya Plibersek, although she will not be delighted by everything in these pages. Even though she did not wish this book to be written, she showed integrity and consideration in her dealings with me and was fair and straightforward in our negotiations. Her staff helped in managing her participation in the project, despite the extra burden in an already considerable workload. I would also like to thank Rose and Ray Plibersek, and Michael, Anna and Joe Coutts-Trotter for their assistance and, particularly in the case of Anna, courage.

My debt to other journalists who have reported on the Plibersek story will be evident from the text and the footnotes.

As is always the case in projects of this kind, librarians and archivists were an enormous help, particularly those at the University of Technology archives, the State Library of New South Wales, the Australian Broadcasting Corporation's archives, the Broken Hill Historical Society and the Baillieu Library, University of Melbourne. Former railway worker Colin Hussey also helped.

My thanks to Stephen Duckett, Julian Disney, Vivienne Milligan, Monika Wheeler and Jane Gilmore for reading and commenting on early drafts of the chapters that concern their areas of expertise. The final draft, including any errors of fact or judgement, is of course my responsibility and not theirs.

Ken Haley assisted me in the early days of the project with sourcing, compiling, and annotating several mountains of media clippings. Ray Cassin helped read the proofs at the point where I could no longer see the errors.

This book was originally the idea of Sophy Williams and Chris Feik at Black Inc. I thank them for their faith in me and the project. Denise O'Dea as copy editor wrangled the book into being with great patience and skill, working to a tight deadline as the events described in the final chapters were still playing out. My agent, Lyn Tranter, was as ever a powerful force in my corner.

Finally, the family shrubbery, the members of which keep me grounded, and sane.

ENDNOTES

1. THE SPIDER

1   Josef Plibersek, oral history interview conducted for SBS documentary *The Snowy*. Producers Lina Safro and Mika Nishimura. 1999. (Unedited raw footage of Josef Plibersek interview provided by the Plibersek family.) Unless otherwise referenced, all direct quotes and recollections from Josef Plibersek in this chapter are from this interview.

2   Quoted in Andrew Markus, 'Labour and Immigration 1946–9: The Displaced Persons Program', *Labour History* 47 (November 1984), p. 78.

3   Ibid, p. 80.

4   National Archives of Australia, Plibersek, Joze, born 18 March 1932 – processing papers. Series number A12081. See also Markus, 'Labour and Immigration 1946–9: The Displaced Persons Program', *Labor History* 47 (November 1984), pp. 73–90.

5   Andrew Markus and Margaret Taft, 'Postwar Immigration and Assimilation: A Reconceptualization', *Australian Historical Studies* 46, p. 240.

6   National Archives of Australia, Plibersek, Joze, born 18 March 1932 – processing papers. Series number A12081.

7   Memories of fettlers' lives on the Broken Hill Railway have been drawn from correspondence with various residents of Broken Hill, notes provided by the Broken Hill Historical Society and John Wilkinson, Bill Crocker, Brain Sear, Jan Phillips, Betty Lutherbarrow, Betty Spargo, Jack Kennedy, Barry Murphy, Jim O'Sullivan, John Hatton, Liz Gammie, Therese Preston, Reg Ryan, Mary Wright, Bruce Heinrich: *'Can You Boil Water?': Memories of Kinalung Fettlers Camp on the Rail Line between Broken Hill and Menindee NSW, 1938–1967*. Self-published book, Orange, NSW, 2016.

8   Ivan Kobal, *The Snowy, Cradle of a New Australia*. Self-published book, Rydalmere, NSW, 1999.

9   Herman, quoted in John Hetherington, *Australian Painters: Forty Profiles*, F.W. Cheshire, Melbourne, 1963, p. 77

10 Recollections from Rose Plibersek are drawn from an interview with her, and from an oral history interview conducted by Louise Darmody of Sound Memories at SABS Studios, Artarmon on 9 October 2017. Unpublished. Copy provided by the Plibersek family.

11   Passenger Arrival Card, Rozalija Repic, National Archives of Australia Series A1225,
     Control Symbol: NSW June 1955, Box 3.
12   Ibid.
13   NSW Land Title Reference 7370/26.
14   Tanya Plibersek, post dated 14 August 2007, on *Remembering Phil Plibersek*,
     a Plibersek family blog.
15   Ibid.
16   Tanya Plibersek, The 38th Archbishop Daniel Mannix Lecture, delivered at Newman
     College, Melbourne, 23 March 2022. Published at www.tanyaplibersek.com.
17   Stewart Burns, post dated 16 January 2011 on *Remembering Phil Plibersek*,
     a Plibersek family blog.

2. SENSE AND SENSIBILITY

1   Harry E. Hand, 'Transducers and Hemingway's Heroes', *The English Journal* 55.7
     (1966), pp. 870–72.
2   Jane Cadzow, 'The Two of Us: Tanya and Michael', *Good Weekend*, 26 November
     2021.
3   Samantha Maiden, 'Pollies Wanna Cracker', *The Advertiser*, 22 December 2013,
     p. 71.
4   Georgia Hitch and Nour Haydar, 'Peter Dutton Seeks to Recast His Image as Tanya
     Plibersek Apologises for Likening Him to Voldermort', ABC News, 26 May 2022.
5   *Hansard*, 20 August 2018, p. 7943.
6   Tory Shepherd, 'Nasty Names Not in Keating League', *The Advertiser*, 14 November
     2013, p. 10.
7   Karen Middleton, *Albanese: Telling It Straight*. Penguin Random House,
     Melbourne, 2017, pp. 126–29.
8   Ibid., p. 130.
9   Cadzow, 'The Two of Us: Tanya and Michael', op. cit.
10   L.S. Burns, 'Reflections: Development of Australian Journalism Education',
     Asia Pacific Media Educator 1.14 (2003), pp. 57–75.
11   Wendy Bacon, www.wendybacon.com/about.
12   Sascha Molitorisz, 'Prime Time', *Sunday Life*, 3 June 2012, p. 12.
13   Amanda Phelan, Tanya Plibersek and Rebecca Dodd, 'Lucas Heights: Fears Over
     Storage Safety', *The Sydney Morning Herald*, 30 June 1991, 18.
14   Tanya Plibersek, 'Reactor Reactions', *Vertigo*, 30 March 1993, pp. 10–11.
15   Tanya Plibersek, 'Hot Bitches', *Vertigo*, 10 September 1991, p. 5.
16   Steve Lewis, letter to the editor, *Vertigo*, 27 September 1991, p. 4.
17   Tanya Plibersek, letter to the editor, *Vertigo*, 10 October 1991, p. 4.
18   Tanya Plibersek and Cassandra Bennett, 'Elections 1991 – Candidates Statements',
     Vertigo, 27 September 1991.
19   *Vertigo*, 23 October 1991, p. 5.
20   Tanya Plibersek, 'Salvation Jane', *Vertigo*, 11 June 1992, p. 30.
21   Tanya Plibersek, 38th Daniel Mannix Lecture, 23 March 2022.
22   Michael Coutts-Trotter, speech delivered at Riverview, 19 September 2007.
     Copy held by the author.

23 Bruce Pennay, 'John Meagher', *Australian Dictionary of Biography*.

24 'Women's Votes', *The Australasian*, 11 February 1928, p. 11.

25 New South Wales Register of Deaths, registration number 1032/1977.

26 Details of Coutts-Trotter's life are drawn partly from interviews with him, and from previous interviews by Stephen Gibbs and Roger Coombs: Stephen Gibbs, 'From Junkie to Justice Boss: Former Drug Smuggler in Charge of Australia's Biggest Prison System', *Daily Mail Australia*, 7 April 2019; Roger Coombs, 'School of Hard Knocks', *The Daily Telegraph*, 14 April 2007, p. 5.

27 Coombs, 'School of Hard Knocks', op. cit., p. 5.

28 Michael Coutts-Trotter (as 'Con'), 'A Letter from the Can', *Billy Blue Magazine*, November 1986, p. 17. Copy held by the author.

29 Michael Coutts-Trotter, 'Big Window', *Billy Blue Magazine*, January 1987, p. 19. Copy held by the author.

30 Cadzow, 'The Two of Us: Tanya and Michael', op. cit.

31 Tanya Plibersek, 'Smoke Signals: Cigarette Advertising Aimed at Women in Developing Countries', honours thesis, University of Technology, Sydney, 1992.

32 Tanya Plibersek and Cassandra Bennett, 'Biteback at Fightback', *Vertigo*, 11 May 1992, p. 26.

33 Tanya Plibersek, 'Balkan at the Very Thought of It', *Vertigo*, 10 March 1993, pp. 25–27.

34 Tanya Plibersek, 'Toy Soldiers Return to Song Ba', *Vertigo*, 17 March 1993, pp. 16–17.

35 Letters to the Editor, *Vertigo*, 20 March 1993, p. 7.

36 Tanya Plibersek, 'Welcome to Her Majesty's Ministry of Fun', *Vertigo*, 3 April 1993, p. 10.

3. SEEKING SYDNEY

1 Andrew Leigh, 'Factions and Fractions: A Case Study of the Power Politics in the Australian Labor Party', *Australian Journal of Political Science* 35.3, pp. 427–48.

2 Meredith Burgmann, 'Albo in the 80s', *Challenge*, magazine of the Left of the Labor Party, Special Platform Conference 2021 edition, pp. 34–36.

3 Middleton, *Albanese*, op. cit., p. 206.

4 Burgmann, 'Albo in the 80s', op cit.

5 Ibid.

6 For this account of the fractional war, I am indebted to Leigh, 'Factions and Fractions', op. cit., and Middleton, *Albanese*, op. cit.

7 Middleton, *Albanese*, op. cit., pp. 211–14.

8 NSW Parliament *Hansard*, Budget Estimates and Related Papers, 25 October 1994.

9 NSW Parliament *Hansard*, Budget Estimates and Related Papers, 25, 26 and 27 October 1994.

10 Sonya Voumard, 'Sack "Calamity Jane", Government Urged', *The Sydney Morning Herald*, 21 October 1994, p. 4.

11 NSW Parliament Hansard, Budget Estimates and Related Papers, 25 October 1994.

12 Tanya Plibersek, maiden speech, Federal Parliament *Hansard*, 11 November 1998, p. 82.

13 'Bruce Kenneth Childs', *The Biographical Dictionary of the Australian Senate*, Parliament of Australia.

14 'Book Launched on St Pat's Day: History of St Pat's College', *Sutherland St George and Sutherland Leader*, 31 March 2017.

15 Anne Summers, 'Cool, Calm, Elected', *The Sydney Morning Herald*, 22 September 2012.

16 Warren Owens, 'Jailed Man Is Government Adviser', *The Sunday Telegraph*, 12 November 1995, p. 5.

17 Ben English and Mark Day, 'Paid My Debt – Minister's Adviser Speaks Out', *Daily Telegraph Mirror*, 14 November 1995, pp. 1–2.

18 Mark Day, 'A Promise Carr Should Break', *Daily Telegraph Mirror*, 14 November 1995, p. 10.

19 Chris Masters, *Jonestown: The Power and Myth of Alan Jones*, Allen & Unwin, Sydney, 2006.

20 'Tribunal Rules Alan Jones Incited Hatred', ABC News, 2 October 2012.

21 *Alan Jones Breakfast Show*, 2GB, 6 July 2012.

22 Peter Rees, 'Baldwin Quits Unique Career', *The Sunday Telegraph*, 3 August 1997, p. 3.

23 David Forman and Nicholas Way, 'Labor Buries Keating', *The Sydney Morning Herald*, 3 March 1997, p. 40.

24 Mark Latham, *The Latham Diaries*, Melbourne University Press, Melbourne, 2005, p. 47.

25 Rachel Morris, 'Four Women Contest ALP Seat', *The Daily Telegraph*, 28 July 1997, p. 4.

26 David Humphries, 'Left Gives Nori Little Chance in Race for Sydney', *The Sydney Morning Herald*, 29 July 1993, p. 2.

27 Middleton, *Albanese*, op. cit., p. 280.

28 Tanya Plibersek (ed.), *Upturn: A Better Normal After Covid*, NewSouth Publishing, Kensington, NSW, 2020.

29 Anne Summers, 'Cool, Calm, Elected', op. cit.

30 Stuart Washington, 'Youth Victory in Sydney', *Australian Financial Review*, 15 December 1997, p. 8.

31 Rachel Morris, 'Youth in the Seat of Power', *The Daily Telegraph*, 16 December 1997, p. 15.

32 *Remembering Phil Plibersek*, a Plibersek family blog.

33 Sandra Lee, 'Litter You Find in the Letterbox', *The Daily Telegraph*, 2 October 1998, p. 10.

4. WE ARE LABOR

1 Tanya Plibersek, maiden speech, op. cit.

2 Ibid.

3 Jenny Tabakoff, 'Life of the Party', *The Sydney Morning Herald*, 13 February 1999, p. 3.

4 Ali Lawlor, 'Young Women Prove Their Place Is in the House', *The Courier-Mail*, 18 August 1999, p. 16.

5   Catherine Lumby, 'Politics, Power and the Personal: A Conversation with Tanya Plibersek', in Kate Deverall, Rebecca Huntley, Penny Sharpe and Jo Tilly, *Party Girls: Labor Women Now*. Pluto Press, Sydney, 2000, p. 37.

6   Anne Summers, *The End of Equality: Work, Babies and Women's Choices in 21st Century Australia*. Random House, Sydney, 2003, p. 215.

7   Tanya Plibersek, 'Censorship: Lolita and Modern Society', speech given at the Sydney Institute, published in *Sydney Papers*, Autumn 1999, pp. 126–30.

8   Christopher Pearson, 'Saving Not Such a Super Idea for Same-Sex Couples', *Australian Financial Review*, 3 May 1999, p. 19.

9   Kate Jenkins, *Set the Standard: Human Rights Commission Report on the Independent Review into Commonwealth Parliamentary Workplaces*, November 2021.

10 Malcolm Farr, 'Male MPs: They Have to Come Over and See What We Are Talking About', *The Daily Telegraph*, 23 October 1999, p. 27.

11 Damien Murphy, 'Souths Unite MPs in Rage at Murdoch', *The Sydney Morning Herald*, 23 November 1999, p. 11.

12 Peter Holder and Jo Casamento, 'Baby Boom a Capital Idea', *The Daily Telegraph*, 1 November 2000, p. 23.

13 Tanya Plibersek, 'It's Time Working Mothers Received a Fair Go', *The Sunday Telegraph*, 12 November 2000, p. 107.

14 Cadzow, 'The Two of Us: Tanya and Michael', op. cit.

15 Andrew Clark, 'Sydney Turns Hard Left', *Australian Financial Review*, 1 May 2001, p. 60.

16 Federal Parliament *Hansard*, 20 June 2001, p. 28251.

17 Federal Parliament *Hansard*, 21 June 2001, p. 28401.

18 Federal Parliament *Hansard*, 26 June 2001, p. 28591.

19 Federal Parliament *Hansard*, 28 June 2001, p. 29075.

20 David Marr and Marian Wilkinson, *Dark Victory*, Allen & Unwin, Sydney, p. 89.

21 Federal Parliament *Hansard*, 23 August 2001, p. 30100.

22 Marr and Wilkinson, *Dark Victory*, op. cit., p. 92.

23 Louise Dodson, 'MPs Fear for *Tampa*', *The Age*, 29 August 2001, p. 2.

24 Federal Parliament *Hansard*, 29 August 2001, p. 30518.

25 Federal Parliament *Hansard*, 17 September 2001, p. 30767.

26 Annabel Crabb, *Losing It: The Inside Story of the Labor Party in Opposition*, Picador, Sydney, 2005, pp. 67–68.

27 'NSW Keneally Tapes Mouth Shut for Refugees', 31 January 2002, Australian Associated Press.

28 Louise Dodson and Kerry Taylor, 'MPs in Row on Detention Policy', *The Age*, p. 1.

29 Dennis Atkins, 'Lawrence Loss Blow to Crean', *The Courier-Mail*, 6 December 2002, p. 2.

30 Kirsten Lawson, 'Lawrence Quits Front Bench Over Refugees', *The Canberra Times*, 6 December 2002, p. 3.

31 Mike Seccombe, 'MPs Tell Crean to Tread Carefully on Iraq', *The Sydney Morning Herald*, 23 September 2002, p. 6.

32 *The Australian*, 12 August 2002.

33 Phillip Coorey and John Kerin, 'Jewish Leaders Defuse Plibersek Row', *The Sydney Morning Herald*, 17 October 2013.

34 Tanya Plibersek, Statement on the death of former Israeli prime minister Ariel Sharon, Federal Pariament *Hansard*, 11 February 2014, p. 29.

35 Latham, *The Latham Diaries*, op. cit., p. 211.

36 'High Profile Visits Prompt Soul Searching for Australian Law Makers', Agence France Presse, 15 October 2003.

37 Crabb, *Losing It*, op. cit., pp. 121–24.

38 Steve Lewis, 'Crean Faces Party-Room Fight on Airport', *The Australian*, 28 July 2003, p. 1.

39 Middleton, *Albanese*, op. cit., p. 334.

40 Brendan Nicholson and Michelle Grattan, 'Beazley Has One Shot at Regaining the Reins', *The Sunday Age*, 8 June 2003, p. 1.

41 Steve Lewis, 'Crean on Track to Defeat Beazley', *The Australian*, 12 June 2003, p. 1.

42 Quoted in Alex Greenwich and Shirleene Robinson, *Yes, Yes, Yes: Australia's Journey to Marriage Equality*, NewSouth Press, Kensington, NSW, 2018, p. 13.

43 Federal Parliament *Hansard*, 17 June 2004, p. 30735.

44 Latham, *The Latham Diaries*, op. cit., p. 365.

45 Latham, *The Latham Diaries*, op. cit., p. 366.

46 Latham, *The Latham Diaries*, op. cit., p. 392.

47 Alexandra Kirk, 'Latham Scorns Labor in Vitriolic Diary', *The World Today*, ABC Radio National, 15 September 2005.

5. LEADERS AND TEAMS

1 Margaret Simons, *Penny Wong: Passion and Principle*, Black Inc., Melbourne, 2019, pp. 156–58.

2 Penny Wong, 'Jenny Macklin', media release, 6 July 2018.

3 Bill Shorten, Twitter, 6 July 2018.

4 'Call for Overhaul of Childcare System', Organisation of Asia Pacific News Agencies, 16 January 2006.

5 Maria Hawthorne, 'Doctors' Wives Make Comeback in Political Debate', Australian Associated Press, 20 May 2005.

6 Iola Mathews, *Winning for Women: A Personal Story*, Monash University Publishing, Melbourne, 2019, chapter 10.

7 'Minchin Scorns Leave for Mothers', *The Sydney Morning Herald*, 3 June 2002.

8 Helen Brown, '76 per cent of Australians Support Paid Maternity Leave', *Lateline*, ABC TV, 13 July 2007.

9 Malcolm Farr, 'Sisters Emerge Out of a Shadow', *The Daily Telegraph*, 11 March 2006, p. 1.

10 Tanya Plibersek, 'Upfront', *The Sydney Morning Herald*, 22 March 2006.

11 Tanya Plibersek, 'Upfront', *The Sydney Morning Herald*, 5 April 2006.

12 Tanya Plibersek, 'Upfront', *The Sydney Morning Herald*, 19 April 2006.

13 Tanya Plibersek, 'Upfront', *The Sydney Morning Herald*, 14 June 2006.

14 Tanya Plibersek, 'Upfront', *The Sydney Morning Herald*, 7 February 2007.

15   Tanya Plibersek, 'Upfront', *The Sydney Morning Herald*, 9 August 2006.

16   Julia Gillard, *My Story*, Knopf, Sydney, 2014

17   Federal Parliament *Hansard*, 13 October 2005, p. 75.

18   Paul Strangio, 'If Beazley Had Become Prime Minister Instead of Rudd, Might We Have Had More Stable Government?', *The Conversation*, 23 November 2016.

19   Gillard, *My Story*, op. cit., p. 4.

20   Kevin Rudd, *The PM Years*, Macmillan, Sydney, 2018, p. 8.

21   Gillard, *My Story*, op. cit., pp. 6–7.

22   Maria Hawthorne, 'Beazley's Future to Be Known on Monday', Australian Associated Press, 1 December 2006.

23   Matthew Franklin and Cath Hart, 'Rivals Are Running Neck-and-Neck', *The Australian*, 2 December 2006, p. 1.

24   Fleur Anderson, 'Double Shocks Cast a Sombre Mood', *Australian Financial Review*, 5 December 2006, p. 11.

25   Patricia Karvelas, 'Latham Supporters Emerge on Right Side', *The Australian*, 5 December 2006, p. 1.

26   Strangio, 'If Beazley Had Become Prime Minister', op. cit.

27   'NSW Government Under Fire Over Coutts-Trotter Appointment', *PM*, ABC Radio National, 11 April 2007.

28   Ibid.

29   Dylan Welch and Anna Patty, 'Give Me a Chance: Schools' Chief', *The Sydney Morning Herald*, 11 April 2007.

30   'NSW Government Under Fire Over Coutts-Trotter Appointment', op.cit.

31   'NSW Government Under Fire Over Coutts-Trotter Appointment', op.cit.

32   Linda Silmalis, 'I Didn't Think I Would Survive Being in Jail', *The Sunday Telegraph*, 15 April 2007.

33   Malcolm Farr and Bruce McDougall, 'Drug Lesson: Wife of New School Boss Tells: He's an Inspiration', *The Daily Telegraph*, 12 April 2007.

34   Ibid.

35   Coombs, 'School of Hard Knocks', op. cit.

36   Karen Heinrich and Amanda Woodard, 'What Makes Women Happy?', *Sunday Life*, 22 April 2007.

6. HOMES

1   Gillard, *My Story*, op. cit.

2   This discussion of the history of housing policy is drawn from: J. Walter and C. Holbrook, 'Housing in a Federation: From Wicked Problem to Complexity Cascade?', *Australian Journal of Public Administration* 74.4 (2015), pp. 448–66; Vivienne Milligan and Anne Tiernan, 'No Home for Housing: The Situation of the Commonwealth's Housing Policy Advisory Function', *Australian Journal of Public Administration* 70.4 (2011), pp. 391–407; and Vivienne Milligan and Simon Pinnegar, 'The Comeback of National Housing Policy in Australia: First Reflections', *International Journal of Housing Policy* 10.3 (2010), pp. 325–44.

3   Australian Government Productivity Commission, *First Home Ownership*, report no. 28, 31 March 2004.

4   Interview with Steve Austin, ABC Radio Brisbane, 19 September 2003.

5   Milligan and Tiernan, 'No Home for Housing', op. cit.

6   Tanya Plibersek, 'Upfront', *The Sydney Morning Herald*, 21 February 2007.

7   Tanya Plibersek, 'Upfront', *The Sydney Morning Herald*, 25 July 2007.

8   Tanya Plibersek, 'Upfront', *The Sydney Morning Herald*, 19 April 2007.

9   Kevin Rudd, speech delivered in Brisbane, 14 November 2007, published by the Museum of Australian Democracy at electionspeeches.moadoph.gov.au.

10   Tanya Plibersek, 'Upfront', *The Sydney Morning Herald*, 28 November 2007.

11   Tanya Plibersek, 'Upfront', *The Sydney Morning Herald*, 12 December 2007.

12   Roger Coombs, 'Having It All Comes at a Price', *Daily Telegraph*, 9 February 2008.

13   Milligan and Tiernan, 'No Home for Housing', op. cit.

14   Australian National Audit Office (ANAO), Administration of the National Rental Affordability Scheme, 18 November 2015; and National Rental Affordability Scheme – Administration of Allocations and Incentives, 7 November 2016.

15   Lenore Taylor, 'US Brickies Could Put Our House in Order', *Australian Financial Review*, 1 March 2008, p. 63.

16   Wayne Swan, *The Good Fight*, Allen & Unwin, Sydney, 2014, p. 58.

17   *KPMG Social Housing Initiative Review*, Housing Ministers' Advisory Committee, September 2012.

18   ANAO, op. cit.

19   Marcus Luigi, 'Spiller Don't Tear It Down: The Idea Behind Labor's National Rental Affordability Scheme Is Worth Saving', *The Conversation*, 23 September 2019.

20   Tom McIlroy, 'Super Funds Excited by Housing Opportunities: Chalmers', *Australian Financial Review*, 20 September 2022.

21   Rudd, *The PM Years*, op. cit., p. 317.

22   Milligan and Tiernan, 'No Home for Housing', op. cit.

23   Australian Government Productivity Commission, *In Need of Repair: The National Housing and Homelessness Agreement Study Report*, October 2022.

7. WOMEN AND THEIR CHILDREN

1   Tanya Plibersek, 'A New Conversation about Equality', speech delivered at the Sydney Institute, 6 November 2008.

2   Rudd, *The PM Years*, op. cit., p. 161.

3   Gillard, *My Story*, op. cit., p. 39.

4   Swan, *The Good Fight*, op. cit., p. 131.

5   Tanya Plibersek, 'Rudd Government Acts to Promote the Rights of Women in Australia', media release, 26 August 2008.

6   Tanya Plibersek, 'Government Boosts the Voice of Women', media release, 9 March 2010.

7   Tanya Plibersek, 'The Commonwealth's Role in Improving the Safety of Women and Children', speech delivered at the NSW Legal Aid Women's Domestic Violence Court Assistance Program Annual Conference, Sydney, 2 August 2007.

8   Tanya Plibersek, 'Prevention and Protection: Federal Labor's National Plan to Reduce Violence Against Women and Children', media release, 18 November 2007.

9   Kevin Rudd, 'Respecting Women and Leading Men', speech delivered at the White
     Ribbon Foundation Annual White Tie Dinner, Sydney, 17 September 2008.
10   National Council on Violence Against Women and Their Children, *Time for Action:
     The National Council's Plan for Australia to Reduce Violence against Women and their
     Children 2009–2021*, March 2009.
11   Jane Gilmore, 'Men's Violence Against Women Is Not a PR Problem', janegilmore.
     com, 7 March 2022.
12   Monash University Gender and Family Violence Prevention Centre, *National Plan
     Stakeholder Consultation: Final Report*, February 2022.

8. BIRTH RIGHT

1   Gillard, *My Story*, op. cit., pp. 35–36.
2   Stephanie Peatling, 'Full House for Expectant MP', *The Sun Herald*, 9 May 2010,
     p. 26.
3   'Abbott Stars at Sexist Award Night, Australian Associated Press', 17 September 2010.
4   Phillip Coorey and Laura Tingle, 'Gillard Faces Surplus Backlash from Labor MPs',
     Australian Financial Review, 14 December 2012.
5   Middleton, *Albanese*, op. cit., p. 394.
6   Middleton, *Albanese*, op. cit., p. 390.
7   See Middleton, *Albanese*, op. cit., p. 402 for a full exploration of Albanese's positon.
8   Middleton, *Albanese*, op. cit., p. 410.
9   Tanya Plibersek, 'A Dash of Compromise is Character Building', *The Sydney
     Morning Herald*, 9 September 2010.
10   Malcolm Farr, 'Baby Bounces Numbers', *The Daily Telegraph*, 25 September 2010.
11   Malcolm Farr, 'A Lot Rests on Louis – Bouncing Boy Arrives to a Fragile
     Parliament', *The Sunday Mail*, 10 October 2010.
12   Mark Latham, 'No Exit: The ALP', *The Monthly*, November 2010.
13   Tanya Plibersek, 'Australia's Social Inclusion Heritage: Past, Present, Future',
     speech delivered at the Sydney Institute, 27 September 2011.
14   Brotherhood of St Laurence, *What Next for Place-Based Initiatives to Tackle
     Disadvantage? A Practical Look at Recent Lessons for Australian Public Policy*, August
     2015, p. 22.
15   Mark Coultan and Joe Kelly, 'The Complex Life of a Political Odd Couple',
     The Australian, 15 October 2013.
16   Simons, *Penny Wong*, op. cit., p. 144.
17   Federal Parliament *Hansard*, 9 February 2011, p. 287.
18   Sean Nicholls and Anna Patty, 'Labor Support for Same-Sex Marriage, But No
     Vote', *The Daily Telegraph*, 11 July 2011.
19   Michelle Grattan, 'Pincer Move on Gillard Over Gay Marriage', *The Sydney
     Morning Herald*, 1 December 2011.
20   'What They Said', *The Sunday Age*, 4 December 2011, p. 5.
21   Barrie Cassidy, interview with Tanya Plibersek, *Insiders*, ABC TV, 4 December
     2011.
22   Sabra Lane, 'Cabinet Refresh Raises Eyebrows', *AM*, ABC Radio National,
     12 December 2011.

23   Tanya Plibersek, 'My Dad Had the Right to Die with Dignity', *Mamamia*,
     24 March 2015.
24   Plibersek, 'Australia's Social Inclusion Heritage', op. cit.

9. END OF GOVERNMENT

1   Jenny Campbell, 'Strewth', *The Australian*, 20 February 2012.
2   Summers, 'Cool Calm and Elected', op. cit.
3   Janet Albrechtsen, 'Waste and Fat Guaranteed When Governments Spend Our
     Money', *The Australian*, 19 September 2012.
4   Rudd, *The PM Years*, op. cit., p. 256.
5   Ibid.
6   Gillard, *My Story*, op. cit., p. 431.
7   Sue Dunlevy, 'Dental Care Top Focus: Plibersek, Heath, Gillard's Reshuffle',
     The Australian, 13 December 2011.
8   Ibid.
9   Federal Parliament *Hansard*, 9 February 2012.
10   Federal Parliament *Hansard*, 21 November 2013.
11   'Albanese Declares Hand for Rudd', ABC News, 25 February 2012.
12   Chris Uhlmann, 'Health Minister Gives Assessment of ALP Leadership Issues',
     7.30, ABC TV, 23 February 2012.
13   Gillard, *My Story*, op. cit., p. 128.

10. AMBITION AND DEFEAT

1   David Speers, interview with Bob Hawke, SkyNews, 7 September 2013.
2   Destroy the Joint, Facebook post, 9 September 2013.
3   'The Contenders', *The Sydney Morning Herald*, 9 September 2013.
4   Christian Kerr and Troy Bramston, 'Deluge of Ballots Arrive in Labor Leadership
     Poll', *The Australian*, 10 October 2013.
5   Don Woolford, 'It May Be Albanese v Shorten on Leadership', Australian
     Associated Press, 8 September 2013.
6   Patricia Karvelas and Ben Packham, 'Plibersek Willing to Be Shorten's Deputy',
     The Australian, 4 October 2013.
7   Middelton, *Albanese*, op. cit., p. 445.
8   'Plibesek Deputy in New Labor Frontbench', Australian Associated Press,
     14 October 2013.
9   'Crikey Says: Plibersek Is the Real Labor Winner' (editorial), *Crikey*, 14 October
     2013.
10   Middleton, *Albanese*, op. cit., p. 452.
11   Craig Emerson and Jay Weatherill, *Review of Labor's 2019 Federal Election
     Campaign*, Australian Labor Party, Canberra, 2019.
12   Summers, 'Calm, Cool, Elected', op. cit.
13   Tanya Plibersek, speech to the National Press Club, 10 February 2016.
14   Leigh Sales, interview with Tanya Plibsersek, *7.30*, ABC TV, 25 November 2015.
15   Interview with Tanya Plibersek, *Lateline*, ABC TV, 9 September 2015.

16 Tanya Plibersek, 'National Interest, Good International Citizenship and Labor's Foreign Policy', speech to the Lowy Institute, 1 June 2016.

17 Brendan Nicholson and Joe Kelly, 'Brandis Shoots Down *Guardian* Metadata Leak', *The Australian*, 3 December 2013.

18 Latika Bourke, '"Lightweight" Tanya Plibersek Certainly No Kevin Rudd, Says Julie Bishop', *The Age*, 24 November 2014.

19 Federal Parliament *Hansard*, 12 February 2015.

20 Phillip Coorey and John Kerin, 'Jewish Leaders Defuse Plibersek Row', *Australian Financial Review*, 17 October 2013.

21 Barrie Cassidy, interview with Tanya Plibersek, *Insiders*, ABC TV, 24 November 2013. 4

22 Dan Harison, 'Acting PM Pays Tribute to Sharon', *The Sydney Morning Herald*, 12 January 2014.

23 Mark Dreyfus, 'Labor's Policy on Israel and the Palestinian Territories', media release, 12 April 2021.

24 Phillip Hudson, 'Unions Save Labor from Single Issue Lefties', *The Australian*, 27 July 2015.

25 'Plibersek Supported New Boat Policy: Carr', Australian Associated Press, 26 July 2015; and Gabrielle Chan, 'Bill Shorten Wins Freedom to Use Boat Turnbacks, but Leadership Split on Issue', *The Guardian*, 25 July 2015.

26 Anthony Galloway, 'Border Protection in Spotlight after Albanese Said He Favours Boat Turnbacks Over Offshore Detention', *The Sydney Morning Herald*, 14 April 2022.

27 Federal Parliament *Hansard*, 15 September 2015, p. 10228.

28 Annabel Crabb, 'What Two Rats Taught Us About Politicians This Week', *The Sydney Morning Herald*, 3 June 2016.

29 Phil Coorey, 'Factions Line Up Behind Shorten', *Australian Financial Review*, 4 July 2016, p. 4. See also: Sid Maher, 'Federal Election 2016: Bill Shorten Bolsters His Spot', *The Australian*, 4 July 2016.

30 Middleton, *Albanese*, op. cit., p. 444.

31 Tanya Plibersek, 'Tanya Plibersek on Same-Sex Marriage', *Mamamia*, 15 September 2016.

32 Federal Parliament *Hansard*, 11 October 2016.

33 Federal Parliament *Hansard*, 7 December 2017.

34 'Tanya Plibersek Speaks to Bill Shorten MP's Children', Channel Seven News, Facebook post, 7 December 2017.

35 Australian Government Productivity Commission, *The Demand Driven University System: A Mixed Report Card*, June 2019.

36 Federal Parliament Hansard, 20 August 2018, p. 7943.

37 Emerson and Weatherill, *Review of Labor's 2019 Federal Election Campaign*, op. cit.

11. THE COUNTRY THAT WE MAKE

1 Renee Viellaris, 'Labor's Report Card for 2019', *The Courier Mail*, 15 December 2019.

2   Emerson and Weatherill, *Review of Labor's 2019 Federal Election Campaign.*

3   Molloy and Clench, op cit.; staff reporters, 'Shorten Backs Plibersek as Labor Leader, *Herald Sun*, 18 May 2019.

4   Judith Ireland, 'Seven Days a Week on the Road Not Something I Wanted for My Kids: Pliberesk and Gillard Talk Leadership,' *WA Today*, 14 July 2019.

5   Jenna Price, 'Tanya, I Would Gladly Retire from My Career to Help Care for Your Kids', *Sydney Morning Herald*, 21 May 2019.

6   Ben James, 'Tanya Plibersek's Daughter Anna Coutts-Trotter Handed Special Award', *Southern Courier*, 25 September 2018.

7   Sarah Dean, 'Police Defend Their Investigation into Bill Shorten', *Daily Mail*, 2 October 2014.

8   Samantha Hutchinson and Kylar Loussikian, 'CBD Melbourne: Plibersek – She's Right Behind You', *The Sydney Morning Herald*, 2 March 2020.

9   Samantha Maiden, 'Self-indulgent: MP's Brutal Message', News.com.au, 18 November 2020.

10   Tanya Plibersek (ed.), *Upturn: A Better Future after Covid*, NewSouth Publishing, Kensington, 2020.

11   Richard Hill and Stuart Rees, 'A Tepid Cry for Change: Tanya Plibersek's Book *Upturn* and Labor's Prospects', Pearls and Irritations (johnmenadue.com), 5 March 2021.

12   Alice Workman, 'You Only Serve Twice', *The Australian*, 19 January 2021.

13   Troy Bramston, 'Sharks Circle Labor Leadership as Anthony Albanese Dead in the Water', *The Australian*, 1 February 2021.

14   Nick Tabakoff, 'Plibersek Plays the Media Game', *The Australian*, 28 February 2021.

15   Katherine Murphy, 'Anthony Albanese Reaches Out to Business as Labor's Internal Instability Continues', *The Guardian*, 18 November 2020.

16   Guy Rundle, 'Albo's Labor: A Party in Search of a Story about What We Are Not – But Should Be', *Crikey*, 5 February 2021.

17   Samantha Maiden, 'Scott Morrison Hauls in COVID Quack Pusher Craig Kelly and Declares "Enough Is Enough", News.com.au, 3 February 2021

18   Samantha Maiden, 'Dark Past of Michael Coutts-Trotter, NSW Premier Dominic Perrottet's New Right Hand Man', News.com.au, 8 October 2021.

19   Paul Daley, 'We Know Where Perrottet Stands, but Is He Pragmatic Enough to Be Popular?', *The Guardian*, 23 October 2021.

20   Sean Kelly, 'Albanese Says He's in the Final Quarter, So When Is He Going to Start Kicking Goals?', *The Sydney Morning Herald*, 25 October 2021.

21   Katherine Murphy, 'Anthony Albanese Commits Labor to Emissions Reduction Target of 43 per cent by 2030', *The Guardian*, 3 December 2021.

22   James Massola, 'The Chosen and the Frozen: Plibersek, Shorten Benched During Labor's Campaign', *The Sydney Morning Herald*, 27 April 2022.

23   Gareth Evans, email to Penny Wong, 27 April 2022. Provided to the author by Evans.

24   Gareth Evans, email to Tim Gartrell, 9 May 2022. Provided to the author by Evans.

25 Greg Combet and Lenda Oshalem, *Election 2022 Review: An Opportunity to Establish a Long-term Labor Government*, Australian Labor Party, 5 December 2022.

26 Lisa Cox and Ben Smee, 'Tanya Plibersek Confirms New Environmental Protection Agency to Enforce Conservation Laws', *The Guardian*, 8 December 2022.

INDEX